Research-Based Strategies for Improving Outcomes for Targeted Groups of Learners

R. A. McWilliam

Siskin Children's Institute

Bryan G. Cook

University of Hawaii

Melody Tankersley

Kent State University

PEARSON

Boston   Columbus   Indianapolis   New York   San Francisco   Upper Saddle River
Amsterdam   Cape Town   Dubai   London   Madrid   Milan   Munich   Paris   Montreal   Toronto
Delhi   Mexico City   São Paulo   Sydney   Hong Kong   Seoul   Singapore   Taipei   Tokyo

Vice President and Editorial Director: Jeffery W. Johnston
Executive Editor: Ann Castel Davis
Editorial Assistant: Andrea Hall
Vice President, Director of Marketing: Margaret Waples
Marketing Manager: Joanna Sabella
Senior Managing Editor: Pamela D. Bennett
Project Manager: Sheryl Glicker Langner
Senior Operations Supervisor: Matthew Ottenweller
Senior Art Director: Diane C. Lorenzo

Cover Designer: Candace Rowley
Cover Image: Background: © Lora liu/Shutterstock; Photo: © Jaren Jai Wicklund/Shutterstock
Full-Service Project Management: S4Carlisle Publishing Services
Composition: S4Carlisle Publishing Services
Printer/Binder: Edwards Brothers Malloy
Cover Printer: Lehigh-Phoenix Color/Hagerstown
Text Font: Times LT Std

Credits and acknowledgments for material borrowed from other sources and reproduced, with permission, in this textbook appear on the appropriate page within the text.

Photo Credits: Chapter-opening photo: © Jaren Jai Wicklund/Shutterstock. Design images (from left to right): © Orange Line Media/Shutterstock; © kali9/iStockphoto; © Nailia Schwarz/Shutterstock; © iofoto/Shutterstock; © Jaren Jai Wicklund/Shutterstock.

Every effort has been made to provide accurate and current Internet information in this book. However, the Internet and information posted on it are constantly changing, so it is inevitable that some of the Internet addresses listed in this textbook will change.

Library of Congress Cataloging-in-Publication Data is available upon request.

10 9 8 7 6 5 4 3 2 1

ISBN 10:   0-13-703133-5
ISBN 13: 978-0-13-703133-7

Dedication

We dedicate this to our families, who help us remember what life is really about.

To Tinsley. – RAM

To Lysandra, Zoe, and Ben. – BC

To Bebe and Jackson. – MT

Preface

Research-Based Strategies for Improving Outcomes for Targeted Groups of Learners was born of discussions over many years between special education practitioners and researchers regarding the need for a reliable and practical guide to highly effective, research-based practices in special education. Providing this type of information is a primary focus of the Council for Exceptional Children's Division for Research (CEC-DR), which the Division has pursued in many ways—sometimes with considerable success, sometimes with disappointment. At a meeting of the Executive Board of CEC-DR, then President Dr. Robin A. McWilliam suggested that the division consider producing a textbook to meet this need that would be unique in its emphasis on research-based practices. And so began concrete discussions that led to the book you are now reading.

You have probably read or heard something about the research-to-practice gap in special education—when practice is not based on research and, although less often emphasized in the professional literature, when research is not relevant to practice. This gap is not unique to special education; it occurs in general education and many other professional fields, including medicine. It is unlikely that the gap between research and practice will ever disappear entirely; indeed, it may not be desirable to thoroughly commingle the worlds of special education research and practice. However, when the gap between research and practice becomes a chasm, with practice being dictated more by tradition and personal trial-and-error than reliable research, the outcomes and opportunities of students suffer unnecessarily. Simply stated, special educators need to use the most effective instructional practices so that students with disabilities can reach their potentials; all too often, that does not occur.

We believe that this text is made all the more timely and important given the recent explosion of information on the Internet. The wealth of information available on the Internet (as well as from other, more traditional sources of recommendations on instructional practices such as professional development trainings, textbooks, and journals) can be an important asset in helping to determine what works. However, much of the information on the Internet and other sources is not research based and therefore is often inaccurate. Thus, although having thousands of pieces of information about various teaching techniques at one's fingertips may seem wonderful, it often has a stultifying effect, leaving many educators drowning in a sea of information overload, without the time or necessary information (i.e., research findings) to determine what is truly credible and what is not. Rather than unsubstantiated promotion of scores of techniques, special educators need in-depth information on the practices shown by reliable research to be most effective for improving important outcomes of learners with disabilities, which is our aim in this text. By focusing on practices with solid research support, such as those featured in this text, special educators can feel confident that they are implementing approaches that are most likely to work for learners with disabilities.

It is important to realize, though, that research support is not an iron-clad guarantee of effectiveness for each and every learner. Even the most effective, research-based practices do not work for everyone (there are nonresponders to every practice); and contextual factors (e.g., school and classroom environments, student characteristics) found in practice seldom align perfectly with the research studies supporting most practices. Therefore, teachers will have to rely on their professional wisdom to select and adapt the research-based practices targeted in this text to make them work in their classrooms, for their learners. Nonetheless, having practices identified as effective on the basis of sound research, knowing what the research says about those practices, and understanding how those practices work are critical first steps in effective special education practice.

We believe that *Research-Based Strategies for Improving Outcomes for Targeted Groups of Learners* will be counted as one of the considerable successes of CEC-DR because it provides researchers, teacher trainers, policy makers, practitioners, family members, and other stakeholders information about research-based practices shown to generally produce desirable outcomes for targeted populations of learners. Moreover, this text provides readers with sufficient information about the practices and their research support to make informed decisions about which practices are right for them and their learners, and whether and how they might adapt the practices to fit their setting.

Acknowledgments

Very little is accomplished in isolation, and that was certainly true for this text. It is important for us to acknowledge the many professionals whose hard work is responsible for this text. We first acknowledge the chapter authors. We were fortunate to have the participation of the foremost authorities in the topics of focus in this work. We thank them for sharing their expertise and working so diligently and agreeably with us throughout the entire process. We thank Ann Davis, our editor at Pearson, for her unflagging support and insightful assistance. We also express our appreciation to Dr. Christine Balan, Dr. Lysandra Cook, Luanne Dreyer Elliott, and Norine Strang for their excellent and professional editing. Thank you to our reviewers: Mary E. Cronin, University of New Orleans, and E. Paula Crowley, Illinois State University. And most importantly, we acknowledge our families, without whose support and forbearance this work could not have been accomplished.

Robin A. McWilliam
Siskin Children's Institute

Bryan G. Cook
University of Hawaii

Melody Tankersley
Kent State University

Contents

1 Introduction to Research-Based Strategies for Improving Outcomes for Targeted Groups of Learners   **1**

Bryan G. Cook and Melody Tankersley

Limitations of Traditional Methods for Determining What Works   2
Benefits of Using Research to Determine What Works   3
The Research-to-Practice Gap in Special Education   6
This Textbook and Addressing the Research-to-Practice Gap   6
Conclusion   7

2 Research-Based Practices in Early Childhood Special Education   **8**

Mary Jo Noonan and Patricia Sheehey

Review of Research-Based Practices   9
Summary   18

3 Teaching Students with High-Incidence Disabilities   **19**

Thomas E. Scruggs and Margo A. Mastropieri

Mnemonic Strategies   20
Differentiated Curriculum Enhancements   26
Summary   29

4 Teaching Individuals with Severe Intellectual Disability: *Effective Instructional Practices*   **30**

Susan R. Copeland and Kay Osborn

General Learning Characteristics of Persons with Severe Intellectual Disability   31
Prompting   31

Task Analysis   36
Self-Management   39
Conclusion   43

5 Effective Reading Interventions for English Language Learners Who Are Struggling Readers or Identified with Learning Disabilities   **44**

Kathleen A. King Thorius, Alfredo J. Artiles, and Amanda L. Sullivan

Setting the Context   44
Review Methods   46
Research-Based Literacy Interventions for ELLs   47
Good, Research-Based Practices for Supporting Literacy Development of ELLs Who Are Struggling Readers or Identified with LD   51
Conclusion and the Road Ahead: Toward Culturally Responsive Literacy Interventions for ELLs Who Are Struggling Readers or Identified With LD   53
Appendix 5.1   Summary Information on Interventions Reviewed   56

6 Teaching Students with Language Disorders   **61**

Laura M. Justice, Sandra Gillam, and Anita McGinty

Review of Effective Practices   63
Conclusion   72

**7 Teaching Students with
   Autism Spectrum Disorders   73**

Rose Iovannone

Peer-Mediated Interventions to Enhance
   Social Skills   74
Functional Approach to Problem Behaviors   79
Summary   85

**8 Effective Practices for
   Promoting Literacy with
   Individuals Who Have
   Physical Disabilities   86**

Mari Beth Coleman and Kathryn Wolff Heller

Characteristics of Individuals with Physical
   Disabilities That Impede Literacy
   Acquisition   86
The Nonverbal Reading Approach   88
Assistive Technology to Promote Writing   93
Summary   99

**9 Teaching Students Who
   Have Sensory Disabilities   100**

*Deborah Chen, Rachel Friedman Narr, and
Diane P. Wormsley*

Visual Phonics with Deaf and
   Hard-of-Hearing Students   100

Early Identification of Braille as the
   Primary Reading Medium for
   Students with Visual Impairments   105
Tangible Symbols with Students
   Who Are Deaf-Blind   108
Conclusion   112
Appendix 9.1   Available Studies
   on Braille Reading   113
Appendix 9.2   Available Studies
   on Tangible Symbols   114

**10 Teaching for Transition
   to Adulthood   115**

*David W. Test, Kelly R. Kelley,
and Dawn A. Rowe*

Self-Determination   116
Community-Based Instruction   119
Instructional Approaches   125
Analysis of the Research Base   126
Recommendations for Practice   127
Conclusion   127

References   129

Name Index   155

Subject Index   161

CHAPTER 1

Introduction to Research-Based Strategies for Improving Outcomes for Targeted Groups of Learners

Bryan G. Cook | *University of Hawaii*

Melody Tankersley | *Kent State University*

This is not a typical introductory textbook in special education that provides brief overviews of a large number of student characteristics and instructional practices. Textbooks with this focus serve important purposes. For example, individuals who are just beginning to explore the field of special education need to understand the breadth of student needs and corresponding instructional techniques that have been and are being used to teach students with disabilities. This text addresses a different need—the need for extensive information on selected, highly effective practices in special education. Stakeholders such as advanced pre-service special educators, practicing special education and inclusive teachers, administrators, parents, and many teacher-educators are more directly involved with the instruction and learning of children and youth with disabilities and as a result need in-depth treatments of the most effective practices that they can use to meaningfully impact and improve the educational experiences of children and youth with and at risk for disabilities.

In this textbook we provide extensive (rather than cursory) information on selected, highly effective practices (rather than on many practices, some of which may be less than effective) in special education. This endeavor begs an important question: What are the most highly effective practices identified in special education? That is, how do we tell "what works" for children and youth with and at risk for disabilities?

Traditionally, special educators have relied on sources such as personal experience, colleagues, tradition, and experts to guide their instructional decision making (e.g., B. G. Cook & Smith, 2012). These resources have served teachers well in many ways. Special education teachers are skilled professionals who learn from their personal experiences and refine their teaching accordingly. Traditions and custom represent the accumulated personal experiences of whole groups and cultures and therefore can be imbued with great wisdom. And experts most often know of which they speak (and write) and make many valid recommendations. Yet, just as in other aspects of life, the personal experiences that lie at the root of these sources of knowing are prone to error and can lead special educators to false conclusions about which practices work and should be implemented with students with disabilities.

Limitations of Traditional Methods for Determining What Works

Chabris and Simons (2010) described five everyday illusions documented in the psychological literature (i.e., illusions of attention, memory, confidence, knowledge, and cause) that cast doubt on whether teachers can use personal experiences (their own, or those of their colleagues) to determine reliably whether practices work for their students. Chabris and Simons noted that although people assume that they attend to everything within their perceptual field, in reality many stimuli—especially those that contrast with one's expectations—"often go completely unnoticed" (p. 7). That is, people tend to focus their attention on what they expect to happen. Moreover, even when people actively attend to phenomena, their memories are unlikely to be wholly accurate and also are biased by their preconceptions. "We cannot play back our memories like a DVD—each time we recall a memory, we integrate whatever details we do remember with our expectations for what we should remember" (p. 49). Moreover, people tend to hold false illusions of confidence (e.g., most people think of themselves as above-average drivers) and knowledge (e.g., people tend to falsely believe that they know how familiar tools and systems work). Finally, "Our minds are built to detect meaning in patterns, to infer causal relationships from coincidences, and to believe that earlier events cause later ones" (p. 153), even though many patterns are meaningless, many associations are coincidental, and earlier events often simply precede rather than cause later occurrences.

Special education teachers—just like other people in their professional and day-to-day lives—may, then, not attend to events in a classroom that they do not expect (e.g., when using preferred practices, teachers may be more likely to focus on students who are doing well but not recognize struggling students); may construct memories of teaching experiences that are influenced by their preconceptions of whether a practice is likely to work; may be more confident than warranted that a favored instructional approach works when they use it; may believe that they fully understand why and how a practice works when they do not; and may believe that a practice causes positive changes in student outcomes when it does not. We are not suggesting that special educators are more gullible or error prone than anyone else. Nonetheless, these documented illusions show that using one's perceptions of personal experiences is an error-prone method for establishing whether instructional practices cause improved student outcomes.

Traditional wisdom shares many important traits with scientific research (e.g., refining understanding based on empirical input over time; Arunachalam, 2001). Indeed, many traditional practices are shown to be valid when examined scientifically (Dickson, 2003). Yet, tradition and custom often are based on incomplete science or consist of inaccurate superstition and folklore. History is replete with examples of traditional thinking that science subsequently has shown to be incorrect—from the flat-earth and geocentric models of the solar system to the direct inheritability of intelligence and ineducability of individuals with various disabilities. Accordingly, although many traditional instructional practices for students with disabilities may be effective, others have been passed down through generations of teachers even though they do not have a consistently positive effect on student outcomes. Basing instruction on the individual learning styles of students with disabilities, for example, is an accepted, traditional teaching practice despite the lack of supporting evidence (see Landrum & McDuffie, 2010).

As with personal experience and tradition, expert opinion is often faulty. Indeed, a common logical fallacy is the appeal to authority, in which one argues that a statement is true based on the authority of who said it. Not surprisingly, so-called authorities such as new-age gurus and celebrities often support less than effective products. But experts more commonly considered credible, such as textbook authors, also frequently provide inaccurate guidance. "The fact is, expert wisdom usually turns out to be at best highly contested and ephemeral, and at worst flat-out wrong" (Freedman, 2010, p. 7). In special education, "experts" have a long history of advocating for ineffective practices such as avoiding immunizations, facilitated communication, colored glasses or prism lenses, and patterning (e.g., Mostert, 2010; Mostert & Crockett, 2000). Thus, special educators need to be wary of basing instructional decisions on unverified expert recommendation.

Unlike their nondisabled peers, who often experience success in school while receiving mediocre or even poor instruction, students with disabilities require the most effective instruction to succeed (Dammann & Vaughn, 2001). As Malouf and Schiller (1995) noted, special education serves "students and families who are especially dependent on receiving effective services and who are especially vulnerable to fraudulent treatment claims" (p. 223). It appears, then, that those who teach and work with students with disabilities need a more reliable and trustworthy method for determining what works than personal experience, tradition, or expert opinion. Scientific research can provide a meaningful guide to special educators and other stakeholders when making decisions about what and how to teach learners with disabilities.

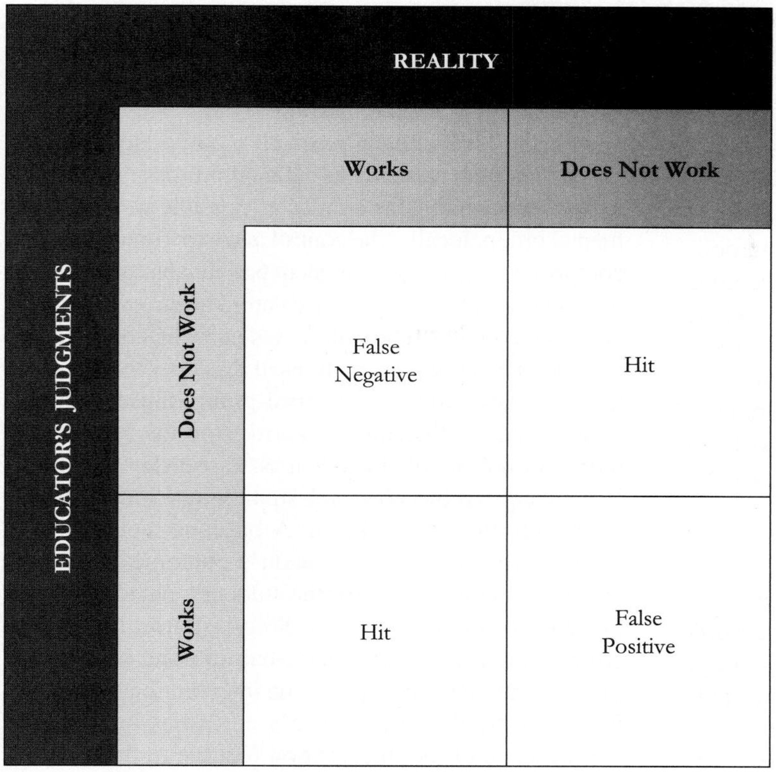

Figure 1.1   Relation between educator's judgments and reality regarding the effectiveness of instructional practices.

Benefits of Using Research to Determine What Works

It is the professional and ethical duty of special educators to implement the instructional techniques most likely to benefit the students they serve. Indeed, the Council for Exceptional Children's (CEC) standards for well-prepared special education teachers specify that special educators should keep abreast of research findings and implement research-based practices with their students (CEC, 2009). Moreover, the No Child Left Behind Act and the Individuals with Disabilities Education Act of 2004 both place considerable emphasis on practices that are supported by scientifically based research (e.g., Hess & Petrilli, 2006; A. Smith, 2003; H. R. Turnbull, 2005). Using research as the preferred method to determine what and how to teach makes sense because research can address many of the shortcomings of other traditional approaches for identifying what works.

False Positives and False Negatives

When examining a practice's effectiveness, four possibilities exist to represent the relation between reality (Does the practice actually work for the children in question?) and educators' judgments (Do I believe that the practice works?) (see Figure 1.1). Educators can be right, or hit, in two ways: they can conclude that the practice (a) works, and it actually does, or (b) does not work, and it actually does not. They can also be wrong, or miss, in two ways. First, educators can commit a false positive by concluding that the practice works when it actually *is not* effective. Second, educators can commit a false negative by concluding that the practice does not work, when it actually *is* effective. The goal of any approach to determining what works is to maximize the number of hits while minimizing the likelihood of false positives and false negatives.

As discussed in the previous section, using personal experience, colleagues, tradition, and expert opinion leaves the door open to false positives and false negatives, which results in ineffective teaching and suboptimal outcomes for students with disabilities. Sound scientific research reduces the likelihood of false positives and false negatives in a number of ways, such as (a) using credible measures of student performance, (b) involving large and representative samples, (c) using research designs that rule out alternative explanations for change in student performance, and (d) engaging in the open and iterative nature of science (Lloyd, Pullen, Tankersley, & Lloyd, 2006).

Safeguards in Scientific Research

Credible Measures

Teachers' perceptions of students' behavior and academic performance are often based on subjective perceptions and unreliable measures and therefore do not correspond strictly with actual student behavior and performance (e.g., Madelaine & Wheldall, 2005). In contrast, sound scientific research uses trustworthy methods for measuring phenomena. Whether using direct observations of behavior, formal assessments, curriculum-based measures, or standardized rating scales, high-quality research utilizes procedures and instruments that are both reliable (i.e., consistent) and valid (i.e., meaningful) to accurately gauge student behavior and performance.

Large and Representative Samples

Educators typically interact with a limited number of students, whose performance and behavior may differ meaningfully from other students. Consequently, personal experience (as well as the experiences of colleagues or experts) may not generalize to other students. That is, just because a practice worked for a few students does not mean that it will work for most others. In contrast, research studies typically involve relatively large and often representative samples of student participants across multiple environments and educators. When research has shown that a practice has been effective for the vast majority of a very large number of students, the results are likely to generalize to others in the same population. It is true, however, that most single-subject research studies and some group experimental studies involve a relatively small number of participants. In these cases, confidence in research findings is obtained across a body of research, when multiple studies with convergent findings show that an intervention works for a substantial number of students within a population.

Ruling Out Alternative Explanations

When educators informally examine whether a practice works, they might implement the technique and observe whether students' outcomes subsequently improve. If outcomes do improve, it might seem reasonable to conclude that the intervention worked. However, this conclusion might be a false positive. The students may have improved because of their own development, or something else (e.g., a new educational assistant, a change in class schedule) may be responsible for improved outcomes. Group experimental and single-subject research studies are designed to rule out explanations for improved student outcomes other than the intervention being examined. In other words, causality (i.e., an intervention generally *causes* improved outcomes) can be inferred reasonably from these designs (B. G. Cook, Tankersley, Cook, & Landrum, 2008).

Group experimental research incorporates a control group (to which participants are randomly assigned in true experiments) that is as similar as possible to the experimental group. Ideally, the control and experimental groups comprise functionally equivalent participants, and the only differences in their experiences are that the experimental group receives the intervention whereas the control group does not. Under these conditions, if the experimental group improves more than the control group, those improved outcomes must logically be ascribed to the intervention (e.g., L. Cook, Cook, Landrum, & Tankersley, 2008).

In single-subject research studies, individuals provide their own control condition. A baseline measure (e.g., typical instruction) of a student's outcomes over time serves as a comparison for the student's outcomes in the presence of the intervention. Single-subject researchers strive to make conditions in the baseline and intervention phases equivalent, except for the intervention. Of course, it is possible that the student's outcomes improved in the presence of the intervention relative to the outcome trend during baseline because of a number of phenomena outside the control of the researcher (i.e., not the intervention; e.g., new medication, a change in home life). Accordingly, single-subject researchers must provide at least three demonstrations of a functional relationship between the intervention and student outcomes. When the intervention is introduced or withdrawn and student outcomes change in the predicted direction at least three times, educators can then be confident that the intervention was responsible for changes in the student outcomes (e.g., Tankersley, Harjusola-Webb, & Landrum, 2008).

Open and Iterative Nature of Science

Although many safeguards exist at the level of individual studies to protect against false positives and false negatives, scientific research is inevitably an imperfect enterprise. No study is ideal, and it is impossible for researchers to control for all possible factors that may influence student outcomes in the real world of schools. Furthermore, researchers can and sometimes do make mistakes, which may result in reporting misleading findings. The more general process and nature of scientific research protects against spurious findings in at least two additional ways: public examination of research and recognizing that knowledge is an iterative process.

When reporting a study, researchers must describe their research (e.g., sample, procedures, instruments) in detail. Additionally, before being published in a peer-reviewed journal (the most common outlet for research studies), research studies are evaluated by the journal editors and blind-reviewed (the reviewers' and authors' identities are confidential) by a number of experts in the relevant field. Authors also must provide contact information, which readers can use to make queries about the study or request the data for reevaluation. These processes necessitate that published research undergoes multiple layers of scrutiny, which are likely to (a) weed out most studies with serious errors before being published and (b) identify errors that do exist in published studies.

Finally, it is critical to recognize that research is an iterative process in which greater confidence in a practice is accrued as findings from multiple studies converge in its support. Even with the safeguard of peer review and public scrutiny of research, published studies do sometimes report inaccurate findings. However, the iterative nature of science suggests that conclusions are best examined across entire bodies of research literature made up of multiple studies. For truly effective practices, the possible erroneous conclusions of one or two studies will be shown to be incorrect by a far larger number of studies with accurate findings. Thus, in contrast to relying on personal experience or on expert opinions, science has built-in self-correction mechanisms for identifying spurious results (Sagan, 1996; Shermer, 2002).

Caveats

Research-based practices represent powerful tools for improving the educational outcomes of students with disabilities, yet special educators need to understand a number of associated caveats and limitations. Specifically, research-based practices (a) will not work for everyone, (b) need to be implemented in concert with effective teaching practices, (c) must be selected carefully to match the needs of targeted students, and (d) should be adapted to maximize their impact.

Special educators cannot assume that a practice shown by research to be *generally* effective will be automatically effective for *all* of their students. No number of research participants or studies translates into a guarantee that a practice will work for each and every student, especially for students with disabilities who have unique learning characteristics and needs. Nonresponders, or treatment resistors, will exist for even the most effective instructional approaches. Therefore, although research-based practices are highly likely to be effective and special educators should therefore prioritize these practices, special educators should also always systematically evaluate the effects of these practices through progress monitoring (e.g., Deno, 2006).

Furthermore, research-based practices do not constitute good teaching but represent one important component of effective instruction. Research on effective teaching indicates that effective instruction is characterized by a collection of teacher behaviors, such as pacing instruction appropriately, emphasizing academic instruction, previewing instruction and reviewing previous instruction, monitoring student performance, circulating around and scanning the instructional environment to identify learner needs, recognizing appropriate student behavior, exhibiting enthusiasm, displaying "withitness" (an awareness of what is happening throughout the classroom), and using wait time after asking questions (Brophy & Good, 1986; Doyle, 1986). When educators implement research-based practices in the context of generally *ineffective* instruction—instruction that occurs in the absence of these hallmarks of effective teaching—the practices are unlikely to produce desired outcomes. As such, research-based practices cannot take the place of and should always be applied in the context of good teaching (B. G. Cook, Tankersley, & Harjusola-Webb, 2008).

Another important caveat is that a practice demonstrated by research studies to be effective for one group may not work for others. It is therefore important that special educators are aware of the student group for which a practice has been demonstrated to be effective when selecting instructional and assessment practices to use with their students. For example, although a practice may have been shown by research studies to be effective for elementary students with learning disabilities, it may not work or even be appropriate for high school students with autism. However, highly effective practices tend to be powerful and their effects robust, and as such, they typically work for more than one specific group of children. For example, the use of mnemonic strategies has been shown to be effective for nondisabled students, students with learning disabilities, students with emotional and behavioral disorders, and students with intellectual impairments at a variety of grade levels (Scruggs & Mastropieri, 2000). Therefore, when reading about a practice that has been validated by research as effective with, for example, students with learning disabilities, special educators working with children and youth with other disabilities should not simply assume that the practice will be similarly effective for their students. But neither should they automatically assume that the practice will be ineffective. Rather, we recommend that special educators use their unique insights and knowledge of their students to evaluate the supporting research, underlying theory, and critical elements of a practice to determine the likelihood that a research-based practice will work for them.

Furthermore, special educators will need to consider whether and how to adapt research-based practices to meet the unique needs of their students. Although implementing a practice as designed is important (e.g., if a practice is not implemented correctly, one cannot expect it to be as effective as it was in the supporting research), recent research has indicated that overly rigid adherence to research-based practices may actually reduce their effectiveness (e.g., Hogue et al., 2008). It appears that teachers should adapt research-based practices to match the unique learning needs of their students and make the practice their own (McMaster et al., 2010). Yet they must do so in a way that preserves the integrity of the essential elements of the research-based practice to avoid rendering it ineffective.

These caveats notwithstanding, because of its many safeguards protecting against false-positive and false-negative conclusions regarding what works, scientific research is the best method available for special educators to identify effective instructional practices. By making decisions about how to teach on the basis of collective bodies of peer-reviewed research studies, special educators can identify with confidence practices that are likely to work for their students.

The Research-to-Practice Gap in Special Education

"Educational research could and should be a vital resource to teachers, particularly when they work with diverse learners—students with disabilities, children of poverty, limited-English speaking students. It is not" (Carnine, 1997, p. 513). The research-to-practice gap describes the commonplace occurrence of children and youth being taught with unproven practices while practices supported through research are not implemented. It is a complex phenomenon with many underlying causes that defies simple solutions. Kauffman (1996) suggested that the research-to-practice gap may be particularly extreme in special education, illustrating that an inverse relationship may actually exist between research support and degree of implementation for instructional practices in special education.

Despite reforms and legislation supporting the role of research in education, research findings indicate that the gap between research and practice continues to persist. For example, special educators reported using research-based practices no more often than ineffective practices (Burns & Ysseldyke, 2009; Jones, 2009). Jones also observed that some special education teachers over-reported their use of research-based practices, suggesting that the actual implementation rate of research-based practices may be even lower than reported. To make matters worse, when special educators do implement research-based practices, they often do so with low levels of fidelity (or not as designed; e.g., B. G. Cook & Schirmer, 2006)—potentially rendering the practices ineffective. Furthermore, many special educators report that they do not trust research or researchers (Boardman, Arguelles, Vaughn, Hughes, & Klingner, 2005) and find information from other teachers more trustworthy and usable (Landrum, Cook, Tankersley, & Fitzgerald, 2002, 2007).

The research-to-practice gap has clear and direct implications for the educational outcomes of students with disabilities. Using practices shown to have reliable and positive effects on student outcomes is the most likely way to improve student performance. Using research-based practices should, therefore, be a professional and ethical imperative for educators. This is true for all teachers. But as Dammann and Vaughn (2001) noted, whereas nondisabled students may perform adequately even in the presence of less than optimal instruction, students with disabilities require that their teachers use the most effective instructional practices to reach their potentials and attain successful school outcomes.

This Textbook and Addressing the Research-to-Practice Gap

Bridging the research-to-practice gap in special education represents a significant challenge. Many issues will have to be addressed, such as improving teachers' attitudes toward research, providing ongoing supports for teachers to adopt and maintain research-based practices, and conducting high-quality research that is relevant to special education teachers (see B. G. Cook, Landrum, Tankersley, & Kauffman, 2003). But perhaps the most fundamental issues for bridging the research-to-practice gap are (a) *identifying* those practices that are research-based in critical areas of special education and (b) *providing the relevant information* (e.g., supporting theory, critical elements of the research-based practices, specific information on the supporting research studies) necessary to guide special educators in deciding whether the practice is right for them and their students and how to implement it. Without these critical first steps of identifying and providing special educators relevant information about research-based practices, the field of special education is unlikely to make significant progress in bridging the gap between research and practice.

Turning to original reports of research is an unsatisfactory alternative for the vast majority of special educators. Most teachers do not have the training to critically analyze technical research reports that often are geared for audiences with advanced training in statistics and research (Greenwood & Abbott, 2001). And even for those educators with advanced training in these areas, their full-time teaching jobs should and typically do occupy their time. It is simply not realistic for teachers to read through, synthesize, and critically analyze entire bodies of research literature for every instructional decision with which they are faced.

Textbooks focused on methods of instruction and assessment seem an ideal place to provide educators with useful information on research-based practices that can be used to bridge the research-to-practice gap. Unfortunately, much of teacher education—both preservice and in-service—is based on expert opinion and the personal experiences of those conducting the training or writing the training materials (e.g., textbooks). For example, textbook authors frequently recommend practices with little justification. Discussion of supporting research, if provided at all, is often too brief and incomplete for educators to make informed decisions about the appropriateness of the recommended practice for their classrooms. For example, Dacy, Nihalani, Cestone, and Robinson (2011) analyzed the content of three teaching methods textbooks and found that when prescriptive recommendations for using practices were supported by citations, authors predominantly cited secondary sources (e.g., books, position papers) rather than provide discussions of original research from which their readers might arrive at meaningful conclusions regarding the effectiveness of the practices.

To address special educators' need for trustworthy, detailed, and teacher-friendly summaries of the research literature regarding what works in special education, the chapters in the complete, four-part text (B. G. Cook & Tankersley, 2013) provide thorough synopses of the research literature supporting research-based practices in core areas of special education: academics, behavior, assessment, and targeted groups of learners.

Specifically, in this volume on improving the academic outcomes of targeted groups of students with disabilities, chapter authors, who are documented experts on the topics of focus, identify research-based practices to address critical and unique areas of need for the following groups of children and youth with disabilities: young children with disabilities, English language learners, students with language disorders, students with autism spectrum disorders, students with high-incidence disabilities, students with severe intellectual disabilities, students with sensory disabilities, students with physical disabilities, and students transitioning to adulthood. Chapter authors discuss and recommend practices and approaches based on supporting research. Chapter authors also provide readers with descriptions of the underlying theory supporting the practices; supporting research studies, including information such as the research designs, the number and type of participants, and the degree to which the recommended practices positively affected student outcomes; and the critical elements of each research-based practice. Using this information, special educators can (a) make informed decisions about which research-based practices best fit their needs and (b) begin to implement the practices and improve the educational outcomes of their students with disabilities.

Conclusion

Special educators clearly want to use the most effective practices to enhance the educational outcomes and opportunities of the students they teach. However, given traditional methods for determining what works and the rapid proliferation of information on teaching techniques on the Internet (Landrum & Tankersley, 2004), much of which is misleading, it is increasingly difficult and complicated to know what works, what doesn't, and how to know the difference. Research is the most trustworthy method for determining what works in special education. This text provides readers with a wealth of information on specific research-based practices for improving outcomes for targeted groups of learners in special education.

CHAPTER 2

Research-Based Practices in Early Childhood Special Education

Mary Jo Noonan and **Patricia Sheehey** | *University of Hawaii at Manoa*

Early childhood special education (ECSE) addresses the needs of young children with disabilities, birth through age 8. The intent of ECSE is to optimize developmental outcomes for children with delays or disabilities by providing individualized, specialized services. ECSE has its roots in compensatory education: In 1972, Head Start began requiring that 10% of their enrollment be children who have disabilities (Economic Opportunity Act Amendments). Although the Education for All Handicapped Children Act (EHA) of 1975 mandated special education for school-age students, it *permitted* but did not *require* states to provide services to infants, toddlers, and preschoolers. Not until the EHA Amendments of 1986 were states mandated to provide preschool special education to 3- to 5-year-olds with disabilities. These amendments also provided grants and incentive monies to states to encourage them to develop early intervention services for infants and toddlers (birth through age 2) with disabilities.

Since the establishment of early intervention and preschool special education programs through the EHA Amendments of 1986, the numbers of infants and young children with disabilities served through EHA—now known as the Individuals with Disabilities Education Improvement Act (IDEA, 2004)—have grown steadily. The 2007 *Annual Report to Congress* (U.S. Department of Education, 2007) indicated that slightly over

1 million young children, birth through age 5, received early intervention and preschool special education through IDEA (298,150 children received early intervention services, and 704,087 received preschool special education). The most frequently identified disabilities among the preschool children served through IDEA in 2005 were speech or language impairments (46.4%) and developmental delay (27.8%). Given that speech and language impairments and developmental delay are relatively mild disabilities, it is not surprising that approximately one third of these children received all of their special services in typical early childhood environments (U.S. Department of Education, 2007).

Three major philosophical perspectives have influenced the development of research-based practices in ECSE: inclusion, natural environments, and developmentally appropriate practice. The philosophical perspective of *inclusion* has a long history dating back to the deinstitutionalization, normalization, and integration movements of the 1970s (cf., Schalock, Harber, & Genung, 1981; Scheerenberger, 1977; Wolfensberger, 1972). The basic tenet of these movements was that all individuals have a right to fully participate in society. For young children with disabilities, this means that most children should receive their specialized services in day-care and preschool programs that serve primarily children who do not have disabilities, rather than attend segregated preschools enrolling only children with disabilities (Division for Early Childhood [DEC] and the National Association for the Education of Young Children [NAEYC], 2009). As educational environments, quality early childhood programs provide children with disabilities a varied and rich curriculum of play, exploration, socialization, communication, and other developmental activities. And as social environments, inclusive early childhood programs afford children with disabilities and their families opportunities to develop friendships and social networks with children who do not have disabilities and their families.

Special education legislation also supports the philosophy of inclusion—especially the least restrictive environment (LRE) policy of the IDEA (2004). Furthermore, the effectiveness and feasibility of inclusive early childhood programs have been demonstrated since the early 1970s, when Head Start began requiring that 10% of its enrollment be children with disabilities (P.L. 92-424, Sec. 3[b]) and when the U.S. federal government funded the model, inclusive of ECSE preschool programs (cf., D. Bricker & Bricker, 1971; D. Bricker, Bricker, Iacino, & Dennison, 1976; W. Bricker & Bricker, 1976). Since these initial efforts, inclusive ECSE programs have shown their effectiveness throughout the United States, serving children with disabilities who have a wide range of special needs (cf., Guralnick, 2001).

The *natural environments* perspective was described in IDEA (1991) to clarify the meaning of least restrictive settings for young children who are not yet school age. According to IDEA, natural environments are "home and community settings in which children without disabilities participate" (Section 303.12), such as preschools, day-care settings, and other community groups serving same-age peers. The opportunity for young children to participate in these natural environments is further supported by the Americans with Disabilities Act (ADA, 1990), which prohibits private programs that serve the public from discriminating against individuals on the basis of disability. The perspective of natural environments exceeds the legal preference for these typical settings, however, and suggests that interventions be provided through *natural learning opportunities* within the settings. Natural learning opportunities are routines and activities that occur in the everyday lives of young children, especially routines and activities that appear to be of high interest to the child (Bruder, 2001; Dunst & Bruder, 2006). When children show high interest, they are focused and engaged in the routine or activity and their learning is enhanced (Dunst et al., 2001). Teaching through natural learning opportunities thereby uses the inherent motivational qualities of inclusive, natural environments (McWilliam & Casey, 2008).

And finally, the third perspective that has strongly influenced the development of research-based practices in ECSE is developmentally appropriate practice (DAP). DAP is a philosophy and a set of principles of the National Association for the Education of Young Children, the leading professional organization for early childhood education (Bredekamp, 1987; Bredekamp & Rosegrant, 1992; Copple & Bredekamp, 2009), which guides the development and assessment of high-quality early childhood programs. Programs that adhere to DAP *facilitate* learning by following children's interests and natural inquisitiveness. Children are encouraged to explore, and teachers respond by arranging related learning activities. Early academics are not the focus; instead, play, social, community, and daily living activities appropriate to the children's developmental levels make up the curriculum.

The earliest publications of DAP did not mention young children with disabilities, and subsequently, the professional community has addressed and debated the applicability and appropriateness of DAP for ECSE in the past (cf., Berkeley & Ludlow, 1989; Carta, Schwartz, Atwater, & McConnell, 1991; Cavallaro, Haney, & Cabello, 1993; J. E. Johnson & Johnson, 1992). Although it may not always provide sufficient structure, supports, and specialized instruction for young children with disabilities through its curricular approach, DAP has come to characterize most preschool settings that serve primarily children without disabilities and therefore represents the targeted inclusion model for most young children with disabilities. The challenge is to identify research-based intervention practices that can be implemented in programs that adhere to DAP (Hemmeter, 2000).

Review of Research-Based Practices

Together, the perspectives of inclusion, natural environments, and DAP have influenced the development of research-based practices for ECSE. Research-based practices are not just those shown to produce developmental gains for young children with disabilities; they are also practices that have been demonstrated to be successful and practical in inclusive and natural environments (Hemmeter, 2000). Two ECSE practices with empirical support for their effectiveness in natural contexts are (a) activity-based intervention (ABI) and (b) milieu teaching.

Activity-Based Intervention

As noted previously, a significant challenge of ECSE is to provide effective, specialized instruction to young children with disabilities in inclusive, natural environments. In a 1989 book chapter, D. Bricker and Cripe defined and proposed ABI as an approach for addressing this challenge. The chapter was soon followed by a detailed textbook on developing and implementing ABI (D. Bricker & Cripe, 1992). As suggested by the title of the approach, ABI provides interventions *during* activities, rather than *as* activities. More specifically, ABI is characterized by four major elements: (a) child-directed instructional interactions; (b) instruction embedded in child-directed, teacher directed, and routine activities; (c) logically occurring antecedents and consequences; and (d) functional and generative skill outcomes. It was developed as a framework for providing special education in conjunction with DAP (D. Bricker & Cripe, 1992).

In linking ABI and DAP, children with disabilities attend inclusive early childhood programs and participate in the same developmentally appropriate activities as their peers who do not have disabilities; specialized interventions are infused into the developmentally appropriate activities. This is in direct contrast to traditional, separate special education preschool programs where activities were defined by individualized education program (IEP) objectives and focused on developmental areas of need (e.g., "motor time," "language time"). A major difference in the two approaches is the *context* of instruction: In ABI, children's special needs are addressed *within* a developmentally appropriate activity; in separate special education preschool programs, children's intervention needs are addressed in isolation of contextually meaningful activities.

A second important difference between separate ECSE programs and inclusive programs that implement ABI is the manner in which specialized interventions are provided. Separate ECSE programs have primarily implemented highly structured, one-on-one, didactic behavioral interventions. Instead, ABI emphasizes a more general, incidental approach to intervention. Using ABI, the special education teacher is guided by broad goals and follows the child's interest to determine when and where to provide specialized instruction (D. Bricker & Cripe, 1992). This child-directed approach to intervention is exemplified in milieu teaching, the second research-based practice we discuss in this chapter.

Theoretical Underpinnings

As described by D. Bricker and Cripe (1992), the ABI model is based on several related conceptual and theoretical frameworks. These include theoretical assumptions of early intervention, a psychoeducational framework, and learning theories. Foundational assumptions of early intervention are two: (a) delays and/or disabilities can be positively affected by intervention, and (b) early

experiences are an important factor in early development. Related assumptions are that (a) young children with disabilities need more and/or different experiences than children who do not have disabilities; (b) personnel must be well-trained in providing formal, early intervention to address children's special needs; and (c) children with delays or disabilities experience improved developmental outcomes if they participate in early intervention. Taken together, these assumptions posit that young children with delays or disabilities will benefit from high-quality, specialized early intervention.

ABI curricula are contextualized by a psychoeducational framework that targets generative, functional, and adaptive skills (D. Bricker & Cripe, 1992). *Generative* means that a child can modify an existing response and formulate a novel and appropriate response to fit a new situation. This is sometimes referred to as response generalization (Carr, 1988). *Functional* skills are immediately useful responses. Pointing to a photo of a cup when a teacher says, "Show me the cup," may be considered nonfunctional; whereas handing a cup to the teacher when told, "Give me your cup if you want water," would be considered a functional skill. And finally, *adaptive* responses are those that are modified to fit a social or physical constraint or need. In other words, a child's repertoire should be flexible enough that if one response is ineffective, one or more additional responses can be used. ABI focuses on teaching generative, functional, and adaptive skills that help children meet the ever-changing demands of natural environments.

Interventions to teach generative, functional, and adaptive skills using ABI are influenced by the learning theories of Vygotsky, Piaget, and Dewey (D. Bricker, 1986; D. Bricker & Cripe, 1992). These three theories share the common thread that the child's interaction with the environment is fundamental to development and learning. Vygotsky's child development theory emphasized the role of social interaction in the learning process, and noted that interaction has a reciprocal effect: The environment affects the child, and the child, in turn, affects the environment (Vygotsky, 1978). While Piaget believed that child development was primarily a biological process, he stressed that it also required environmental interaction because of the feedback obtained through the interaction. Focusing on children's cognitive development, Piaget proposed that children construct their intelligence as they actively engage in the world (Piaget, 1954). Dewey (1916), an educational theorist, emphasized that learning is an experiential process. He suggested that children learn from *all* of their experiences; and educational goals are maximized when teachers orchestrate thoughtfully planned, sequenced, and well-organized activities that allow for children's full participation. D. Bricker and Cripe (1992) based ABI on three themes drawn from the theoretical frameworks of Vygotsky, Piaget, and Dewey: "1) the influence and interaction of both the immediate and larger social-cultural environment, 2) the need for active involvement by the learner, and 3) the enhancement of learning by engaging children in functional and meaningful activities" (p. 16).

Research Base

D. Bricker and Cripe (1992) summarized initial research on ABI in four manuscripts (Bailey & Bricker, 1985; D. Bricker, Bruder, & Bailey, 1982; D. Bricker & Gumerlock, 1988; D. Bricker & Sheehan, 1981). These studies were conducted as program evaluations of a model ABI demonstration project for infants and preschoolers with and without disabilities. All four studies were pretest/post-test comparisons, and included norm-referenced and criterion-referenced measures addressing developmental milestones and preacademic skills. Although none of these program evaluation studies included control/comparison groups, the data did indicate that children made significant progress over spans of 5 months to 2 years. In a more controlled single-subject alternating treatments study of object naming with six preschool children who were at risk or had developmental delays, results indicated that direct instruction was associated with more rapid skill acquisition than ABI; however, ABI was more effective in promoting generalization and maintenance of the newly acquired object names (Losardo & Bricker, 1994).

Concurrent with the development of ABI by Bricker and her colleagues, other researchers investigated what is probably the most distinctive feature of ABI, *embedded instruction.* Embedded instruction is also known as embedded learning opportunities (Dunst, Hamby, Trivette, Raab, & Bruder, 2000; Horn, Lieber, Li, Sandall, & Schwartz, 2000), routines-based instruction (Pretti-Frontczak, Barr, Macy, & Carter, 2003; Schepis, Reid, Ownbey, & Parsons, 2001), and participation-based practices (Campbell, 2004; Fleming, Sawyer, & Campbell, 2011). Consistent with the description in ABI, embedded instruction means that intervention to address the needs of children with disabilities is incorporated into ongoing, functional, age-appropriate activities. These activities can be in preschool, home, or community environments.

Researchers have shown that embedded instruction is an effective technique across a wide range of skill areas (Fox & Hanline, 1993; Grisham-Brown, Schuster, Hemmeter, & Collins, 2000; Horn et al., 2000; Kohler, Strain, Hoyson, & Jamieson, 1997; McBride & Schwartz, 2003), including communication (McBride & Schwartz, 2003; Peck, Killen, & Baumgart, 1989; Warren & Gazdag, 1990), social (Macy & Bricker, 2007; Venn & Wolery, 1992), play (Schepis et al., 2001),

self-help (McBride & Schwartz, 2003; Schepis et al., 2001; Sewell, Collins, Hemmeter, & Schuster, 1998), cognitive/preacademic (Daugherty, Grisham-Brown, & Hemmeter, 2001; McBride & Schwartz, 2003; Venn et al., 1993), and transition (Bakkaloglu, 2008). A number of teaching strategies have been used as the intervention method during embedded instruction, such as time delay (Daugherty et al., 2001; Grisham-Brown et al., 2000), incidental teaching (Bakkalogu, 2008; Horn et al., 2000; Macy & Bricker, 2007; Mudd & Wolery, 1987; Warren & Kaiser, 1986), discrete trial training/systematic instruction (Grisham-Brown et al., 2000; McBride & Schwartz, 2003; Sewell et al., 1998), and peer-based strategies (Kohler et al., 1997). And finally, research has demonstrated that embedded instruction can be implemented effectively in inclusive early childhood settings and home environments, even by relatively inexperienced student teachers, teaching assistants, and family members (Dunst et al., 2001; Fox & Hanline, 1993; Kaiser, Hancock, & Hester, 1998; Kohler et al., 1997; Macy & Bricker, 2007; Schepis et al., 2001).

Despite the large number of studies indicating that embedding is an effective strategy that does not require extensive training or support to implement, some studies have indicated that embedding is not used to the extent that it could be, even following training on its implementation (Horn et al., 2000; Pretti-Frontczak & Bricker, 2001). Pretti-Frontzcak and Bricker found that teachers were most likely to embed instruction during one-on-one activities and in situations that were more teacher directed than child directed. This finding was concerning for two reasons: first, one-on-one activities did not occur very often in the inclusive environments observed during the study, and thus, very little instruction was occurring for the targeted skills. Second, the procedure was designed to be implemented as teachers followed the children's lead. The multitude of demands on teachers' attention and responsibilities during the school day as well as their concerns about stigmatizing children with disabilities by implementing specialized interventions also seem to influence the extent to which the embedding strategy was implemented (Horn et al., 2000). Although Pretti-Frontzcak and Bricker emphasized that teachers must learn to identify opportunities for embedded instruction as they naturally occur, they also recommended that providing some planning—such as engineering opportunities for instruction (cf., Grisham-Brown et al., 2000) or establishing a minimum number of opportunities for instruction within an activity (cf., Macy & Bricker, 2007)—may help to increase teachers' use of embedding.

Unlike ABI, embedded instruction is not a comprehensive curricular approach; instead, it focuses solely on providing specially designed instruction to students with disabilities during meaningful, developmentally appropriate activities. Results of the related research on embedded instruction, however, lend support to ABI as a research-based practice in early childhood special education. ABI—and its most recognized component, embedded instruction—is now considered a recommended practice in ECSE (Sandall, Hemmeter, Smith, & McLean, 2005). Next we provide a description of the procedures for implementing embedded instruction as described in the ABI model.

Implementation of ABI/Embedded Instruction

In the following sections, we provide guidelines for planning and implementing ABI/embedded instruction.

Planning for ABI/embedded instruction.   Planning the embedded instruction component of ABI involves three steps: First, the intervention itself must be developed; second, individual and group activity schedules are designed; and third, meaningful, age-appropriate activities are prepared (D. Bricker & Cripe, 1992). The intervention is a detailed instructional plan that is written in behavioral terms, specifying general antecedents (i.e., prompts or environmental arrangements provided *before* the child is expected to respond), responses (i.e., child behaviors that meet the objective), and consequences (i.e., teacher responses that correct, extend, or reinforce the child's behavior after its occurrence). The procedures delineated in the intervention are conducted in a similar manner each time it is embedded. For example, if an intervention to teach a child with physical disabilities to reach for a desired object is developed, it might be embedded one or more times during arrival at preschool, large-group morning circle, center activities, and snack time. When the intervention plan is implemented in each of these activities, the antecedents, response, and consequences will be nearly identical (some slight differences may be necessary to fit the activity). In this example, the antecedent could be that highly preferred items are placed within the child's reach, but at a distance requiring the child to extend her elbow and shoulder in order to obtain the items. The response could be stated as any arm movement that results in the child's touching the item. And the consequence might be that a teacher physically assists the child in grasping and obtaining the item as soon as the child touches the item. If the child doesn't reach the object within 6 seconds, the teacher assists the child in reaching and grasping the item.

When this intervention is embedded throughout the school day, the materials and activities will vary. During arrival at preschool, the child may reach for a book to look at while waiting for school to begin; in the large-group morning circle, the child may reach for a magnifying glass to use in the science center for a new activity; and at snack time, the child may reach to indicate a preferred type of cracker. Because the intervention is implemented in a nearly identical manner each time it is embedded, the child is likely to learn that given a particular antecedent situation (e.g., when an item is out of reach), a specific response (e.g., reaching with extended shoulder and elbow) consistently results in a given consequence (e.g., obtaining a desired item). Thus, systematic instruction is provided across a variety of meaningful activities. The variety of activities, and the associated variations in materials, peers, adults, and other situational stimuli, have an added benefit of promoting generalization (Stokes & Baer, 1977).

The second step in planning embedded instruction in the ABI model is to design individual and group activity schedules. This step is critical because it ensures that children receive both one-on-one and group instruction. It also provides an accountability mechanism to ensure that children receive an adequate amount of instruction on priority objectives, while at the same time allowing teachers to schedule a manageable amount of embedded instruction. Individual and group activity schedules are created as matrices (Noonan & McCormick, 2006, pp. 94–95). The group activity schedule is created by listing the daily schedule of home, community, and/or classroom activities down the left side of a grid, and the children's names/objectives to be embedded throughout the day across the top of the grid. The schedule should include a balance of child-initiated (e.g., child-directed play during centers time), teacher-directed (e.g., group science lesson), and routine activities (e.g., cleanup in preparation for recess). Check marks are placed in the cells of the grid corresponding to objectives that will be taught during each activity (see Figure 2.1). A teacher can then review a group activity schedule before an activity and note which children's objectives are to be embedded during that activity.

The individual activity schedules are similar to the group activity schedules. Instead of placing check marks in the cells of the grid specifying when objectives are embedded, a brief description of how the objective will be addressed within the corresponding activity is noted in the cell. Continuing with the example discussed previously, "Reaches to indicate book choice" is written in the cell corresponding to morning arrival time in the schedule and the objective of "reaches for an item." The individual activity schedule is developed for each child and operationalizes the form that objectives take when embedded in activities.

Preparing activities is the third step in implementing embedded instruction in the ABI model. Selection or creation of activities is a critical step in ABI: activities

Figure 2.1   Group activity matrix.

Schedule	Students and Embedded Objectives					
	Jacob: makes two-word requests	Sara: names item	Keoni: takes two conversational turns	Mia: points to symbol on board	Sam: points to indicate choice	Malia: Looks at speaker and makes audible request
Arrival			✓	✓		✓
Group Exercise		✓			✓	
Snack	✓	✓	✓	✓	✓	✓
Hygiene		✓		✓		
Morning Circle	✓		✓	✓		✓
Centers	✓	✓				✓
Recess			✓		✓	
Lunch	✓				✓	✓

must be developmentally appropriate, that is, age appropriate, meaningful, and of high interest to the children (with and without disabilities). As indicated, the plans are written for child-directed activities, teacher-directed activities, and routines. The plan includes a detailed description/sequence of the activity, variations that might be included, and required materials. An example of a description/sequence of a "Trip to the Store" activity is provided by D. Bricker and Cripe (1992), and begins as follows:

> The activity area is set up as a pretend store. The interventionist is positioned at the cash register and the children are near the shelves or pushing shopping carts. The interventionist has materials such as bags and shopping lists behind the cash register at the beginning of the activity. (p. 117)

The description continues and explains that the children may decide how they get to the store, what they might talk about during the activity, and what they might do while in the store. The use of various materials (e.g., purses, play money, food items) is also described. The "variations" section of the activity plan suggests alternative approaches to the activity, such as stocking the store or shopping for a specific purpose, such as a birthday party. The intent of the activity plan is to provide a general guide (script) of the activity, keeping in mind the need for naturally or logically occurring opportunities to embed instruction on children's selected objectives. The activity plan also includes situations that facilitate learning opportunities (e.g., surprising students with items that are new to the classroom or are highly preferred items).

Implementing ABI/embedded instruction.   To implement ABI, activities are conducted as indicated on the activity schedules and activity plans. During an activity, the teacher carefully attends to the children with embedded objectives and watches for opportunities for instruction (transactions). The teacher is responsive to the children and may facilitate an instructional opportunity by following a child's lead and/or interacting in a reciprocal manner. If a preschool child is playing with toy cars and has an embedded objective to initiate interactions with peers, the teacher may begin by playing responsively with the child. For instance, the teacher may pick up a car and roll it behind the child's car. If the child directs the teacher to move the car along a particular path, the teacher complies and allows the child to lead the play. If the child changes the type of play with the car (perhaps moving the car toward the teacher's car), the teacher may reciprocate by moving the car in a novel fashion. By following the child's lead and interacting reciprocally, the teacher has entered the child's play. As the play continues, the teacher may use a number of strategies to embed learning opportunities to address the objective of initiating interaction with peers.

One example of an embedding strategy to teach social interactions is to bring a peer into proximity with a new and unique toy car. Novelty often attracts attention and may provide a naturalistic prompt for the target child to initiate interaction. When the target child shows attention in any way to the peer with the new toy car, the teacher responds to the child's interest by embedding and implementing the instructional plan (providing the prompts, corrections, and other consequences indicated in the plan) to teach the child to initiate interaction with a peer. Another strategy might be to introduce materials that have been shown to facilitate child interaction, such as building blocks. A peer can be guided to play next to the target child, building bridges and roads with blocks. When the child looks at or approaches the block roads or bridges, the teacher notices the learning opportunity and embeds the instructional plan.

Other strategies for embedding suggested by D. Bricker and Cripe (1992) include:

1. *Forgetfulness:* The teacher prompts a response from the child by *forgetting* to provide a necessary material or step for an activity. During tooth brushing, for example, toothbrushes and cups might be lined up on the counter, but the toothpaste is missing.

2. *Visible but unreachable:* Highly desirable items are placed in view, but at a distance beyond where a child can access them independently. This strategy prompts interaction to obtain the items.

3. *Violation of expectations:* A step or component of a familiar routine or activity is changed or omitted. Instead of saying, "And the pig says oink-oink," while reading a favorite story, the teacher might say, "And the pig says meow-meow." Similar to the forgetfulness strategy, the violation of expectations encourages or evokes a response from the child as the child is surprised and recognizes the error.

4. *Piece by piece:* When an activity involves several pieces or components, the teacher can provide one piece at a time, requiring the child to request each piece throughout the activity time (e.g., child must ask for each item of a tea set when setting a table).

5. *Assistance:* Materials that are highly desirable, but difficult to use independently (e.g., starting an electronic toy, putting on tie-shoes in preparation for recess), can encourage children to interact or attempt various problem-solving strategies, potentially including a target objective.

6. *Sabotage:* To promote problem solving and child interaction with materials, peers, or adults, the teacher can intentionally interrupt or interfere with the workings of an item. For example, a computer mouse can be hidden, or children can be told to get art materials only to find that the art cabinet is locked.

7. *Interruption or delay:* When used judiciously (as to not cause too much upset), stopping or pausing an activity or routine—especially a very familiar one—can be highly effective in prompting initiations and requests from children. When singing

the itsy-bitsy spider song with a toddler, for example, the teacher might pause the song's words and hand motions just after singing, "Down came the rain and . . ." prompting the child to look at the adult and either indicate what comes next (singing "washed the spider out," or taking the teacher's hands to make the washing-out motion) or requesting that the adult continue.

The techniques are designed to increase opportunities to embed instruction. The keys to embedded instruction are to ensure that instructional plans are implemented at times that are typical or logical for the targeted skills. Embedding instruction involves naturally occurring stimuli and consequences that will ultimately promote and support the maintenance and generalization of newly acquired skills. In summary, the components that must be present if an intervention is adhering to the guidelines of ABI (Losardo & Bricker, 1994) are listed in Table 2.1.

Table 2.1   Essential Activity-Based Intervention Components

Component	Characteristics
1. Nature of Transactions	• Teacher directs attention to child's interests, actions, and motivations.
	• Teacher follows child's lead.
	• Teacher responds reciprocally to child's initiations.
2. Goals and Objectives	• Teacher targets goals and objectives during naturally occurring opportunities.
	• Teacher ensures adequate instructional time by planning embedded goals and objectives.
	• Teacher plans beginning and end of transitions.
3. Antecedents and Consequences	• Teacher uses antecedents that are inherent or logical to the activity.
	• Teacher uses consequences that are inherent outcomes or are logical to the activity.
4. Generalization	• Teacher uses multiple antecedents to elicit a range of appropriate child responses.
	• Teacher assesses for generalization of newly acquired skills.

Source: Adapted, with permission, from p. 747 of Losardo, A. & Bricker, D. (1994). Activity-based intervention and direct instruction: A comparison study. *American Journal on Mental Retardation, 98,* 744–765.

Milieu Teaching

Perhaps the earliest demonstration of embedded instruction was Hart and Risley's (1968) language intervention study using incidental teaching, later subsumed under the naturalistic language teaching strategies known as milieu teaching (Hart & Rogers-Warren, 1978) and enhanced milieu teaching (EMT) (Kaiser, 1993). Incidental teaching was originally developed and demonstrated with preschoolers with language delays who were from economically disadvantaged backgrounds. The procedure was designed to address the challenges of generalizing newly acquired language skills to spontaneous use in new situations (Hart & Risley, 1980).

Incidental teaching is a child–adult teaching interaction that occurs during natural, unstructured times. A hallmark of incidental teaching is that teaching interactions follow the child's attentional lead. The teacher follows the child's attentional lead by approaching the child, moving to the child's level, and visually attending to what the child is attending to. Specifically, incidental teaching interactions occur in *child-selected* situations that are identified in advance as an *occasion for instruction,* such as, "when the child requests assistance, either verbally or nonverbally" (Hart & Risley, 1975, pp. 411–412). In addition to occurring under naturalistic conditions and following the child's lead, incidental teaching and its variations (milieu teaching and EMT) share the common features of using multiple examples to teach elaborated linguistic forms, explicitly prompting for child language, and providing natural consequences for children's use of targeted language (Kaiser, Yoder, & Keetz, 1992).

As described by Hart and Risley (1975), incidental teaching includes a series of decisions as the teacher responds to the child's request:

1. whether to use the occasion for incidental teaching; if yes, then

2. a decision concerning the language behavior to be obtained from the child, and

3. a decision concerning the cue to be used to initiate instruction, whether

   a. the cue of focused attention alone [following the child's attentional lead], or

   b. the cue of focused attention plus a verbal cue.

   And, if the child does not respond to the cue,

4. a decision concerning the degree of prompt to be used, whether

   a. fullest degree: a request for imitation

   b. medium degree: a request for partial imitation, or

   c. minimal degree: a request for the terminal language behavior. (p. 412)

This sequence of decision making is followed each time an incidental teaching interaction is implemented.

Theoretical Underpinnings

Developmental and behavioral perspectives have been described to explain the effectiveness of incidental and milieu teaching (Hart & Risley, 1980; Warren & Kaiser, 1986); Warren and Kaiser (1988) referred to these joint perspectives as an interactionist or hybrid framework. From a developmental perspective, incidental and milieu teaching mirror the natural social and communication interactions of parents who are responsive to their children (Bruner, 1975). For example, parents tend to reply to the meaning of their child's communication, rather than the grammatical correctness of the utterance. In other words, if a child says, "Want cookie," the parent might typically respond, "Oh, you'd like one of these chocolate chip cookies!" and gives the child the cookie. In contrast, it is unlikely for parents' replies to address the grammatical correctness of their children's requests (e.g., "No. Say, 'I want a cookie, please'"). In addition to responding to meaning rather than grammar, parents tend to reply with extensions and expansions, adding content and modeling more structure to the child's utterance. Researchers in child language development believe that this style of responsive parent interactions supports the development of more sophisticated language development (McCormick, 2003). Further, correcting grammar tends to interrupt communicative interactions and decrease subsequent language use.

Hart and Risley (1980) posited that, from a behavioral perspective, incidental teaching establishes language use as a generalized class of behavior. Children learn through incidental teaching that language use gains close, receptive adult attention and access to reinforcers. That is, the procedures of incidental teaching function to reinforce and thereby increase children's use of language. Moreover, language use transfers across settings and occasions because of reinforcement in a rich variety of stimulus conditions.

At a finer level of behavioral theoretical analysis, incidental teaching incorporates at least three stimulus conditions that promote generalization (Stokes & Baer, 1977). First, incidental teaching is conducted in natural environments that include a rich array of naturally maintaining reinforcers. As children acquire and demonstrate targeted language skills, the natural communities of reinforcers (e.g., adult attention, access to preferred items) function to maintain and increase future use of the new skills. Second, the varied array of stimulus conditions (e.g., requesting juice at snack time, requesting a favorite book during centers time, or requesting a peer-partner for a field trip) under which the child initiates language and responds with elaborations provides multiple exemplars, a procedure that promotes generalization. And third, the naturalistic conditions under which incidental teaching is implemented are inherently loosely structured, meaning that stimulus and response characteristics of environments change slightly from occasion to occasion because events rarely repeat in an identical manner. The fluid and changeable structure of the naturalistic environment functions as the *train-loosely* technique for facilitating generalization (Stokes & Baer, 1977). Together, the developmental and behavioral bases for incidental and milieu teaching provide a strong theoretical explanation for the effectiveness of the procedures.

Research Base

Beginning with the 1968 seminal study by Hart and Risley, incidental and milieu teaching have been shown to be effective strategies for increasing overall language use and rate (Halle, Baer, & Spradlin, 1981; Rogers-Warren & Warren, 1980); increasing vocabulary, linguistic complexity, and length (Hart & Risley, 1980; Warren, McQuarter, & Rogers-Warren, 1984); and teaching specific linguistic forms and functions in young children with delayed speech or mild developmental delays. The most important finding regarding incidental and milieu teaching strategies was their effectiveness in achieving generalization *concurrently* with the acquisition of new language skills (Alpert & Kaiser, 1992; Alpert & Rogers-Warren, 1984; Halle, Marshall, & Spradlin, 1979; Hart & Risley, 1974, 1975, 1980; Kaiser & Hester, 1994; Rogers-Warren & Warren, 1980; Warren et al., 1984). This was significant because it contradicted the widely held belief that generalization was an advanced stage of the learning process that could occur only after the stages of acquisition, maintenance, and fluency (R. H. Horner, Sprague, & Wilcox, 1982).

Linguistic forms and functions taught through incidental and milieu teaching include descriptive adjectives (Hart & Risley, 1968, 1974), prepositions (McGee, Krantz, & McClannahan, 1985), nouns and compound sentences (Hart & Risley, 1974), two- and three-word semantic relations (Hancock & Kaiser, 2002), receptive object labels (McGee, Krantz, Mason, & McClannahan, 1983), initiations (Halle et al., 1979), affirmations and negations (Neef, Walters, & Egel, 1984), requests (Cavallaro & Bambara, 1982; Halle et al., 1981), and responses to questions (Rogers-Warren & Warren, 1980; Warren et al., 1984). Milieu teaching has also been shown to be a research-based strategy for increasing nonverbal, prelinguistic requesting and commenting (Warren, Yoder, Gazdag, Kim, & Jones, 1993; Yoder, Warren, Kim, & Gazdag, 1994), as well as teaching the

use of augmentative/alternative communication systems such as sign language (Kaiser, Ostrosky, & Alpert, 1993; Oliver & Halle, 1982), communication boards (Kaiser et al., 1993), and voice output communication aids (Schepis, Reid, Behrmann, & Sutton, 1998).

Critical reviews have suggested that incidental and milieu teaching are most effective in teaching basic vocabulary and simple two- and three-word semantic relationships (e.g., agent–action–object) to children in the early stages of language development (Kaiser, 1993; Warren & Yoder, 1997, Yoder et al., 1995). Although initially developed and demonstrated with preschoolers from economically disadvantaged backgrounds (Hart & Risley, 1968, 1974, 1975) and with language delays (Alpert & Rogers-Warren, 1984; Rogers-Warren & Warren, 1980; Warren et al., 1984), their effectiveness has also been demonstrated with children who have disabilities such as developmental delay/intellectual disabilities (Halle et al., 1979; Halle et al., 1981; Kaiser et al., 1993; Oliver & Halle, 1982) and autism (Charlop-Christy & Carpenter, 2000; Hancock & Kaiser, 2002; McGee et al., 1985; Schepis et al., 1998).

One of the most appealing findings concerning incidental and milieu teaching strategies is that they can be implemented effectively in home and school environments, by parents (Alpert & Kaiser, 1992; Alpert & Rogers-Warren, 1984; Charlop-Christy & Carpenter, 2000; Kaiser & Hancock, 2003) and even siblings (Hancock & Kaiser, 1996). The effectiveness data on parents' implementing milieu teaching are compelling: In 2003, Kaiser and Hancock reported that 94% of the more than 200 parents trained to implement milieu teaching in their homes completed the training, and 97% of those completing the training reached the accuracy criterion. The training effectiveness and integrity resulted in secondary effects on their children (many of whom demonstrated significant language delays): nearly 90% of the children maintained and generalized language skills learned through the incidental teaching provided by their parents. Teachers have also been trained, with graphical feedback, to increase their use of milieu teaching (Casey & McWilliam, 2008).

The overwhelming majority of the research on incidental and milieu teaching has been conducted using single-subject research designs. This is both a weakness and a strength of the research base. It is a weakness because generalization of research findings is usually dependent on randomized assignment of participants and control groups. However, in the case of incidental and milieu teaching, with over 40 years of single-subject research studies (see reviews in Hancock & Kaiser, 2006; Kaiser et al., 1992; Warren & Kaiser, 1986), it can be considered a strength. The extensive number of replications across procedures and procedural variations, participant age groups (e.g., toddlers through adults), language needs/disabilities (e.g., speech delays, cognitive impairments, prelinguistic communicators, autism, disadvantaged backgrounds), targeted language responses, settings (e.g., home, school), and interventionists (e.g., researchers, graduate students, special education teachers, parents) builds a strong case for the generalizability of its effectiveness. Moreover, the single-subject research designs have allowed for cross-case intrasubject analyses that have suggested that the children who are likely to show the greatest improvements in language skills through incidental and milieu teaching are those who are verbally imitative, have at least 10 productive words, and have mean length of utterances between 1.0 and 3.5 words (Kaiser et al., 1992).

Implementation of Milieu Teaching

Incidental teaching is currently subsumed under the procedures of *milieu teaching* (Kaiser, 2000), a set of four language teaching procedures:

1. In the *model* procedure, the teacher notices the occasion for instruction, approaches the child, demonstrates the target communication response ("I need help"), and waits a few seconds. If the child imitates the model, the teacher provides what the child requested. If the child does not imitate within the specified time, the teacher judges the child's level of interest. If the teacher believes the child is still very interested, the teacher repeats the model and waits again. If the teacher believes the child is losing interest, the teacher repeats the model and gives the child the requested item.

2. The *mand-model* procedure builds on the *model* procedure by first offering a less-intrusive prompt than the model (a mand) when the teacher notices the child-determined occasion for instruction. Instead of modeling the target response, the teacher provides a mand (e.g., a directive, an indirect verbal prompt), such as, "Tell me what you need." If the child responds correctly, the teacher immediately provides what the child requested. If the child does not respond within the specified time period (usually 4 or 5 seconds) and the child's interest level is still high, the teacher repeats the mand; if the child's interest is waning, the teacher provides a model of the target response, for example, "I need help." From this point on, the *model* procedure is followed. In summary, one or two mands may be provided as prompts for the target response (depending on the child's level of interest); if the mand is an ineffective prompt, the teacher shifts to the model procedure, and may provide one or two models (depending on the child's level of interest).

3. When a child has demonstrated acquisition of a target response but does not use that response frequently, consistently, or independently (as an initiation), the *delay* procedure is used. A less-intrusive procedure than the model or mand-model procedure, the delay procedure begins as all incidental teaching interactions begin, with the teacher noticing the child-determined occasion for instruction, approaching the child, and sharing the child's focus of attention. Unlike the model or mand-model procedure, the teacher says nothing. Instead, the teacher implements a delay by continuing to focus on the child and the child's activity and waiting expectantly for several seconds (usually 4 or 5 seconds) for the child to provide the target response. If the child responds correctly, the teacher immediately provides what the child requested. If the child does not respond and shows high interest, the teacher may continue to the delay for a few more seconds. If the child does not provide the target response, the teacher shifts to the mand-model procedure (if the child shows a moderate level of interest) or the model procedure (if the child shows a low level of interest).

4. And finally, the *incidental teaching* procedure includes the model, mand-model, and delay procedures with the teacher selecting one of the three procedures based on the difficulty level of the target response and the apparent level of child interest at the time. The model procedure is generally used with basic vocabulary, conversational, and imitation skills, or when the child's interest level appears to be relatively low. It is the most intrusive of the milieu teaching procedures, providing the child with a clear demonstration of the target response. The mand-model procedure is most appropriate for promoting generalization of new communication skills across situations and settings; the child should show at least a moderate level of interest. And the delay procedure is best-suited to highlighting environmental stimuli as the prompts to communication (e.g., the natural turn-taking pause in conversational turns or the attention of an adult); the child should show a high level of interest in having a need met.

Other variations of incidental/milieu teaching are EMT, which includes incidental teaching, plus two additional strategies—environmental arrangements and responsive interactions (Kaiser, Hemmeter, & Hester, 1997). Environmental arrangements and responsive interactions are general approaches to setting up the early childhood environment and responding to children in ways that encourage and promote communication. Increasing the overall quantity of communicative interactions, in turn, increases opportunities for incidental teaching.

Environmental arrangements in EMT are much like the environmental arrangements discussed earlier in the description of ABI:

1. Provide interesting materials and activities.
2. Place desired materials in sight but out of reach.
3. Offer small amounts of desired or required materials.
4. Offer choices frequently.
5. Provide activities in which the children will require assistance.
6. Create surprising, unexpected situations.

The common element in these strategies is that they create the need for children to communicate. Multiple environmental arrangement strategies can be used concurrently, and they can be used on a daily basis (although materials and activities should change in keeping with the preschool curriculum throughout the year).

The *responsive interaction* component of EMT requires that adults (e.g., teachers, parents) respond to children in ways that encourage communicative interactions and promote balanced communication exchanges (again, much like the *responsive* interactions described in ABI). When adults are responsive to children, they focus on and attend to the child and follow the child's lead. In EMT—with its specific goal of improving communication skills—adults then attempt to facilitate communication. The teacher might ask a question or comment on the child's play. If the child talks to the teacher, the teacher responds in a manner that encourages sustained conversation. For example, a child holds up a toy dinosaur and says, "blue." Rather than simply replying "Yes," and effectively ending the communication exchange, the teacher might say, "A blue dinosaur! What is your dinosaur doing?"

It is common to see the use of environmental arrangements and responsive interactions in high-quality preschool programs. Environmental arrangements ensure that the setting provides numerous prompts for communication, and responsive interactions ensure that children have adult communication partners who are focused and attentive to their interests. The third component of EMT is incidental teaching (as described previously). As noted, all incidental teaching interactions are embedded at child-determined occasions for instruction. This means that the occasion for instruction is planned ahead of time, and intervention occurs when the teacher observes the occasion (e.g., "When the child approaches a peer and watches the peer play," "When the child notices that a required item is missing and makes a one-word request").

Milieu teaching is a communication intervention approach in ECSE that has a well-established research base in promoting generalized communication skills. It is the most thoroughly researched embedded instruction procedure, beginning with the seminal incidental teaching study by Hart and Risley in 1968. Over the years it has evolved to a set of four milieu teaching procedures (developed primarily by Warren, Kaiser, and their colleagues; e.g., Kaiser et al., 1993; Warren & Gazdag, 1990) and more recently led to the conceptualization of EMT (by Kaiser and her colleagues; e.g., Kaiser & Hester, 1994). Although incidental teaching was originally developed for young children from economically disadvantaged backgrounds, a significant amount of research now demonstrates its effectiveness for young children with disabilities.

Summary

The philosophies of inclusion, natural environments, and DAP have influenced the development of research-based practices in ECSE. We have described two research-based practices, ABI and milieu teaching, that have been shown to be effective intervention approaches in inclusive, developmentally appropriate preschool programs. Diane Bricker and her colleagues (D. Bricker & Cripe, 1992) developed ABI, which provides special education through the use of embedded instruction in naturalistic environments. Incidental teaching, initially developed by Hart and Risley (1968, 1974, 1975, 1980), is an embedded intervention approach to facilitating language development. Incidental teaching is supported by an extensive research base and is now subsumed in a set of naturalistic language teaching procedures known as milieu teaching (Kaiser, 2000; Warren & Kaiser, 1986) and EMT (Kaiser et al., 1997). Both ABI and milieu teaching are well-established research-based procedures considered recommended practices in ECSE (Sandall et al., 2005).

CHAPTER 3

Teaching Students with High-Incidence Disabilities

Thomas E. Scruggs and **Margo A. Mastropieri** | *George Mason University*

S tudents with high-incidence disabilities—including the categories of learning disabilities, mild intellectual disabilities, and emotional disturbance—comprise nearly two thirds of the total population of school-age individuals with disabilities (Mastropieri & Scruggs, 2009; U.S. Department of Education, 2006). Students in these high-incidence disability areas are generally thought to be able to master most, if not all, of the school's general education curriculum and very commonly receive instruction in general education settings. Students in high-incidence categories of exceptionality share a number of characteristics. Some (e.g., intellectual ability) are defining characteristics for particular disability areas (e.g., intellectual disability), whereas others are commonly found in conjunction with one or more categories. Two characteristics very commonly observed across high-incidence disability categories are difficulty with verbal learning and memory, skills and processes critically linked to successful school learning (see Mastropieri & Scruggs, 2009, Chapter 10).

Memory deficits have long been associated with intellectual disability (Kavale & Forness, 1992) and have accompanied many different early theoretical perspectives on this category. Intellectual disability has been associated with deficits in many aspects of memory functioning, including short-term (Henry, 2008) and long-term (Kavale & Forness, 1992) memory, as well as with procedural and declarative memory processes (Vakil, Shelef-Reshef, & Levy-Shiff, 1997).

Researchers in the 1970s began to identify verbal or semantic memory deficits as important characteristics of learning disabilities (Bauer, 1977; Torgesen, 1977; Torgesen & Goldman, 1977). Evidence of memory deficits accumulated in later years (e.g., Ceci, 1984; Cooney & Swanson, 1987), as researchers considered memory deficits in this population as automatic (e.g., spontaneous) or purposive (e.g., intentional strategic) processes (Brainerd, Kingma, & Howe, 1986; Wertlieb, 1992) and established the link between memory and literacy skills (Cornwall, 1992).

Verbal learning and memory have been studied in students with emotional disturbance less overall; however, sustained academic learning deficits (presumably one correlate of verbal learning) have been well documented for this population (Scruggs & Mastropieri, 1986; Reid, Gonzalez, Nordness, Trout, & Epstein, 2004), as have deficits in general information (Mastropieri, Jenkins, & Scruggs, 1985). Further, deficits in verbal learning and memory have commonly been associated with anxiety, depression, and aggressiveness (Günther, Holtkamp, Jolles, Herpertz-Dahlmann, & Konrad, 2004; Mueller, 1979; Seguin, Pihl, Harden, Tremblay, & Boulerice, 1995; Watts, 1995).

Deficits in verbal learning and memory are among the major contributors to another important characteristic of students with high-incidence disabilities: deficits in academic achievement. Given the close association between memory deficits and both academic learning and deficits in purposive (strategic) processing (Kavale & Forness, 1992; Mueller, 1979; Wertlieb, 1992), strategies intended to increase memory for school-related content would seem to be highly appropriate for students with high-incidence disabilities. In addition, because most of these students receive a large portion of their instruction in general education classrooms (Mastropieri & Scruggs, 2009), it also seems appropriate to develop methods for implementing learning strategies in general education classrooms in ways that minimize or eliminate the stigma of working with "specialized" materials. This would involve maximizing individual student engagement, providing appropriate instructional strategies (e.g., rehearsal, elaboration, active engagement), and finding ways to present instructional materials such that instruction can be individualized without appearing to single out individual students.

In this chapter, we describe some successful approaches to these complex problems. One relevant approach to memory and verbal learning deficits, which has received considerable research attention, is mnemonic instruction (Scruggs & Mastropieri, 1990). These strategies have been demonstrated to facilitate very substantial improvements in the amount of information students with high-incidence disabilities have been able to acquire and retain. Next, we describe some relevant approaches to the application of effective instructional strategies, including mnemonic elaboration, in inclusive general education classrooms. These approaches, described as differentiated curriculum enhancements (Scruggs, Mastropieri, Marshak, & Mills, 2009), have recently been employed to increase learning and memory of academic material for both general education and special education students. Finally, we discuss the strengths and weaknesses of these approaches to date and provide suggestions for future research.

Mnemonic Strategies

Whereas a mnemonic is any procedure or operation designed to improve memory, mnemonic strategies described in this chapter are those that involve "a specific reconstruction of target content intended to tie new information more closely to the learner's existing knowledge base and, therefore, facilitate retrieval" (Scruggs & Mastropieri, 1990, pp. 271–272). In this section, we review a number of mnemonic strategies (i.e., keyword method, pegword method, letter strategies,

and reconstructive elaborations) that share the same theoretical rationale of addressing learning needs by capitalizing on student strengths.

Rationale

Mnemonic strategies are intended to be useful because they build on familiarity or meaningfulness (Underwood & Shultz, 1960) and elaboration (Rohwer, Raines, Eoff, & Wagner, 1966; Scruggs & Cohn, 1983) to enhance learning (Mastropieri, Scruggs, & Levin, 1985). These types of mnemonics are expected to be of particular utility to individuals with high-incidence disabilities, because they minimize the effect of relative learning weaknesses (e.g., spontaneous strategy production, verbal fluency, memory for verbal information), while maximizing relative strengths (e.g., memory for pictures, memory for semantically or phonetically elaborated information; see Scruggs, Mastropieri, & Levin, 1987, for a discussion).

Types of Mnemonic Strategies
The Keyword Method

The keyword method has its roots as far back as ancient Greece (Yates, 1966), as do most mnemonic strategies, but its first appearance in modern experimental psychology was in an investigation by Atkinson (1975) on Russian vocabulary learning. The keyword method works by creating concrete, acoustically similar proxies for unfamiliar information and associating it with the to-be-remembered information. For example, to remember that *dorado* is a Spanish word for a type of fish, a keyword is first constructed for *dorado*. In this case, a good keyword would be "door," because it sounds like the first part of *dorado* and is easily pictured. Learners are then shown (or asked to imagine) a picture of the keyword and associated information interacting, for example, in a picture of a *fish* (meaning for *dorado*) knocking at a *door* (keyword for *dorado*). When asked for the meaning of *dorado*, then, learners are taught to first think of the keyword, *door,* think of the picture with the door in it, remember *what else* was in the picture (a fish), and retrieve the answer, fish (McLoone, Scruggs, Mastropieri, & Zucker, 1986). For another example, consider the scientific name, *ranidae,* which refers to the family of common frogs. A good keyword for ranidae would be *rain,* and a picture would be shown of a *frog* (or family of frogs) sitting in the *rain.* When asked the meaning of ranidae, then, learners first think of the keyword, *rain,* think of the picture with the rain in it, remember what else was in the picture (frog), and retrieve the answer, frogs (Mastropieri, Scruggs, Levin, Gaffney, & McLoone, 1985).

Table 3.1 Example Applications of Keyword Mnemonics

Subject Area	Target Word	Key Word	Meaning	Interactive Picture
English	Vituperation	Viper	Abusive speech	A *viper speaking abusively*
Foreign language	*Barca* (Italian)	Bark	Boat	A *barking dog* in a *boat*
Science	Erode	Road	To wear away, by wind or water	A *road*, *eroding* from wind and water runoff
Social studies	Lusitania	Lucy	Passenger ship sunk by German submarine	*Lucy* (from Peanuts) on the deck of a sinking passenger ship, shaking her fist at a submarine

Keywords have been shown to be very versatile, and have been applied in many domains, including foreign language vocabulary; English vocabulary; social studies content, including people, places, and concepts; and science concepts and classifications. Some examples of applications of keyword mnemonics in different subject areas are provided in Table 3.1. The keyword method, as with all mnemonic techniques, cannot be considered a panacea for all school learning. The keyword method is best when used to promote initial acquisition of unfamiliar names, facts, and concepts. Additional activities can easily be combined with the keyword method, including activities designed to promote fluency, comprehension, and applications.

The Pegword Method

Pegwords are rhyming proxies for numbers (e.g., *one* is *bun, two* is *shoe, three* is *tree*) and can be used when numbered or ordered information needs to be remembered. For example, to help students remember that a *rake* is an example of a third-class lever (fulcrum at one end, force applied in the middle), show them a picture of a *rake* leaning on a *tree* (pegword for *three*). To help students remember that insects have *six* legs, show a picture of *insects* on *sticks* (pegword for *six*). To help students remember that spiders have *eight* legs, show a picture of a *spider* weaving a web on a *gate* (pegword for *eight*).

Pegwords can also be combined with keywords when unfamiliar terms are associated with numbers. For example, to help students remember that Andrew Jackson was the *seventh* president, show a picture of angels playing *jacks* (keyword for Jackson) in *heaven* (pegword for seven) (Mastropieri, Scruggs, Bakken, & Whedon, 1997). Or, to help students remember that the mineral *wolframite* has a hardness level of approximately *four,* show a picture of a *wolf* (keyword for *wolframite*) at a *door* (pegword for *four*). When asked about wolframite, then, learners think of the keyword, *wolf,* think back to the picture of the wolf, remember

the wolf was at a door, remember that *door* is a pegword for *four,* and retrieve the answer, hardness level four (Mastropieri et al., 1986).

Additional information has also been successfully integrated into mnemonic pictures involving pegwords; for example, to teach that wolframite is hardness level four, is commonly *black* in color, and is used in the manufacture of tungsten for *lightbulb* filaments, show a picture of a *black* (color) *wolf* (keyword for *wolframite*) pulling a cord on a *lightbulb* (common use) in front of a *door* (pegword for *four*). Although this may seem a complicated strategy, it has been successfully employed with students with learning disabilities (e.g., Scruggs, Mastropieri, Levin, & Gaffney, 1985). Pegwords higher than 10 can include numbers for the teens, (e.g., *lever* (11)), and combinations used for number decades (e.g., *twin* for 20, *twin doors* = 24).

Letter Strategies

Letter strategies are probably the most familiar of mnemonic strategies, as most individuals can remember learning that HOMES could represent the first letters of the Great Lakes (i.e., Huron, Ontario, Michigan, Erie, and Superior). Letter strategies include acronyms—in which each letter represents a word, as in the HOMES example; and acrostics—in which the first letters of words in a sentence are used to remember a list or sequence of information. For example, the sentence, "King Phillip's class ordered a family of gentle spaniels," could be used to prompt recall of the taxonomic order: kingdom, phylum, class, order, family, genius, species. The sentence, "My very educated mother just served us nine pizzas" has been used to prompt the recall of the planets in order: Mercury, Venus, Earth, Mars, Jupiter, Saturn, Uranus, Neptune, Pluto.

Letter strategies can also be combined with keywords. For example, in social studies, to remember that the members of the Central Powers during World War I were Turkey (Ottoman Empire), Austria-Hungary, and Germany, students can be shown a picture of children playing *TAG* (acronym for Turkey, Austria-Hungary, and Germany) in *Central Park* (keyword for *Central Powers*). When students are asked the names of the countries in the Central Powers, they remember the keyword, *Central Park,* think of the children playing *TAG* in Central Park, and remember the countries that begin with T, A, and G (Scruggs & Mastropieri, 1989b). Because letter strategies such as this provide only a first-letter prompt, teachers must be certain to practice the relevant names sufficiently so that students can remember them, given only the first letter.

Reconstructive Elaborations

School curriculum is complex and diverse, requiring a number of different mnemonic strategies to effectively encompass all important content. Scruggs and Mastropieri (1989b) suggested a model referred to as *reconstructive elaborations* to address this issue. They suggested considering the familiarity and concreteness of relevant content, and constructing mnemonic elaborations relative to these features (see also Mastropieri & Scruggs, 1989c). For example, *earthworm* is concrete and familiar to most learners and needs no reconstruction. To-be-associated information can simply be shown in a representative interactive picture (a *mimetic* reconstruction). For example, to remember that earthworms are *segmented,* have *many hearts,* and live *in the ground,* a picture can be developed of an earthworm with many segments, and showing a number of hearts, living in the ground. Similarly, to help students remember that many World War I soldiers became *ill* in the *trenches* (all familiar concepts), simply show a picture of *sick soldiers* in *trenches.*

Other content is familiar but not concrete. For example, the concept of *U.S. policy* may be familiar to students but not easy to represent. Therefore, teachers can use a *symbolic* reconstruction, in this case, the figure "Uncle Sam," to represent U.S. policy. For information that is unfamiliar, acoustic reconstructions in the form of the keyword method can be employed. These reconstructions also can be combined with letter strategies or pegwords, as needed, and have been effective in teaching content in U.S. history (Scruggs & Mastropieri, 1989a) and science (Scruggs & Mastropieri, 1992).

Description and Fidelity Checklist

Implementation of mnemonic instruction depends on development of appropriate mnemonic elaborations of target content. In most cases, this involves developing relevant illustrations. First, identify critical target content that students may have difficulty remembering. For

example, a list of SAT vocabulary words may include the following:

Vocabulary Word	Meaning
Martinet	A strict disciplinarian
Turbulent	Violent, stormy
Truculent	Fierce, cruel, aggressive
Vociferous	Loud and noisy

Because vocabulary words lend themselves to the keyword method, construct a keyword for each target word. A good keyword is familiar to learners, sounds like an important part of the target word, and can be included in a picture. Good keywords for these words may include the following:

Vocabulary Word	Keyword	Meaning
Martinet	Martian	A strict disciplinarian
Turbulent	Turtle	Violent, stormy
Truculent	Truck	Fierce, cruel, aggressive
Vociferous	Voice	Loud and noisy

Now, create an illustration of the keyword and meaning interacting in some way that is memorable. This interaction is important so that the retrieval of the illustration prompts recall of the word meaning. For example, a good illustration for *martinet* would be a Martian being a strict disciplinarian, for example, in a school classroom. Possible mnemonic illustrations include the following:

Word	Keyword	Meaning	Picture
Martinet	Martian	A strict disciplinarian	A Martian being a strict disciplinarian
Turbulent	Turtle	Violent, stormy	A turtle swimming through a violent storm
Truculent	Truck	Fierce, cruel, aggressive	A truck with an aggressive driver
Vociferous	Voice	Loud and noisy	A baby with a loud and noisy voice

Once mnemonic elaborations have been constructed, it is best to develop mnemonic illustrations. Although imagery can also be used (by prompting students to imagine mnemonic pictures), it is generally less effective (Scruggs & Mastropieri, 1992). Good pictures should contain clear and direct representations of the necessary information, but not any additional information. For example, in our earlier research, we used no color, unless it was important for the mnemonic picture (as in the *wolframite* example, described previously). Fortunately, mnemonic illustrations, to be effective, do not need to be creative or particularly artistic, if they adequately portray the important information. Other alternatives are using stick figures and cutouts from magazines, selecting an artistic student to draw the appropriate illustrations, or using computer clip art to create relevant illustrations. Such clip art programs can be found installed with some computers, can be purchased at computer stores, or can be found online by searching (e.g., "turtle clip art") and selecting from the alternatives. For example, to represent a turtle in a violent storm, clip art for "turtle" and "storm" can be identified and combined into an effective mnemonic illustration, as shown in Figure 3.1. Such an illustration can be displayed on an overhead projector, on a PowerPoint slide, or on student handouts. The presentation should employ something like the following dialogue:

> *Turbulent* means *violent* or *stormy.* The keyword (or word clue) for *turbulent* is *turtle.* What is the keyword for *turbulent*? [students respond] Good, *turtle.* Remember this picture of a *turtle* in a *violent storm.* Remember this picture of what? [students respond] Good, a turtle in a violent storm. When I ask you for the meaning of *turbulent,* first think back to the keyword, which is . . .? [students respond] *Turtle,* good. Now think back to the picture of the turtle, and remember *what else* is in the picture. In this case, the turtle is . . .? [students respond] In a violent storm, good. So *turbulent* means . . .? [students respond] *Violent* or *stormy,* good. And what word means *violent* or *stormy?* [students respond] *Turbulent,* good.

In some cases, particularly in early stages of mnemonic instruction, students may reply that *turbulent* means *turtle.* In such cases, simply state that *turtle* is not the meaning, but it is the word clue that will help find the meaning, and then repeat the strategy.

Figure 3.1 Mnemonic illustration of *turbulent = violent* or *stormy.*

Turbulent (turtle)   **Violent, stormy**

It is also important to consider that mnemonic strategies are intended to facilitate recall of verbal information and are not in themselves strategies for facilitating comprehension. Although mnemonically trained students typically outperform traditionally taught students on comprehension tests (e.g., Mastropieri, Scruggs, & Fulk, 1990), this is because mnemonically instructed students recall more information, which they can bring to bear on comprehension tests. Nevertheless, it is important to determine that students taught mnemonically (or otherwise) understand what they are learning. For these purposes, comprehension strategies (e.g., content elaboration, discussion, examples, applications, hands-on activities, multimedia presentations) can be employed. Above all, memory and comprehension should not be looked at as mutually exclusive competitors, but as important components of all learning tasks. Although students might acquire new verbal information without comprehending it, it is also true that information must first be remembered before it can be employed in any meaningful way.

Table 3.2 provides other examples of how mnemonics might be applied, in this case in a U.S. history class. Examining the content for the World War I unit, a teacher may consider the target information shown in Table 3.2 (Scruggs & Mastropieri, 1989a). Using the method of reconstructive elaborations, effective mnemonic elaborations can be developed for the information, as represented in the table. The teacher then constructs the appropriate mnemonic pictures, using the methods described previously. In a U.S. history lesson, the teacher would select a number of mnemonic illustrations (usually, three to five in a lesson) to present along with the content, using dialogue such as the following:

> The *Zimmerman note* was an important cause of U.S. entry into World War I. Zimmerman was the German Foreign Secretary, who sent a coded note to Mexico asking them to join Germany against the United States, in case the United States entered the war on the side of the Allied Powers. In return, Germany promised former Mexican territory in Texas, Arizona, and New Mexico. This note was intercepted and decoded, caused public outrage in the United States, and contributed to the declaration of war against Germany and its allies.
>
> To help you remember about the Zimmerman note, remember the keyword for *Zimmerman, swimmer.* What is the keyword for *Zimmerman?* [students respond]. *Swimmer,* good. Now [shows picture] remember this picture of a *swimmer* swimming from Germany to Mexico with a *coded note* saying "Mexico: Join us." Remember this picture of what? [students respond]. Good, a *swimmer* with a *coded note.* So when I ask what the Zimmerman note is, what do you answer? [students respond]. Good, a coded note from Germany to Mexico.

Teachers should practice the content and the mnemonic strategy with students several times, until students

Table 3.2 Target Information from a Unit on World War I

Question	Response	Mnemonic Elaboration
What were the countries in the Central Powers?	Turkey (Ottoman Empire), Austria-Hungary, Germany	"TAG" (Turkey, Austria-Hungary, Germany) in *Central Park*
What were the countries in the Allied Powers?	France, Italy, Russia, England	"FIRE" (France, Italy, Russia, England) in an ALLIED van (keyword for *Allied Powers*)
Who was William Jennings Bryan?	Secretary of State, opposed war	A *lion* (keyword for *Bryan*) as secretary at a desk (Secretary of State), urging other animals to *stop fighting* (opposed war)
What was the first U.S. policy?	Not to get involved	*Uncle Sam* (symbol for U.S. policy) looking over at Europe and saying, "*It's not my fight*"
What was the *Lusitania*?	Passenger ship sunk by a German submarine	*Lucy* (keyword for *Lusitania*) on a sinking passenger ship sunk by a German submarine
What was the Zimmerman note?	Coded note from Germany to Mexico, urging Mexico to fight the United States	A *swimmer* (keyword for *Zimmerman*) carrying a coded note from Germany to Mexico
What were the conditions of trench warfare?	Unhealthy, many soldiers became sick	A mimetic (representational) picture of *sick soldiers* in *trenches*
Who was Eddie Rickenbacker?	U.S. flying ace, shot down many enemy airplanes	A *linebacker* (keyword for Rickenbacker) *flying* over a football field, *shooting down* enemy aircraft
Who was George M. Cohan?	Patriotic songwriter, wrote "Over There"	Someone asking a person with an ice cream *cone* (keyword for Cohan) "Where did you get that cone?" with person responding, "*Over There, Over There*"

can clearly retrieve the information. Although mnemonic strategies frequently improve memory, they must be presented clearly, practiced several times by students, and reviewed periodically to be maximally effective.

Fidelity Checklist

Mnemonic instruction is versatile and can be applied in different ways in many different subject areas. For example, Mastropieri et al. (1998) employed mnemonic instruction for important science vocabulary in the context of a hands-on unit on ecosystems. However, in all cases, the following steps should be taken:

- Critical target content identified
- Appropriate mnemonic elaborations constructed
- Clear, relevant mnemonic illustrations developed
- Appropriate delivery of strategy information, with questioning and feedback
- Sufficient guided and independent practice activities
- Periodic review of content and mnemonic strategies

Research Base

Applications

Mnemonic strategies are among the most thoroughly researched techniques in the field of special education and have been applied effectively in a wide variety of content areas, from English vocabulary instruction (Mastropieri, Scruggs, Levin, et al., 1985) to foreign language vocabulary (McLoone et al., 1986), state (Mastropieri & Scruggs, 1989b) and U.S. history (Mastropieri & Scruggs, 1988), and life and earth sciences (King-Sears, Mercer, & Sindelar, 1992; Scruggs & Mastropieri, 1992). These strategies have been successfully employed on elementary (Uberti, Scruggs, & Mastropieri, 2003) and secondary levels (Bulgren, Schumaker, & Deshler, 1994) as well as with students with learning disabilities (Mastropieri, Scruggs, & Levin, 1985), intellectual disability (Mastropieri, Scruggs, Whittaker, & Bakken, 1994), and emotional/behavioral disabilities (Mastropieri, Emerick, & Scruggs, 1988). In addition, students who are normally achieving (Scruggs et al., 1986) and those who are gifted (Scruggs & Mastropieri, 1988) have also benefitted from mnemonic strategies.

Settings

Most of the earlier investigations were conducted in laboratory-type settings, where participants were seen individually in a private area removed from the classroom (e.g., Mastropieri, Scruggs, Levin, et al., 1985). Once the potential efficacy of mnemonic strategies had been demonstrated in these laboratory studies, later investigations were conducted in special education classrooms over longer periods of time (e.g., Mastropieri & Scruggs, 1988). More recently, mnemonic strategy research has been conducted in inclusive classrooms (Fontana, Mastropieri, & Scruggs, 2007; Mastropieri, Sweda, & Scruggs, 2000; Uberti et al., 2003). Fontana et al. (2007) investigated the use of mnemonic strategies in high school history classes, and they reported that students who were English language learners (ELLs) benefited most from the strategies.

Diversity of Participants

Mnemonic strategy research studies have also included substantial diversity among participants. For example, African American students represented 49% of the sample in the Scruggs, Mastropieri, Brigham, and Sullivan (1992) investigation, 40% of the Scruggs and Mastropieri (1989a) investigation, and 56% of the Mastropieri and Scruggs (1988) investigation. Hispanic students represented 7% of the Scruggs and Mastropieri (1989b) investigation and 19% of the Scruggs, Mastropieri, McLoone, Levin, and Morrison (1987) investigation. In the second experiment of the Mastropieri et al. (1986) investigation, all of the participants were Native Americans. The Mastropieri, Scruggs, Levin, et al. (1985) investigation included 11% Hispanic and 6% Native American students. The Fontana et al. (2007) investigation, in inclusive high school history classes, included 17% African American, 19% Hispanic, and 7% Asian participants. As mentioned, in that investigation, the students who benefited most from the mnemonic strategies were ELLs.

Levels of Support and Fidelity of Implementation

In the earliest mnemonic laboratory investigations, researchers delivered the treatments, and all dialogue was read from prepared scripts at a prespecified pace (e.g., Mastropieri, Scruggs, & Levin, 1986; Mastropieri, Scruggs, Levin, et al., 1985). In some classroom applications (e.g., Mastropieri & Scruggs, 1988), teachers were given prepared scripts for the mnemonic portion of the classroom activities and a videotape model for implementing instruction, and observers attended class regularly and evaluated treatment fidelity (Fontana et al., 2007). In some inclusive classes (e.g., Mastropieri et al., 2000; Uberti et al., 2003), teachers had less support, developed their own materials, and were more independent with their implementation. Similarly positive outcomes were consistent across these investigations. In other inclusive implementations (Fontana et al., 2007; Marshak, Mastropieri, & Scruggs, 2009), fidelity was monitored through teacher logs and direct observation with checklists and was found to be high (e.g., 95% in the Marshak et al., 2009).

Meta-Analysis

Several quantitative research syntheses have been published on the effectiveness of mnemonic instruction in general (Levin, Anglin, & Carney, 1987) and for students with disabilities (Mastropieri & Scruggs, 1989b; Scruggs & Mastropieri, 2000). With respect to high-incidence disabilities, Mastropieri and Scruggs (1989a) summarized the outcomes of 24 experimental investigations of mnemonic instruction, involving 983 students, and reported a very large overall mean effect size of 1.62 ($SD = 0.79$) on criterion-referenced content and vocabulary tests. An effect size of this magnitude means that the average-performing student receiving mnemonic instruction would have scored at the 94.7th percentile of the comparison conditions, who generally received direct-instruction rehearsal, free study, or visual-spatial displays. Stated another way, the average proportion of items correct after instruction for all the comparison conditions, as reported in the original studies, was 43.8%, as compared with 75.0% correct for students instructed mnemonically, an overall difference of nearly 2-to-1.

An updated meta-analysis of mnemonic strategy instruction for students with high-incidence disabilities of 34 experiments was reported by Scruggs and Mastropieri (2000), who identified a virtually identical mean effect size of 1.62 ($SD = 0.84$). Effect sizes were found to be similar across a number of variables, including grade levels, content areas, type of disability of participants, laboratory or field-based setting, and whether Scruggs and Mastropieri were involved as authors. More recently, Wolgemuth, Cobb, and Alwell (2008) summarized all mnemonic research for students with high-incidence disabilities on the secondary level only and reported a mean overall effect size of 1.38. Taken together, these effect sizes are among the largest of any intervention in special education (Forness, 2001).

Adaptations and Modifications

Because mnemonic strategy instruction has itself been considered an adaptation for students who exhibit difficulty learning and remembering new content, adaptations or modifications have not been typically employed. In all cases, students received very direct, explicit instruction on the strategy and, specifically, how it was to be employed, with the assumption that students with high-incidence disabilities would need more support than other types of learners (Scruggs & Mastropieri, 1988). Researchers found that additional instructional sessions were necessary for students with intellectual disability to master mnemonic pegwords (Mastropieri et al., 1986), an issue probably associated with observed rhyming difficulties of students with this disability (M. S. Scott, Perou, Greenfield, & Swanson, 1993). In inclusive settings, it may be that all students do not require mnemonic strategies to learn content adequately. In such cases, adaptations have been created in the form of *differentiated curriculum enhancements,* which employ differential exposure to different instructional procedures (including mnemonics), in order to maximize learning for all students.

Differentiated Curriculum Enhancements

As students with high-incidence disabilities have moved from self-contained to more inclusive settings, concurrently addressing the needs of diverse learners has become a more important issue. One common approach to this problem is *differentiated instruction* (e.g., Tomlinson, 2001), in which students receive different materials or instructional strategies depending on their individual learning needs. One potential problem with such differentiation, however, is that students with high-incidence disabilities may be perceived to be receiving "dumbed-down" materials and instruction and may become stigmatized by this perception. To address this significant problem and to preserve the concept of appropriately differentiated instruction, a model referred to as *differentiated curriculum enhancements* was proposed (Mastropieri et al., 2006). Using this model, all students receive the same materials, and differentiation is built into the instructional program so that each student can differentially benefit, according to individual learning needs. In all cases, class-wide peer tutoring (Greenwood, 1997) or small-group learning is used to individualize instruction.

Rationale

Research has indicated that students with high-incidence disabilities, who generally exhibit relatively low levels of achievement, learn better when (a) time on task is maximized, (b) they are engaged with activities directly relevant to learning objectives, (c) they receive questioning directly relevant to learning objectives, and (d) to-be-learned information is elaborated and effectively linked to prior knowledge (Mastropieri & Scruggs, 2004, 2009). In addition, research has consistently supported the use of peer tutoring for increasing the outcomes of students with high-incidence disabilities (e.g., Greenwood, 1997; Osguthorpe & Scruggs, 1986; Sáenz, McMaster, Fuchs, & Fuchs, 2007). Differentiated curriculum enhancements represent an attempt to place these considerations within a context in which all students work with the same instructional materials. The differentiation occurs when students with special learning needs receive (a) more practice, (b) more time with lower-difficulty levels of the materials, or (c) elaborative learning strategies to be used when needed.

Description and Implementation Procedures

To date, three separate approaches have been applied to enhance learning in inclusive science and social studies classrooms. These approaches are (a) fact sheets, (b) differentiated activities, and (c) embedded mnemonic elaborations.

Fact Sheets

The simplest method of differentiated curriculum enhancements is the development of "fact sheets" to promote learning of critical content area information. Teachers develop a number of fact sheets and corresponding quizzes, which include questions and answers of relevance to unit tests or high-stakes (i.e., state proficiency) tests. For example, one question (of about five per sheet) might be "What kind of molecule is DNA?" with the answer, "Double helix molecule." These sheets are duplicated and placed in folders. Teachers then construct multiple-choice quizzes designed to match the content of fact sheets. Teachers select the frequency of quiz administration but typically administer them before and after a chapter of content. The multiple-choice format of the quizzes enables students to easily administer and score their partner's quizzes.

Students are placed in tutoring pairs using the following process. Students are (discreetly) listed from highest to lowest in terms of academic performance on the target content. Then, the list is divided in the middle. The highest-performing student on the first half of the list is paired with the highest-performing student in the second half of the list, the second highest on the first half with the second highest on the second half, and so on. In this way, student pairs differ in skill level, and the difference in skill level is similar in all peer-tutoring dyads. Students are then informed of their tutoring partners, and given the following directions, in sequence: get with your partner and pick up a tutoring folder; write date, time, and names on the record sheet; take out fact sheets, and begin asking and answering questions with your partner. Students are divided into groups (e.g., "Admirals" and "Generals"), where one group represents the higher-functioning partner.

The higher-functioning tutor begins asking questions of the other student. After a certain amount of time, the students switch roles. Students are provided with rules, including speaking with a quiet voice, cooperating with partners, and correcting responses appropriately. For instance, when a partner answers incorrectly, the tutor might say, "You missed that one, can you try again?" If partially correct, the tutor might say, "Almost—can you think of anything else?" If the partner does not answer within 3 seconds, the tutor might say, "The answer is ____," and then repeat the question. As students master the fact sheets, scores (based on number of correct responses) are recorded, and tutoring pairs move on to the next fact sheet (see also McMaster, Fuchs, & Fuchs, 2006, for a discussion of class-wide peer-tutoring procedures). At designated times partners administer and score quizzes that correspond with the fact sheets, and students record their own performance. Teams may or may not be established within a class to compete against one another.

Using fact sheets, all students receive the same materials, and tutoring sessions can be implemented two or three times a week, for 20 or 30 minutes. Differentiation occurs in the manner in which the fact sheets are implemented. That is, students work on individual fact sheets until they achieve mastery using a predetermined criteria such as 100% on two consecutive trials, pass the quiz, and record the score. Then students practice new fact sheets. Given the peer-tutoring framework, each student receives appropriate individualized practice with the materials as needed. Fact sheets are the simplest of the differentiated curriculum enhancements, with materials that are the easiest to develop and implement, and for this reason may be of particular value to teachers.

Essential components of implementing fact sheets that could be included on fidelity of implementation checklists include:

- Fact sheet materials are designed to cover critical content at appropriate level of difficulty.

- Teachers effectively start and monitor tutoring session.

- Students have appropriate tutoring materials.

- Students administer appropriate prequiz measures.

- Students tutor one another for designated amount of time.

- Students remain on task during tutoring.

- Students administer appropriate postquizzes.

- Students record performance and progress.

- Teachers and students make decisions based on data whether to proceed to the next level of fact sheets.

- Students replace tutoring materials.

- Teachers record anecdotal observation notes from the session.

Differentiated Activities

Some content does not lend itself as readily to question-and-answer tutoring formats. In such cases, students can work in small peer groups to complete comprehension/application tasks on relevant content, depending on student skill level. For example, students in a science unit on scientific methods may need to learn about independent and dependent variables, qualitative and quantitative research questions, and to include data into various graphs and charts. Activities can be provided at three graduated levels, progressing generally from identification (where students identify a correct response from an array) to production (where students produce the correct response) with prompting when needed, to production responses without prompts. As students complete activity areas, they progress toward more complicated applications of the same content.

For each level of difficulty, activity materials are created. For example, for the "Quantitative/Qualitative" activities, Level 1 materials can direct students to read statements on each of a series of cards, and identify whether it was a quantitative or qualitative statement. Level 2 materials may direct students to generate three quantitative and three qualitative observations from each of a series of illustrations, with prompting provided by partners when needed. The final level (Level 3) materials could direct students to generate quantitative and qualitative observations, without any prompting. For an activity on experimental design, students could be directed to match independent with dependent variables (Level 1), and then produce independent and dependent variables, and hypotheses, given one of a series of scenarios, with prompts when needed (Level 2) or without prompts (Level 3). Record-keeping sheets can also be developed, on which students record progress on each of the levels of each of the activities.

Differentiation occurs on several levels. First, some students may not require participation in all levels. For example, when students have demonstrated they have previously identified content, they may be told to skip the identification-level activities. Second, no specified time limit is associated with the activities. In this way students can repeat levels as necessary before proceeding to more advanced levels. Differentiated activities are appropriate when content includes comprehension and application objectives. These are more difficult to develop than fact sheets, and also require some creativity in coming up with relevant game-like activities for each unit. However, once developed (and preferably, laminated), materials can be used over and over again, over a period of years, with different classes. Essential components of implementing differentiated activities that could be included on fidelity of implementation checklists are highly similar to the one described for fact sheets. However, differentiated activities should be designed to directly reflect the learning objectives and be appropriate for the targeted difficulty levels.

Embedded Mnemonic Elaborations

Peer tutoring using fact sheets can also be combined with mnemonic or other elaborative strategies, to be used when needed. For example, tutors can be directed to ask tutoring partners the meaning of *mole* in a chemistry class (i.e., atomic weight in grams of a compound or element). Because *mole* is a complicated concept, additional questioning can be provided when students give the correct answer, such as, "Can you give me an example of a mole?" and, "What else is important about moles?" If tutoring partners have difficulty retrieving the meaning of *mole,* they can be shown a mnemonic elaboration, for example, a picture of a mole (the animal) sitting on a scale, getting its weight in grams. The tutor can read from a supplied script, for example, "To remember that a mole is the atomic weight in grams of a compound or element, remember this picture of a mole on a scale, getting its weight in grams. So, what is a mole?" Other mnemonic strategies could include, for example, for *groups* and *periods* in a periodic table, "*Groups* sounds like *grows,* and plants *grow* up and down, like the groups in the periodic table. *Periods* are at the end of sentences, and sentences are horizontal like the periods on the periodic table."

Embedded mnemonic elaborations are differentiated in that the mnemonic strategies are provided only if students are having difficulty remembering important words (they can be on a separate page or attached to the back of the tutoring sheet). Nevertheless, all students receive the same materials and can use as many, or as few, elaborations as needed. Essential components of implementing embedded mnemonic elaborations that could be included on fidelity of implementation checklists are highly similar to those described for fact sheets and for differentiated activities. However, embedded mnemonic elaborations should be designed to directly reflect the learning objectives and should be concrete, familiar, and meaningful for the targeted sample.

Research Base

Applications

To date, the applications of differentiated curriculum enhancements are far fewer than those of mnemonic strategy instruction, but the number of studies conducted is sufficient to draw some tentative conclusions (Scruggs, Mastropieri, Marshak, & Mills, 2009). These studies include investigations of the use of fact sheets (Mastropieri, Scruggs, & Marshak, 2008; McDuffie, Mastropieri, & Scruggs, 2009; Scruggs, Mastropieri, & Marshak, 2009), differentiated activities (Mastropieri et al., 2006; Simpkins, Mastropieri, & Scruggs, 2009),

and differentiated mnemonic elaborations (Marshak, 2008; Mastropieri, Scruggs, & Graetz, 2005). In each of these studies, students engaged in differentiated curriculum enhancements statistically outperformed students taught by traditional methods, including lecture, questioning, work sheet, and independent study activities.

Settings

Studies to date have been conducted mostly in junior high settings, with one study of Earth and physical science learning (Simpkins et al., 2009) conducted in fifth-grade classes, and one (Mastropieri et al., 2005) conducted in high school chemistry classes. In all cases, students were taught in inclusive science or social studies classrooms, both individually taught and co-taught.

Diversity

Considerable diversity was represented in this set of investigations. For example, the Simpkins et al. (2009) investigation included 23% Asian, 18% African American, 3% Hispanic, and 5% biracial participants. The Mastropieri et al. (2006) investigation included 27% African American, 17% Hispanic, 4% Asian, and 5% multiracial students; whereas the Marshak (2008) investigation included 12% African American, 16% Hispanic, 22% Asian, and 3% multiracial students. Students who were ELLs frequently participated in these studies, however, the sample sizes were often small, and in many cases students were also identified as having other primary disabilities. One qualitative study, however, specifically described ELLs' interaction with differentiated science curriculum enhancements (Norland, 2005). These students reported that the materials contributed to the learning success and that they enjoyed using them more than their traditional science instruction (Norland, 2005).

Levels of Support and Fidelity of Implementation

Although all studies in this area to date employed teachers as intervention agents, in every case teachers received considerable support from research staff, including materials development and training. In some investigations (e.g., Scruggs, Mastropieri, & Marshak, 2009), teachers played a role in content selection and material development. In all cases, teachers kept logs documenting their implementation practices, and classes were observed regularly with fidelity checklists to ensure materials and methods were implemented appropriately. Fidelity ranged from 95% to 100% in Scruggs, Mastropieri, and Marshak (2009) and was 95% in Marshak et al. (2009). In other investigations (e.g., Fontana et al., 2007;

McDuffie et al., 2009), implementation integrity was reported as number of minutes per teaching component across conditions.

Research Support

In all cases, students in classes employing differentiated curriculum enhancements outperformed students taught by more traditional methods. In the differentiated activities studies (Mastropieri et al., 2006; Simpkins et al., 2009), mean effect sizes were in the mid 0.30s. However, these included a significant effect for the standardized end-of-year high-stakes test in science in the Mastropieri et al. investigation. This outcome was somewhat surprising, because that study was conducted over a small proportion of the entire school year (12 weeks). It was hypothesized that the effect may have been greater because the content selected (scientific method) had applications to all other science units.

For the fact sheet investigations (Mastropieri et al., 2008; McDuffie et al., 2009; Scruggs, Mastropieri, & Marshak, 2009), effect sizes were somewhat higher, in the 0.50 to 0.60 range. These effect sizes are consistent with, or a little larger than, previous meta-analyses of peer tutoring (e.g., S. Cook, Scruggs, Mastropieri, & Casto, 1985–1986). The embedded mnemonic elaborations yielded much higher mean effect sizes, of 0.84 (general education) and 1.22 (special education), more consistent with effect sizes found in meta-analyses of mnemonic instruction in content area learning (Scruggs, Mastropieri, Berkeley, & Graetz, 2010). Overall, research outcomes to date have been in the moderate-to-high effect range and have been consistently positive. In addition, in all studies to date, students and teachers have commented positively on the procedures.

Overall, seven experimental studies on differentiated curriculum enhancements have been conducted in science and social studies, with implementation periods of 8 to 18 weeks ($M = 11.14$ weeks). All interventions produced a statistically significant advantage over traditional instruction. The studies included 940 students (702 general education students and 315 special education and ELL students). Across all models, the overall average effect size was 0.55 for typical learners and 0.76 for at-risk students, ELLs, and students with disabilities. The higher overall effect size for students with disabilities and other special learning needs may indicate that these students benefit differentially from enhanced practice, activities, and learning strategies. Nevertheless, the effect size of 0.55 for general education students is sufficiently substantial to merit the use of these strategies in inclusive classrooms.

Summary

Overall, existing research provides strong support for both mnemonic strategy instruction and differentiated curriculum enhancements. The research base for mnemonics is among the most substantial in special education; research supporting differentiated curriculum enhancements is more limited but includes a substantial number of students, classrooms, and content areas across seven replication studies. Perhaps one reason for the success of these approaches is that they interact favorably with the characteristics of students with high-incidence disabilities. It appears that students with problems with verbal learning and memory benefit from mnemonic strategies, and that generalized low achievement is ameliorated by increased academic engagement afforded by peer mediation and learning materials targeted to learning needs.

In spite of the observed positive outcomes, several limitations can be noted. Mnemonic instruction has been demonstrated to be very effective; however, these effects are generally limited to initial acquisition and retention of specified verbal content. Such objectives are of great importance but are not the only school learning objectives. Additional strategies are needed to address other objectives, such as fluency development, comprehension, and application. Future research could address how mnemonic instruction can effectively be combined into an integrated program of instruction, incorporating a variety of instructional objectives, over significant instructional periods.

Research in differentiated curriculum enhancements is recent and in need of further replication, particularly across grade levels and subject areas. In addition, evidence is needed about teacher receptivity to the approaches, particularly with respect to issues of materials development and classroom organization. Scruggs, Mastropieri, and McDuffie (2007) observed that general education teachers may be reluctant to depart significantly from traditional classroom routines, and strategies for encouraging teachers to implement more research-based practices in inclusive classrooms could be of particular importance.

Mnemonic strategies and differentiated curriculum enhancements represent only a small fraction of the range of instructional and behavioral strategies now available for students with high-incidence disabilities (Chard, Cook, & Tankersley, 2013; Lane, Cook, & Tankersley, 2013). Taken in conjunction with these other strategies, teachers have a wide variety of effective treatments available for substantially improving the school experiences of students with high-incidence disabilities.

CHAPTER 4

Teaching Individuals with Severe Intellectual Disability: *Effective Instructional Practices*

Susan R. Copeland and **Kay Osborn** | *University of New Mexico*

*B*efore beginning a discussion of effective interventions for persons identified as having severe intellectual disability, it is useful to first describe who these individuals are. The most widely used current definition of intellectual disability states that it is "characterized by significant limitations both in intellectual functioning and in adaptive behavior as expressed in conceptual, social, and practical adaptive skills. This disability originates before age 18" (Schalock et al., 2010, p. 5). To better provide services, researchers and others have further classified individuals within this broad disability based on a measure of the severity of their disability. Before 1992, IQ scores were the major method used to classify individuals with intellectual disability. Some organizations, such as the World Health Organization, continue to use this method of classification. According to this system, individuals scoring between 25 and 40 on a standardized assessment of intelligence were classified as having severe intellectual disability. Beginning in 1992, the American Association on Mental Retardation (now known as the American Association on Intellectual and Developmental Disability [AAIDD]) eliminated IQ-based

categories and instead recommended categorization based on the level and intensity of individuals' needs for support (i.e., the activities, resources, or strategies that assist individuals to function more successfully in their environment) (Schalock et al., 2010). The underlying premise of a supports-based classification model is that provision of necessary supports will result in improved outcomes for the individual. In a supports-based classification system, individuals with severe intellectual disability would be those most likely to require support across the majority of areas of their life for sustained periods of time (Beirne-Smith, Patton, & Kim, 2006).

Research reviewed for this chapter spans several decades, so participants in reviewed studies were likely assigned classifications based on different systems, depending on the time period within which they were identified as having an intellectual disability. To ensure consistency in the manner in which we use the term *severe intellectual disability,* we will adhere to Beirne-Smith and colleagues' (2006) statement that "the 'severe' label encompasses the groups specifically designated as having moderate, severe, and profound levels of mental retardation" (p. 294).

General Learning Characteristics of Persons with Severe Intellectual Disability

Individuals with severe intellectual disability comprise a heterogeneous group (Beirne-Smith et al., 2006). Each individual has unique learning needs and also skill areas that are relative strengths. The effect of low expectations on the learning abilities of this group of individuals must be considered. Historically, educators and others have had few expectations for individuals with severe intellectual disability to acquire skills beyond basic functional tasks (Browder, Spooner, Wakeman, Trela, & Baker, 2006), which too often resulted in limited opportunities for these students to learn more complex skills. Given the pervasiveness of these limited opportunities, it is not always possible to make completely definitive conclusions about what these individuals can and cannot learn.

Nonetheless, a number of learning challenges widely observed with this group of individuals merit consideration when selecting content for instruction and instructional methods. Many individuals with severe intellectual disability, for example, experience difficulty in both understanding spoken language and producing it (Reichle, 1997). Because of the foundational nature of language, language and communication delays and impairments significantly affect all areas of learning. This includes social and behavioral skills and the ability to acquire related academic skills, such as literacy.

Difficulty attending to relevant cues in a given situation is another learning challenge for many persons with severe intellectual disability (Heller, Forney, Alberto, Best, & Schwartzman, 2009). Sensory and motor challenges may further affect the ability to focus or respond to instruction (Heller et al., 2009). A related problem is difficulty with memory, particularly short-term memory. These complexities, combined with language impairments, can affect the ability of individuals with severe intellectual disability to organize and synthesize several different skills needed to complete activities comprised of multiple components (L. Brown et al., 1983). For example, a student may have learned the component skills necessary to purchase lunch in the school cafeteria in a classroom setting (i.e., coin identification, basic sight-word vocabulary, social greeting responses). However, when faced with buying lunch in the actual cafeteria during the lunch period, the student may not be able to use the necessary skills to accomplish the task.

Another common learning challenge for persons with severe intellectual disability is transferring (generalizing) information learned in one context to a novel or different context or to novel materials or people (L. Brown et al., 1983). This problem requires instructors to teach in a manner that facilitates generalization, such as carefully selecting multiple teaching examples that represent the range of situations in which targeted skills may be needed (i.e., general case instruction), using authentic materials that are common to the environments that individuals will encounter, and teaching skills that are likely to be reinforced in natural settings (Fox, 1989).

Difficulty establishing social relationships is another widespread challenge for individuals with severe intellectual disability (Heller et al., 2009). Multiple factors contribute to this difficulty, such as having limited communication skills and trouble reading social cues, as well as a lack of access to peers because of receiving educational services exclusively with other individuals who also have significant limitations in social competence (Schwartz, Staub, Peck, & Gallucci, 2006). Effective means to address these issues seem to combine teaching social skills directly in inclusive settings where the skills will be used and where individuals with severe disability can observe competent peer models (Schwartz et al., 2006).

Researchers and others have developed and examined a number of highly effective instructional practices that assist persons with severe intellectual disability across the age range to acquire and use skills in many different environments. In the following sections, we describe three such research-based practices: prompting, task analysis, and self-management. Within each of these sections, we define the practice, describe the research base supporting it, describe how to implement it successfully with this population of students, and provide suggestions for continued research on the practice. We selected these three practices because of their foundational nature. These practices can be used in home, school (general and special education settings), community, and employment settings; and research supports their use with individuals ranging from young children to adults. All are derived from behavioral theory, specifically, from the field of applied behavior analysis.

Prompting

A prompt is a stimulus that sets the occasion for the targeted response when it is paired with the natural cue (i.e., the discriminative stimulus) (J. O. Cooper, Heron, & Heward, 2007). A prompt provides information that lets a student know how or when to perform a task. Educators use prompts to reduce errors when individuals are acquiring new skills but then fade the prompts as the new skill becomes more fluent. Prompts are considered to be an antecedent strategy (i.e., specific, planned actions before a student responds) and are derived from the field of applied behavior analysis (Browder, Ahlgrim-Delzell, Spooner, Mims, & Baker, 2009).

Response Prompts

Researchers categorize instructional prompts in several different ways. Response prompts are the actions a teacher takes before the student responds or after an incorrect response that help the student make a correct response (J. O. Cooper et al., 2007). These include verbal cues, gestures, modeling, or full or partial physical assistance. Prompts may be provided before a student responds, such as with simultaneous prompting, or provided in the form of feedback after a student responds (e.g., "That isn't correct. Do that problem again."). Research supports use of response prompts in teaching both discrete and chained (i.e., multistep) tasks (Wolery, Ault, Gast, Doyle, & Griffen, 1990).

Simultaneous prompting is a type of response prompt that is considered an errorless learning strategy. It may be effective for individuals with severe intellectual disability who become upset when they make a mistake or those who are easily confused by errors (Browder, 2001). When using this strategy, the teacher presents the natural cue for the targeted behavior and simultaneously provides the controlling prompt (Morse & Schuster, 2004). A controlling prompt is one that "consistently produces the target behavior" (Wolery et al., 1992, p. 240). For example, a teacher using this strategy to teach sight words shows the student a printed word (the natural cue) (e.g., milk) while simultaneously reading the word aloud (modeling the correct response), and then instructs the student to read the word using simultaneous prompting (e.g., "This word is *milk*. Read *milk*."). The teacher's model demonstrates to the student how to respond, increasing the likelihood of success.

After several trials using the simultaneous prompt, the teacher assesses the student's performance by presenting the natural cue without the prompt. These trials are called probes and occur before the instructional session so the teacher can assess whether stimulus control has shifted from the controlling prompt to the natural cue. Returning to our sight-word example, after one or more sessions using the model as a controlling prompt, the teacher would present the printed target word(s) and ask the student to read the word without providing the model. She would then record the student's performance and use this information to determine whether the student needed additional sessions with the simultaneous prompt or was ready to move to new words.

Morse and Schuster (2004) reviewed 17 studies examining simultaneous prompting on acquisition of both discrete and chained tasks in one-to-one and small-group instructional arrangements. Individuals with severe intellectual disability across the age range from preschool to adulthood made up a large segment of the participants in these studies (approximately 19 of 74 total participants). Findings indicated that simultaneous prompting was effective in helping participants with severe intellectual disability acquire a range of skills including communication, vocational, and self-care/domestic skills within school and vocational training settings. Participants acquired skills with generally low error rates and generalized and maintained the skills they learned.

Simultaneous prompting has also been used to teach academic skills. Rao and Kane (2009) used simultaneous prompting to teach two middle school students with intellectual disability (one who had severe intellectual disabilities) in a self-contained classroom to subtract decimals using regrouping. Both students acquired the skill, maintained it, and demonstrated generalization of the skill across settings, materials, and persons.

Morse and Schuster (2004) noted that simultaneous prompting is easy for teachers to learn and implement. It doesn't require students to have a wait time that teachers must monitor or for teachers to set up a predetermined hierarchy of prompts (e.g., starting with a verbal prompt, then using a model prompt if the student doesn't respond, and finally using a physical prompt if the student still does not respond). Use of a single controlling prompt rather than a hierarchy may also make it a more time-efficient procedure than other prompting methods.

Typically, teachers or other adults have been the instructors in studies examining response prompts. Nevertheless, some researchers have successfully trained parents to use response prompts to teach skills (e.g., Denny et al., 2000). Other researchers have examined use of response prompts to teach academic skills to small groups of students versus in one-to-one formats. Some of these groups have included individuals with severe intellectual disabilities as well as peers who are typically developing (e.g., Fickel, Schuster, & Collins, 1998; Schoen & Ogden, 1995). This group of studies demonstrated positive outcomes for all students in the instructional groups and support use of response prompts within general education settings, thereby adding evidence of their utility with students with diverse abilities.

Fading Response Prompts

To avoid prompt dependency, the teacher should transfer stimulus control from the prompt to the natural cue as soon as the student's performance warrants this. Researchers have developed several systems to promote stimulus transfer. These include the most-to-least prompting hierarchy (sometimes called *the system of most prompts*), the least-to-most prompting hierarchy (sometimes called *the system of least prompts*), graduated guidance, and time delay.

A *most-to-least prompting hierarchy* begins with the instructor providing the maximum level of prompt required for the individual to be successful and then fading to a less intrusive level of prompt as the individual begins to acquire the new skill (Demchak, 1990). Often this begins with a physical prompt, gradually moving to a verbal prompt, and then to no external prompt. This strategy has been used successfully to teach individuals with severe intellectual disability functional tasks such as self-care, dressing, and food preparation (Demchak, 1990).

When using the *least-to-most prompting hierarchy*, the teacher provides the natural cue and waits a predetermined amount of time for the student to respond (e.g., 3 seconds). If the student gives no response or an incorrect response, the teacher provides the least-intrusive level of prompt possible and again waits for the student to respond. If the student still gives no response, the teacher then provides the next most-intrusive prompt, and so on, until the student successfully responds. The system of least prompts has been used to teach both discrete and chained tasks and is one of the most widely used techniques for learners with severe intellectual disability (P. M. Doyle, Wolery, Ault, & Gast, 1988). Diverse tasks involving language, social, employment, self-care, and motor skills have been successfully taught to this group of learners using a system of least prompts.

Time delay is a stimulus-fading procedure with a strong evidence base (Browder et al., 2009). The two types of time delay are constant and progressive. A teacher using constant time delay secures the student's attention, presents the natural cue, asks the student to make the correct response, and then gives a several-second delay before providing an additional prompt. On the initial trials, the teacher uses a 0-second delay by modeling the correct response immediately after providing the natural cue (just like simultaneous prompting, described earlier). As soon as the student responds correctly, the teacher provides reinforcement for correct responding. Once the student has had several opportunities to succeed with a 0-second delay, the teacher increases the time-delay interval to a predetermined length (e.g., 4 seconds) and continues this delay interval until the student consistently responds without need of prompts. The increased delay gives the student an opportunity to make a correct response. If the student does not respond within the delay interval or makes a mistake, the teacher provides error correction and prompts the student to perform the task correctly (e.g., "No, write the number 6."). Constant time delay is an especially useful strategy for individuals who do best when they make few errors in acquiring a new skill or who might become dependent on the teacher's prompts (Miller & Test, 1989). Numerous research studies have shown constant time delay effective in teaching discrete and chained tasks to individuals with severe intellectual disability in both one-to-one and small-group teaching formats using teachers and peer tutors to deliver instruction (e.g., Collins, Branson, & Hall, 1995; Schoen & Ogden, 1995).

With *progressive time delay*, the length of the delay after the 0-second delay trials is gradually and systematically extended across time (Demchak, 1990). The teacher may go from a zero delay to a 2-second delay for several sessions and then to a 4-second delay, then a 6-second delay, and so on. Although more complex to implement than constant time delay, it can be useful for persons who need a gradual withdrawal of prompts. For example, researchers have successfully used progressive time delay to teach purchasing skills (Frederick-Dugan, Test, & Varn, 1991), recreation skills (S. Chen, Zhang, Lange, Miko, & Joseph, 2001), and vocational skills (e.g., Walls, Dowler, Haught, & Zawlocki, 1984).

Graduated guidance, a variation of using physical prompts, is most often used with chained tasks (Snell & Brown, 2011). The teacher begins by using hand-over-hand guidance to assist the student to perform the targeted task. Next, the teacher moves his or her hand either slightly away from the student and shadows the required movement or changes the position of the physical prompt (J. O. Cooper et al., 2007). For example, to teach students to write their names, teachers first put their hand over their students' hands as students form the letter. Once students have acquired some fluency, teachers move their hand to students' wrists, then to students' elbows, and then fade the physical prompt completely. Graduated guidance has been used to successfully teach a range of functional and play skills to individuals with severe intellectual disability (e.g., Reese & Snell, 1991). Denny and colleagues (2000), for example, described parents using graduated guidance to teach their preschool child with severe intellectual and motor disabilities to feed himself and engage in a play activity. The mother used a four-level procedure to teach the child to spoon feed, and the mother and father used a three-level procedure to teach the child to roll a ball back and forth to another individual. The child maintained both skills across a 1-year period. Snell and Brown (2011) recommended using graduated guidance when other prompting systems have not succeeded and using it during early acquisition stages of learning a new task.

Comparison of Response Prompting Procedures

Research comparing use of each type of prompting system with individuals with severe intellectual disability in terms of efficiency (e.g., number of trials to criterion, number of errors) and effectiveness has found each of these systems more effective than simple error correction (P. M. Doyle et al., 1988). Constant and progressive time delays appear more efficient than a system of least prompts with both discrete and chained tasks (Demchak, 1990; Wolery et al., 1990, 1992). Comparisons between the most-to-least prompting and system of least prompts have yielded mixed results (P. M. Doyle et al., 1988). Demchak's review of the literature indicated that the most-to-least prompting might be more effective when teaching for acquisition, whereas the system of least prompts might be more effective in teaching for fluency (i.e., building accuracy and speed).

Stimulus Prompts

Many individuals with severe intellectual disability have difficulty attending to the relevant aspect of a stimulus, making it difficult to discriminate between two stimuli. Stimulus prompts (sometimes called *stimulus modification*) are changes to instructional materials that cue the student to make a correct discrimination (i.e., response) (J. O. Cooper et al., 2007). For example, color coding the start and stop buttons on a portable DVD player make it easier to choose correctly when operating the machine. Ault and colleagues (1989) reviewed research comparing stimulus prompts with other prompting systems and found stimulus prompts to produce fewer errors for individuals with severe intellectual disability than response prompting or simple error correction. Combining stimulus prompts with response-prompting methods was found to be especially effective.

Just as with response prompts, it is critical to transfer stimulus control from a stimulus prompt to the natural cue. The first method of stimulus transfer, stimulus fading, involves changing one or more dimensions of the stimulus prompt to make it more salient to the learner and fading this change over time. For example, in our previous DVD player example, we could make the color on the buttons more and more transparent across time until it is completely eliminated. Researchers have used this method successfully with learners with severe intellectual disability to teach skills such as word and shape recognition (e.g., McGee & McCoy, 1981; Schreibman, 1975; Sheehy, 2002; Strand & Morris, 1986).

Stimulus shaping, another stimulus transfer method that facilitates skill acquisition, is done by presenting incorrect items (i.e., distractor stimuli) with the natural stimulus that are initially very different from the natural stimulus on one or more dimensions (e.g., size and color). Over time, distractor stimuli are changed to be more like the natural stimulus, requiring the student to make increasingly fine discriminations between the two. For example,

to teach recognition of the letter *b,* the teacher would first pair it with letters that look very different (e.g., *w, z*) and gradually add pairings with letters of a similar shape (e.g., *p, d*). Using this method, individuals with severe intellectual disability have successfully learned skills such as self-care (Mosk & Bucher, 1984), number and word recognition (e.g., Repp, Karsh, & Lentz, 1990; Walsh & Lamberts, 1979), and discrimination between photographs (Graff & Green, 2004).

Utilizing Prompting with Fidelity

Selecting and implementing the most effective prompting strategy for a given individual requires paying careful attention to the individual's learning history and characteristics and to the type of task being taught. Figure 4.1 provides general considerations for implementation of the various response-prompting strategies based on reviews of the research. Many excellent resources describe in detail how to implement prompting strategies effectively (e.g., Dogoe & Banda, 2009; Morse & Schuster, 2004; Snell & Brown, 2011); the reader is encouraged to consult one of these for additional information on how to implement prompting as designed.

Summary

A broad research base that spans over 30 years and comprises over 100 studies supports the use of response and stimulus prompts to teach individuals with severe intellectual disability. Researchers examining prompting with this population have primarily used single-case research designs. Examination of the research in this area indicates that the majority of studies are methodologically sound. Researchers demonstrated reliable measurement of participants' behaviors, and many, but not all, assessed procedural fidelity.

Prompting often forms the underlying basis on which other instructional approaches are founded. For example, task analysis instruction, discussed in the next section, typically incorporates prompting to teach each task step. Given the strong empirical support for the use of prompting and the fact that it is more effective than simple error correction (P. M. Doyle et al., 1988), it is critical that educators and others understand how to use prompting effectively with individuals with severe intellectual disability.

One aspect of response prompting that appears to be under-researched is its use in general education and inclusive community settings. Researchers have expressed concern that use of highly specialized instructional practices, such as response prompting, within general education settings may stigmatize students with extensive

Figure 4.1 Checklist for use of response prompts.

Simultaneous Prompting

1. Select a task that is meaningful for the individual student.

2. Choose the least-intrusive controlling prompt that has been shown previously to be successful for that individual and that matches the features of the teaching task. Modeling has been used most often in research studies in this area (e.g., Rao & Kane, 2009).

3. Secure the student's attention before teaching on each trial during instruction.

4. Provide the target stimulus and the controlling prompt simultaneously (0-second delay). Consider providing a minimum of two instructional sessions at this level before conducting probe sessions.

5. Provide specific feedback after the student responds versus more general (e.g., "Good, you read *milk*" instead of "Great work").

6. Provide probe sessions immediately before each teaching session, and collect data on student's error rate. Use these data to determine when to introduce new items to instruction. Criterion most often used in research was 100% correct responding for 3 consecutive probe sessions (e.g., Fickel et al., 1998).

Most-to-Least Prompting Hierarchy

1. Choose which prompts fit the student's learning needs, and arrange in order from most to least intrusive; select a length of delay between the natural cue and the prompt (e.g., 3 second). Base this on knowledge of the student's prior learning.

2. Decide what will be the criterion to move from one prompt level to the next (e.g., 5 trials with 100% accuracy). Base this on the student's prior learning history.

3. Provide the natural cue (instruction for the task); wait using the delay time. If the student fails to respond or responds incorrectly, provide the first level of prompt. Reinforce any correct prompted or unprompted responses using specific feedback.

4. Collect data on student's error rates. Use these data to determine when to move up the prompt levels according to the predetermined criterion.

Least-to-Most Prompting Hierarchy

1. Choose which prompts fit the student's learning needs, and arrange in order from least to most intrusive; select the length of delay time between presentation of the natural cue and the prompt based on the student's prior learning history (e.g., 3 second). Note that the research literature generally used 4 or more prompt levels for individuals with severe intellectual disability.

2. Choose the criterion to move from one prompt level to the next (e.g., 5 trials with 100% accuracy). Base this on the student's prior learning history.

3. Provide the natural cue (instruction for the task); wait using the delay time (researchers have used 2- to 30-second delays, with most using 4- to 10-second delays; e.g., P. M. Doyle et al., 1988). If the student fails to respond or responds incorrectly, provide the first level of prompt. Reinforce any correct prompted or unprompted responses using specific feedback. If the student gives no response or an incorrect response, present the next most-intrusive prompt on the next trial.

4. Collect data on student's error rates. Use these data to determine when to move down the prompt levels according to the predetermined criterion.

Constant Time Delay

1. Choose the most effective prompt for the individual that is also the least intrusive; this should be based on the student's learning history.

2. Select the delay interval. Researchers have used 2- to 5-second delays; some experts recommend use of a 4-second delay (e.g., Snell & Brown, 2011). Consider the student's learning characteristics, the features of the task, and observations of peers who are typically developing performing the task.

3. Begin with one or more trials at 0-second delay (i.e., providing natural cue and controlling prompt simultaneously), and then move to trials using the predetermined delay interval. Criteria to increase the delay varied across studies; most researchers used 1, 2, or 3 consecutive correct 0-second delay sessions as the criterion to move to the longer interval (e.g., Dogoe & Banda, 2009).

(continued)

Figure 4.1   Checklist for use of response prompts. (*Continued*)

Constant Time Delay (*continued*)

4. Interrupt errors with the predetermined prompt. Reinforce correct unprompted and prompted responses using specific feedback. Plan to thin the reinforcement schedule as the student becomes more proficient.

5. Collect data on student error rates, and use these to make instructional decisions. If errors do not decrease, return to several trials at 0-second delay.

Progressive Time Delay

1. Choose the most effective prompt for the individual that is also the least intrusive; this should be based on the student's learning history.

2. Select the delay intervals. Consider the student's learning characteristics, the features of the task, and observations of peers who are typically developing performing the task. Researchers have typically used 3- to 5-second delays (e.g., Collins et al., 1993).

3. Decide what will be criterion to move from one delay level (i.e., time interval) to another. Researchers have used varied criteria, ranging from 67% to 100% correct responding on a single trial to 100% correct on 2 to 5 consecutive trials (e.g., Collins et al., 1993).

4. Begin with one or more trials at 0-second delay (i.e., providing natural cue and controlling prompt simultaneously) and then move to trials using the first predetermined delay interval. After criterion is reached at this level, move to the next level, and so on.

5. Interrupt errors with the predetermined prompt. Reinforce correct unprompted and prompted responses using specific feedback. Plan to thin the reinforcement schedule as the student becomes more proficient.

6. Collect data on student error rates and use that information to make instructional decisions. If errors do not decrease, return to several trials at previous delay interval.

Graduated Guidance

1. Determine each level of physical guidance for the individual student (e.g., full physical prompt at hand, gradual lessening of pressure to light touch, shadowing). Selection should be based on student's individual learning characteristics. Arrange these in order from most intrusive to least intrusive.

2. Determine a delay interval to use before providing a level of physical guidance (researchers often used 5-second delay). Select a criterion for moving from one level to the next (e.g., 3 consecutive trials with 100% accuracy).

3. Provide the instruction to begin the task, use the predetermined wait time, and provide the first level of physical guidance if student does not respond or responds incorrectly. When student meets criterion, move to next level of physical guidance and so on until student is performing task independently.

4. Interrupt errors with the level of guidance used on a prior trial; reinforce correct prompted and unprompted responses using specific feedback.

5. Collect data on student error rates. Use these data to determine when to lessen physical guidance according to the predetermined criterion. Researchers' criteria varied, but many used 3 consecutive trials of correct response at one prompt level before moving to a less-intrusive prompt (Denny et al., 2000).

---

support needs or that their use might disrupt the typical routines in these settings (McDonnell, 1998). Some evidence suggests that prompting can be used within general education environments in nonstigmatizing ways with individuals with severe intellectual disability (e.g., see the work of McDonnell and colleagues on embedded instruction, e.g., Jameson, McDonnell, Johnson, Riesen, & Polychronis, 2007). A small group of studies has examined use of prompting strategies with students without disabilities. This is promising and is also an area in need of additional research. Finally, relatively few studies have investigated prompting to teach complex academic tasks (Dogoe & Banda, 2009). As educators

provide more students with severe intellectual disability the opportunity to acquire academic skills, this is also an area for future research.

Task Analysis

Task analysis essentially involves breaking a complex skill or activity down into a series of smaller steps and teaching someone to perform the steps in sequence. Its origins, like many other successful practices for persons with severe disabilities, are within applied behavior analysis. The steps in a task analysis are called a *behavioral chain* (Alberto & Troutman, 2009). Each response in the behavior chain acts as a cue (i.e., a discriminative stimulus) for the next behavior in the chain. Individuals perform one step in the chain, which cues them to perform the next step, and so on until they reach the end of the chain and receive some type of reinforcement. Consider, for example, that many of us download driving directions from Mapquest to travel from where we live or work to a new destination. We carefully follow each step in the directions (task analysis), with each step prompting the next until we arrive at the desired location. Our reinforcement consists of the satisfaction of having arrived without getting lost.

Task analysis is one of the most commonly used instructional strategies with students with extensive support needs. Task analysis instruction may be especially helpful for individuals with severe intellectual disability because it supports difficulties with short-term memory by breaking a complex task down into single, discrete steps that can be mastered and chained together. A task analysis is also easily individualized for a student's particular needs. This feature can be particularly important for students with severe intellectual disability who may have additional conditions that affect their learning and require individualization. Reese and Snell (1991), for example, designed individualized task analyses for three young students with intellectual disability and accompanying sensory and motor difficulties that took into account each student's unique learning challenges (e.g., modifying steps for a child who had difficulty using one arm) so that all the students could succeed.

Task analyses are also useful instructional tools because they can perform several functions. These include serving as (a) an initial form of assessment to determine which component skills within a task or activity a student may have already mastered; (b) a plan for instruction (breaking down a task into teachable steps); and (c) a means of progress monitoring (collecting frequent information on student progress in acquiring a targeted skill) (F. Brown, Lehr, & Snell, 2011).

Types of Task Analyses

Behavior chains can be taught using three methods: forward chaining, backward chaining, and total task presentation. Forward chaining begins by teaching the first task step and then proceeding sequentially through the steps as each is mastered. Training does not proceed to the next step until a preset criterion is mastered on the first step. Researchers have used forward chaining to teach a variety of skills. For example, McDonnell and McFarland (1988) used forward chaining to teach four high school students with severe intellectual disability

to operate a commercial washing machine and laundry soap dispenser. They taught students these behavioral chains beginning with the first step. Once students could perform that step independently for three consecutive trials, instruction began on the next step in the chain and so on until the entire chain was performed independently.

Backward chaining, another method of teaching chained tasks, involves beginning instruction with the last step; and when that is mastered, teaching the last two steps, then the last three steps, and so on (Farlow & Snell, 2006). It has been widely used with individuals with severe intellectual disability (McDonnell & Laughlin, 1989). For example, Hagopian, Farrell, and Amari (1996) taught a 12-year-old boy with intellectual disability and autism to swallow liquids from a cup using a backward chaining procedure. They noted that if an individual does not display a target behavior at all or very infrequently, then backward chaining may be a useful instructional procedure. This may be because this method makes a more salient connection for the student between the final step (which can act as a natural reinforcer) and the preceding steps. In other words, it promotes understanding of how the steps are linked and creates more immediate access to reinforcement.

Total task presentation (sometimes called *whole task* or *total task approach*) requires teaching each step of the behavioral chain every time the skill is taught (J. O. Cooper et al., 2007). Many academic chains, such as addition with regrouping, are taught in this manner (Alberto & Troutman, 2009). An advantage of using this format is that the student can experience the functional outcome of the task (i.e., receive the natural reinforcer for the task) every time the skill is practiced (similar to backward chaining). This outcome may enhance students' understanding of why an activity is being taught and what is its purpose. However, with long and complex tasks, total task presentation may require large amounts of instructional time and may be so complicated that it interferes with student learning (Farlow & Snell, 2006). Despite this, numerous researchers have used total task presentation successfully in teaching a range of tasks: self-care and domestic skills (e.g., R. D. Horner & Keilitz, 1975; Miller & Test, 1989); purchasing skills (e.g., McDonnell & Laughlin, 1989; Morse & Schuster, 2004), cooking skills (e.g., Griffen, Wolery, & Schuster, 1992; Wright & Schuster, 1994), vocational skills (e.g., Chandler, Schuster, & Stevens, 1993; Walls et al., 1981), safety skills (e.g., Collins, Stinson, & Land, 1993), and academic skills (Rao & Kane, 2009).

Several researchers have compared the effectiveness of these three methods of teaching task analysis (e.g., McDonnell & McFarland, 1988; Walls et al., 1981). Results indicate that total task presentation is more efficient and effective in teaching complex, chained tasks to individuals with severe intellectual disability, although some results are mixed (McDonnell & Laughlin, 1989). Particular aspects of certain tasks or unique learning characteristics of some individuals likely make one method more effective than another in different circumstances. Therefore, teachers and other instructors should take into consideration their knowledge of the student and the task being taught when selecting the type of task analysis.

Task Analysis Instruction

A response prompt method typically is used to teach the steps of a task analysis, regardless of which task analysis format is being used. An examination of the literature indicates that all the response prompt procedures have been used to successfully teach chained tasks. Certain prompting systems seem more effective or efficient in certain situations, however. A comparison of using least-prompts hierarchies with constant time delay to teach chained tasks to individuals with severe intellectual disability found constant time delay most efficient (P. M. Doyle et al., 1988). Comparisons of the effectiveness of constant time delay versus a system of most prompts to teach chained tasks via task analysis have shown mixed results. Miller and Test (1989) compared these two prompting systems and found that although both methods assisted students with severe intellectual disability in acquiring task-analyzed laundry skills, constant time delay resulted in less instructional time and fewer student errors. However, McDonnell and Ferguson (1989) compared the two methods in teaching banking skills to high school students with severe disability and found time delay less efficient. These findings suggest that the instructor should take the learning characteristics of each student and the features of the task into consideration when selecting a prompting system to teach the task analysis.

Instruction using task analysis has been criticized by some experts as being too focused on teaching subskills and not focused on teaching for understanding (M. Carter & Kemp, 1996). Yet, careful construction of a task analysis can create opportunities for individuals to acquire more than merely the motor skills involved in a task (Browder, 2001). In fact, students can learn what F. Brown and colleagues (2011) called "extension skills" (p. 93) within the context of task analysis instruction. These critical skills include self-initiating the task, making choices, problem solving, using social or communication skills, or self-monitoring performance. K. J. Cooper and Browder (1998), for example, described a study in which three adults with severe intellectual disability increased independent performance on the steps of a purchasing task when choices were included within

the task analysis (e.g., selecting which door to enter the restaurant, selecting which food item to order). These individuals knew how to make choices but did not do so until choices were embedded within the task and they were taught to make selections. The authors suggested that adding choice-making instruction to the task analysis may have enhanced the participants' motivation to perform other task steps, or it may have increased the salience of the discriminative stimulus for each step, and thus helped participants recognize what behaviors were required.

Although most often teachers use task analysis instruction for one student at a time, research supports using small-group instruction (e.g., three to four students) to teach chained responses (Reese & Snell, 1991; Wall & Gast, 1999). Griffen and colleagues (1992), for example, described a study in which the classroom teacher taught three elementary students with moderate or severe intellectual disability to prepare snacks using a total task presentation format combined with constant time delay. The teacher taught each student one snack preparation task directly, while the other students merely observed and turned pages in a pictorial recipe book as the lesson progressed. The teacher praised the observers, gave them tokens, and prompted them to praise and give a token to the student being directly instructed. All the students acquired three snack preparation tasks, including those they had only observed. This research finding is promising because it indicates that students with severe disabilities can acquire skills through observational learning in small groups, thus increasing instructional efficiency.

Another promising line of research has investigated using peers who are typically developing to teach or model chained tasks with students with severe intellectual disability (Kohl & Stettner-Eaton, 1985). Werts and colleagues (1996), for example, taught 12 peers who were typically developing to model several school skill task chains (e.g., sharpening a pencil) while verbally describing each step as three students with disabilities, including one with severe intellectual disability, observed. Each of the students with disabilities acquired the targeted skills, and all generalized at least some of the new skills to different materials. These findings support the inclusion of students with severe intellectual disability within inclusive environments where they can acquire useful skills through observing competent peer models.

Some researchers have investigated the effect of requiring students to perform steps in a task chain in a specific, predetermined order, in comparison to letting the students perform the steps out of order as long as this did not keep them from completing the tasks successfully (called a *functional order*). Of course, some tasks should be completed in a specific order (e.g., crossing a street), but rearranging step order within other tasks will not necessarily affect the outcome. Wright and Schuster (1994), for example, taught four elementary students with moderate or severe disabilities to make two simple snacks, one using the specific task step format and one using the functional order format. Students acquired the preparation tasks using both formats and maintained them up to 3 weeks, but required fewer instructional sessions during the functional order task instruction. Three of the four students made fewer errors when taught with this format. Because reducing error rates is associated with increased instructional efficiency, this is a potentially useful strategy for teachers to consider as they design task analysis instruction.

Implementing Task Analysis Instruction with Fidelity

Research examining task analysis instruction for individuals with severe intellectual disability reveals a few key instructional considerations. A first critical decision in teaching with a task analysis is whether the student has all the prerequisite skills needed to perform the steps in the task analysis (Alberto & Troutman, 2009). If the student lacks one or more of these, then the first step is to teach these individual, necessary skills. Next, it is important to individualize the task analysis for the learner. Generally, learners with severe intellectual disability require smaller steps—more explicit individual skills—than do persons with no or milder disability. A next step is to determine which format to use in teaching the task. Although all three formats have been found to be effective, total task presentation seems in general to be more effective across most tasks for learners with severe intellectual disability. Finally, the instructor must select a prompting system with which to teach the task analysis. Results of studies comparing these methods are not completely clear. What seems most effective is to consider the student's past learning history and the specific features of the task to be taught. As with prompting, many excellent resources describe in detail how to use task analysis instruction (e.g., Browder, 2001); the reader is encouraged to consult one of these for additional information.

Summary

In summary, numerous research studies have examined task analysis instruction. Much of this research involved participants with severe intellectual disability ranging in age from preschool through adulthood. Tasks taught in these studies have included self-help, motor, community, leisure, vocational, and academic skills. However, we located only one study that examined a chained academic task taught to participants with severe intellectual

disability (Rao & Kane, 2009). This seems to be an area for future research, particularly, as students with severe disability should now be given access to the core academic content (IDEA, 2004).

The majority of studies examining the utility of task analysis as an instructional tool used single-case research designs. Research design and methodology in the studies were adequate. Not all studies assessed procedural fidelity, but the majority of the studies included many design components needed for quality single-case research.

Although some studies examining the utility of task analysis occurred in community settings or generalization was probed within inclusive school environments (e.g., the school cafeteria), the majority took place in settings where most of the individuals present had disabilities (e.g., self-contained classrooms). Only three of the studies located were conducted in general education settings (Arntzen, Halstadtro, & Halstadtro, 2003; Kohl & Stettner-Eaton, 1985; Werts et al., 1996). This finding substantiates Wolery and Schuster's (1997) observation that relatively little research that includes participants with severe disabilities has been conducted in inclusive settings. It is now required that these students have access to the general curriculum, and research indicates that providing this access to the curriculum within general education settings can be highly beneficial for students (Ryndak, Moore, Orlando, & Delano, 2008/2009). Researchers should, then, further examine some of the research-based strategies used in special education settings, such as task analysis, within general education settings. These strategies likely will be effective in general education settings, but more evidence is needed about implementation techniques that do not disrupt ongoing instruction or that inadvertently stigmatize students (McDonnell, 1998).

Self-Management

Self-management strategies are actions individuals take to manage or regulate their own behavior (Agran, King-Sears, Wehmeyer, & Copeland, 2003). These are sometimes called *student-directed learning strategies* because their use allows students to direct their learning rather than relying solely on teachers to do so (Agran et al., 2003). Self-management employs behavioral strategies that come from behavioral theory (J. O. Cooper et al., 2007). From this perspective, an individual who uses self-management engages in a behavior that affects or modifies the environment in some manner that makes it more likely that the target behavior will occur again (Agran et al., 2003). For example, checking off a picture representing a step on a task list helps individuals understand that this step is accomplished, and that they need to initiate the next step on the list.

Self-management strategies comprise some of the component skills of self-determination, which has been defined as the "skills, knowledge, and beliefs that enable [individuals] to engage in goal-directed, self-regulated, autonomous behavior" (Field, Martin, Miller, Ward, & Wehmeyer, 1998, p. 2). Research has demonstrated that providing instruction on the component strategies of self-determination is highly effective in helping individuals improve a range of skills, including academic skills in core content areas (e.g., Fowler, Konrad, Walker, Test, & Wood, 2007). These instructional strategies also teach broader skills (e.g., problem solving) that individuals with severe intellectual disability can use across the lifespan in different life areas.

Additional advantages of self-management strategies are that they can be effective with behaviors that are not readily observable (e.g., problem solving). Consequently, an individual can use them even when an external change agent, such as a teacher, cannot easily observe the behavior. Self-management strategies can also help persons with severe intellectual disability to gain increased control of their lives. These individuals may look frequently to others to guide their behavior rather than manage it themselves. Acquiring self-management skills can decrease reliance on external assistance and help them provide their own supports. Individuals may be motivated to use self-management strategies because they, not someone else, direct their own actions. This may result in higher performance rates of target behaviors than in teacher-directed interventions (Fantuzzo, Polite, Cook, & Quinn, 1988).

Self-management strategies also facilitate maintenance and generalization of newly acquired behaviors because individuals can provide their own prompts and consequences across settings. Indeed, L. K. Koegel and colleagues (1999) considered self-management to be a pivotal behavior because acquiring a self-management strategy allows an individual to apply it to a wide range of behaviors across settings and people without need for an external change agent to be present. Because many individuals with severe intellectual disability struggle with generalizing skills, this is an important benefit for this population of learners. Some experts have suggested that self-management strategies can increase instructional efficiency because teachers will spend less time managing students' behaviors if the students are taught to manage their own behaviors (Ganz, 2008). Ganz also suggested that learning to implement self-management instruction is relatively simple and does not require obtaining materials or resources beyond those found in most classrooms. This characteristic makes it appealing to classroom teachers and others who often work with large numbers of students and have limited time and resources to develop instructional materials.

Individuals with diverse abilities have used self-management to acquire new skills, build fluency of previously acquired skills, and facilitate generalization of skills across settings, materials, time, and persons. Self-management strategies have assisted individuals with severe intellectual disability improve performance of a variety of skills including social (e.g., C. Hughes et al., 2000), employment (e.g., Moore, Agran, & Fodor-Davis, 1989), classroom (Agran et al., 2005), recreational (e.g., C. Hughes et al., 2004), and academic skills (e.g., Copeland, Hughes, Agran, Wehmeyer, & Fowler, 2002).

Numerous self-management strategies are available. In the following sections, we describe two of the most widely used strategies: antecedent prompts and self-monitoring. We describe the research base supporting both strategies and offer research-based suggestions about successful implementation with individuals with severe intellectual disability. We also refer readers to additional sources that provide extensive information on implementation of both strategies (e.g., Agran et al., 2003; Ganz, 2008).

Antecedent Prompts

Antecedent prompts are cues added to the environment that help individuals guide their behavior. They differ from consequences, which are stimuli that occur after a behavior and affect its future occurrence, because antecedent prompts are used before a behavior to signal a response. Many people use antecedent prompts in their daily lives. Writing the date for an important meeting on a calendar is a form of antecedent prompting. Seeing the written date prompts you to gather your materials and attend the meeting. Similarly, individuals with disabilities may use visual, tactile, or auditory prompts to assist them in learning the steps for a new behavior or remembering to initiate a behavior. Some individuals require these prompts only temporarily, but others may continue to need them each time they perform a targeted skill (Agran et al., 2003).

Antecedent prompts have many benefits for persons with severe intellectual disability, such as increasing independence. Some individuals may master a skill but may not always be certain when to use the skill. Rather than relying on others for cues to begin a task, use of antecedent prompts allows individuals to initiate and complete tasks on their own. These prompts can also act as a memory aid for individuals who have difficulty with short-term memory that hampers their ability to complete complicated routines or activities. Antecedent prompts can provide the support needed to successfully complete complex tasks. Because these prompts typically are easily moved from one setting to another (i.e., they are portable), an individual can easily use them across different settings and with different tasks, thus facilitating generalization of learned skills.

Types of Antecedent Prompts

Picture prompts are a common form of antecedent prompts that can include graphic images, line drawings, or photographs. Research supports their successful use with individuals with severe intellectual disability across the age span to increase independent performance of many different types of skills such as social (e.g., C. Hughes et al., 2000), vocational (e.g., Lancioni & O'Reillly, 2001), leisure (Bambara & Ager, 1992), and functional tasks (e.g., Irvine, Erickson, Singer, & Stahlberg, 1992), among others. These prompts have been used with both multicomponent tasks (e.g., assembly tasks) and to help individuals perform a series of activities (e.g., follow an activity schedule).

Auditory prompts are another form of antecedent prompting that research has found is successful in teaching new skills to individuals with severe intellectual disability. Skills taught have included vocational (e.g., Grossi, 1998) and functional skills (e.g., Lancioni, Klaase, & Goossens, 1995). Most often, researchers have used a portable audio cassette player to provide either single- or multiple-word prompts to participants. Post and Storey (2002) noted that auditory prompting has been used to (a) help individuals remember to perform steps in complex multistep tasks, (b) stay focused on a task long enough to complete it, and (c) reduce errors in completing tasks. In a review of the auditory-prompting literature, Mechling (2007) stated that auditory-prompting systems may be easier for individuals with physical disabilities to use than systems that require manipulation of the picture prompts. Post and Storey (2002) also pointed out in their review of this literature that some participants in research studies were able to fade their use of auditory prompts once they had acquired the targeted skills.

Recently, researchers have begun to examine the use of computer-based systems to provide antecedent prompts, teaching skills ranging from daily living, employment, and school routines (Mechling, 2007). Mechling listed several advantages of computerized systems. First, computer use is a highly valued skill in our society, so prompting systems making use of this technology may be less stigmatizing than systems based on use of picture cards. It is also possible to easily individualize a computerized prompting system for an individual's needs. Use of touch screens, for example, can be helpful for individuals with physical challenges who may have difficulty manipulating a picture card system. Computerized systems also combine auditory and picture cues, for example, in video clips. Computers can also be used to provide varied types of cues, which can help individuals with severe intellectual disability attend more consistently to the task. Handheld computers are also small and easily portable, which is another advantage for their use across settings.

Several studies have compared computerized systems with picture prompts and have found computerized systems to be more effective in teaching persons with severe intellectual disability to complete daily living and vocational tasks (e.g., Davies, Stock, & Wehmeyer, 2003). Researchers speculated that these systems helped participants focus on the relevant cues within the task so that they made more correct decisions in completing the task steps. Generalization may also be enhanced with this type of antecedent prompting (e.g., Cihak, Kessler, & Alberto, 2006).

Implementing Antecedent Prompt Interventions with Fidelity

Implementing picture prompt interventions requires matching of the type of graphic to the individual's unique learning needs. Some persons with severe intellectual disability will do best with actual photographs, and others may be able to use line drawings or other graphic images. Organization of the graphic cues is another area for consideration. Short tasks can be represented with a few pictures arranged sequentially. More complex tasks will require a different arrangement. A common solution for complex tasks is to place photographs of each step of the task within a booklet. Individuals refer to each picture as they complete each step of the task. Copeland and Hughes (2000), for example, taught two high school students with severe intellectual disabilities to successfully and independently complete multistep work tasks using a picture prompt strategy that included self-monitoring. Students learned to refer to a picture of a task step, perform the step, and then turn the page to the next step, complete it, and so on, until the entire task was finished.

When teaching individuals to use auditory prompts, some researchers have interspersed verbal task step instructions with music (e.g., C. A. Davis, Brady, Williams, & Burta, 1992), and others have used a tone (beep) to cue participants to pause the audio and perform the verbalized step. Other researchers (e.g., Mechling & Gast, 1997) have taught students with intellectual disability to perform tasks by combining both auditory prompts and visual prompts. These researchers pointed out that using two sensory systems may be a way to provide additional information about task completion to students with extensive support needs.

Teaching individuals with severe intellectual disability to use computer prompting systems requires similar considerations to picture and auditory prompting.

Selection of graphics, complexity of auditory prompts, size (complexity) of prompted steps, and physical access of the device (e.g., using a touch screen, pushing keys) must be based on the individual's unique learning characteristics. Additional considerations include device cost and availability of someone to provide technical support.

Self-Monitoring

Self-monitoring, the most widely used and researched self-management strategy, is often used in conjunction with other self-management strategies (J. O. Cooper et al., 2007). Self-monitoring requires individuals to observe one of their behaviors and indicate its occurrence in some way, such as by making a checkmark on a form. Self-monitoring assists students in becoming more aware of their own behavior. D. J. Smith and Nelson (1997) noted that becoming more aware of one's own behavior, called *reactivity,* may act as a discriminative stimulus for that behavior.

Self-monitoring can be used to increase or decrease a behavior and typically is used with behaviors a student already knows how to perform (Agran et al., 2003). In other words, it can be useful in increasing the fluency of a behavior or in maintaining it across time, but not for learning a new behavior. Individuals can be taught to self-monitor specific behaviors (e.g., check off each step that is required to access a favorite Web site as it is completed) or can learn to self-monitor broader categories of behavior such as on-task behavior (Agran et al., 2003). This makes it a very flexible strategy that can be applied to widely varying situations.

Individuals with severe intellectual disability have used self-monitoring with a range of skills including academic (e.g., L. K. Koegel et al., 1999), social (e.g., C. Hughes et al., 2002), exercise (e.g., D. N. Ellis, Cress, & Spellman, 1992), and vocational (e.g., Ganz & Sigafoos, 2005) behaviors. Individuals have used self-monitoring strategies to increase independence of previously acquired skills and decrease problem behaviors (e.g., L. K. Koegel et al., 1999). Interventions have been used successfully in both general and special education settings across age ranges from kindergarten to adulthood (see Ferretti, Cavalier, Murphy, & Murphy, 1993; Ganz, 2008). In addition to adults, peers who are typically developing have successfully taught individuals with severe intellectual disability to self-monitor (e.g., Gilberts, Agran, Hughes, & Wehmeyer, 2001).

Implementing Self-Monitoring Interventions with Fidelity

When teaching an individual with severe intellectual disability to self-monitor, it is important to explicitly teach the individual to recognize the target behavior when it occurs and to select a form of marking its occurrence based on the individual's age, ability level, and learning characteristics (e.g., checking a small box on a form each time an elementary student raises his hand). Researchers have frequently used modeling and role-play to explicitly teach the self-monitoring system selected. Often researchers set criteria for accurate self-monitoring that must be met before the individual begins independent self-monitoring (e.g., self- and teacher-recording of the occurrence of behavior must match on 80% of opportunities). However, research indicates that even if the individual's self-recorded data are not completely accurate, positive behavioral changes often result (e.g., Gilberts et al., 2001). If the individual fails to maintain self-monitoring after initial training, some researchers have provided brief booster sessions to retrain participants in the system, which has proved successful with a variety of participants across settings and tasks (e.g., Ganz & Sigafoos, 2005).

Summary

As with the other reviewed practices, a solid empirical basis supports teaching individuals with severe intellectual disability to use antecedent prompts and self-monitoring to self-manage their behaviors. Most studies in this area employed single-case research designs and were methodologically sound. Most, however, used an intervention package, meaning that more than one strategy was used within an intervention (e.g., antecedent prompts and self-monitoring), making it difficult to isolate the individual effects of a particular strategy. Studies included participants across the age range from kindergarten to adulthood and examined self-management with diverse skill areas and across environments. Because self-management has been documented to decrease reliance on others and to promote generalization of skills, it is especially promising for use within inclusive school and community settings.

Despite the documented effectiveness of self-management strategies with individuals with severe intellectual disability, research has shown that these individuals may not be given opportunities to acquire these valuable skills. Wehmeyer and colleagues (2000) surveyed 1,200 high school teachers of students with disabilities regarding self-management instruction. Although the majority of the responding teachers recognized the importance and potential benefit of teaching self-management strategies to their students, 41% of them did not think that their students had the resources or skills to do this successfully. Teachers of students with severe intellectual disability were less likely than teachers of students with other disabilities to provide self-management instruction and less likely to recognize potential benefits of providing this instruction. This finding is troubling, because self-management strategies increase independence and autonomy, promote generalization of adaptive skills, and may be an effective way to increase access to the general curriculum for individuals with severe intellectual disability. Future research should investigate how to increase acceptance of this important strategy among instructors of individuals with severe intellectual disability.

Conclusion

Individuals with severe intellectual disability have significant learning challenges that affect all aspects of their lives. The instructional practices reviewed within this chapter address the particular learning characteristics of this group in ways that help them successfully acquire new knowledge and skills. Studies examining these practices provide a strong research-based foundation for their effectiveness.

Because of low expectations frequently held about the learning potential of individuals with severe intellectual disability, these individuals have not always been provided opportunities to acquire complex skills. Thankfully, expectations are changing, and increasingly these individuals receive challenging and meaningful instruction in content areas valued by society within settings that include individuals with and without disabilities. Researchers and practitioners now have the challenge of taking the instructional strategies found to be effective with learners with severe intellectual disabilities such as those reviewed in this chapter, and extend their use within inclusive school, community, and employment settings.

CHAPTER 5

Effective Reading Interventions for English Language Learners Who Are Struggling Readers or Identified with Learning Disabilities

Kathleen A. King Thorius | *Indiana University—Indianapolis*

Alfredo J. Artiles and **Amanda L. Sullivan** | *Arizona State University*

Setting the Context

As the U.S. population grows and becomes more diverse, so does the enrollment of public schools, which comprises 43% racial minority students and students who are learning English (Planty et al., 2008). In the West, Latino/a students constitute nearly 45% of the 7.9 million students in the region, and 22% of students are considered English Language Learners (ELLs). This increasing diversity, paired with anti-immigrant and anti-bilingual discourses (Chávez, 2008), further complicates the educational opportunities and outcomes for the 10.8 million students classified as Limited English Proficient (LEP),[1] the majority of whom speak Spanish as their primary language (Planty et al., 2008).

Educators are increasingly challenged to meet the educational needs of students who are ELLs, yet barriers to effective supports exist. For example, in states with large ELL populations, teachers reported having received little professional development to prepare them to teach these students (Gándara, Maxwell-Jolly, & Driscoll, 2005). Further, many educators view students' linguistic diversity as a problem rather than a resource that enriches teaching and learning (S. G. Law & Lane, 1987; Obiakor, 1999). Such attitudes manifest themselves in low expectations expressed in watered down, fragmented curriculum for students of diverse abilities, languages, and cultures (Steinberg & Kincheloe, 2004). Consequently, these students have a greater chance of receiving low grades, dropping out, and not going on to postsecondary schools (Durán, 2008).

Authors' note: The second author acknowledges the support of the Equity Alliance at ASU under grant #S004D080027 awarded by the U.S. Department of Education. Funding agencies' endorsement of the ideas expressed in this manuscript should not be inferred.

[1]The phrases *Limited English Proficient* and *English Language Learner,* and their respective acronyms, *LEP* and *ELL,* are similar in meaning. The primary difference is that LEP students are identified through testing, while ELL is a more general term referring to any student who is learning English as a second or additional language. Therefore, while Planty et al. (2008) reported on LEP students, this term also refers to ELLs.

Latino/a students, who are disproportionately represented in the ELL population, continue to have the highest dropout rate in the United States as compared to all other ethnic groups (U.S. Department of Education, 2010), and the Education Trust (2009) reports that 4 of every 10 Latino/a children who enroll in U.S. schools fail to graduate.

Moreover, students who are ELLs may have a higher probability of being placed in special education in some school contexts, and researchers have expressed concern that such educational decisions are made without ensuring access to high-quality opportunities to learn, providing instruction in the students' primary language, or ensuring the application of culturally and linguistically appropriate pre-referral interventions (Bernhard et al., 2006). Many ELLs, who often have immigrant backgrounds, do not receive curriculum in a language they understand and are taught by educators who only speak English and may not know or use techniques for working effectively with them (Suárez-Orozco, Roos, & Suárez-Orozco, 2000). Scholars point out that increasing special education referrals are also affected by (a) providing instructional services to foster English proficiency and academic content mastery simultaneously and (b) premature exiting from language support programs (Ochoa, Robles-Piña, Garcia, & Breunig, 1999).

Unfortunately, the connection between language and disability is not fully understood. For many educators, distinguishing between limited English proficiency and reading disability is exceedingly difficult (Keller-Allen, 2006); educators often confuse language acquisition with learning problems (Artiles & Klingner, 2006). In addition, no instruments are available to reliably assess limited English proficiency versus potential learning disability (LD) (Keller-Allen, 2006). These challenges have contributed to questions as to whether ELLs are misidentified for special education because educators do not adequately understand language acquisition processes and the influence of language acquisition on the academic content mastery (Case & Taylor, 2005) or, conversely, because educators fail to identify students with LD for special education because they are ELLs (Zehler et al., 2003). Indeed, emerging evidence indicates that ELLs in the Southwestern United States are overrepresented in special education (Artiles, Klingner, Sullivan, & Fierros, 2010; Artiles, Rueda, Salazar, & Higerada, 2005; De Valenzuela, Copeland, Qi, & Park, 2006). Further, the rate of ELLs identified as LD is growing significantly, quite often related to reading difficulties (Artiles, Trent, & Palmer, 2004; Donovan & Cross, 2002; Losen & Orfield, 2002).

Not surprisingly, emerging research has demonstrated teacher ratings of literacy skills and reading proficiency are significant predictors of eventual special education placement (Samson & Lesaux, 2009). However, considering the high proportion of ELLs who struggle academically, a significant challenge for researchers, policy makers, and practitioners is to elucidate whether disabilities or other factors shape ELLs' poor educational performance. Scholars have discussed that ELLs' disproportionate special education placement is likely shaped by complex interactions between factors such as ELLs' limited access to effective instruction and interventions, structural barriers (e.g., low funding, low teacher quality), and systematic disadvantages (e.g., poverty rates) (Artiles & Klingner, 2006). Thus, the necessity for supporting educators' development of culturally responsive research-based practices for intervening with struggling ELLs' literacy cannot be understated.

Exploring ELLs' Literacy Needs

The literacy outcomes of ELLs differ from those who are language-majority learners (i.e., students for whom English is their primary language). ELLs tend to perform less well on reading and writing assessments than their English-speaking peers; the gap is smaller on math, science, and social studies tests (Abedi, 2006). Nationwide, less than 20% of ELLs met state standards in reading (Genesee, Lindholm-Leary, Saunders, & Christian, 2005) and large-scale reading assessments show that at all grade levels, ELLs perform nearly 2 standard deviations below peers (Durán, 2008). Factors that contribute to these disparities vary across multiple levels (e.g., student, teacher, family, community/culture) and include demographics (e.g., economic status) (Snow, Burns, & Griffin 1998), sociocultural influences (Goldenberg, Rueda, & August, 2006), instructional quality (Téllez & Waxman, 2006), and those related to the developmental processes associated with literacy in second-language learners (Francis, Rivera, Lesaux, Kieffer, & Rivera, 2006). Despite considerable educational and language research around supporting ELLs' literacy development, a large research–practice gap remains.

This chapter offers a description of research-based practices that are effective in improving literacy outcomes for ELLs who are either identified as struggling readers or as having LD. The implications for this chapter are twofold. First, we hope educators may apply this review and description of effective research-based practices to a better understanding of how the research on literacy for ELLs is grounded. The goal of such awareness is to provide educators and leaders at different levels of the educational system with insights about how a general literacy curriculum is conceptualized; what underlying assumptions exist about the nature and purpose of literacy for ELLs who are struggling learners, and in turn, how are literacy interventions designed and implemented to support ELLs' literacy development?

Second, we hope educators find this chapter a useful support to increase their capacity to design, select, and implement literacy interventions with ELLs who are struggling to read or who have been identified with LD, while being mindful of histories of marginalization and unfavorable outcomes many students in such groups have faced in U.S. schools (e.g., Gitlin, Buendía, Crosland, & Doumbia, 2003; Valdés, 2001). Implications for this enhanced understanding of appropriate literacy interventions are improved instruction and support for ELLs, including better services for ELLs identified as having LD, as well as the prevention of unwarranted referrals for special education eligibility evaluations and the reduction of disproportionate representation of ELLs in special education for literacy difficulties.

Definition of Terms

First, we define what we mean by *intervention* and describe multiple positions held by those who design, implement, and study interventions with regard to what *reading* or *literacy* entails. Although *reading* and *literacy* are sometimes used interchangeably, specific definitions of each term appear to inform particular types of supports, which we discuss in detail in subsequent sections. *Intervention* is a word commonly used in education policy, practice, and research, yet its meaning is rarely addressed in sources on the subject. Even in the federal No Child Left Behind Act, despite the call for educational practitioners to apply "scientifically based research" to guide their decisions about which interventions to implement to have an impact on student achievement, the criteria for defining an intervention are not provided. For the purposes of this chapter, we use the following definition of *intervention:* "The direct manipulation by the researchers of psychological, medical, or educational variables for the purpose of assessing learning efficiency, learning accuracy, learning understanding or the combination of all three" (Swanson, 2000, pp. 4–5). In this chapter we focus on interventions to improve reading/literacy performance for ELLs. This is one of the most critical issues in the national education policy and practice discourse, because federal and state policies require success on standardized measures of reading for all student subgroups and schools experience difficulties understanding and implementing curriculum and instruction that ensure this outcome.

Two competing conceptualizations of literacy account for opposite ends in a continuum that defines conceptions of literacy (Snow, 2006) and guides the research and practice of designing and implementing literacy interventions with ELLs who are struggling to read, who have been identified with LD, or both. One side of the continuum defines literacy as a set of discrete skills to be taught explicitly; skills that, when applied by readers, allow them to obtain meaning from print for a functional purpose (Lyon, 1998; Reyna, 2004). Reviews of research demonstrate that these skills, commonly referred to as the five core areas of

reading instruction (i.e., phonemic awareness, phonics, fluency, vocabulary, and comprehension), apply similarly to reading instruction for ELLs (August & Shanahan, 2006; Shanahan & Beck, 2006). On the other side of this continuum are conceptions of literacy as an integrated, collaborative, empowering social activity that can be understood and facilitated by attending to the process by which readers make sense of texts (Gee, 1996; Street, 1995).

Proponents of either end of this continuum have engaged in long-standing debate, in which skill-based approaches to teaching reading were pitted against process-oriented approaches. Buried deep within the debate, which raged during the 1980s and 1990s, are assumptions about literacy's nature and purpose. These assumptions become more complex as related to a particular group of students with histories of exclusion and marginalization in U.S. schools (Willis & Harris, 2000). Testing these assumptions requires that we ask: (a) What are the goals of literacy development for ELLs in schools? (b) How has literacy been used as a political tool that has both afforded and constrained social access and power for ELLs? (c) What are individuals' and groups' reasons for becoming literate (Ladson-Billings, 1992)? These questions underlie competing views of literacy that shaped our approach to this review of literacy interventions for ELLs who are struggling readers and those identified with LD.

We review research on two categories of literacy interventions for these groups of ELLs. The first of these are interventions grounded in the notion that literacy is a set of cognitive reading and writing skills that collectively allow one to advance socially, economically, and engage in individual decision making. This first group of interventions bases effective interventions for ELLs on the teaching of specific subskills delivered as *explicit* or *direct* instruction. The second category of literacy interventions we review are those grounded in the notion that literacy is a sociocultural process between the learner and the text, which therefore emphasizes the provision of opportunities for individuals to engage in *reciprocal, interaction-oriented* strategies of reading and more broadly defined literacy practices as part of a larger process of inquiry. Finally, we provide a model of literacy and accompanying interventions for ELLs grounded in the research base of both literacy models, with approaches that use the resources of the multiple literacies ELLs bring to their classrooms to develop basic literacy skills.

Review Methods

To locate research studies as a basis for our description of effective literacy interventions for ELLs struggling with reading or identified with LD, we conducted a title, abstract, and full-text search of the ERIC and EBSCO host databases for research-based journal articles published between 2003 and 2008. This is the 5-year period immediately following the unprecedented emphasis placed on the academic achievement of students classified as Limited English Proficient by the 2002 reauthorization of the Elementary and Secondary Education Act (i.e., No Child Left Behind Act) and its Title III, the English Language Acquisition, Language Enhancement, and Academic Achievement Act. To find articles concerned with the particular groups of children on whom this chapter is focused, we used the keywords *English* AND *Learner* AND *disability* OR *struggling* AND *reading* OR *literacy*. Our search excluded articles about research with ELLs who were not having learning difficulties at school.

Participants in Identified Studies

Articles were coded on the basis of the target group identified for the interventions and the type of intervention used. We found 16 studies that appeared in a total of 11 educational research journals. Of the 16 articles, 14 were focused on ELLs identified as struggling readers (i.e., at risk for reading failure or for identification as having LD). The remaining articles were concerned with ELLs who struggled with reading within *both* special and general education; no articles researched interventions *solely* for ELLs who were eligible for and received special education.

Types of Interventions in Research

We found a pattern in the types of interventions that corresponded with the two ends of the literacy continuum in the relevant literature: (a) interventions concerned with the direct instruction of a specific set of reading subskills and (b) interventions focused on social, reciprocal (i.e., transactional) interactions around text, primarily concerned with students' literacy as making meaning from texts. Descriptive features (i.e., intervention, setting, participants, measures, duration, level of support, fidelity, and outcomes) of the studies reviewed are provided in Appendix 5.1, at the end of this chapter.

In the subsequent sections, we describe briefly these two broad categories of interventions located in the recent literature by highlighting the features of each and, given the relatively few studies located, providing an overview of each.

Research-Based Literacy Interventions for ELLs

Interventions for Specific Reading Subskills

Just under 88% (i.e., 14 of 16) of the studies included in this review of the literature were grounded in the premise that effective instruction and intervention for ELLs who are struggling, ELLs identified with LD, or both is based on the teaching of specific reading subskills. Some studies focused more explicitly on intervention in one specific subskill (e.g., phonological awareness, or the ability to recognize the many ways sounds function in words). Others used a combination of several skills, either as a prepackaged literacy intervention program such as *Reading Recovery* (e.g., Scull & Bianco, 2008) or as an intervention for which the researchers combined a number of interventions to account for various dimensions of decoding, fluency, and comprehension (e.g., Linan-Thompson, Vaughn, Hickman-Davis, & Kouzekanani, 2003).

Interventions Targeting Phonological Awareness Skills

Of the articles that reported results of interventions implemented around one specific reading subskill, several demonstrated the effectiveness of intensive phonological awareness instruction for ELLs. For instance, a study with ELL kindergarteners by Leafstedt, Richards, and Gerber (2004) found that when intensive phonological awareness instruction was provided as an intervention within one self-contained kindergarten class, students demonstrated significantly greater growth in word reading as compared to students in another class who did not receive this intervention. Vaughn and colleagues (Vaughn, Linan-Thompson, et al., 2006; Vaughn, Mathes, et al., 2006) demonstrated the efficacy of intervention consisting of explicit instruction in oral language and reading skills based on lesson plans of integrated literacy content strands. The experimental group intervention was delivered in small-group settings for 50 minutes every day and led to improved ELL performance on letter naming, phonological awareness, word attack, and comprehension compared to peers receiving standard English reading interventions. It is important to note that although both of these studies demonstrated the intervention's efficacy, the intervention for the Vaughn, Linan-Thompson, et al. (2006) study involved students who were considered at risk for reading problems in Spanish; the intervention was conducted only in Spanish, and effects were observed in Spanish, but not English. In contrast, the Vaughn, Mathes, et al. (2006) study involved students who were assessed to be at risk for reading problems in both Spanish and English. The intervention was delivered in English. Effects were strongest on English measures but were evident on some Spanish measures.

Gerber et al. (2004) demonstrated the positive relationship between strong foundational primary language skills and reading skill acquisition in English as a second language. This study looked at an intensive phonological skills training intervention for Spanish-speaking kindergarteners considered to be at risk. The intervention model focused on direct instruction strategies, in addition to the support for the development of phonological skills.

Interventions Based on Prepackaged Literacy Programs

Five research studies on prepackaged literacy intervention programs investigated the efficacy of the following published materials with ELLs who were struggling readers, some of whom were identified with LD: *Reading Recovery, Fast ForWord Language, Reading Mastery,* and *Read Well.* Two studies assessed the efficacy of *Reading Recovery* (Kelly, Gomez-Bellenge, Chen, & Schulz, 2008; Scull & Bianco, 2008). Kelly et al. (2008) analyzed data collected as part of the national program evaluation for *Reading Recovery.* Participants were among the lowest 20% in reading performance at their school in the fall of their first grade year. Among children who completed the full *Reading Recovery* intervention, 69% of ELL students and 76% of Native English Speaking (NES) children achieved grade-level performance in reading at the end of the school year. The authors concluded that, although the ELLs' achievement on levels of text reading and phonological awareness was significantly lower than their NES peers, the effect ($d = 0.18$) was not large enough to exclude ELLs from *Reading Recovery* as an effective intervention and considered it part of the spectrum of best practice for ELLs who are struggling readers.

Scull and Bianco (2008) approached the study of *Reading Recovery* from a more critical stance, in response to earlier findings that a percentage of ELLs continued to struggle with literacy, even after receiving the *Reading Recovery* intervention. The researchers used ethnographic observation strategies and analysis of the nature of specific examples of teaching and learning in *Reading Recovery* with 10 young (6.5 to 8 years) ELLs identified as progressing below expected levels, and their 10 literacy teachers, compared to a group of students who were making "accelerated" progress. The authors found that student progress was related to teachers' capacity to understand the varying skill levels of students and to match supports to their level of need. Teacher–learner interactions were the key mechanism by which ELLs became more independent learners. One type of interaction the authors found particularly supportive in this acceleration was teachers' "verbal accompaniment to reading" (p. 145). Furthermore, the authors concluded that oral language is of central importance as a contributor to early literacy development.

Fast ForWord Language is a program that provides students with instruction in receptive English language skills through the use of interactive exercises that provide ELLs practice discriminating nonverbal and verbal sounds, recognizing vocabulary, and comprehending language. These exercises lengthen and, at times, amplify portions of recorded sounds students listen to, with the aim of speeding up the learning of English by ELLs. The method employed by Troia (2004) is based on findings of August and Hakuta (1997) that demonstrated some ELLs' difficulty with the perception of phonemes that were not part of their native language. Researchers assigned first- through sixth-grade ELLs ($n = 191$) to a treatment and control group, and used a pre- and post-test design with a no-contact control group. The author reported limited statistically significant differences between the treatment and control group; of the five domains (English language proficiency, oral language competence, phonological processing, basic reading, and classroom behavior), the treatment group showed significantly greater gains in the basic reading domain only. Based on this finding, Troia questioned media claims of *Fast ForWord's* efficacy, its popularity with educators and researchers, and called for additional research on the effectiveness of this program and caution when applying it systematically as an intervention for ELLs who are struggling readers.

The last program studied within the period included in this review was the *Reading Mastery* program, in combination with a parent training component entitled *Incredible Years* (Webster-Stratton, 1992). The *Reading Mastery* intervention was delivered as a 2-year supplemental reading program for 299 students "at risk for reading failure" (p. 66), in kindergarten through third grade, who were randomly assigned to a treatment and control group (Gunn, Biglan, Smolkowski, & Ary, 2005). *Reading Mastery* focuses specifically on the development of fluency and decoding, and students' capacity in these areas was assessed before intervention, once a year in the spring during the intervention years, and then annually for 2 more years. Students who were Latino and non-Latino, and who were both ELLs and non-ELLs, benefited from the intervention as much as or significantly more than non-Latino students (all of whom spoke only English) with matched baseline achievement levels. Evidence of smaller intervention effects on the non-Latino students was demonstrated, but effects for ELLs and non-ELLs as separate groups were not provided. Instead, on the basis of 84% of the Latino students' parents reporting that the primary language of the home was Spanish, the authors concluded that supplemental instruction focused on the development of word-recognition skills that is part of the *Reading Mastery* program is an effective intervention for both ELL and non-ELL students at risk for reading failure.

Multiple-Strategy Interventions Targeting Reading Skills

The remaining intervention studies with the target group of children used methods that combined strategies for teaching a number of specific reading subskills. For example, Lovett et al. (2008) investigated how struggling readers from varied linguistic backgrounds responded to phonologically based reading interventions by randomly assigning 166 struggling elementary students to one of three reading intervention programs (the *Phonological and Strategy Training (PHAST) Decoding Program;* the *Phonological Analysis and Blending/Direct Instruction Decoding Program,* with spelling and writing components added; or the *PHAST Decoding Program* with additional spelling and writing components) or to a special education curricular control group. The authors found that all of the interventions were significantly more effective than the special education curriculum exposure and that, regardless of students' first language, growth rate and outcomes for the three interventions were not statistically different.

A similar study by Denton, Wexler, Vaughn, and Bryan (2008) also divided students between an intervention group and a control group that provided their school's remedial or special education classes. The intervention included 40 minutes of daily small-group instruction with a modified version of the Wilson Reading System (Wilson, 1996) for 38 students, of whom a majority were Spanish-speaking ELLs identified with what the authors termed "significant reading disabilities" (p. 79). The authors found that in general, the intervention was no more effective than the control instruction, and they recommended further design and study of effective interventions for ELLs with identified disabilities.

K. Y. Tam, Heward, and Heng (2006), in a multiple-baseline across-subjects design, provided three components of reading instruction—vocabulary instruction, error correction, and fluency building on oral reading rate and comprehension—with five ELL struggling elementary school readers. There were two intervention conditions: The first provided students with a new passage during each intervention session; the second condition used the same passage each session until a predetermined criterion was achieved. Each student received between 73 and 79 intervention sessions. Despite these differences in conditions, the students improved fluency and comprehension under both; and in the second condition, four of the five reached the predetermined fluency criterion.

Kamps and colleagues (2007) found that second-tier direct instruction of a reading subskills intervention delivered in a three-tiered model of intervention (i.e., Response to Intervention; RtI) was effective with ELLs across urban and suburban schools, compared to instruction provided in nontreatment schools. The participants consisted of 170 ELLs and 148 English-only speakers. The ELLs in the experimental schools received an intervention that combined elements of three direct-instruction curricula: *Reading Mastery* (Engelmann & Bruner, 1995), *Early Interventions in Reading* (Mathes & Torgesen, 2005),

and *Read Well* (Sprick, Howard, & Fidanque, 1998). For second-grade students only, the *Read Naturally* (Ihnot, 1991) program was also implemented, and materials from the *Open Court* program (Adams, Bereiter, McKeough, Case, Roit, Hirschberg, et al., 2002) were used as reading texts. Nonexperimental schools provided students with an "ESL/balanced literacy intervention," which focused on word study, writing activities, and group and individual story reading in addition to primary reading instruction. Overall, ELLs in the experimental schools had a statistically higher performance level on all outcome measures (i.e., $p < 0.001$) as compared to control schools, especially for students who received the intervention in small groups.

Linan-Thompson et al. (2003) studied the impact of an intervention that combined research-based instructional strategies for ELLs and effective skill-based reading interventions based on research with monolingual English speakers. The intervention, which consisted of 58 sessions provided 30 minutes daily for 13 weeks in small groups of two to three students, focused on specific activities that addressed students' oral reading fluency, phonological awareness, instructional level reading, word study (word analysis strategies), and writing. Practices grounded in research on effective instruction for ELLs included the provision of opportunities for students to learn skills in isolation and then practice them in context, redundancy in the daily lesson format, frequent guided and independent skill practice opportunities, and discussion between students about what they were learning. The researchers found a statistically significant time effect (e.g., significant increases from pretest to post-test measures) on all reading subskills incorporated in the intervention (Linan-Thompson et al., 2003).

Finally, Sáenz, Fuchs, and Fuchs (2005) studied the impact of Peer-Assisted Learning Strategies (PALS) for 132 third- through sixth-grade ELLs identified with LD and their classroom peers of all achievement levels, implemented three times a week for 15 weeks. Six classes were randomly assigned to the PALS condition, and six classes to a control condition. The PALS intervention is a reciprocal whole-class peer-tutoring strategy that includes a different literacy focus at different grade levels (Sáenz et al., 2005). The PALS Grades 2 to 6, the intervention studied, is focused on increasing strategic reading, reading fluency, and comprehension. ELLs were paired with students who were low, medium, and high achieving, and pairings were switched every 3 to 4 weeks. Within the pairs, both students were tutors and tutees. The students who participated in PALS significantly outperformed those who did not on reading comprehension questions answered correctly across student groups, after a 15-week intervention. The largest effect size (1.03) was associated with ELL students with LD. Large and moderate effect sizes that were not statistically significant were achieved, respectively, for ELL students with LD for words read correctly and correct words selected on a maze measure. Notably, although a classroom teacher facilitated this intervention strategy, this was the only intervention study in the identified research pool in which students worked collaboratively to support each other's literacy development, rather than a teacher or instructional staff member holding responsibility for direct intervention delivery.

For the most part, the research reviewed appeared to measure literacy in relation to the interventions designed and implemented to improve a set of cognitive skills measurable by standardized tests (e.g., Vaughn, Linan-Thompson, et al., 2006, Vaughn, Mathes, et al., 2006) or locally normed curriculum-based assessments (e.g., Scull & Bianco, 2008). The emphasis on the development of basic literacy skills by ELLs, particularly those who are struggling, those with disabilities, or both, is important in order for them to access the general education curriculum and experience favorable participation and outcomes. However, the autonomous model of literacy (Street, 1984), as these intervention studies appear to reflect, has been criticized in relation to an assumption that teaching and learning of literacy skills can occur independently of the cultural context in which they are applied (Street, 1995). This criticism has highlighted the emphasis in the autonomous model on one standard form of literacy (i.e., English language practices used among U.S. middle class speakers) and that a major goal of becoming literate is to demonstrate mastery of this standard set of cognitive skills (Delpit, 1986). This pattern of reading instruction has been documented as prevalent by research on instruction provided for the lowest reading groups and remedial reading classes, as well as in reading lessons with ELLs (Au & Raphael, 2000).

Interventions for Reading as a Reciprocal, Interaction-Oriented Process

We located only two research articles on literacy interventions for ELLs who were struggling readers or identified with disabilities, despite over a decade having past since Gee (2000) promoted "a broader view of both what constitutes empirical research and what sorts of empirical evidence are relevant to complex issues that integrally involve culture, social interaction, institutions, and cognition" (p. 126). These two studies differed markedly in terms of sample size, methods, and implications.

The first study focused on the relationship between a struggling high school ELL and tutor in a summer university tutoring course (Cohen, 2007). The tutoring focused on intensive strategy instruction between 13 graduate students and 13 ELL readers and writers.

The 4-week program included a variety of interactions around texts, writing, and discussing literacy content. Interactions included think alouds, K-W-L charts (described later), reading aloud quietly, and mental imagery of what was read (Gambrell & Jawitz, 1993) as a way to monitor comprehension. These were taught and practiced in pairs with tutors and in whole-group sessions. Students selected a person about whom they wanted to research and present about at the course end. One student participant, Mario, selected Julio Cesar Chavez, a famous boxer from his Mexican hometown. The discussion between the researcher/tutor and Mario emphasized how Mario would have reacted to the situations Chavez encountered throughout his life and career. Lower-level texts about Chavez were provided in both English and Spanish. Throughout the intervention, Mario learned to make K-W-L charts (Ogle, 1986) about what he already Knew (K), what he Wanted to know (W), and what he had Learned after interacting with the text (L), with his tutor, and during sustained silent reading periods.

Findings indicated that Mario reported liking reading, and he visited the library and checked out books on his own, which was new for him. He got a B in his high school English class, and he reported getting along better with teachers and feeling more confident about reading. Additionally, the research design used the Qualitative Reading Inventory—3 (Leslie & Caldwell, 2001) as a pre- and post-assessment. The preassessment was applied to the design of Mario's literacy instructional plan. On the preassessment, although Mario was able to decode most words, he had limited reading comprehension, while at the end of the course, he answered all reading comprehension questions without difficulty.

The final study presented results of a 1-year language intervention program called the Early Authors Program (EAP) (Bernhard et al., 2006), which is grounded in principles of transformative education (Freire, 1970) as well as other sources including Bransford, Brown, and Cocking's *How People Learn* model (2000), and Cummins's Academic Expertise framework (2000). The intervention randomly selected 367 children enrolled at early childhood centers in Miami Dade County and placed them in experimental ($n = 280$) and control ($n = 87$) groups.

The primary component of the EAP involved preschool ELLs writing and illustrating autobiographical bilingual books, which were shared with peers, parents, and teachers. The program also included on-site coaching from literacy specialists who supported educators to implement the EAP in technology-enriched classrooms. Other EAP elements included (a) monthly parent meetings to facilitate families' roles in reading and communicating with their children about their self-created texts and (b) training for assessors of children's performance on pre- and post-test measures that measured expressive language, auditory comprehension, cognition, and fine motor skills and were administered in Spanish or English, depending on students' dominant language. Students demonstrated improved language and early literacy scores, expressed pride in themselves as readers, and developed "affective bonds to literacy" (Bernhard et al., 2006, p. 2399).

The literacy interventions employed in these two research studies focused on providing students with opportunities to engage in inquiry, connect with self-selected and self-generated texts, and learn strategies for making meaning of texts, in order to enhance multiple forms of literacy, including oral language development. These interventions characterize what has been called an *ideological model of literacy* (e.g., Street, 1995), which emphasizes the purposes of and uses for literacy within a social system and does not focus on the teaching of discrete and separate reading subskills. Criticisms of these types of approaches, and of this conceptualization of literacy, argue that such practices rely on context and authentic texts as a proxy for decoding skills (Lyon, 1998).

Good, Research-Based Practices for Supporting Literacy Development of ELLs Who Are Struggling Readers or Identified with LD

To provide concrete illustrations of how research-based interventions can be applied with struggling ELL readers, we present in this section a detailed description of two strategies, one explicit and one reciprocal, supported by the reviewed research. Further, we expand these strategies by providing teachers with a set of considerations to guide their use of these interventions within the unique local contexts of their own classrooms.

Before we present these examples, we discuss briefly what is regarded as "best practice" and offer guidelines to consider when identifying "good practices." We address this point as a means to transcend simplistic analyses of the intervention research literature that tend to focus on narrow aspects of the interventions at the expense of considering equally substantive aspects in the design and implementation of interventions. Although a universally accepted notion of what constitutes a best practice does not seem to exist, we find the definition of best practice presented by the United Nations Educational, Scientific, and Cultural Organization (UNESCO) useful for the purposes of this chapter. Best practices, according to UNESCO (n.d.), are innovative (i.e., they are new and creative) solutions to common problems, demonstrate positive and tangible impact, have sustainable effect, and serve as a model for policy and practice elsewhere. We ask, therefore, what should be considered when identifying good practices?

What Are Good Practices?

To call any one practice or group of practices *best* is to suggest that there is one superior way to teach, which neglects careful consideration of context within which the practice is to be applied. Alexander's (1996) model of good practice is a potentially useful heuristic in this discussion; it consists of five considerations that interact and balance each other and that view good practice as an aspiration as much as an accomplishment. The first two shape teaching in general and inform the latter three, which together contribute to a model of *good practice:*

1. *Political considerations:* Practices are shaped by institutional and historical norms, as well as the expectations of professionals, parents, communities, and other political players.

2. *Pragmatic considerations:* Practices are implemented within an awareness of the opportunities and constraints of a particular educational context (e.g., district, school, classroom).

3. *Conceptual considerations:* The practice is shaped by the essential elements of teaching, learning, and the curriculum, and the relationship between them.

4. *Value considerations:* The practice is shaped by views about students' needs, societal needs, and necessary knowledge, all of which inform what is taught.

5. *Empirical considerations:* Evidence supports the effectiveness of the practice to result in learning.

Good, research-based practices in ELL literacy interventions provide students with direct instruction in a set of reading subskills relevant to the development of access to and understanding of written language. Simultaneously, however, such practices incorporate the multiple literacies that students who are ELLs bring to their classrooms and connect them to literacy practices with purposes of developing oral language through engaging students in social interaction with texts and those around them. Further, "good, research-based practice" in literacy intervention for ELLs includes teachers' analysis of and attention to the contexts of their classrooms within which they are creating the opportunities for struggling ELLs to improve their literacy skills, as much as any specific set of replicable recommendations that teachers are to deliver to students.

We expect, therefore, that this discussion will help us transcend simplistic policy, research, or practice questions about interventions that privilege exclusively empirical considerations. Although it is critical to maintain empirical considerations at the center of discussions about good practice, it is also necessary to take into account the comprehensive perspective we outline in this section. Next, we describe in more detail two reading interventions used for ELLs who struggle with reading.

We encourage readers to bring to bear the considerations about good practice that we outline in this section as they review these exemplars.

Supplemental Direct Instruction of Phonological Awareness

A report published by the National Center for Education Evaluation and Regional Assistance (Gersten et al., 2007) recommended focused, intensive small-group interventions for elementary-grade ELLs who are struggling readers. This recommendation parallels those included in the reviewed literacy interventions that we described as skills-based approaches. The research provides evidence of the effectiveness of direct small-group instruction in a combined set of skills: phonological awareness, phonics, reading fluency, vocabulary, and comprehension. Based on our review of the recent research literature for this type of instruction for ELLs who are struggling readers or who are identified as having LD (Gunn et al., 2005; Vaughn, Linan-Thompson, et al., 2006; Vaughn, Mathes, et al., 2006), we decided to focus on a particular subset of these areas for direct instruction—phonological awareness— because it was the only reading subskill included across all 14 skills-based intervention studies.

Phonemic awareness, the basis for learning phonics, is the understanding that the sounds of spoken language are combined together to form words. *Phonological awareness* refers to the ability to key in on and manipulate phonemes, the smallest units of sound connected with independent meaning, into spoken words (Adams, Foorman, Lundberg, & Beeler, 1998). A core assumption of this type of intervention is that ELLs, particularly those who are struggling readers, need early, direct, and intensive instruction in phonological awareness in order to develop the building blocks for decoding skills. Research shows that as early as kindergarten it is possible to identify ELLs who are at risk for becoming struggling readers in relationship to their weaknesses with phonological awareness (Gunn et al., 2005; Leafstedt et al., 2004). Additional research shows that many schools delay in addressing the needs of ELLs who are experiencing reading difficulty, and instead take the approach that these students are simply learning English and developing literacy skills in typical ways due to their limited oral proficiency in English (Limbos & Geva, 2001). It is very important, it is argued, not to delay intervention until English proficiency is gained.

As summarized briefly in the preceding section entitled "Multiple-Strategy Interventions Targeting Reading Skills," Linan-Thompson et al. (2003) provided supplementary phonological awareness instruction as part of a focused literacy intervention for ELLs with Spanish as their primary language who were struggling readers. Of all the 14 skills-based intervention studies we reviewed (which were grounded in previous research on effective literacy

interventions for monolingual English speakers who were also struggling readers), this was the only skill-based intervention study that also incorporated strategies vetted in previous research on effective instructional strategies for ELLs. To provide sufficient detail so that readers can apply findings from this study to their own practice, we next detail Linan-Thompson and colleagues' approach to phonological awareness in combination with the instructional strategies for ELLs. Phonological awareness intervention was provided 5 minutes per day, following a period of 5 minutes of intervention in fluent reading, and followed by 10 minutes of instructional level reading and 5 minutes of word-study activities within a 30-minutes' total intervention block. Specifically, the phonological awareness portion of the intervention block consisted of students engaging in activities in which they had to "blend, segment, delete, substitute, and manipulate phonemes in words" (Linan-Thompson et al., 2003, p. 228). Teachers used activities from existing programs (e.g., *Ladders to Literacy,* Notari-Syverson, O'Conner, & Vadasy, 1998; *Phonemic Awareness in Young Children: A Classroom Curriculum,* Adams et al., 1998) and also created their own, grounded in research on effective instruction for ELLs, to assist students with auditory recognition of words, one strategy involved the teacher's showing picture cards while pronouncing the words illustrated by the cards. Another strategy informed by ELL instruction research was teacher identification of real and nonsense words; many real words encountered in the phonological awareness activities were not already part of the students' vocabulary, so teachers provided quick definitions of real words and identified nonsense words as students practiced blending, segmenting, and other phonemic manipulations of presented words. Further, if students could already manipulate phonemes efficiently in Spanish, the phonological awareness intervention focused instead on teachers' direct instruction of sounds that are similar in both Spanish and English, and then on those that are often more difficult for students who speak Spanish to distinguish, "such as minimal contrast pairs (e.g., /d/ and /th/)" (Linan-Thompson et al., 2003, p. 229). The 13-week intervention was conducted in small groups of two to three students per teacher for 30 minutes per day. For further reference, blending and segmenting are listed in a table of subskills most commonly addressed in phonological awareness interventions (see Table 5.1), because they have been found to have the greatest impact on overall phonological awareness (Yopp, 1988).

Considerations for Phonological Awareness Interventions with ELLs

When implementing phonological awareness interventions, a number of considerations are necessary to make them appropriate for ELLs. First, a primary focus in learning another language is on making meaning of sounds one hears in order to comprehend what is being said.

Table 5.1 Examples of Subskills Addressed in Phonological Awareness Interventions

Specific Skill	Example
Blending	Teacher: What word do you get when you put together these four sounds? /m/ /e/ /s/ /a/? Students: *Mesa.*
Segmenting	Teacher: How many sounds are in *map*? Students: /m/ /a/ /p/ three (students tap out sounds on table as they say them).
Deleting	Teacher: What is *hand* without the /h/? Students: *Hand* without the /h/ is *and.*
Substituting	Teacher: The word is *grade.* Change /d/ to /p/. What's the new word? Students: *Grape.*
Discriminating between real and nonsense words	Teacher: Which word is real? *Table* or *Pable?* Students: *Table.*

However, many phonological awareness interventions instead ask ELLs to manipulate individual meaningless units of speech. Phonological awareness for ELLs therefore should be paired with strong support for language learning in comprehensible contexts (Cummins, 2000). Further, although English and some languages, such as Spanish, share similar sounds and have many polysyllabic words, some languages, such as Mandarin and Thai, have many monosyllabic words with very few final consonant sounds that may have many different meanings, depending on the speaker's tone. These variations across languages may mean some students, especially those experiencing reading difficulties, will struggle to discriminate sounds in words because of differences in their primary language structure. Thus, phonological awareness interventions may better support students when incorporating knowledge about the structure of the ELLs' primary language.

Intervention Concerned with Sociocultural Process of Literacy

The EAP (Bernhard et al., 2006, 2008), as mentioned earlier, is a literacy program that provides ELL struggling readers with opportunities to be writers and readers of their own books, supported by adults who facilitate this process. The EAP is one of several literacy interventions concerned with multiple forms of literacy described by Ada and Campoy (2003). The EAP intervention (Bernhard et al., 2006) included several components as students self-authored their own identity texts (i.e., autobiographies), facilitated by a teacher or other instructional personnel over a 12-month period. Educators required professional development to facilitate their effective teaching; they attended three community events in which the principles of

the program were presented, in addition to 2 days of on-site training led by bilingual literacy specialists.

Students authored, read, and used their books with each other, teachers, and their families and caregivers over the intervention period. Parents were involved in the authorship process by guiding students along the way. Four 2-hour meetings with parents/family members were held over the course of the intervention. During the meetings, family members participated in writing activities based on prompts about their life histories, which formed the basis for discussions about key themes in family writing. Additionally, teachers taught students to recite poems and rhymes in their home language. The EAP intervention provided teachers with books and other texts that included "children's oral folklore, including traditional art, literature, and sayings" (Bernhard et al., 2006, p. 2390). Teachers received training in how to relate letters of the alphabet with letters in children's names and with those of their family members and friends. Students who participated in the EAP demonstrated significant improvement in language skills compared to children in the control group, as measured by pre- and post-assessment with the Learning Accomplishment Profile–Diagnostic Edition (LAP-D; Nehring, Nehring, Bruni, & Randolph, 1992) and the Preschool Language Scale–Revised Fourth Edition (PLS-R; Zimmerman, Steiner, & Evatt Pond, 2002).

Bernhard et al. (2006) caution that the EAP is not a program that should or could be replicated exactly, because it is so highly driven by the context within which it is enacted and is informed by the settings, students, and families who participate in it. Instead, they recommend that similar interventions should adhere to the principles that inform the approaches presented in the study and should account for the unique resources and needs of the students in the processes of authorship and sharing of texts detailed within the program design. For further reference, these principles are listed and described in Table 5.2.

Conclusion and the Road Ahead: Toward Culturally Responsive Literacy Interventions for ELLs Who Are Struggling Readers or Identified with LD

Despite the unprecedented growth of the ELL population in schools around the United States and their long-standing negative educational outcomes, relatively few intervention studies have been conducted regarding literacy for this population in recent years. The theoretical underpinnings of the existing research continue to index the opposing views that have historically pervaded in the debates about reading and literacy. On one hand,

Table 5.2 Principles of Process-Oriented Literacy Intervention

Principle	Description
Student authorship of bilingual autobiographical texts	Students author books in which they are featured as protagonists of their life story.
Teacher facilitation of authorship process	Teachers engage in professional learning in the principles of the intervention and in their classrooms by bilingual literacy specialists to support students in the authorship process. Teachers have access to material resources that allow students' books to be published in high-quality format (e.g., laid out on computer, printed in black and white and color, bound, laminated).
Family facilitation of authorship process	Families receive training over time in community settings from bilingual literacy specialists about how to (a) support their children in developing ideas about self to include in auto-biographical texts, (b) assist their children with taking pictures or finding print objects to be included in their texts, and (c) involve family members in related writing activities of their own.
Teacher-led instruction on phonological awareness grounded in students' cultural and linguistic contexts	Teachers instruct students to recite poems and rhymes in their home language through the use of texts that included "children's oral folklore, including traditional art, literature, and sayings" (Bernhard et al., p. 2390). Teachers receive training by bilingual literacy specialists about how to relate letters of the alphabet with letters in children's names and in the names of their family members and friends.
Students' texts used as school curriculum and family resources	Students' texts are frequently used as the basis for school and home storytelling and literature-based discussion with teachers, other students, and family members.

Source: Information from Bernhard, J. K., Cummins, J., Campoy, F. I., Ada, A. F., Winsler, A., & Bleiker, C. (2006). Identity texts and literacy development among preschool English language learners: Enhancing learning opportunities for children at risk for learning disabilities. *Teachers College Record, 108,* 2380–2405.

the bulk of the work is founded on a skill-based perspective, partly because federal and state funding have prioritized this model (M. L. Smith, 2004). Moreover, more skill-oriented research has been produced because this perspective has received greater attention over time in the special education research community, where most of this research is conducted (Swanson, 2000; Swanson, Trainin, Necoechea, & Hammill, 2003). On the other hand, the bulk of process-oriented literacy research has historically relied on qualitative methodologies, which have a different approach to the transportability of findings across populations and contexts (Flood, Heath, & Lapp, 2008; C. Lee & Smagorinsky, 1999).

With the goal of transcending unproductive dichotomies in intervention work and as a means to pose a challenge to this field for future research, we conclude with discussion of a third model: culturally responsive literacy interventions for ELLs who are struggling with reading, identified with LD, or both. We frame this model as a set of the most promising practices from both types of interventions (i.e., skills based and socioculturally based) described earlier.

Culturally Responsive Literacy Interventions

Culturally responsive literacy interventions bridge a gap between the models discussed previously, while addressing histories of marginalization that many ELL groups

have experienced in U.S. schools. Specifically, these interventions provide explicit, small-group instruction in discrete reading skills that are informed by knowledge of students' primary language structures. Further, these interventions engage students in the use of authentic texts and purposes for using texts in ways that draw on and build on the multiple ways of being literate that ELLs bring into classrooms. ELLs use their cultures and languages as a basis for understanding themselves and others, as a foundation for structuring social interactions around literacy practices, and to provide frameworks for conceptualizing new learning and knowledge (Ladson-Billings, 1992) as they receive direct instruction in reading subskills. Culturally responsive literacy interventions are:

1. *Relevant:* They use the cultural knowledge, prior experiences, and performance styles of diverse students to make learning more appropriate and effective; teaching to and through the strengths of ELLs (Gay, 2000).

2. *Multifaceted:* Their goals are to develop a variety of forms of literacy in ELLs, to provide opportunities to participate in critical inquiry about their world, and to work for social change. Multiple literacies include language-based, mathematical, scientific, historical, cultural, and political aspects (Ladson-Billings, 1992).

3. *Explicit:* ELLs receive direct instruction in basic literacy skills required in order to fully participate in the dominant culture (Delpit, 1988).

Table 5.3 Practitioner Considerations in Designing Culturally Responsive Literacy Interventions

Element	Questions
Goal of Instruction	How do I establish students' ownership of literacy as the overarching goal of the curriculum, while maintaining a systematic instruction in the cognitive processes of reading and writing?
	How do I make literacy personally meaningful and viewed as useful for the student's own purposes?
Role of Home Language	How do I allow students' primary language to exist in the classroom and build upon this language to achieve English literacy proficiency?
Instructional Materials	In what ways can I use materials that present diverse cultures in an authentic manner? Does the literature accurately depict the experiences of diverse groups?
	How do I increase students' motivation to read, their appreciation and understanding of their own language and cultural heritage, and their valuing of their own life experiences as a topic for writing?
Classroom Management and Interaction with Students	How do I create and adjust the classroom environment (organization and management system) to allow for genuine literacy activities through which students can feel ownership and learn through collaboration and engage in conversations with rules more like those for everyday talk rather than for classroom recitation?
Relationship to the Community	How do I make stronger links to the community, restructure the power relationships between the school and community, and involve parents and other community members in the school?
	How do I make specific connections to communities to which students belong?
Instructional Methods	In what ways can I provide students with authentic literacy activities, while providing instruction in specific literacy skills needed for full participation in the culture of power?
	How do I teach basic literacy skills within authentic literacy activities?
Assessment	What strategies could I use to prepare and analyze my assessments prior to implementation that would help reduce or eliminate sources of bias and more accurately reflect students' literacy achievement?

Source: Reprinted with permission from National Center for Culturally Responsive Educational Systems (2008). *Culturally responsive literacy. Professional Learning Series.* Tempe, AZ: Author.

We also wish to engage teachers in consideration of their unique classroom and community contexts as they implement the types of interventions described here. Thus, we provide a list of considerations for practitioners as they design culturally responsive literacy interventions (see Table 5.3). The questions in the table first appeared in our work with the National Center for Culturally Responsive Educational Systems, as part of a larger professional learning module on Culturally Responsive Literacy (National Center for Culturally Responsive Educational Systems, 2008). They are grouped by elements for improving school literacy learning of students of diverse backgrounds (Au, 1998) and reflect key areas of research on school literacy learning.

To conclude, we identified specific strategies with demonstrated effectiveness in promoting acquisition of reading subskills and other literacy practices. However, much work remains related to the advancement of a model that integrates insights derived from alternative models of reading and literacy. Furthermore, educators face substantial challenges in the institutionalization and scaling up of the research knowledge produced in this domain of study. It is encouraging that the bulk of intervention studies focused on prevention, that is, on ELLs who struggle with learning to read before diagnosis with LD. This is a needed perspective that can save significant resources to school districts (e.g., assessment costs) while enhancing the power of general education to address the needs of all students. Simultaneously, our review clearly suggests an urgent need to invest in research that addresses the needs of ELLs with LD, particularly because students in this disability category constitute the largest population served under IDEA funding. The increasing investment in preventive approaches as well as the growing concern with the seamless integration of general and special education are undoubtedly welcome developments that we expect will benefit significantly the growing population of ELLs in U.S. schools. We hope to see the consolidation of such trends in years to come.

Appendix 5.1

Summary Information on Interventions Reviewed

Study	Intervention	Setting	Participants	Measures	Duration	Level of Support	Fidelity Measures	Outcome
Bernhard et al., 2006	Early Authors Program	32 child-care centers in Miami-Dade County	1,179 randomly selected children ages 2–4	Learning Accomplishment Profile—Diagnostic Edition; Preschool Language Scale—Revised Fourth Edition; teacher survey of literacy skills; Early Steps to Reading Success survey	1 year	Support provided to classroom teachers by 13 trained literacy specialists	Not reported	Significant gains in language development compared to pretest measures and control children; prevented increasing lag compared to national age norm groups
Cohen, 2007	Summer literacy program of individualized instruction, Sustained Silent Reading, dialogue journals, and whole-group activities	Collaborative program between university and school district	One 17-year-old ELL	Qualitative Reading Inventory—3	4-week, full-day program	Individualized tutoring and group instruction by trained graduate students	Not reported	Increased enjoyment of reading, transactions with text, completion of oral reading activities, improved responses to reading comprehension items
Denton, Wexler, Vaughn, & Bryan, 2008	Modified phonics-based remedial program incorporating ESL practice, vocabulary instruction, fluency, and comprehension strategies	Southwest, urban middle school serving predominantly Hispanic, economically disadvantaged population	38 sixth- to eighth-grade students with DIBELS words correct per minute <80; randomly assigned to treatment or typical practice group	Peabody Picture Vocabulary Test in English and Spanish (receptive vocabulary); WJ-III Passage Comprehension, Letter-Word Identification, and Word Attack subtests; DIBELS reading fluency; Test of Word Reading Efficiency; Social Skills Rating System	47–55 daily 40-min sessions over 13 weeks	Instructional groupings of 2–4 students taught by 2 teachers with ≥ 10 hr training and ongoing coaching	Observations 3 times using treatment integrity checklist; rating between 91% and 98% for both teachers	Improved Sight Word Efficiency on the TOWRE

Study	Intervention	Setting	Sample	Measures	Duration	Delivery	Monitoring	Results
Gerber et al., 2004	Core Intervention Model: supplemental direct instruction in phonological skills	3 California school districts of predominantly Latino students identified as ELLs	37 Spanish-speaking kindergartners	Phonological awareness tasks (rime, onset detection, and phoneme segmentation); WJ-III English Word Attack and Letter-Word Identification	10 half-hr sessions	Small-group, direct instruction provided by trained bilingual undergraduates	Monitoring and feedback by senior researchers	Significant gains from beginning of kindergarten to end of 1st grade; caught up with high-performing peers
Gunn et al., 2005	Supplemental Reading Program emphasizing instruction in phonemic awareness and phonics; Incredible Years parent training program; Contingencies for Learning Academic and Social Skills	13 schools across 4 communities in Oregon	148 K–3 students identified with poor reading skills ($n = 80$) or aggressive social behavior ($n = 80$) (17 in special education; 27 receiving Title I services)	WJ-III English Word Attack, Letter-Word Identification, Vocabulary, Comprehension; Oral Reading Fluency words/minute	30 min daily for 3 days/week for 6–7 mo in 1st year, 9 mo in 2nd year	30 min/day supplemental reading instruction, parent training, social skills intervention, provided by 9 instructional assistants with 10 hr of training	Weekly observations during first month, monthly observations thereafter, 90% to 100% fidelity reported across observations	Significant improvement in letter-word identification, oral reading fluency, and reading comprehension relative to control group; continued improvement in reading fluency following intervention
Kamps et al., 2007	Small-group direct instruction in phonemic awareness, letter-sound recognition, decoding, fluency, and comprehension skills	16 Kansas schools over a 5-year period	170 ELL and 148 English-only 1st- and 2nd-grade students	DIBELS, Woodcock Reading Mastery Test	Not stated	Groups of 3–6 students using Reading Mastery, Early Interventions in Reading, Read Well, or Reading Naturally by general education teachers or read-ing specialists	Fidelity checklists of procedures, instructional features, instruction in key skills, and management features; mean scores of 82% to 98% across schools	Significant gains in Nonsense Word Fluency and Oral Reading Fluency; direct instruction intervention more effective than ESL literacy services
Kelly et al., 2008	Reading Recovery intensive tutorial intervention	U.S. schools participating in Reading Recovery	8,581 ELLs from schools throughout U.S.	An Observation Survey of Early Literacy Achievement	Average of 15–16 weeks	Daily, individual 30-min lessons from 12–20 weeks from a trained teacher	Not reported	69% achieved grade-level performance

Study	Intervention	Setting	Participants	Measures	Duration	Level of Support	Fidelity Measures	Outcome
Leafstedt, Richards, & Gerber, 2004	Intensive phonological awareness direct instruction based on Core Intervention Model	Semi-rural California community of predominantly Spanish-speaking families	1 kindergarten class of ELLs ($n = 18$)	WJ-III Word Identification, Word Attack	300 min over 10 weeks (15 min twice per week)	Intensive instruction provided by researcher to groups of 3–5 students using Early Reading Project Curriculum	Not reported	Significant growth in word reading compared to ELLs receiving general kindergarten instruction ($n = 46$)
Linan-Thompson et al., 2003	Supplemental reading instruction in English	11 schools participating in a multistate longitudinal project	26 ELLs identified as at risk for reading difficulty	Texas Primary Reading Inventory Woodcock Reading Mastery Test—Revised Test of Reading Fluency DIBELS—Segmentation Fluency Woodcock-Muñoz Language Survey	30 min daily for 13 weeks (58 sessions)	Small groups	Not reported	Significant gains from pre- to post-test measures on all outcome measures
Lovett et al., 2008	Remedial reading instruction emphasizing word attack and word identification, randomly assigned to 1 of 3 groups focusing on (a) decoding only, (b) decoding plus writing and spelling, (c) phonological analysis plus writing and spelling	16 schools from a diverse, urban school district in Toronto, Canada	166 students identified with reading disabilities (76 ELL, 90 non-ELL)	Comprehensive Tests of Phonological Processing, Woodcock Reading Mastery Tests—Revised	1 hr daily for 4–5 weeks, totaling 105 hr	Intervention classes taught by certified special education teachers, grouped by reading level	Fidelity checked once for every 35 hr of instruction	No differences in outcomes between ELL and non-ELL groups; significant gains in overall scores and growth rates over students receiving equivalent amount of special education reading instruction

Author / Year	Intervention	Setting	Participants	Measures	Duration	Instruction	Observation	Results
Sáenz, Fuchs, & Fuchs, 2005	PALS: reciprocal, class-wide peer-tutoring strategy	12 transitional, bilingual education classrooms in a South Texas school district	132 native Spanish-speaking ELLs, 3rd to 6th grades, 10 with learning disabilities	Comprehensive Reading Assessment Battery	35 min, 3 times per week for 15 weeks	Classes taught by teachers who completed full-day PALS workshop	Observation checklist assessed during weeks 6 and 12 by 2 observers, 100% at Time 1, mean accuracy between 93% and 95%	More growth in reading comprehension for ELLs with and without LD relative to comparison group receiving normal instruction
Scull & Bianco, 2008	*Reading Recovery* intensive tutorial intervention	10 schools in Victoria, Australia	10 students 6 to 8 years old, 4 ELLs	Observations, survey of early literacy achievement, record of reading difficulty level	30 min daily instruction for 12–20 weeks	Individualized instruction by teachers with at least 2 years' experience teaching RR	Not stated	Improved independent reading confidence and skill
K. Y. Tam, Heward, & Heng, 2006	Intervention program of vocabulary instruction, error correction, and fluency building	Public elementary school of 500 students	5 ELLs, 3 with disabilities	Reading rate, correct answers to comprehension questions	65 daily sessions	Individualized instruction by researcher	Not stated	4 of 5 reached fluency criterion of 100 words correct per minute
Troia, 2004	*Fast ForWord Language* computer-assisted instructional program, training in auditory perception and spoken language comprehension skills	7 rural public schools in Central Washington	99 first- to sixth-grade ELLs, 92 in control group	Lindamood Auditory Conceptualization Test; WJ-III Sound Blending, Word Identification, Word Attack; experimental rhyming and segmentation tasks	Five 20-min computer exercises per day for 4 weeks	Individualized computer-based exercises	Not stated	Greater gains compared to control group in basic reading, with greater gains among students with lower English proficiency in word recognition

Study	Intervention	Setting	Participants	Measures	Duration	Level of Support	Fidelity Measures	Outcome
Vaughn, Linan-Thompson, et al., 2006	Direct instruction in oral language and reading in Spanish following predetermined lesson plans of integrated literacy content strands	20 classrooms in 7 schools from 3 school districts	69 first-grade, Spanish-speaking ELLs	Woodcock Language Proficiency Battery—Revised	50 min/day for 8 mo	Small-group (3–5 students) instruction by 6 trained bilingual intervention teachers	Intervention validity checklist, field notes, teacher checklists of daily preparedness	Higher performance in Spanish on measures of basic reading and reading comprehension relative to student receiving standard interventions
Vaughn, Mathes, et al., 2006	Direct instruction in oral language and reading in English following predetermined lesson plans of integrated literacy content strands	14 classrooms in 4 schools in 2 districts in Texas	48 first-grade, Spanish-speaking ELLs	Letter naming, letter-sound identification, Comprehensive Tests of Phonological Processing; Test of Phonological Processes—Spanish; Woodcock Language Proficiency Battery—R: English and Spanish Forms; DIBELS	50 min/day for 7 mo	Small-group (3–5 students) instruction by 4 trained bilingual reading interventionists	Intervention validity checklist, field notes, teacher checklists of daily preparedness	Higher performance in letter naming, phonological awareness, word attack, and comprehension compared to students receiving standard instruction. Largest effects on these performance measures were in English; smaller effects on outcomes were in Spanish

Note: DIBELS = Dynamic Indicators of Basic Early Literacy Skills; ELL = English Language Learner; ESL = English as a Second Language; LD = Learning Disability; PALS = Peer-Assisted Learning Strategies; RR = Reading Recovery; WJ-III = Woodcock-Johnson III Tests of Achievement.

CHAPTER 6

Teaching Students with Language Disorders

Laura M. Justice | *The Ohio State University*

Sandra Gillam | *Utah State University*

Anita McGinty | *University of Virginia*

The term *language* refers to the socially shared code of symbols that people use to represent the world to others using speech (spoken language), sign (sign language), or writing (written language). Language, which draws on a set of basic and higher-order processes based largely within the left hemisphere of the human brain, is often confused with such closely related terms as *speech* and *communication*. Speech is the neuromuscular process through which humans express language, whereas communication is the process through which information is shared between humans using speech, language, and other means, such as gestures and facial expressions (Justice, 2010).

Language processes are often differentiated into two modalities—comprehension (i.e., the reception of language) and expression (i.e., the production of language)—and four domains. These domains consist of (a) grammar, referring to the set of rules that govern word and sentence structure (e.g., using the conjunction *and* to join two independent clauses); (b) semantics, referring to the set of rules that govern word meanings and word relationships (e.g., recognizing that *couch* and *chair* are categorically related); (c) phonology, referring to the set of rules that govern speech sounds (e.g., knowing that the sound /g/ never follows the sound /n/ at the start of spoken English words); and (d) pragmatics, referring to the set of rules that govern the social use of language (e.g., entering conversations using specific strategies, such as commenting on the topic currently being discussed).

Language involves a highly complex set of processes specific to the human species that facilitates participation in life from home to the community. Language abilities are intricately tied to children's ability to form attachment relationships with their earliest caregivers, to succeed academically, and to form positive peer relationships. Beyond the years of schooling, language ability is necessary to perform most if not all activities required to participate fully in society, including basic and advanced work functions (e.g., responding to e-mail, leading meetings) and civic functions (e.g., voting by ballot). Given the relevance of language skill to human development from birth forward, it is not surprising that educators are greatly concerned when children are not meeting their full potential in language acquisition, as may be the case when children have a language disorder.

Language disorders are a specific type of disability that can affect individuals across the lifespan, from infants to the elderly. A language disorder occurs when one's language skills or processes in any one of the four domains are not consistent with expectations based on normative references (i.e., the language abilities expected based on a person's age and social background, including educational history). A long history of developmental research has informed our understanding of when specific language skills and processes typically emerge during the course of human development (as well as how variability in developmental experiences can have an impact on emergence of language), and these normative references are useful for identifying when language acquisition is not proceeding at a typical rate. For instance, we generally expect infants to begin to babble by about 6 months of age and to produce their first word by about 12 months. By 18 months, it is common to see children begin to combine two words to make very short sentences (e.g., *mommy up*). Such developmental data make it possible to recognize when language development is not following its expected courses (e.g., Ganger & Brent, 2004). For instance, in infancy, characteristics of a language disorder typically include (a) delayed use of babbling and restricted range of babbled sounds, (b) delayed gesturing and other nonverbal means of communicating, and (c) delayed production of the first word. In addition, infants with language disorder will accrue their first 50 vocabulary words relatively slowly and will begin to combine words to make two-word sentences later than other children (Rescorla, Roberts, & Dahlsgaard, 1997; Scarborough, 1990).

Language disorders, when present from infancy forward, are referred to as *developmental language disorders* to distinguish them from language disorders that occur later in life, often because of some sort of acquired brain damage (most commonly stroke or a traumatic brain injury). Language disorders that result from damage to the brain are typically described as acquired language disorders, or aphasia. In this chapter, we focus exclusively on developmental language disorders. Some cases of developmental language disorder occur for no known reason; in such instances, a significant disability in the area of language is the child's only impairment, as the language disorder occurs in the absence of any intellectual (e.g., cognitive disability), neurological (e.g., autism), motor (e.g., cerebral palsy), or sensory (e.g., hearing loss) disturbances. When a language disorder occurs in isolation, it is referred to as *primary language disorder* or, more commonly, *specific language impairment (SLI)*. SLI affects an estimated 7% to 10% of school-age children, thereby making it one of the most common reasons for which children receive special education services (Tomblin et al., 1997). Language disorders can also occur concomitantly with other disabilities; for instance, children who experience cognitive disability (e.g., Down syndrome), autism, and hearing loss often experience a language disorder as a result of their primary disability.

Whether a language disorder is a child's primary disability or occurs secondary to another type of impairment, difficulties with language ability can cause children to have significant challenges in two pivotal areas of development: (a) social competence, including engagement and interactions with parents, teachers, and peers; and (b) academic achievement, including the development of skills specific to reading development and the use of these skills to gain access to the entire curriculum. Because of its far-reaching impact on children's social and academic development, treatment of language disorders is a significant component of special education services for children within public schooling. In fact, the costs of such services are estimated at $36 billion annually (Chambers, Parrish, & Harr, 2004).

Intervention for language disorders is often introduced early in a child's life, perhaps as early as infancy for children who exhibit specific recognizable conditions that heighten risks for language disorders. This includes early-identified cognitive disability (e.g., as associated with fetal alcohol syndrome and Down syndrome) and significant hearing loss, as well as prematurity/low birth weight. Intervention for children who are not yet talking (e.g., babies with Down syndrome) will focus on helping them to develop *prelinguistic* skills, such as engaging in periods of sustained attention with their caregivers and babbling (Warren, Yoder, Gazdag, Kim, & Jones, 1993). In the years following infancy, including toddlerhood and the preschool years, most language disorders are recognized among children who do not exhibit other identifiable disabilities, because this is when children must draw on their linguistic resources to interact with the world around them (e.g., by producing sentences to make requests and to ask questions). Warning signs that can signal presence of a language disorder include (a) having a very small vocabulary and having difficulty learning new words; (b) using very short sentences and omitting grammatical markers (e.g., plurals, articles) when other children are using them; and (c) being unable to use language instrumentally with peers and others, such as asking questions to gain information and making requests. These and other indicators of language disorders characterizing children in the preschool and primary grades appear in Table 6.1.

Educators, parents, and allied professionals (e.g., speech-language pathologists) use a number of practices to address the core language difficulties of children with language disorders. These practices can vary substantially with respect to *how* they go about changing a child's language abilities; for instance, one practice may feature the child's participation in highly decontextualized repeated drill-and-practice routines with a professional, whereas another practice may feature the child's participation in classroom-based curricular activities with a peer. Often, decisions about the specific techniques one uses (the *how* of intervention) are based on one's theoretical paradigm and personal experience. As a general rule, a variety of practices are potentially effective for bringing about change in a child's language

Table 6.1   Common Indicators of Language Disorder

Age	Language Difficulties
Infancy and toddlerhood	Delayed production of babbling
	Late appearance of first word
	Delayed use of simple grammatical markers (present progressive *-ing*, plural *-s*, possessive *-'s*)
	Late emergence of two- and three-word combinations
	Less variety of verbs
	Slow development of pronouns
Preschool	Omission of *to be* verbs (e.g., "he going," "dolly coming")
	Omission of articles
	Pronoun errors
	Shorter sentence length
	Lack of coherence in stories
	Problems comprehending complex directions
	Overreliance on nonspecific nouns
	Difficulty initiating conversations with peers
	Difficulty sustaining conversations over multiple turns
	Limited diversity in vocabulary
Early and later elementary	Word-finding problems
	Slow naming speed and naming errors (e.g., *shoes* for *pants*)
	Use of earlier-developing pronoun forms
	Difficulty maintaining conversational topics over multiple turns
	Difficulty/reluctance initiating conversation with peers
	Difficulty understanding abstract vocabulary terms
	Shorter sentence length
	Lack of coherence in connected discourse (e.g., story retelling)
	Problems with reading development (including reading comprehension)
	Problems comprehending figurative language (e.g., riddles, idioms)

Sources: Conti-Ramsden & Jones (1997); Leonard (2000); McGregor & Leonard (1995); Ratner & Harris (1994); Watkins, Rice, & Molz (1993).

abilities. What seems to be particularly important is that a selected language-intervention practice is offered with reasonable intensity/frequency and explicitly targets the domains of language developing slowly (Fey, Cleave, &

Long, 1997; S. Gillam, Gillam, Petersen, & Bingham, 2008; J. Law, Garrett, & Nye, 2004).

In the remainder of this chapter, we'll discuss two specific language-intervention practices adhering to these parameters that also have a reasonable amount of quality research supporting their effectiveness with children with language disorders: *focused stimulation* and *story structure intervention*. We have selected these two practices not only because they are scientifically supported but also because they represent how approaches may vary when used with younger versus older children. Specifically, focused stimulation is primarily used with toddlers and preschoolers, whereas story structure intervention is primarily used with school-age children.

Review of Effective Practices
Focused Stimulation
Definition and Overview

Focused stimulation is a language-intervention practice commonly used with toddlers and preschoolers exhibiting significantly delayed language development. To implement this practice, a parent, teacher, or therapist provides *highly concentrated presentations* of specific linguistic targets, which include words, sounds, or grammatical structures, within such naturalistic routines as play or storybook reading (Girolametto, Pearce, & Weitzman, 1996, p. 1275; see also Fey, 1986). These "presentations" often take the form of repeated *models, contrasts,* and *recasts.* Contrasts and models tend to follow and thus build on the child's communicative contributions. These three examples target the child's use of "is" as a main (copula) verb:

Example 1:   *Teacher (models):* This boy *is* sad. The boy *is* so sad.

   Child: He sad.

   Teacher (recasts): He *is* sad.

Example 2:   *Child:* He sad.

   Teacher (recasts): Is he sad?

Example 3:   *Child:* Him sad.

   Teacher (contrasts and recasts): He is sad.

In the first example, the teacher initially models the targeted form. The child responds and omits the targeted form, to which the teacher then recasts the child's utterance to model again the targeted form. Note that the teacher's recast retains the child's statement verbatim with the exception of providing the copula form. In the third example, the teacher uses a contrast for the pronoun form (*him/he*) along with the recast for the copula form: the teacher uses the correct form of the subjective pronoun (*he*) as contrasted against the child's form (*him*): Models, contrasts, and recasts can be used to target a variety of specific linguistic structures, including such semantic targets as individual words and word combinations (Girolametto et al., 1996):

Example 1: *Child:* That. (individual word)

Teacher (models, recasts): That's a *baby.*

Example 2: *Child:* Baby sleeping. (word combination)

Teacher (models, recasts): The *little baby's* sleeping. He's a *little baby.*

Phonological targets might include eliminating cluster reduction (i.e., when the child reduces consonant clusters to single sounds) and eliminating final consonant deletion (Tyler & Sandoval, 1994).

Example 1: *Child:* It's a "tain." (cluster reduction)

Teacher (recasts, contrasts): It's a *train.* Is it a tain or a *train?*

Example 2: *Child:* My "boa." (final consonant deletion)

Teacher (recasts, models): That's your *boat.* It's a *boat.*

Grammatical targets might include use of articles and use of word inflections (e.g., -*ing* for present progressive) (Cleave & Fey, 1997).

Example 1: *Child:* I need book. (use of articles)

Teacher (recasts, models): You want *the* book.

Example 2: *Child:* He walk. (use of word inflections)

Teacher (recasts): He is *walking.*

In addition to using models, recasts, and contrasts to provide children with high-density exposure to targeted linguistic forms, focused stimulation procedures also commonly feature several additional strategies designed to elicit the child's productions of targeted forms explicitly. These descriptions and definitions are adapted from Cleave and Fey's (1997) description of each strategy. The first strategy involves using *false assertions and feigned misunderstandings* designed to evoke responses from the child that include targeted forms, as in this false assertion which evokes the child's use of the targeted present-progressive verb form:

Example 1: *Adult (pointing to a sleeping baby):* The baby is *eating.*

Child: No, baby sleeping.

Forced-choice questions are another strategy for eliciting the child's production of targeted forms, as in this

example designed to elicit the child's use of subjective pronouns:

Example 1: *Adult (holding two baby dolls):* Do you want *him* or *her?*

The third strategy is *requests for elaboration,* which are used specifically to elicit the child's use of more complex sentence structures and to include omitted information:

Example 1: *Child:* Want that one.

Adult: Which one do you want?

Child: That one.

Adult: Why do you want that one?

Child: That one strawberry.

Adult: Oh, you like strawberry. That's your favorite flavor.

An important aspect of focused stimulation is that it is to be implemented within naturalistic contexts. This approach to intervention is designed to leverage children's desire to communicate with others in functional circumstances that approximate typical communicative experiences. Within these naturalistic contexts, such as interactive play, the adult might use specific strategies to manipulate the environment so as to encourage the child's use of targeted words, sounds, or grammatical structures (Cleave & Fey, 1997). For instance, again drawing on our goal for a child to use *is* as a main verb, a teacher might engage a child in an activity that involves taking turns, such as building a tower out of blocks in which opportunities to add to the tower are rotated across teacher and child. During the activity, the teacher might withhold blocks from the child (e.g., place them behind her back) so that the child must communicate to participate in the activity; this is sometimes referred to as *sabotage.* This presents the opportunity for the teacher to model the targeted grammatical form frequently, as in "It *is* my turn" and "It *is* your turn." Should the child comment "It my turn," this also provides the opportunity for the teacher to recast the child's contribution by responding, "It *is* your turn."

A particularly important feature of focused stimulation concerns the selection of linguistic targets (also called *goals*), which requires careful examination of the child's current vocabulary, phonological, or grammatical abilities. In other words, goal selection is highly individualized. Goals are typically selected based on (a) communicative need (the goal will in some way help a child communicate more effectively) and (b) readiness (the child shows some cognitive readiness for the goal) (Cleave & Fey, 1997). For instance, vocabulary goals for a given child might be a small set of words that are highly functional to a child (e.g., *eat, want, my, bottle*) and are comprehended but are not used in any context. That the words are comprehended suggests that the child may be "ready" to use the words productively. Grammatical goals for a child might represent grammatical forms used infrequently and inconsistently; a typical benchmark for selection of a grammatical form as an appropriate target for intervention is use of the form less than 50% of the time in obligatory contexts (Cleave & Fey, 1997). Selection of goals for a specific child typically requires one to have a strong understanding of typical language development (so as to select developmentally appropriate targets) as well as sophisticated knowledge of that child's language abilities across grammar, semantics, phonology, and pragmatics. This knowledge is typically attained not only by standardized assessments but also through language-sampling procedures, in which children's language production is studied and analyzed across a variety of different contexts, including everyday routines.

Theoretical Underpinnings

Focused stimulation is highly influenced by social-interactionist theories of language acquisition. Interactionist perspectives view language acquisition as a psychobiological process in which "frequent, relatively well-tuned affectively positive verbal interactions" are critical for supporting language growth in early childhood (Chapman, 2000, p. 43). This perspective emphasizes the importance of children's socially embedded, mediated interactions with more knowledgeable conversational partners as a critical developmental mechanism (Bruner, 1983; Justice & Ezell, 1999). Within such interactions, the more knowledgeable partner (e.g., teacher) fine-tunes her verbal input to scaffold the child's communicative engagement and gradual movement from dependent to more independent levels of linguistic skill in semantics, phonology, grammar, and pragmatics. This partner is seen as a critical resource for fostering the language skills of children with language disorders, in that she can provide "enhanced or optimized levels" of linguistic input that provide increased opportunities for children to learn specific dimensions of language (Girolametto et al., 1996, p. 1274). Drawing on the perspective that interactions with others is a critical context in which children acquire language skills, focused stimulation embeds intervention within naturalistic conversational routines; within these routines, the adult provides the child with highly concentrated exposures to specific language-acquisition targets, based on the theory that children with language-learning difficulties may require a higher concentration of exposures to specific words, sounds, or grammatical forms to acquire them.

Developmental research provides considerable empirical support for social-interactionist perspectives regarding the influence of linguistic input on children's

rate of language acquisition (e.g., Baumwell, Tamis-LeMonda, & Bornstein, 1997; Hart & Risley, 1995; Pellegrini, Galda, Jones, & Perlmutter, 1995; Tamis-LeMonda, Bornstein, & Baumwell, 2001). Although much of this research has focused on parents and their children, some studies have looked outside the home to study associations between the linguistic input children hear in other environments and their rate of language growth. For instance, Girolametto and Weitzman (2002) described the rate of child-care providers' use of specific language-modeling strategies (e.g., imitations, labeling, expansions) to explain variation in preschoolers' semantic and syntactic skills. Additionally, a number of studies (several of which we describe shortly) have directly tested the effects of focused stimulation for accelerating the language growth of children with language disorders, supporting the efficacy of this approach (e.g., Cleave & Fey, 1997; Girolametto et al., 1996).

Implementation Guide

Implementation of focused stimulation typically involves three primary considerations: (a) establishing and manipulating the intervention context, (b) selecting intervention targets, and (c) implementing focused stimulation procedures. Figure 6.1 provides an overview of each of these three components of focused stimulation based on published reports in the literature (Cleave & Fey, 1997; Fey, Long, & Finestack, 2003; Girolametto et al., 1996). It is also worth noting that a comprehensive manual for implementing a variation of focused stimulation is available from the nonprofit Hanen Centre, located in Canada; this guide (*It Takes Two to Talk;* Pepper & Weitzman, 2004) was developed specifically for parents as a means to support their use of focused stimulation procedures within the home environment with their toddlers with language disabilities. This manual presents complex concepts regarding language facilitation in parent-friendly terms and offers numerous examples of specific facilitation techniques. Also available is a teacher-oriented manual, *Learning Language and Loving It* (LLLI; Weitzman & Greenberg, 2002), which was designed to teach early childhood educators how to use focused stimulation procedures with young children in their classrooms. The Hanen Centre has implementation checklists available for LLLI that can be used to promote teachers' learning of these techniques (Girolametto & Weitzman, 2002, includes a copy in the appendix).

Research Base

Among the variety of language-intervention approaches available in the research literature, focused stimulation is likely the most strongly supported. This support is

Figure 6.1   Implementation guide for focused stimulation.

A. Intervention Context

— Intervention implemented in naturalistic contexts/activities

— Intervention features natural adult–child conversations

— Context manipulated to entice child to engage in communicative participation (e.g., withholding objects, use of interesting toys)

B. Intervention Targets

— Targets selected based on analysis of conversational language sample

— Targets represent obstacles to child's communication success

— Targets are linguistic forms that the child uses infrequently and/or inconsistently

C. Intervention Procedures

1. Adult provides a high density of linguistic targets by using:

— **simple models** of linguistic targets in a range of possible contexts

— **recasts** that follow the child's use of linguistic targets

— **contrasts** between target forms and more advanced forms

2. Adult elicits child's attempts at linguistic targets by:

— **false assertions** and **feigned misunderstandings**

— **forced-choice questions**

— **requests for elaborations**

Sources: Cleave & Fey (1997); Fey (1986); Fey, Long, & Finestack (2003); Girolametto, Pearce, & Weitzman (1996).

---

derived in part from descriptive or correlational studies that support a positive and significant relationship between child exposure to specific stimulation procedures (e.g., recasts) and their language gains (Girolametto & Weitzman, 2002; M. W. Smith & Dickinson, 1994). Girolametto and Weitzman, for instance, reported correlations of 0.51, 0.41, and 0.48 between day-care providers' use of three stimulation strategies combined (i.e., models, expansions, recasts) and preschool-age children's verbal productivity, syntactic complexity, and lexical diversity. Perhaps more convincingly, experimental studies training parents, teachers, and therapists to use specific stimulation techniques have consistently shown these strategies to foster early language achievements in young children (e.g., Cole, Dale, & Mills, 1991; Fey, Cleave, & Long, 1997; Fey, Krulik, Loeb, &

Proctor-Williams, 1999; Fey & Loeb, 2002). We describe two such studies here to illustrate the type of evidence available in support of this approach to language intervention with young children.

Focused stimulation with toddlers with vocabulary delays.   Girolametto and colleagues (1996) conducted a randomized controlled trial of focused stimulation as implemented by parents of toddlers with expressive vocabulary delays. A total of 25 mother–child dyads participated, with 12 dyads assigned to an experimental treatment group, and the remainder ($n = 13$) assigned to a control group. Demographically, the sample comprised primarily middle- to upper-socioeconomic status (SES) families, all of whom were native English speakers. Children ranged in age from 23 to 33 months of age, and all had significant delays in vocabulary development (i.e., all were in the lower fifth percentile on a standardized measure of language expression, based on parent report).

Parents assigned to the treatment group participated in an 11-week program involving eight 2.5-hour evening training sessions (completed as a group) and three home visits; training sessions and home visits were conducted by certified speech-language pathologists (SLPs). The parent training used the Hanen Centre's variation of focused stimulation and taught parents how to use specific stimulation techniques, particularly modeling and recasting, to target 10 vocabulary words across a variety of naturalistic contexts within the home environment. Treatment fidelity was assessed for all parents, to include attendance data showing that parents completed training sessions and observation data showing that parents used the stimulation techniques they were taught.

To assess the efficacy of focused stimulation for these toddlers with expressive-vocabulary delays, researchers assessed children's vocabulary growth pre- and post-intervention, using several measures, including parent report of child vocabulary size based on a standardized parent questionnaire and analysis of children's vocabulary expression during structured observations. Compared to children in the control group, at post-intervention the children whose parents used focused stimulation had significantly larger vocabularies and used a significantly greater variety of words when interacting with their parents. Study findings suggest that parent implementation of focused stimulation within the home environment is an efficacious means for promoting the vocabulary development of toddlers with vocabulary delays.

Focused stimulation with preschoolers with SLI.   A hallmark characteristic of SLI is its negative impacts on children's development of grammar (e.g., Rice & Wexler, 1996; Rice, Wexler, & Hershberger, 1998). Children with SLI, during the preschool years, commonly exhibit late onset of specific grammatical forms (e.g., objective pronouns: *she, he, they*) as well as protracted use of more immature forms (e.g., substituting subjective pronouns for objective pronouns: *Her did it*). A number of experimental studies have sought specifically to determine whether focused stimulation procedures are efficacious for resolving the grammatical deficits of preschoolers with SLI (see Cleave & Fey, 1997; Fey et al., 1997; Fey, Cleave, Long, & Hughes, 1993).

Likely the most extensive study addressing this question to date was that of Fey and colleagues, described in a 1993 publication. This study involved 30 children with SLI who ranged in age from 42 to 70 months. All had grammar-specific deficits in conjunction with additional difficulties with language (e.g., vocabulary and phonological weaknesses). The children were randomly assigned to one of three groups, two of which involved focused stimulation, and one of which involved a delayed-treatment (control, $n = 9$) group. The two focused stimulation groups, comprising a total of 21 children, featured a planned comparison of parent- and clinician-implemented language interventions ($n = 10$ and $n = 11$, respectively). As this design indicates, in addition to assessing the efficacy of focused stimulation for influencing the language skills of children with SLI, this study also sought to compare the efficacy of parent- and clinician-implemented treatment variations.

Children in both treatment conditions received focused stimulation for 4.5 months. Children in the clinician-implemented condition received treatment in three sessions per week by a licensed SLP, consisting of one 1-hour individual session and two 1-hour group sessions involving four to six children. Children in the parent-implemented condition received treatment at home by their parents, who completed weekly 2-hour group sessions (in which only parents participated) for 12 weeks and then monthly for two additional months. For children in both treatment groups, four specific grammatical goals were selected for each child, and one goal was targeted each week; goals were cycled through the course of the 4.5 month treatment. Focused stimulation procedures used by clinicians and parents largely adhered to those listed in Figure 6.1.

The effects of the focused stimulation treatment programs on children's language development were determined using a single measure of grammatical complexity collected from children pre- and post-intervention. Children in the control group exhibited no gains on the grammatical complexity measure from pre- to post-test, whereas children in both treatment programs exhibited gains on the magnitude of about 1 standard deviation unit. This is generally considered to be a large treatment effect. Interestingly, the difference between the two treatment conditions (parent- or clinician-implemented) was not statistically significant, indicating that whether children received focused stimulation from an SLP or a parent was not an important consideration when considering intervention efficacy. In this regard, findings of this study converge with those discussed previously concerning parental implementation of focused stimulation with their toddlers experiencing vocabulary delays.

Story Structure Intervention

Definition and Overview

Story structure intervention is a practice commonly used with school-age children who have a language disorder. It is designed to increase children's comprehension and production of relatively "large" units of language (e.g., stories, also called *narratives*). Story structure instruction typically involves teaching the components of a story, modeling the use of the components in stories, identifying story elements, answering questions about stories, retelling stories, or generating new stories containing the elements that were taught. Many of the instructional strategies include graphic visual representations of specific elements, ideas, and causal connections contained in stories, which we refer to as *story maps*. Originally, the goal of story structure instruction was to improve children's reading comprehension (Z. T. Davis, 1994; Gardill & Jitendra, 1999; Reutzel, 1985a, 1985b; Short & Ryan, 1984). However, later studies of story structure instruction have focused on improving children's story-telling skills. A number of story elements have been taught in story structure intervention, often called story grammar (D. Hughes, McGillivray, & Schmidek, 1997; Labov, 1972; Stein & Glenn, 1979); elements of story grammar often taught in the intervention are summarized in Figure 6.2.

Some story grammar elements are associated with more sophisticated conceptual and linguistic knowledge than others. For example, for a child to understand or employ the use of *planning* in a story, he must have knowledge of mental state verbs such as *thought* or *decided* and attribute them to characters. Plans are usually expressed with a complex syntactic structure called a *clausal complement* (e.g., "Superman thought he should save Lois Lane."), in which the object of the mental state verb is an entire clause. Similarly, *internal responses* require an understanding of the ways characters feel about events in the story and how they may motivate their actions. Attributing mental states and feelings to characters can be particularly difficult for children with language problems (Ford & Milosky, 2003; Spackman, Fujiki, & Brinton, 2006) or with

Figure 6.2 Elements of story structure often targeted in story structure instruction.

Character	Agents who perform actions in stories
Setting	References to time or place in stories
Initiating events	Central problems in the story requiring some action be taken for resolution
Internal responses	Statements indicating how characters feel about an initiating event
Plan	Character's thoughts about potential solutions to a problem
Attempts	Actions taken by a character to resolve a central problem
Complications	Obstacles impeding the resolution of central problems
Consequences	Statements about whether actions taken by characters in response to central problems were successful or unsuccessful
Reactions	Statements indicating how characters feel about the consequences
Closing	Statements that bring the story to a close or explain the general meaning of the story

autism spectrum disorders (Bartsch & Wellman, 1995; Silliman et al., 2003; Wellman, 1990) and may require more explicit, intensive instruction. Thus, decisions regarding the kinds of story grammar elements to include in story structure instruction will involve careful consideration of a child's level of conceptual development as well as linguistic proficiency.

Educators can use story maps to specifically teach children the causal connections between story elements, as in the following example:

$$\text{Character} \rightarrow \text{Problem} \rightarrow \text{Action}$$
$$\rightarrow \text{Consequence} \rightarrow \text{Reaction}$$

In this story map, the character encounters a problem and takes a corresponding action, which is then followed by a consequence and a subsequent reaction. These story grammar elements occur in temporal order, as indicated by the direction of the arrows, and these elements together form the basis for understanding the story. The story also involves a causal order of events; for instance, the problem "causes" the character to act, which in turn results in a consequence.

The use of "why" questioning techniques has been recommended as a useful way to highlight causal networks in stories (Trabasso & Magliano, 1996). For example, using the example from the preceding causal map, a teacher or clinician might ask, "Why did [character] do [action]?" The correct answer would require the child to make a causal connection between the *problem* in the story and the *action* taken by the character to solve that problem, as in "Eleanor *ran away* (action) *because* (causal connection) *the bear was chasing her* (initiating event/problem)."

Theoretical Underpinnings

Teaching procedures commonly associated with story structure intervention, particularly the use of story maps and graphic organizers, align well with the theoretical literature on text structure (see Hoggan & Strong, 1994). Mapping allows a visual depiction of the overall structure and theme of the story as well as the sequence of events. The theory of text structure (Kintsch & van Dijk, 1978) is relevant to the story structure approach because it includes descriptions of text microstructure (e.g., vocabulary, sentences), macrostructure (e.g., overall structure or theme of the text, specific to different genres), and cohesion (i.e., devices used to relate microstructures to each other and to the macrostructure). Kintsch and van Dijk proposed that comprehension is accomplished by integrating these sources of information to construct a coherent situational representation of the text through the use of semantic relationships and causal connections contained therein.

Schema theory (Rumelhart, 1975; Stein & Glenn, 1979) is another theoretical basis for the use of story structure instruction that focuses on story episodes in comprehension instruction. Helping children gain explicit knowledge of text structures may improve the conceptual knowledge that supports their understanding and use of oral and written discourse structures. *Text structure* refers to the ways in which texts are organized: in narrative stories, a common text structure is problem–solution, whereas in expository text, a common text structure is compare–contrast. Text structures are associated with specific vocabulary as well as specific grammatical forms. Comprehension processes can be facilitated through knowledge of underlying text structure (Graesser, Singer, & Trabasso, 1994; Trabasso, Secco, & van den Broek, 1984). One of the most salient features of narrative texts is its predictable and stable causal structure (Trabasso, van den Broek, & Suh, 1989). Adults and children are better able to recall relevant information and answer comprehension questions about texts when they attend to the underlying text structures that are contained therein (Goldman & Varnhagen, 1986; Trabasso & Magliano, 1996; Trabasso & van den Broek, 1985; Trabasso, Suh, Payton, & Jain, 1995). Providing children with a highly specific scaffold or story map for narrative discourse should improve a child's understanding of the "structure" of oral and written texts. This knowledge may

Figure 6.3   Implementation guide for story structure intervention.

A. Intervention Context

— Intervention implemented in literature-based contexts/activities

— Intervention features identification of story grammar elements and causal connections using visual graphic organizers or symbols

— Complexity of stories manipulated to highlight different linguistic targets (e.g., subordinated adverbial clauses, relative clauses, causal compliments, later developing infinitives)

B. Intervention Targets

— Intervention targets story grammar elements (character, setting, initiating event, internal response, attempts, complication, consequence, ending)

— Intervention targets causal connection words (e.g., *because, so, since, therefore, thus*)

— Intervention targets linguistic forms that the child uses infrequently, inconsistently, or both in narrative production (e.g., subordinated adverbial clauses, relative clauses, causal compliments, later-developing infinitives) to improve story complexity and use of literate language

C. Intervention Procedures

1. Adult models, scaffolds, and supports independence in:

— **identification** of story grammar elements and causal connections in a variety of contexts (e.g., listening and reading, question-answer)

— **production** or use of story grammar elements and causal connections in supported and self-generated stories (e.g., retelling sequenced pictures, wordless picture books and single scenes, drawing/pictography)

— **contrasts** between complete (e.g., initiating event, attempt, consequence), incomplete (e.g., initiating event, attempt), and complex (initiating event, attempt, complication, consequence) episodes

2. Adult highlights linguistic forms, causal connections, or both through the use of contingent facilitation strategies:

— **modeling/demonstration** (Adult: She ran BECAUSE she was afraid of the bear.)

— **prompts/questions** (Child: She ran away. Adult: Why do you think she ran away?)

— **vertical structuring** (e.g., Child: The girl is running. Adult: Why is she running? Child: She sees a bear. Adult: The girl is running BECAUSE she sees a bear.)

— **growth-relevant recasts** (e.g., Child: That girl is running. Adult: Yes, she is running SO THAT the bear can't catch her.)

Source: Information from Gillam, S., Gillam, R., Petersen, D., & Bingham, C. (2008). *Narrative language intervention program: Promoting oral language development.* Technical session presented at The Annual Convention of the American Speech Language and Hearing Association, Chicago, IL.

be applied regularly to future encounters with similar texts (Pearson & Duke, 2002) to aid in comprehension and generation of summaries.

Implementation Guide

Figure 6.3 provides a general implementation guide for story structure interventions. In general, story maps may be developed for an entire story or for certain subcomponents of a story (e.g., mapping a cause-and-effect sequence of events); as a result, these may be very specific or more general in nature. As may be seen in Figure 6.4, a story map may be used to elaborate on any one aspect of story grammar with which children may be having particular problems or to assist them in deeper processing of information for use in elaboration. The story map shown in Figure 6.5 was designed to assist children in thinking

Figure 6.4   Story map for character elaboration.

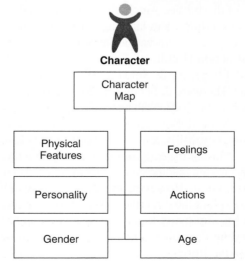

Figure 6.5   Child-generated story map based on a clinician-led, progressive, group story-generation activity.

Source: Information from Gillam, S., Gillam, R., Petersen, D., & Bingham, C. (2008). *Narrative language intervention program: Promoting oral language development.* Technical session presented at The Annual Convention of the American Speech Language and Hearing Association, Chicago, IL.

about the attributes of the characters who took part in the story for use in answering more elaborative questions after reading. As a rule, there is considerable flexibility in using story maps to promote language and reading skills.

Research Base

The practice of teaching story structure through the use of story maps and graphic organizers has been widely applied in regular and special education contexts. School-age children who are developing typically as well as those with a wide range of disabilities—including learning disabilities, reading disabilities, and language disorders—have been shown to benefit from various approaches to story structure instruction (Boulinea, Fore, Hagan-Burke, & Burke, 2004; Fitzgerald & Spiegel, 1983; Gordon & Pearson, 1983; Hayward & Schnieder, 2000; Idol, 1987; Montgomery & Kahn, 2003; Nathanson, Crank, Saywitz, & Ruegg, 2007; Nolte & Singer, 1985; Singer & Donlan, 1982; Swanson, Fey, Mills, & Hood, 2005; Westerveld & Gillon, 2008). Most of the early studies on story structure focused on improving reading comprehension rather than language expression. However, more recent research has begun to explore the effectiveness of story structure intervention for improving aspects of spoken language ability, including the ability to summarize, retell, and generate narrative stories.

Several well-conducted studies have provided empirical support for the use of story structure intervention for children with language disorders and, more generally, learning disabilities (see Hayward & Schnieder, 2000; Nathanson et al., 2007; Westerveld & Gillon, 2008). As an example, Nathanson and colleagues (2007) investigated the effects of story structure instruction for improving children's recall of a history lesson. Study participants were 39 children with learning disabilities, 7 to 12 years old, who were randomly assigned to either a story structure instruction group, referred to as *narrative elaboration treatment (NET),* or a control group. Children in the NET group were given verbal descriptions and simple cue cards depicting information in four overarching categories: (a) character details, (b) setting details, (c) actions/behaviors, and (d) feelings of characters. After explaining the meaning of the cue cards, teachers used a think-aloud process to demonstrate their use. Children practiced describing pictures and used the cue cards to recount video vignettes. During training, children received corrective feedback with respect to the completeness and accuracy of their recounts and their accuracy in using the pictorial cues. Children in the control condition performed similar storytelling activities but did not receive instruction in using cue cards. Instead, these children were told to "do their best" and "remember as much information as you can" when describing pictures and recounting the video vignettes.

All the children in the study had participated in a history lesson 2 weeks before the intervention sessions. Each child received individual instruction in recalling the video vignettes in two 30-minute sessions held 2 days apart. At the end of the second session, children participated in free- and prompted-recall tasks regarding the previous history lesson. Children were asked to recount what they remembered about the history lesson they had received 2 weeks earlier. Children in the NET group recalled 25% more information from history lessons during free recall (Cohen's $d = 0.37$) than children in the control group, although this difference did not reach statistical significance. However, for cued-recall children, the NET group recalled significantly more information (Cohen's $d = 2.87$) than children in the motivating instructions group. The results of this study are very encouraging because they suggest that the use of story maps or visual graphic organizers may be useful in improving the content and quality of information children report even after a significant delay between exposure to information and oral reporting of the information.

Researchers have begun to investigate whether instruction in story structure is associated with gains in narrative production and general language skills such as syntax or morphology (e.g., Swanson et al., 2005). As an example, S. Gillam et al. (2008) sought to determine whether a story structure instruction program improved the comprehension and production of narratives and general language abilities for 16 children with language disorders between the ages of 6 and 9 years. Children were randomly assigned to a socialization-first or concurrent-socialization group. Children in the socialization-first group engaged in free play together for 4 weeks (i.e., the control block). After the free-play block, these children received narrative intervention from SLPs for 4 weeks (i.e., the intervention block). The concurrent socialization group stayed at home and did not receive any services for 4 weeks (i.e., the control block), then received narrative intervention followed by free play each day for 4 weeks (i.e., the cross-over intervention block). The focus of the 4-week intervention was on story structure, emphasizing both story retelling and story generation in the context of simple and complex episodes. As in earlier studies of story structure instruction (e.g., Swanson et al., 2005; Westerveld & Gillon, 2008) graphic organizers or story maps were used to teach the elements of story grammar and to assist children in retelling and generating their own stories. Children were seen in groups of three or four for 90 minutes, 4 days per week by certified SLPs in a university setting.

The basic session format included instruction on meaning of the story element icons. Then, clinicians and children created stories using the icons. The visual icons representing story structures were also used during story comprehension activities to cue children to answer questions about specific information related to particular story elements. Children participated in group retelling activities, progressive story generation tasks, and independent story generation tasks with and without the visual icons to assist them. In group retelling, children listened to stories that they had heard repeatedly and then received all of the relevant icons in a random fashion. For example, Child A might be given icons representing *character, plan,* and *resolution;* Child B might be given *setting, complication,* and *consequence;* and Child C might be given *initiating event, internal response,* and *attempts.* As the group retold the story, each child was responsible for filling in the story grammar elements represented on their cue cards in the appropriate order in the story. Progressive story generation involved a similar process, except children drew stick figures of elements in their "group-created" stories on story maps containing the icons and later without the icons. An example of a child's map of a story generated through progression is shown in Figure 6.5. In this map, a spider and a fly are the characters; the basic premise of the story is as follows:

> The spider wants to live in his web and catch flies, but he has a medical issue regarding his spinner mechanism, which has made him sad. He decides to get some medication for his spinner. After obtaining the medication, he applies it to his spinner. The medicine heals his spinner, and he builds a web for future fly catching and yummy meals and is very happy about it.

Independent story generation was similar to progressive story generation, except children designed and told their own stories using the story structure instruction process with and without icons. Children took turns telling their peer's independently generated stories while peers tracked story grammar elements on Bingo cards containing the iconic representations. Children were tested immediately after random assignment (pretest), after the control blocks (midtest), and after intervention (post-test) with the Test of Narrative Language (TNL; R. B. Gillam & Pearson, 2004) and the Clinical Evaluation of Language Fundamentals, Fourth Edition (CELF-4; Semel, Wiig, & Secord, 2003). Children did not make improvements in narration (TNL) or in general language proficiency (CELF-4) after the control blocks. After the intervention blocks, children in both groups made significant improvements on the TNL production composite score but not on the TNL comprehension composite score or on the CELF-4 standard score. The results suggest that for some children with language disorders, a narrative intervention program that focused on story structure using story structure procedures was associated with significant gains in oral narrative production but not in narrative comprehension (TNL) or in general language proficiency.

This finding is similar to that of Swanson et al. (2005), in which researchers reported that story structure intervention resulted in improved oral narrative skills but not in general language abilities. In the S. Gillam et al. (2008) study, the findings may reflect the intensive focus on storytelling rather than story comprehension or specific grammatical or syntactic targets. That is, children spent the majority of their time developing and producing stories, and less time answering questions about them. Instruction in more authentic contexts and texts may be required to activate the mechanisms involved in bringing about change in specific linguistic domains (morphology, syntax). In terms of the comprehension findings, children with language disorders may require the same type of intensive, explicit instruction and practice in story comprehension that they received in story production. That is, children with language disorders do not appear to be adept at transferring skill from one situation (e.g., story production activities) to another (e.g., story comprehension activities) or in generalizing information or knowledge that they have in one context to another.

To summarize, the use of story structure instruction to improve the comprehension and production of oral stories is generally well-supported in the literature for increasing the language skills of children developing typically as well as those with language disorders and more general learning disabilities. The research that has been summarized in this chapter supports the use of story mapping procedures within story structure instructional programs. Specifically, good results have been obtained when children are explicitly taught the components of a story using visual (graphic) representations of specific story elements or story content. Researchers typically model the use of the target story components in stories and ask children to identify story elements in model stories, answer questions about stories, retell stories using the graphic representations as guides, or generate new stories containing the elements that were taught.

One limitation in the research base related to story structure intervention using story mapping procedures is the lack of high-quality, randomized, clinical trials with large numbers of children with language disorders. To date, we are aware of no meta-analyses, systematic reviews, or large-scale randomized controlled trials examining this approach for improving story comprehension or production. Positive outcomes for story structure interventions have been demonstrated in a range of contexts with a variety of interventionists. Children have been shown to benefit from instruction provided in intensive individual intervention contexts delivered by SLPs as well as in less-intensive group settings delivered by regular and special educators, SLPs, and teachers of English Language Learners. Practitioners can feel relatively comfortable that children will respond favorably to story structure interventions that involve (a) explicit instruction with the use of visual, graphic organizers in the context of stories, (b) repetitive practice in identification and use of story elements and

causal connections, (c) frequent opportunities for children to generate their own stories, and (d) directed practice in answering questions about story grammar elements and causal connections contained in texts.

In addition, we also want to point out several shortcomings associated with current approaches to story structure instruction. Most approaches have focused on teaching children to produce simple single-episode narratives. These narrative language targets are qualitatively and quantitatively different from the longer and more complex age- and content-appropriate narratives that students routinely encounter in daily academic instruction (Lynch et al., 2008). In addition, existing narrative interventions often focus on story retelling to the exclusion of story generation or do not place enough emphasis on language features such as vocabulary, sentence structure, and causal connections. We were surprised to note that there were no studies of the generalization from oral story comprehension and production to reading comprehension and writing in children with language disorders. Story structure instruction may need to include explicit print-based experiences within the context of authentic literature in order to support generalizations to broader language skills and to written language. Finally, additional research is necessary to tease apart the underlying mechanisms that contribute to positive outcomes in other language abilities such as grammatical morphology and syntax and the associated procedures that will facilitate their emergence.

Conclusion

A variety of intervention approaches are available to address the language difficulties of children with language disorders, many of which can be used in classroom settings; however, not all approaches have a sufficient research base showing their efficacy or effectiveness. Two approaches to language intervention described in this chapter, focused stimulation and story structure intervention, have reasonable research support demonstrating the positive effects that might be expected with their use. Focused stimulation involves highly concentrated delivery of targeted language forms and functions in naturalistic contexts and is typically used with toddlers and preschoolers. Story structure intervention involves explicit teaching of story grammar and other aspects of narratives using story maps and graphic organizers. Both interventions require professionals to have a well-developed understanding of a child's linguistic strengths and needs to select appropriate targets for intervention. Nonetheless, the extant literature also suggests that both interventions can be used by a range of potential interventionists, including parents, teachers, and allied professionals, such as SLPs.

CHAPTER 7

Teaching Students with Autism Spectrum Disorders

Rose Iovannone | *University of South Florida*

The education of students with autism spectrum disorders (ASD) presents ongoing and increased programming challenges to education professionals (National Research Council, 2001). Although substantial research related to autism, including etiology, characteristics, and interventions has been conducted, it remains a complex and not fully understood developmental disorder that begins at a very young age and continues throughout the lifespan of an individual. Contributing to the ongoing challenges are the widely disparate display of atypical characteristics and patterns of behavior, uneven developmental rates, diversity in responding to interventions, and reported increase in prevalence (e.g., in 2010 the Centers for Disease Control and Prevention [CDC] reported that the prevalence of ASD had risen to 1 in 110 children).

To date, the characteristics of ASD have been distributed into a triad of domain impairments consisting of social interaction, communication, and repetitive behaviors and fixated interests (American Psychiatric Association, *Diagnostic and Statistical Manual of Mental Disorders,* 4th ed. [DSM-IV], 1994). Examples of social interaction impairments include difficulties using and understanding nonverbal behavior, lack of spontaneous sharing and social-emotional reciprocity, and failure to develop peer relationships. Features of communication impairment are manifested by a delay or lack of development of spoken language, difficulty initiating and maintaining conversation, repetitive and idiosyncratic use of language, and lack of pretend play. Repetitive behaviors and fixated interests include preoccupations with restricted areas of focus, inflexible adherence to routines, recurring movements, and preoccupation with parts of objects. Although the DSM-IV provides thresholds of the number of symptoms to be displayed within each domain, the specific features and intensity of symptoms exhibited by individuals within the spectrum are heterogeneous; thus, the needs of individuals with ASD are diverse, which further contributes to the challenge of effective education. In addition to the core features used for diagnostic purposes, students with ASD manifest unique learning characteristics such as stimulus overselectivity, reduced motivation, behavioral excesses, and generalization difficulties that require specialized attention and intervention before planning instruction (Simpson & Myles, 1998).

Developing defensible instructional programs is daunting, primarily due to the paucity of agreement on appropriate practices for students with ASD (Detrich, 2008). Although the literature related to interventions for students with ASD is plentiful, it is remarkably varied, lacks a unifying theory, and can create more confusion than clarification. In addition, new, unproven treatments continue to inundate the media and Internet—treatments that require professionals and parents to differentiate between practices that have strong empirical evidence and those that have no or inadequate efficacy (Detrich, 2008).

Since the 1990s, researchers have attempted to respond to the lack of program guidance by offering reports identifying and describing the core factors shared by effective interventions for young children with ASD. Reports have originated from states and provinces (e.g., New York Department of Health, 1999; Perry & Condillac, 2003), specialized task forces and councils (e.g., Hurth, Shaw, Izeman, Whaley, & Rogers, 1999; National Research Council, 2001), and various individual authors (e.g., Dawson & Osterling, 1997; Dunlap & Robbins, 1991; Powers, 1992; Simpson, 2005). Although the outcomes of the reports are varied, researchers generally agree on the core features present in most effective programs for young children with ASD, including structured learning environments, specialized curriculum, early initiation of intervention, instructional foundation built on behavioral principles, and active family involvement. These reports have contributed valuable programming guidance to educational professionals, yet they are primarily focused on features present in early intervention programs.

More recently, the National Autism Center (2009) prepared a comprehensive report called the National Standards Project that evaluated the strength of research evidence for educational and behavioral strategies currently used for individuals with ASD, aged birth through 21 years. The report used a threshold method to establish the category of evidence for each practice. After identifying and evaluating 775 intervention articles to be included in the review, 38 treatments were identified. Four hierarchical categories provided the evidential basis, with interventions identified as (a) established, (b) emerging, (c) unestablished, or (d) ineffective/harmful. Of the 38 treatments, 11 were identified as established or having multiple studies showing effectiveness for students with ASD, 22 were classified as emerging or having few studies showing effectiveness, and 5 were assigned as unestablished or having limited or low-quality research. No treatments were identified as ineffective or harmful.

Even with the provision of the reports of recommended practices, educators continue to need specific and clear teaching guidelines to support students with ASD. An early attempt to provide such guidelines was made by Iovannone, Dunlap, Huber, and Kincaid (2003) by reviewing the literature on young children with ASD and identifying six core components of effective educational practices: (a) systematic instruction, (b) individualized supports and services, (c) comprehensible and structured learning environments, (d) specialized curriculum focus, (e) functional approach to problem behavior, and (f) family involvement. The same components were further described by Dunlap and Iovannone (2008), with additional guidelines addressing pertinent issues and the infrastructure needed when developing programs for students with ASD. This chapter provides details on two of the six components and their application in typical school contexts. Specifically, we discuss information regarding programs with specialized curricular focus (specifically, peer social-mediation techniques) and a functional approach to problem behavior (specifically, individualized positive behavior support).

Peer-Mediated Interventions to Enhance Social Skills

Social interaction difficulties of individuals with ASD have major, widespread impact on their ability to access inclusive educational and community environments and can lead to social isolation and a reduced quality of life. In comparison to their peers who are typically developing, students with ASD present with qualitatively different social behaviors that are evident at a very young age and include impairments in joint social attention, symbolic play, and nonverbal behaviors such as smiling and eye contact (Clifford & Dissanayake, 2008). As they grow older, the social difficulties students with ASD display effect play skills and social interaction overtures necessary for developing and maintaining friendships.

Given the importance of social relationships, considerable research has been devoted to exploring interventions designed to address the lack of reciprocal social behaviors. Some of the most effective practices for increasing and improving the social behaviors of learners with ASD are those in which peers are the primary interventionists and are taught to interact with specific students with ASD. A wide variety of peer-assisted or peer-mediated interventions exist and have been implemented with learners with ASD, including peer management (nonacademic), peer tutoring (academic), peer modeling, and peer participation in group contingencies (Kohler & Strain, 1990).

All of the variations of peer-mediated interventions are similar in conceptualization: They begin with identifying a student (for our purposes in this chapter, one with ASD) who has social difficulties and one (or more) typically developing peer(s) with intact social behaviors who have opportunities to frequently interact with the learner with ASD. Specific procedural training on how to interact with and support the learner with ASD is provided to the peer. After implementing the intervention with the learner with ASD, the peer is provided ongoing, systematic support and reinforcement to ensure continuation of interactions and strategies. The results of the numerous studies using peer-mediated techniques have shown that the practice is very effective in increasing social skills of students with ASD (e.g., Harper, Symon, & Frea, 2008; Owen-DeSchryver, Carr, Cale, & Blakeley-Smith, 2008; Strain, Kerr, & Ragland, 1979) as well as generalizing and sustaining social skills (e.g., C. D. Jones & Schwartz, 2004; Kamps et al., 1992; Strain & Hoyson, 2000). For the purposes of this chapter, a detailed description of Peer-Mediated Instruction and Intervention (PMI), based on a nonacademic peer-management framework, illustrates the implementation of peer-mediated interventions.

Steps of Peer-Mediated Instruction

Step 1: Get Buy-in from Faculty

Before starting PMI, it is important to have administrative, faculty, and parental support for implementing the practice. Although activities are intended to occur during social times throughout the school day, typical peers will be asked to leave their classrooms for small periods of time to receive training from adults and to serve as the social skills peer mediator for the student with ASD.

Step 2: Select Peers

Peers who are typically developing and who are close to the chronological age of the student with ASD will be recruited to participate in the intervention. Literature has identified that peers with the following characteristics are the most appropriate for participation and have the greatest promise of successful performance (Neitzel, Boyd, Odom, & Edmondson-Pretzel, 2008; Snell & Janney, 2000; Strain & Odom, 1986): competent social skills, well-respected and liked by others, present in classes with focus student or has a similar schedule (if young), ability to attend to tasks or activities at an age-appropriate duration (e.g., 5 to 10 minutes), good school attendance, history of positive interactions with the focus student, generally persistent and positive about individual differences, and willing to participate.

After acquiring parental permission for participation, cohorts of three to six peers for each focus student should be formed, with the intent of having one or two peers paired with the student with ASD for each scheduled social interaction. The cohort allows for rotation of peer pairs, which increases the focus student's acquisition and generalization of specific skills due to exposure to multiple peers over an extended period of time (i.e., minimum of 3 to 4 months). After 4 months, additional peers should be selected and added to the cohort to further enhance skill generalization (E. W. Carter & Kennedy, 2006; Utley, Mortweet, & Greenwood, 1997).

Step 3: Provide Training to Selected Peers

Once appropriate peers have been selected, a block of time is scheduled for direct training. The specific content and number of training sessions depend on the amount of time allotted, the age of the peers, and the quantity and complexity of the interventions. In general, four to five training sessions may be needed for peers to feel competent implementing the strategies with the student with ASD (Strain & Odom, 1986). Training occurs in two distinct sections: the first provides awareness of disabilities, and the second focuses on specific intervention strategies that will be implemented with the student with ASD.

Training content generally begins with appreciation of individual differences. Peers discuss similarities and differences of their friends, classmates, family members, and acquaintances. During this part of the training, a brief description of ASD is provided, specifically, behaviors related to social interaction. The training content is adjusted for the chronological age of the typical peers; for younger students, it is concrete and factual, focusing on observable behaviors, while older students may receive more information about the characteristics in addition to concrete examples. For elementary-age and older peers, relevant information about the student with ASD is also discussed, including social activity preferences that will be used in determining when peer support will be provided.

The next section of training concentrates on teaching peers the specific strategies designed to increase the social skills of the learner with ASD. It is best to present only one strategy at each session so that the peers have ample time to learn it, see it modeled by the trainer, practice it by role-playing with the trainer, and receive feedback on their performance. Examples of typical PMI strategies for young children include organizing play (e.g., "Let's play. Do you want to play with the ball or the puzzles?"), sharing (e.g., "Here is a puzzle piece. Put it in."), providing assistance (e.g., "Do you need help with that puzzle piece?"), and delivering affection and praise (e.g., "Way to go!") (Strain & Odom, 1986). At elementary and middle school grade levels, social behaviors emphasized include initiating and responding to interactions; starting, maintaining, and ending conversations; giving and accepting compliments; taking turns and sharing; asking for help and assisting others; and entering into ongoing social activities and inviting others to participate (Kamps et al., 1992; Thiemann & Goldstein, 2004). More recent literature suggests placing increased emphasis on teaching peers of all ages to make comments about activities, objects, and actions (e.g., "I like to swing." "Swinging is fun.") for the purpose of providing the student with ASD a model of conversational phrases commonly used in an age-appropriate manner (R. L. Koegel & Koegel, 2006).

Figure 7.1 Sample script for peer-mediated instruction—elementary.

Target Skill: Asking a Friend to Play

Introductory Lesson

Teacher: Today, we are going to talk about how to get Noah to play with you during recess. One way is to ask Noah to do something he likes. What is one thing Noah likes to do? (If students do not respond, prompt as necessary.)

Trained Peers: Play with trains.

Teacher: Yes, Noah likes trains. When you ask Noah to play with you, first get his attention by looking at him or touching him on the shoulder and say, *"Hey, Noah. Let's play. Here,"* and put the train in his hand. How are you going to get Noah to play with you?

Trained Peers: Get his attention, say, *"Hey, Noah, let's play. Here,"* and put the train in his hand.

Once targeted skills are selected and the activity preferences of the learner with ASD are considered, peers are asked for examples of age-appropriate words and phrases that can be used that will elicit the desired social behaviors during the preferred activities. Having peers, rather than teachers, generate the phrases ensures that the language used will be age appropriate and will be more natural and comfortable for use by the trained peers. Scripts or other visual cues can be created that include actions to perform and suggestions for responses (Sasso, Mundschenk, Melloy, & Casey, 1998). The script can also be provided as a visual prompt for engaging in the peer-mediated activities. Figure 7.1 gives an example of a script appropriate for an elementary student.

The peers use modeling and role-playing techniques to practice the strategies in relevant activities. Initially, the teacher models by role-playing the use of scripts with a peer acting the part of the student with ASD. Next, peers role-play with each other to increase competency in using the skills. The teacher provides prompts to cue peers of accurate use of the strategies and delivers feedback and reinforcement following each role-play practice.

Step 4: Introduce and Practice Strategy Implementation with Student with ASD in a Structured Social Setting

After peers are sufficiently trained, a time is scheduled to practice the strategies with the student with ASD. A brief social period (e.g., 5 to 10 minutes) is scheduled in which the teacher, similar to Step 3, presents the activity, gives cues to the peers to implement the trained strategies with the student with ASD, and provides them with reinforcement and feedback. The cueing and prompting of the trained peers has been shown to be a vital ingredient in enhancing the strategy's impact on increasing the targeted social behaviors of students with ASD (Storey, Smith, & Strain, 1993). After peers demonstrate competent use of the strategies with the student with ASD,

they can implement them in daily, natural activities with a planned fading of adult prompts and feedback.

Step 5: Implement Strategies in Naturalistic Settings

It is important to determine all of the naturally occurring social activities and routines throughout the day that present opportunities in which the trained peers will use PMI to interact with the learner with ASD. A lesson-planning matrix that identifies key events in which interactions can occur can be a valuable tool for this purpose. After determining appropriate daily opportunities for social interaction activities, the teacher chooses those that can be scheduled consistently (e.g., daily) for 10 to 15 minutes and considers preferred activities for both the focus student and peers to enhance motivation for participating. Then, the teacher selects one or two social skills to be targeted during the social session. For example, responding to play initiations and participating for a brief time (e.g., 2 minutes) can be targeted skills for an elementary student during recess time. This information is provided to the peers, along with a menu of strategies to be implemented that are appropriate for eliciting the selected behaviors. A rotating schedule, identifying which of the trained peers within the cohort will support the student with ASD during the scheduled time, is a useful tool to identify the activity, target skills, interventions, and peer schedule (see Figure 7.2 for an example).

Over time, it is important for the adult to turn more responsibility for initiating the social interactions over to the trained peers. Initially, the adult is in close proximity to the peers and provides verbal prompts, feedback, and reinforcement as necessary. As peers become more proficient in using the strategies, one way to fade support is the adults' carefully eliminating prompts and distancing themselves from physical proximity. Also, the adults can replace verbal prompts and feedback with visual cues and gradually fade the visual tools until peers are

Figure 7.2   Peer-planning form schedule.

Activity	Peer Schedule				
	Monday	Tuesday	Wednesday	Thursday	Friday
	Joey, Elijah	Joey, Gustavo	Elijah, Jeff	Gustavo, Jeff	Joey, Elijah
	Target Skills				
Free Time 10:00–10:15	Respond to request to play	Respond to request to play	Respond to request to play	Respond to request to play Take turns	Respond to request to play Take turns
Recess 12:00–12:30	Respond to request to play	Respond to request to play	Respond to request to play	Respond to request to play Take turns	Respond to request to play Take turns
Lunch 12:30–1:00	Respond a minimum of one time to a comment Use peers' names	Respond a minimum of one time to a comment Use peers' names	Respond a minimum of one time to a comment Use peers' names	Respond a minimum of one time to a comment Use peers' names	Respond a minimum of two times to a comment Use peers' names

Student: <u>Noah</u>   Peer Cohort: <u>Joey, Elijah, Gustavo, Jeff</u>   Week of: <u>10/1/13</u>

performing independently (Odom, Chandler, Ostrosky, McConnell, & Reaney, 1992).

Step 6: Evaluate, Monitor, and Provide Follow-Up Support

Data should be collected to evaluate the effectiveness of the peer-mediated intervention and the fidelity of implementation. Initially, teachers may take the primary role of collecting data, but as the adults fade out their support, the trained peers can measure the focus student's interactions as well as self-monitor their use of peer-mediated strategies. In addition, measurements of teacher fidelity in presenting the PMI procedures to peers should be reviewed. Figure 7.3 shows an example of a fidelity measure that can be used to evaluate the degree to which the teacher implemented the program.

Regularly scheduled debriefing meetings are held to provide follow-up support to the trained peers on a consistent basis. During debriefing sessions, data are reviewed to ensure that the intervention is associated with desirable outcomes for the student with ASD and that the trained peers are implementing the strategies as intended. Group problem solving and identification of any needed adaptations, as well as development of next steps, also occur within the recurring meetings. Trained peers can give their perspective on additional social interaction goals that are relevant for the targeted student with ASD and suggest intervention strategies. Achievements are celebrated during this meeting, and trained peers are provided reinforcement. Although most peer mediators are intrinsically reinforced, it is recommended that various forms of recognition be provided to peers for the time and efforts they exert. Some examples of appropriate reinforcement include verbal praise for specific activities, certificates of recognition, or social events with food that can take place at the end of problem-solving meetings.

Research Support

The extant literature includes numerous research studies examining the effectiveness of PMI to increase, sustain, and generalize social interaction skills of students with ASD. The majority of the studies have focused on young children (i.e., preschool), although recent years have shown an emerging research base examining the use of PMI with older students (i.e., 6 to 13 years of age). Studies focused on young children have shown that PMI is effective in increasing the number and the duration of reciprocal social interactions between children with ASD and trained peers as well as the number of social initiations for play (e.g., Kohler, Greteman, Raschke, & Highnam, 2007; C. Nelson, McDonnell, Hohnston, Crompton, & Nelson, 2007). Studies targeting elementary-aged students have used PMI strategies to increase social engagement while concurrently decreasing stereotypic behaviors (S. Lee, Odom, & Loftin, 2007), to increase social communication skills of students with high-functioning ASD (Chung et al., 2007), and to enhance social overtures between students with ASD and peers in inclusive settings (Owen-DeSchryver et al., 2008). Studies have explored using a combination of

Figure 7.3 Sample fidelity measure for peer-mediated instruction.

Teacher: <u>Smith</u>   Student: <u>Noah</u>   Date: <u>10/5/13</u>

Type of Measure (circle): <u>Observation</u> <u>Self-Assessment</u>

Procedures	Was the step implemented?	Fidelity Score *Y = 1* *N = 0* *NA = NA*
1. Obtained faculty buy-in	Y/N/NA	
2. Recruited multiple peers (3–5 per target student) to participate	Y/N/NA	
3. Obtained parental consent	Y/N/NA	
4. Scheduled training sessions for peers	Y/N/NA	
5. Determined daily activities/routines in which peers and Noah will implement PMI	Y/N/NA	
6. Prepared and gathered all necessary materials for training peers	Y/N/NA	
7. Presented training on appreciation of individual differences to peers	Y/N/NA	
8. Discussed reasons for PMI, expectations, and responsibilities with peers	Y/N/NA	
9. Introduced target skills and presented strategies/script	Y/N/NA	
10. Engaged peers to practice by Q&A and demonstration	Y/N/NA	
11. Engaged peers in role-playing exercises with teacher	Y/N/NA	
12. Engaged peers in role-playing exercises with each other	Y/N/NA	
13. Provided prompts/cues to peers as necessary	Y/N/NA	
14. Delivered appropriate reinforcement to peers and feedback	Y/N/NA	
15. Conducted debriefing session at end of lesson, and provided specific reinforcement and feedback	Y/N/NA	
16. Scheduled a time for peers to practice with Noah before beginning PMI in scheduled routines	Y/N/NA	
17. Provided prompts/cues to peers as necessary	Y/N/NA	
18. Delivered appropriate reinforcement to peers and feedback	Y/N/NA	
19. Conducted debriefing session at end of lesson and provided specific reinforcement and feedback	Y/N/NA	
20. Upon implementation, provided ongoing support to peers by giving them scripts, cues, and other tools to be used	Y/N/NA	
21. Provided prompts/cues to peers as necessary	Y/N/NA	
22. Delivered appropriate reinforcement to peers and feedback	Y/N/NA	
23. Conducted debriefing session at end of lesson, and provided specific reinforcement and feedback	Y/N/NA	
24. Held problem-solving meetings (weekly/biweekly) with peers to celebrate, discuss status, and decide on next steps	Y/N/NA	
25. Systematically faded level of support as peer competence increased	Y/N/NA	
26. Used rotating schedule of peer trainers and identified targeted skills within activities	Y/N/NA	
Implementation Score **(Total Y's/Total Y's + N's in column)**		

Note: Y = 1; N = 0; NA = not applicable.

PMI and pivotal response training during recess to increase social skills (Blauvelt-Harper, Symon, & Frea, 2008) and to explore the effectiveness of using multiple peer trainers to generalize intervention effects (Pierce &

Schreibman, 1997). Thiemann and Goldstein (2004) extended the PMI research by combining it with written text cues to increase the number and quality of social interactions as well as to improve specific social behaviors.

In comparison to studies conducted with young children, relatively fewer studies have explored the effectiveness of PMI with older students (e.g., middle school, high school). However, Morrison, Kamps, Garcia, and Parker (2001) conducted a study that included four students with ASD whose ages were from 10 to 13 years. A group of peers were trained in PMI and self-monitoring strategies. Results indicated that the combination of PMI and self-monitoring increased the quantity of social initiations and length of social interactions along with specific social skill behaviors of the students with ASD.

Finally, Strain and Hoyson (2000) reported on the longitudinal outcomes of a comprehensive intervention approach, Learning Experiences: An Alternative Program for Preschoolers and Parents (LEAP), for children with ASD. The LEAP model, described in detail in Hoyson, Jamieson, and Strain (1984), includes daily peer-mediated interventions embedded in multiple social opportunities throughout the day. Data collected over a period of several years from six children with ASD who were the first recipients of the LEAP procedures showed an increase of intervals engaged in positive social interactions from entry into the program (2%) to exit (23%) and sustainability at age 10 (24%), lending further support for the use of peer trainers to improve and generalize appropriate social behaviors.

In summary, PMI strategies have been effective in increasing the social competence skills of students with ASD. The technique has been successfully used for young students (e.g., preschool) and for older students (e.g., elementary school, middle school). The technology is well developed, is feasible for use by typical school personnel, and is suitable for application in an expansive range of environments.

Functional Approach to Problem Behaviors

Students with ASD frequently display problem behaviors that can be a formidable challenge to address through typical behavior interventions used by teachers. Limited communication skills as well as deficits in social behaviors contribute to the unique types and quality of behavior problems experienced by students with ASD (Heal, Borthwick-Duffy, & Saunders, 1996; R. L. Koegel, Koegel, & Surratt, 1992). Typographies of problem behavior are varied and can include self-injury, pica, tantrums, physical aggression, disruptions, noncompliance, and stereotypy (R. H. Horner, Diemer, & Brazeau, 1992; Reichle, 1990). Problem behaviors are often cited as the primary reason for excluding students with ASD from inclusive educational and community settings and

serve as a barrier in delivering effective and meaningful educational instruction (Sprague & Rian, 1993).

An impressive body of research has been conducted on the effectiveness of using function-based supports to decrease problem behaviors and increase prosocial, appropriate behaviors for students with ASD (National Research Council, 2001). In recent decades, the field has shifted focus from contingency-based interventions to delivering more comprehensive behavior approaches that emphasize contextual adjustments to prevent problem behaviors; teach new, appropriate replacement skills; and change the way others respond to behaviors so that the new skills will be reinforced and repeated and problem behaviors will be extinguished (Carr et al., 2002).

The emerging approach, referred to as *positive behavior support (PBS),* is based on the wealth of applied research taken from the core concepts of operant learning theory (e.g., J. O. Cooper, Heron, & Heward, 2007; B. F. Skinner, 1953) and principles of ecological and contextual systems theories that have contributed to the current work in school-based positive behavior support (Carr et al., 2002). The theory is framed within a three-pronged contingency model in which antecedent (i.e., environmental) events set the stage for problem behavior occurrence that is immediately followed by consequences (e.g., positive reinforcer, punishment) that either strengthen or weaken the behavior (Harrower, Fox, Dunlap, & Kincaid, 2000).

As a first step to intervention in a PBS approach, a functional behavior assessment (FBA) is conducted to identify the contextual conditions eliciting problem behavior and resulting consequences that serve to reinforce and maintain problem behavior. This information leads to development of a hypothesis from which a function-based support plan is built that includes the identification and manipulation of three key components: (a) antecedents associated with identified patterns of responding to prevent problem behavior; (b) strategies for teaching new skills to replace problem behaviors; and (c) consequences, particularly contingent positive reinforcement. The aim is to promote conditions that allow new, appropriate behaviors to occur more frequently and to change responses to problem behavior in order to render them no longer effective or efficient for obtaining the desired outcome (i.e., escape, obtain). Individualized PBS expands on traditional behavioral interventions by collaborating with stakeholders (i.e., teachers), ensuring that interventions have social and ecological validity and contextual fit, and broadening the targeted goals of intervention that impact quality of life (Carr et al., 2002).

Recently, a randomized controlled trial exploring the efficacy of implementing a standardized model of function-based behavior intervention based on the components of PBS was conducted, and outcomes indicated that students receiving the intervention, Prevent-Teach-Reinforce (PTR), had significantly improved outcomes in comparison to the students who received "services as usual" (Iovannone et al., 2009). The intervention is manualized (Dunlap, Iovannone, Kincaid, et al., 2010), with the steps feasible for use by typical school personnel in school settings and detailed in such a way they can be implemented with fidelity across settings. The PTR model, a functional approach to problem behavior, consists of five basic steps that are common to most FBA approaches: (a) forming a team, (b) identifying goals of intervention, (c) conducting an FBA and developing a hypothesis, (d) building a comprehensive function-based support plan, and (e) evaluating and monitoring the impact of the behavior support plan. The following section provides details for each step.

Steps of a Function-Based Approach to Problem Behavior

Step 1: Forming a Team

A team is formed that includes people who have a vested interest in improving the life of the focus student and who will be committed to actively participating in the process. The team includes individuals who have direct knowledge of the student's behavior, such as the primary classroom teacher, paraeducators, primary caregivers, and others with whom the student interacts consistently (e.g., teachers of art, music, PE; speech pathologists; related service providers). In addition, the team includes at least one person who has knowledge of behavioral principles and experience in facilitating FBAs (e.g., school psychologist, special educator, behavior analyst/specialist, guidance counselor, social worker), as well as an individual who has knowledge of the context in which the interventions will be implemented and has the ability to access resources (e.g., administrator).

To enhance team cohesiveness, the roles and responsibilities of each team member should be established before participating in any activities. Deciding the manner in which each team member will provide input and determining how consensus will be reached will increase the likelihood that meetings will be run efficiently and effectively in an environment that is collaborative and nonthreatening. One team member who has competence in collaborative consultation techniques and has a sound knowledge of behavioral principles should be designated as the facilitator.

Step 2: Identifying Goals of Intervention

The primary purpose of Step 2 is to identify and define the behaviors of greatest concern as the targets of intervention. During this step, the team will develop a method of collecting data that is simple to use yet provides enough information to make decisions about the impact of the intervention on student behavior change. Team members identify both the problem behaviors they wish to see decreased, as well as appropriate behaviors to be increased. Once they identify those behaviors, the team clearly describes them in operational terms that are observable and measurable. The definition includes the physical and auditory behaviors that the student performs when engaged in the problem behavior. For example, if the team identifies tantrums as a problem behavior of concern, team members list the behaviors they have observed the student doing when he is engaged in tantrums and develop an operational definition. For one team, tantrum behaviors may include screaming at a high pitch and volume, dropping body to the floor on back, and kicking feet against persons who approach. Another student's tantrum behavior may be defined differently, depending on the actual behaviors exhibited during the episodes.

After the team identifies and defines behaviors, they prioritize the behaviors that are of greatest concern. Although FBA processes can be conducted for more than one problem behavior, it can be quite time-consuming and possibly overwhelming to do so; therefore, the team may wish to start with the one or two behaviors that are considered the most disruptive or severe and are reducing the student's access to inclusive environments and educational instruction.

Next, the team agrees on methods of collecting data on the targeted behaviors and establishes a data plan that includes who will collect the data and how often. Data should be collected frequently (i.e., minimum two times a week, with daily collection preferred) and in a way that is both practical for the teacher and sensitive to behavior variations. Although many observational data methods exist (i.e., interval, partial interval, time sampling), not all teachers are adequately trained to use these techniques, and they can be time-consuming. An emerging method for assessing social behavior, called Direct Behavior Rating (DBR), has been the subject of several recent studies. DBR is a hybrid data technology combining features of systematic direct observation with the efficiency of rating scales (Chafouleas, Riley-Tillman, & Christ, 2009). With DBR, an individual observes the student's behavior and evaluates it by rating its occurrence using a Likert-type scale with anchors representing a standardized coding system (Pelham, Fabiano, & Massetti, 2005). For example, a 5-point scale can be created in which anchor 5 represents the most undesirable presence of the behavior (i.e., excessive frequency, duration, or intensity), a 3 can represent an average presence for that particular student, and a 1

Figure 7.4   Sample behavior rating scale.

Student: <u>Noah</u>   Teacher: <u>Smith</u>   Routine/time for measurement: <u>Transition from preferred to nonpreferred activities</u>

Behavior		Date																		
Screaming	Ear penetrating		5	5	5	5	5	5	5	5	5	5	5	5	5	5	5	5	5	5
	Outside voice		4	4	4	4	4	4	4	4	4	4	4	4	4	4	4	4	4	4
	Loud inside voice		3	3	3	3	3	3	3	3	3	3	3	3	3	3	3	3	3	3
	Inside voice		2	2	2	2	2	2	2	2	2	2	2	2	2	2	2	2	2	2
	Soft squeal		1	1	1	1	1	1	1	1	1	1	1	1	1	1	1	1	1	1
Hitting	≥5 times		5	5	5	5	5	5	5	5	5	5	5	5	5	5	5	5	5	5
	4 times		4	4	4	4	4	4	4	4	4	4	4	4	4	4	4	4	4	4
	3 times		3	3	3	3	3	3	3	3	3	3	3	3	3	3	3	3	3	3
	2 times		2	2	2	2	2	2	2	2	2	2	2	2	2	2	2	2	2	2
	0–1 time		1	1	1	1	1	1	1	1	1	1	1	1	1	1	1	1	1	1
Asking for a Break	≥5 times		5	5	5	5	5	5	5	5	5	5	5	5	5	5	5	5	5	5
	4 times		4	4	4	4	4	4	4	4	4	4	4	4	4	4	4	4	4	4
	3 times		3	3	3	3	3	3	3	3	3	3	3	3	3	3	3	3	3	3
	2 times		2	2	2	2	2	2	2	2	2	2	2	2	2	2	2	2	2	2
	0–1 time		1	1	1	1	1	1	1	1	1	1	1	1	1	1	1	1	1	1

Note: Definitions of Behaviors: Screaming—high pitched, loud piercing cry; Hitting—open-handed slap, pinching delivered to peers and adults; Asking for a break—using voice-output device to ask for a break when transitioning from preferred to nonpreferred activities.

can represent the goal of intervention. An example of a DBR is shown in Figure 7.4. The scale is individualized and reflects the team's prioritized problem and appropriate behaviors, operational definitions, and estimates of behavioral occurrence. The scale can be used to measure behavior presence during a specific routine or time (e.g., centers, math class, writing activities, independent work time), a partial day (e.g., morning, afternoon), or the entire day. At the end of the specified time period, the teacher simply circles the rating that best represents her estimate of behavior performance. Recent studies have shown that DBR has the potential of being both efficient and a reliable and valid method of teacher data collection (Riley-Tillman, Chafouleas, Sassu, Chanese, & Glazer, 2008).

Step 3: Conducting a Functional Behavior Assessment and Developing a Hypothesis

The primary purposes of an FBA are to identify the environmental events consistently associated with the presence of problem and appropriate behaviors, to identify the function(s) of the problem behavior in the specific events, and to lay the framework for building an effective behavior support plan (O'Neill et al., 1997). Since the late 1990s the field of special education has seen an increased focus on developing FBA procedures and accompanying tools that are "school-friendly" while adhering to the foundational behavioral theory. The techniques include development of forms to record direct observations (e.g., O'Neill et al., 1997) and creation of indirect procedures such as checklists and interviews (e.g., Dunlap, Iovannone, Kincaid, et al., 2010; T. M. Scott & Nelson, 1999). In determining the resources to commit to conducting the FBA, the team should attempt to match the intensity of the method with the intensity of the problem behavior (i.e., more severe and complicated problem behavior warrants more intense FBA resources). Regardless of the intensity of the FBA method selected, the assessment should include a way of identifying the events and contexts in which the target problem behavior occurs and does not occur and the consequences or responses that follow the problem behavior.

After the FBA data are collected, the team organizes the information, identifies patterns, and develops a hypothesis statement that summarizes the patterns and surmises the function of the problem behavior. The subsequent hypothesis statement will include, at a minimum, three distinct components: (a) the antecedents to the problem behaviors, (b) the specific behavior that is the focus of the FBA, and (c) the purpose or function of the behavior. An example of a hypothesis statement is:

> *When presented with an academic demand to start a nonpreferred activity or when transitioning from a preferred to a nonpreferred activity, Noah will scream at a high pitch and loud volume for an extended amount of time. As a result, he delays the nonpreferred activity or transition and gets adult attention.*

Once the team reaches consensus on the hypothesis, they are ready to begin to build a function-based support plan.

Step 4: Building a Comprehensive Function-Based Support Plan

After completion of the hypothesis statement, the team develops an individualized behavior support plan. The plan includes strategies linked to the hypothesis components (a) to prevent the problem behavior from occurring, (b) to teach new and appropriate skills that replace the problem behavior, and (c) to arrange responding consequences that reinforce the performance of the new skill so that it is repeated and reinforcement of the problem behavior discontinues.

Prevention strategies aim to alter the circumstances related to behavioral occurrence (i.e., antecedents) in a way that makes the event less aversive, thereby eliminating a need for the student to perform the target behavior. Taking our hypothesis example in the preceding section, one antecedent situation identified is transition from preferred to nonpreferred activities. In this case, the team will design support strategies that modify the transition so that it no longer is a predicting event occasioning the problem behavior. Examples of transitional support interventions are providing visual or auditory transition warnings, developing a visual support (e.g., visual schedule) that prepares the student for transitions, presenting visual checklists or auditory supports that describe appropriate transition behaviors, or giving the student some choices about how the transition will occur.

When the team selects the new skill to be taught that replaces the problem behavior, they carefully consider the function of the behavior and discuss appropriate, alternate ways of getting the same outcomes (e.g., escape; delay or avoidance of an activity, a person, an object, or sensory stimuli; obtaining access to an activity, attention from others, an object, or a sensory event). For example, if a student is screaming to protest and delay a nonpreferred activity, the team would decide which behavior they would prefer the student to perform that would result

in the same outcome (delay the nonpreferred activity) but in an acceptable method. In this case, the team may want to teach the student to request a brief delay of the transition or ask for a time to calm down before transitioning. In selecting the replacement behavior, the team ensures that it is a skill that is already present in the student's repertoire and can be performed as effortlessly as the problem behavior.

Finally, the team develops a strategy to reinforce the use of the replacement skill. Again, they use the function listed on the hypothesis as a guide in identifying an effective approach. That is, if the student's hypothesized function of the problem behavior is to escape, and the new skill they will teach the student is to ask for a break, the reinforcement strategy is to grant the student's request and permit a short delay. In addition to identifying the reinforcement that follows student use of the replacement behavior, the team also considers how to change the current method of responding when the problem behavior occurs so that it defeats the behavior's function. For example, if the student was removed to a cool down after displaying problem behavior resulting in a delay of a nonpreferred activity, the new response strategy may be for the teacher to calmly and efficiently redirect or prompt the student to use the new request for break behavior. When developing the reinforcement strategy, the team carefully ensures that the new behavior results in the student's getting the outcome just as quickly and efficiently as did the problem behavior.

Effective behavior support plans describe each of the intervention strategies with enough detail so that the teacher and any other staff or interventionist understands its implementation. This may be effectively achieved by task analyzing each intervention and including when to do the intervention, what to say to the student, and the specific physical actions that comprise the strategy. To enhance the likelihood of teacher willingness to implement the strategies, careful attention should be given to the classroom context so that the intervention developed is one that is feasible for teachers to do within the classroom dynamics and matched to their skill levels. Moreover, methods for training the teacher how to use the strategy should be prescribed as a part of the plan. Figure 7.5 shows a sample function-based intervention plan developed for the hypothesis described in Step 3.

The next consideration for Step 4 is to plan how the team will provide the teacher with follow-up support and ensure that the interventions are being implemented with fidelity. As discussed in the PMI section, before making any changes to the intervention plan or probing reasons for lack of impact of the plan on student behavior, it is important to first decide if the interventions are being

Figure 7.5 Sample function-based support plan.

Hypothesis: *When presented with an academic demand to start a nonpreferred activity or when transitioning from a preferred to a nonpreferred activity, Noah will scream at a high pitch and loud volume for an extended amount of time. As a result, he delays the nonpreferred activity or transition and he gets adult attention.*

Prevent Interventions	*Teach Interventions*	*Reinforce Interventions*
Providing Choices Noah will be given choices before transitioning from preferred to nonpreferred activities. Choices will be from the following: (a) within—Noah can choose the materials he will use to do the activities; (b) when—Noah can choose the sequence of activities. Steps: 1. Immediately before transitioning, tell Noah, *"Noah, for* (nonpreferred activity), *do you want to use the marker or the pencil to do* (activity)? OR *"Noah, we have 3 things to do in the math center* (show the mini-task schedule icons). *Which do you want to do first?* (Have Noah put icon selected in the first spot on the mini-task schedule.) *Which do you want to do second?* Repeat sequence. 2. Have Noah put each completed activity in the finished pocket.	**Replacement Behavior: Ask for a break** Noah will be taught to ask for a break using his voice-output device (VOD) and will select what he needs to calm down. Steps: 1. Immediately before a transition to a nonpreferred activity, prompt Noah to use his VOD to ask for a break by saying, *"Noah, do you need a break?"* 2. Initially, physically prompt Noah to push the icon for break by using hand-over-hand. 3. When Noah presses the break icon, say *"Noah, you asked for a break. What do you need to calm down?"* Present him with the choices. 4. Initially use hand-over-hand prompting to assist Noah in selecting his calming activity. 5. After he selects the activity say, *"Noah, calm down with a break for 1 minute."*	**Reinforce Replacement Behavior: Ask for a break** Each time Noah asks for a break, honor his request and choices. Steps: 1. When Noah requests a break, say *"Thank you for asking for a break."* 2. When Noah selects his calming activity say, *"Thank you for telling us what you need to calm down."* 3. Use flat affect, flat verbal tone when Noah requests break and choices. Do not provide attention while he is engaged in his calming activity. 4. Use a warm tone of voice with all other peers while Noah is engaged in calming activity. 5. When Noah transitions from the calming activity to the nonpreferred activity, warmly say, *"Thank you, Noah, for joining us!"* **Discontinue Reinforcing Problem Behavior** If Noah engages in screaming or hitting, redirect him to use his VOD to request a break. Steps: 1. Using flat affect and no eye contact, physically prompt Noah to use his VOD to request a break. Say, *"What do you need?"* 2. Repeat sequence for replacement behavior.

implemented accurately. Figure 7.6 provides a fidelity measure sample that can be used as an observational measure as well as a self-assessment. Once it is confirmed that the plan is doable and is implemented with fidelity by the teacher, the team is ready to evaluate the effectiveness of the plan.

Step 5: Evaluating and Monitoring the Impact of the Behavior Support Plan

The evaluation and monitoring step establishes a plan for evaluating the effectiveness of the supports on the student behavior and for making data-based decisions about whether and how to change the behavior support plan. Student outcome data, used consistently throughout Steps 2 through 5, are reviewed to determine whether behavior change is headed in the desired direction. If

behavior is changing as desired, several options are available for the next steps. Teams may decide to expand the interventions for use in other times or routines, systematically fade components of the intervention, or identify another behavior target and add to the plan. The latter option is particularly appealing in cases of multiple behaviors occurring under different situations for different functions. By building on the plan gradually, it is less likely the teacher and/or student will be overwhelmed.

If the student's behavior data indicate a trend that is undesirable, showing no change or worsening of the situation, the team should first examine the fidelity data and, if necessary, address implementation issues. If the fidelity data indicate the teacher has consistently implemented the plan as intended, but the student data show no improvement, the team should revisit the FBA data and hypothesis to determine if the function

Figure 7.6   Sample fidelity measure for function-based support plan.

Intervention Strategies	Was the step implemented?	Fidelity Score Y = 1 N = 0 NA = NA
Prevent Intervention—Providing Choices with Mini-Task Schedule		
1. Presented a valid choice (within or when)	Y/N/NA	
2. Presented the choice prior to transition from preferred to nonpreferred activity	Y/N/NA	
3. Honored the choices	Y/N/NA	
Teach Intervention—Replacement Behavior—Ask for a Break		
1. Prior to transitioning from preferred to nonpreferred activity, prompted Noah to request a break using his Voice Output Device	Y/N/NA	
2. After requesting a break, prompted Noah to select the activity/object for his break time	Y/N/NA	
Reinforce Intervention—Reinforced Replacement Behavior		
1. Immediately after requesting a break, presented the choice activities for calming down	Y/N/NA	
2. Immediately after Noah makes his choice, released him to the activity	Y/N/NA	
3. Used a flat affect and minimal attention while engaged in choice	Y/N/NA	
4. Used a warm tone with peers while Noah engaged in choice	Y/N/NA	
5. Welcomed Noah with a warm tone upon ending break and transitioning to the activity	Y/N/NA	
Discontinue Reinforcing Problem Behavior		
1. If Noah engaged in screaming or hitting behaviors, used flat affect, no eye contact, and minimal verbage to redirect him to use his VOD to request a break.	Y/N/NA	
Implementation Score **(Total Y's/Total Y's + N's in column)**		

Note: Y = 1; N = 0; NA = not applicable.

is correct. For example, suppose the hypothesized function of a student's screaming behavior was to get attention and the plan included a replacement behavior designed to allow the student attention. However, if the primary function of screaming was actually to escape, the plan then does not match the purpose of the behavior. By changing the replacement behavior to one that allows the student escape and examining the student data after the new intervention is implemented, the team can then determine the accuracy of the new hypothesis. A new FBA may need to be conducted, particularly if the behavior is significantly intense and/or occurs in multiple contexts with multiple functions. The team would then develop a revised or new behavior support plan based on the new FBA data and resulting hypothesis.

It is important for the team to continue to review both student performance and fidelity data throughout the process. The information allows the team to make data-based decisions for continuing, discontinuing, or changing the support plan. Using data allows the team to document areas of weakness within the plan, evaluate student progress toward desired goals, identify interventions that require supplemental teacher training, and determine next steps.

Research Support

Addressing problem behaviors through the functional behavior process has been repeatedly documented as effective by extant literature. Functional approaches have been effectively used with students with ASD for a wide range of problem behaviors such as physical aggression and self-injurious behaviors (Christensen et al., 2009; O'Reilly, Sigafoos, Lancioni, Edrisinha, & Andrews, 2005), elopement (Perrin, Perrin, Hill, & DiNovi, 2008), and compliance (Stager, Singer, & Horner, 1987). Research using individualized function-based supports for students with ASD has examined the effectiveness of use by people holding diverse roles including speech-language pathologists (Bopp, Brown, & Mirenda, 2004), families (Lucyshyn et al., 2007; Najdowski et al., 2008; Smith-Bird & Turnbull, 2005), as well as preschool program staff (Duda, Dunlap, Fox, Lentini, & Clarke, 2004). FBA-derived strategies have been shown to be effective for a wide age range including young children (Dunlap & Fox, 1999), elementary-aged students (Lang et al., 2008), and adolescents (Butler & Luiselli, 2007).

More recently, Iovannone et al. (2009) and Dunlap, Iovannone, Wilson, et al. (2010) reported on a randomized controlled trial that examined the effectiveness of a model of function-based supports, PTR, as compared to services as usual for students in grades K–8. Although the study's sample of 245 did not focus solely on students with ASD, they were represented with 24 students (10% of the participants). Results of the study showed that students receiving the PTR intervention increased their social skills and academic engagement, and decreased their problem behaviors at a significant degree, when compared with their control counterparts.

Summary

The literature related to students with ASD is diverse and often consists of unfounded recommendations. The recent attempts to describe and define practices that are supported by research are helpful for the field in selecting interventions. This chapter describes two strategies that have been shown to be efficacious through a multitude of studies. Although the method in which the strategies will be included in educational programs must be flexible to meet the diversity of characteristics displayed by students with ASD, the steps described for each provide a firm foundation for delivery of effective instruction for these students.

It is imperative that educators become proficient in applying social and behavior interventions. Outside of families, education is the main source of treatment for students with ASD (National Research Council, 2001). Educational environments provide wide-ranging natural opportunities for meaningful social exchanges and appropriate behavior skills that will build mastery. In addition, the deficits in social skills and behaviors experienced by individuals with ASD impact all areas of human life (National Research Council, 2001). Without receiving instruction in these core areas, students with ASD will have marked difficulties making and sustaining friendships, engaging in activities with others, gaining access to inclusive environments, engaging in academic instruction, securing or keeping competitive employment, and attaining a high quality of life. Both of the interventions described in this chapter—peer-mediated interventions to enhance social skills and a functional approach to problem behavior—have shown to fit contextually within typical school settings, are easy for teachers to learn, and can be generalized to multiple environments. Both are individualized to meet unique student needs and circumstances and include tools to monitor progress and treatment fidelity. Certainly, more research will be conducted in the future to further substantiate these approaches as research-based strategies; however, both interventions currently enjoy a well-established infrastructure of research support and technology as well as guidelines for implementation that should prove helpful for educational professionals and lead to important life-altering outcomes for students with ASD.

CHAPTER 8

Effective Practices for Promoting Literacy with Individuals Who Have Physical Disabilities

Mari Beth Coleman | *University of Tennessee*

Kathryn Wolff Heller | *Georgia State University*

Reading and writing skills are critical for participation in school, employment, and life activities. Literacy opens doors to academic success; concept development; career possibilities; personal fulfillment; and, in this age of ever-expanding technology, access to real-time information, multimodal text experiences, and social networking (Barone & Wright, 2008; Browning, 2002; Hansford & Adlington, 2009). For individuals who have physical disabilities that impact their ability to perform manual tasks, the ability to read and write is even more essential with regard to an individual's being included in less-restrictive educational settings, finding employment, having access to resources and information, and participating in leisure activities (Heller, Coleman-Martin, & Swinehart-Jones, 2006; Peterson-Karlan, Hourcade, & Parette, 2008). When speech limitations accompany a physical disability, literacy becomes crucial for an individual to be able to communicate (Heller, 2010). This chapter discusses the barriers to literacy experienced by individuals with physical disabilities and two literacy interventions that have a small, but important, research base with this population: the Nonverbal Reading

Approach and the use of assistive technology to promote writing.

Characteristics of Individuals with Physical Disabilities That Impede Literacy Acquisition

The causes and impacts of physical disabilities are, quite possibly, more varied than in any other disability category. Even two individuals who have the same diagnosis (e.g., spastic quadriplegic cerebral palsy) may be on extreme ends between mild and profound in terms of their physical limitations and cognitive abilities (Heller, 2009b). The term referring to physical disabilities in federal legislation is *orthopedic impairments*. The Individuals with Disabilities Education Improvement Act of 2004 provides this definition:

> Orthopedic impairment means a severe orthopedic impairment that adversely affects a child's educational performance. The term includes impairments caused

by congenital anomaly (e.g., clubfoot, absence of some member, etc.), impairments caused by disease (e.g., poliomyelitis, bone tuberculosis, etc.), and impairments from other causes (e.g., cerebral palsy, amputations, and fractures or burns that cause contractures). [20 U.S.C. § 1401 (3); 1401(30)]

Orthopedic impairment is a disability category in which services across different states and even different school systems vary tremendously. Less than one third of states continue to have separate licensure for teachers of students with orthopedic impairments. Often, the cross-categorical certification of special educators creates a situation where students with physical disabilities are served in less-restrictive environments by teachers who are not prepared to deal with their physical, health, and disability-related educational needs, or they are placed in classrooms where their physical and health needs can be met but the instruction does not sufficiently challenge them cognitively and academically (Heller & Swinehart-Jones, 2003). Heller, Fredrick, Dykes, Best, and Cohen (1999) found that one third of cross-categorically licensed teachers who were directly responsible for teaching students with physical disabilities reported feeling unprepared in 60% of the knowledge and skills identified as critical for working with this population. Because students with physical disabilities often require specialized instruction and adaptations to succeed in reading and writing, it is critical to identify interventions that overcome barriers to learning faced by these students and to disseminate knowledge of these strategies to teachers responsible for providing their literacy instruction.

A number of barriers impede successful literacy acquisition for people who have physical disabilities, and these must be addressed in the context of literacy instruction. Barriers to literacy vary depending on the type of disability (e.g., neuromotor impairment, degenerative condition), functional impact of the disability (e.g., sensory loss, health and endurance factors, background experiences), psychosocial impact on the individual (e.g., self-concept, behavioral and emotional functioning), and environmental factors (e.g., physical, learning, and attitudinal barriers) (Heller, 2009a).

The type of disability may have an impact on an individual's acquisition of literacy skills. Neuromotor impairments resulting from damage to the brain (e.g., cerebral palsy, traumatic brain injury) or requiring intracranial medical intervention (e.g., shunting for hydrocephaly in individuals with spina bifida) might result in learning difficulties more significant than a musculoskeletal disability (e.g., scoliosis, arthritis) (Iddon, Morgan, Loveday, Sahakian, & Pickard, 2004; Vermeer & Dekker, 1993). Whereas the physical impact of a neuromotor impairment initially may be more significant than that of a degenerative condition (e.g., muscular

dystrophy, spinal muscular atrophy), issues surrounding the loss of abilities and death and dying may have an impact on a child's progress in learning literacy (Heller, Mezei, & Schwartzman, 2009). The type of disability also plays a role in learning because of the specific functional effects of different disabilities.

Many physical disabilities result in the loss of functional abilities due to atypical motor patterns or restricted motor abilities (Heller, 2009a). The inability to engage with reading and writing materials and to explore the surrounding environment poses important obstacles in early development of literacy skills and basic concepts. The early print experiences of young children without disabilities are very different from those of children with severe physical disabilities. Often, young children will select books from the bookshelf, crawl up into an adult's lap, and engage in a shared reading experience. Children with physical disabilities often do not have the ability to select materials or turn pages in a book, and their parents may have difficulty holding them in their laps while reading. These factors make early literacy learning different for children with physical disabilities. When another barrier, impaired speech, is present, early literacy learning becomes increasingly adult directed. Young children often request the same book repeatedly; however, children who have both physical and verbal limitations cannot do so and thus miss out on the repeated exposure to text that is so important for development of early literacy skills (Heller & Coleman-Martin, 2007). Different early literacy experiences paired with different experiences of the surrounding world (e.g., not playing in the dirt or going to the mall because of mobility difficulties) can play a major factor in the development of concepts necessary for reading comprehension and written productivity.

Many physical disabilities, such as cerebral palsy and spina bifida, are accompanied by concomitant impairments such as decreased visual acuity or visual perception and problems related to memory, attention, or cognitive processing (Junkala & Talbot, 1982; Rowley-Kelly & Reigel, 1993). Finally, functional effects that may impact literacy development of individuals with physical disabilities include physical and health factors such as fatigue, lack of endurance, pain, and medication effects (Heller, 2009a). These functional barriers often contribute to or interact with psychosocial and environmental factors to impair development of reading and writing abilities.

Psychosocial factors such as behavioral, emotional, and social functioning; motivation; and self-efficacy can play a part in reading and writing for individuals with physical disabilities. Behavioral challenges can arise from ineffective discipline and decreased expectations related to the presence of a disability. Some individuals with physical disabilities have lower self-concept or self-esteem that can impact performance in academics or life activities (Heller, 2009a). They may fail to develop appropriate social skills because of isolation or decreased social opportunities (G. A. King, Schultz, Steel, Gilpin, & Cathers, 1993; Magill-Evans & Restall, 1991). Lower self-efficacy and higher levels of learned helplessness have been noted in individuals with physical disabilities, which may impact motivation to read and write (Heller, 2009a; S. F. Tam, 2000). Because learning happens through social engagement with adults and peers, all of these psychosocial factors may have a direct impact on the development of literacy skills.

Finally, environmental barriers such as decreased access to materials, limited participation, ineffective learning environments, and decreased expectations can impede an individual with a physical disability from achieving his full potential in reading and writing (Heller, 2009a). When upper limb function is impaired or problems with positioning are present, access to books and other printed materials as well as writing utensils or keyboards may be limited. Hemmingson and Borell (2002) found that barriers of time, pace, and space had a detrimental effect on the participation in general education classrooms by children with physical disabilities. Because the general education classroom must accommodate large numbers of students, the pace of instruction and amount of time devoted to mastery learning and the amount of space devoted to accessibility may not meet the needs of students with significant physical disabilities. Mike (1995) found that as little as 30 minutes per day was allocated for literacy instruction in a classroom for students with severe physical disabilities because of the increased focus on meeting the physical and health needs of the students.

As previously mentioned, most states do not have certification in orthopedic impairments. Thus, teacher-preparation programs in those states may not provide specific training in teaching literacy to students with physical disabilities. Even in states that continue to have separate teacher licensure in this area, some school systems do not have teachers who are trained to provide literacy instruction that meets the specific needs of students with physical disabilities. One other environmental factor is the incorrect assumption by many people that physical disability is always accompanied by limited learning capacity, which may lead to decreased expectations and inappropriate literacy instruction for students who have physical disabilities.

To reiterate, numerous potential barriers to learning reading and writing exist for individuals who have physical disabilities. Depending on the type of disability, an individual may experience one or more functional or psychosocial effects that may impact learning. Additionally, environmental barriers may exist that result

in inappropriate literacy instruction for students with physical disabilities. Despite the barriers that impede literacy and the increased need for strong literacy skills for individuals who have physical disabilities, the literature examining effective interventions for promoting literacy with this population is sparse (Browning, 2002; Ferreira, Rönnberg, Gustafson, & Wengelin, 2007; Koppenhaver, Hendrix, & Williams, 2007). Two interventions demonstrated to be effective in promoting literacy for individuals with physical disabilities are the Nonverbal Reading Approach and assistive technology for writing.

The Nonverbal Reading Approach

Definition and Theoretical Underpinnings of the Nonverbal Reading Approach

One effective practice that was originally developed for students with physical disabilities is the Nonverbal Reading Approach (NRA; Heller, Fredrick, & Diggs, 1999). The NRA is a systematic instructional strategy for teaching decoding skills to students who have severe speech impairments in addition to their physical disabilities, such as those with severe spastic quadriplegia cerebral palsy who have dysarthric speech (i.e., poor articulation) or anarthric speech (i.e., no intelligible speech). It has also been used with students who have disabilities such as autism, stroke, and intellectual disabilities with speech and physical disabilities. The approach is designed to be used in conjunction with phonics-based reading programs (Heller & Alberto, 2010). It uses the strategies of guided practice, inner speech, self-instruction, diagnostic distractor arrays, and error analysis.

The NRA has been used to teach students specific words in a phonics-based reading program, as well as to teach students a strategy to use when encountering unknown words. It has been used to effectively improve word-recognition and reading levels in conjunction with the Direct Instruction curriculum (Heller, Fredrick, & Diggs, 1999), to promote generalization or faster acquisition of decoding unknown words with similar phoneme sequences (Heller, Fredrick, Tumlin, & Brineman, 2002), to promote decoding when paired with computer-based instruction (Coleman-Martin, Heller, Cihak, & Irvine, 2005), and as a self-instruction strategy to promote decoding unknown words (K. W. Heller & Alberto, 2010; Swinehart-Jones & Heller, 2009).

The theoretical basis of the NRA originates with Lev Vygotsky, who theorized about the development of inner speech and its relationship to thought through the influences of the sociocultural experience (Vygotsky, 1934/1986).

According to Vygotsky, children develop from using language to communicate to using language to guide and monitor their activity. Language, in the form of inner speech, therefore can be used in a self-regulatory capacity, and students can be taught to use inner speech in self-instruction strategies (Diaz, Neal, & Amaya-Williams, 1990). Using the NRA, students are taught to use inner speech as a self-instruction strategy to decode words and monitor progress. This can be an advantage for children who lack the ability to speak or to speak understandably.

Speech production has been found to be important for decoding words, and students with limited speech production are at risk of developing limited reading skills (Peeters, Verhoeven, de Moor, & van Balkom, 2009). However, studies have shown that speech production (i.e., articulatory coding) is not an essential part of the process used for subvocal rehearsal or phonological coding (Baddeley & Wilson, 1985; Bishop & Robson, 1989; Foley & Pollatsek, 1999; Peeters, Verhoeven, & de Moor, 2009; Vallar & Cappa, 1987). For example, in one study by Foley and Pollatsek (1999), children with no intelligible speech and those with severe speech production impairments were able to accurately use phonological coding for reading and short-term memory tasks in the absence of speech. These findings support the use of inner speech to teach word decoding and self-instruction.

Description of the Nonverbal Reading Approach: Guided Practice

The NRA consists of: (a) a guided practice procedure for teaching the target words and decoding process, (b) an evaluation procedure, and (c) expansion strategies. The purpose of the guided practice portion of the NRA is to teach students their targeted words as well as teach them a procedure for decoding unknown words. In this procedure, students are taught to use inner speech to decode words, in a manner similar to that of a more advanced reader (instead of decoding aloud as a beginning reader would do). This allows students who have difficulty speaking to put their efforts into correctly decoding the words subvocally and concentrating on the correct sounds, rather than struggling to pronounce sounds that will sound inaccurate because of their speech impairment. The main part of the guided practice portion of the NRA is a three-step decoding sequence using inner speech and self-instruction of the sequence.

Three-Step Decoding with Inner Speech

The three-step decoding process of the NRA focuses on using inner speech. The teacher needs to consistently use the same phrase when directing students to use inner speech, such as, "Think the sound," "Quietly say

the sound to yourself," "Silently say the sound," or "Say in your head the sound." Teachers should not use the cue "Say the sound in your head," because students may start to vocalize the moment they hear, "Say the sound" before the teacher has a chance to say the rest of the cue. Students may need to be taught directly the concept of using inner speech. This can be done by presenting the student with known items and saying, "Think what this is. Don't say it aloud. Are you doing it? Are you saying it in your head?" Games and songs like BINGO that substitute saying a letter or item with a clap or other action may also assist with teaching the use of inner speech.

Students are taught to decode words using a three-step decoding process with inner speech (see Figure 8.1). In Step 1, the student sounds out each letter (or groups of letters) using inner speech while the teacher models the sounds aloud. For example, for the word *man,* the student is shown the first letter, *m,* and is told to "Say in your head this sound" (or a similar phrase) while the teacher models "/mmm/" aloud. This continues for all of the sounds of the word. Step 2 consists of slowly blending together the letters (or groups of letters). For the word *man,* the teacher directs the student to use inner speech to say all of the sounds together without stopping between the sounds while the teacher says "/mmmaaannn/." In Step 3, the word is blended quickly and the student is told to "Say it in your head fast," as the teacher says the word (e.g., /man/) (K. W. Heller & Alberto, 2010).

Motoric Indicators with the Three-Step Decoding Process

Because using inner speech is a covert process, it is not possible to know with absolute certainty that the student is using inner speech or is using it correctly. However, the teacher can look for indications that the student is using inner speech, such as seeing the student visually track across the written word, attend to the written word, correctly decode the word during the evaluation process, or engage in a motoric indicator.

A motoric indicator is any type of observable movement that the student engages in simultaneously with each step of the decoding process. Not only do motoric indicators provide an observable behavior for the teacher to see, they may also assist the student in remembering the decoding steps. Some examples of movements used by students include moving a finger left to right near the word for each of the three steps, moving an arm up and down, leaning the body forward, and eye blinking. The movement should involve minimal effort for the student to make, and it is important that it does not interfere with the concentration needed to decode the words with inner speech. The use of the motoric indicator is optional.

Figure 8.1   Steps of the Nonverbal Reading Approach.

Guided Practice Component of the Nonverbal Reading Approach

1. *Introduction.* The teacher shows the word to the student and says, "Look at this word. I'll say the sounds, and you think the sound in your head."

2. *Step 1 of saying each sound/unit.* The teacher shows only the first letter of the word (or first word unit) by covering other letters with a piece of paper and says, "Think in your head this sound (unit)," and the teacher models the sound aloud. The teacher uncovers the next letter (or unit), repeats this process, and continues until all of the sounds (word unit) have been modeled.

3. *Step 2 of blending the sounds/units.* The teacher shows the student the word and says, "In your head, think the sounds all together without stopping between the sounds," as the teacher provides a model by slowly saying the word aloud while pointing to the letters across the word.

4. *Step 3 of saying the sounds fast to make a word.* The teacher says, "Think it in your head fast." The teacher then says the word aloud as it would be pronounced when reading text and pointing quickly across the word.

Evaluation Component of the Nonverbal Reading Approach

1. *Introduction.* The teacher says, "I am going to test you on some words. Sound them out first in your head using the three steps, and then I will give you choices." The teacher shows the student the target word and says, "Sound out this word" (or provides guidance by telling the student the steps to decode the word as in the guided practice component, but without providing the sounds).

2. *Provides diagnostic distractor array.* The teacher says, "I'll give you four choices. Listen to your choices. Your choices are: [choice 1], [choice 2], [choice 3], [choice 4]." "Is it [choice 1]?" (waits 3 to 5 seconds for student response). "Is it [choice 2]?" and so on. The teacher gives choices without any cueing.

3. *Records student response.* The teacher watches the student to indicate her choice (e.g., head nod, vocalization, eye blink) and accurately records the one the student selected.

4. *Responding to student's selection.* If the student gave a correct answer, the teacher confirms the correct selection (and gives praise or reinforcement). If the student gives an incorrect answer, the teacher goes through the guided practice procedure while providing sounds.

5. *Error analysis.* The teacher analyzes the data after the session for error patterns to determine additional instructional needs and possible changes in distractor arrays.

In some cases, students may engage in a motoric indicator spontaneously. If that does not occur, a motoric indicator can be selected for use if the teacher elects to have one in place. However, for some students, introducing a motoric indicator after they have learned the three-step decoding process may be better, so their attention is not divided between learning the steps and learning a corresponding movement.

Teaching Self-Instruction of the Nonverbal Reading Approach

One of the goals of the NRA is not only to have students learn the words being targeted for instruction but to be able to decode unknown words. Teachers consistently need to teach students to learn the three-step decoding process and to apply it to unknown words. Some strategies that may be used to teach students to learn the three-step decoding process are systematic instruction of the three steps, modeling the three steps and gradually fading teacher support, using prompt cards with the steps, programming the steps on the students' augmentative and alternative communication (AAC) devices, and using mnemonics. Once the three-step decoding process is learned, teachers need to instruct students when to use it on their own. This can be facilitated by intentionally introducing unknown words and prompting students, "What do you do if you don't know the word?" and prompting them (e.g., on their AAC device, motioning to their prompt card) to use the three-step decoding process. Students then use the strategy, and teachers assess if they did it correctly.

Some students like the use of mnemonics to help remember the steps. One mnemonic is SAM, which can stand for, "Say the sounds, All together, Make it fast"—corresponding to each of the three decoding steps.

Another mnemonic is SAMS, which may be more appropriate if the student is reading sentences. It stands for <u>S</u>ay the sounds, <u>A</u>ll together, <u>M</u>ake it fast, and check if it makes <u>S</u>ense. The last step serves as a self-reflection step to help the students determine if the word they decoded fits the sentence they are reading.

Optional Components

Teachers may add some optional components to the guided practice portion of the NRA. For example, some students can make noises or approximations of letter sounds and want to say the word aloud. Teachers have the option of first modeling the word before sounding it out and having students say the word aloud as well as they can before guiding students through the three-step decoding strategy using inner speech.

Supplementary instruction is often provided along with teaching the decoding process using the NRA. For example, the teacher may compare the word to a previously learned word, examine prefixes or suffixes, provide definitions, and have the student spell and write the word. Often these activities are part of the phonics curriculum that is being used in conjunction with the NRA.

Description of the Nonverbal Reading Approach: Evaluation Component

After using guided practice to teach students to decode words, the teacher will need to evaluate if the students decoded properly. The evaluation component of the NRA consists of several steps: (a) the student decodes the word, (b) the teacher provides a diagnostic distractor array, (c) the student receives confirmation and praise for a correct response or goes through a correction procedure, and (d) the teacher performs an error analysis.

The evaluation component begins by the teacher presenting the word and directing the student to sound out the word using the three-step decoding process and inner speech. For students who have not learned the three steps independently, the teacher guides the students through the steps using the same procedure in the guided practice component, but the teacher does not provide the sounds. This process helps the students learn the decoding steps and decode the targeted word. Next, the teacher encourages the students to remember the word that was just decoded and then listen closely to the verbally presented choices and select the one that matches what the students just decoded. It is important that the teacher uses a diagnostic distractor array when selecting the choices for the student to choose from.

Diagnostic Distractor Arrays

A diagnostic distractor array provides choices to the student designed to evaluate the student's acquisition of the targeted material, which in this case is whether the student correctly decoded the word. Most diagnostic distractor arrays consist of the correct answer and two or three additional choices that have been carefully selected to determine if the student correctly decoded the word. Choices are typically presented orally to the student as the student looks at the written word she decoded. Teachers must be cautious not to inadvertently cue the student to the correct word through intonation or emphasis when saying the words in the diagnostic distractor array.

There is a difference between simply providing an array of words and a diagnositc distractor array. For example, if the student was shown the word *dog,* asked to sound it out, and then was given the verbal choices of *cat, rabbit, dog,* and *car,* a correct answer would indicate only that the student knows the first letter sound or some other sound in the word *dog.* In a diagnostic distractor array, the carefully chosen array assists the teacher in pinpointing the student's errors and helps ensure that the student knows the word. Initially, a diagnostic distractor array may begin by including a word with a different beginning sound, a word with a different ending, and a word with a different vowel sound. In our *dog* example, a diagnostic distractor array could consist of *hog, dug, dog, dot.* If the student selected *dot,* she may not be sounding out the word until the end or may be confusing the *g* and *t* sound. If the student selected *dug,* she appears to have vowel-sound confusion. If the student selected *hog,* she appears not to be sounding out the beginning sound.

Student Response and Consequence

Students should be told when they answer correctly and should be given praise or other reinforcement as appropriate. If the student makes an incorrect response, the teacher should go through a correction procedure that consists of using the guided practice component of the NRA, as well as any additional instruction (e.g., providing more repetition on the word or the sounds that are being confused). In addition, the teacher should record the distractor array that was used and the choice the student made for each word for later error analysis.

Error Analysis

An error analysis is a careful examination of the type of errors the student is making within the trial as well as any error patterns across the different targeted words.

In our *dog* example, let's say the student selects *dot*. And for another choice, the teacher sees that for the word *rat* the student selected *rag*. This may indicate that the student is confusing *g* and *t*. The student needs additional instruction for the *g* and *t* sounds. Also, other diagnostic distractor arrays will need to be examined. For example, after teaching *g* and *t*, the student is answering correctly for the word *dog* and *rat*; however, for a third word, *fit*, which the student has always answered correctly, the teacher sees that the distractors never included a choice with a *g* sound. In this case, the teacher would provide the word *fig* as one of the choices the next time she assesses the word *fit* to be sure the student is no longer confusing *g* and *t* and that the student really knows that word. Careful analysis is important to correctly identify and address any decoding errors that may be occurring.

Description of the Nonverbal Reading Approach: Expansion Strategies

The NRA involves students in a process of (a) sounding out words nonverbally with guided practice, (b) sounding out words using the NRA independently (i.e., self-directed instruction) with words in isolation and words in sentences, and (c) achieving automaticity on targeted words (i.e., recognizing words without decoding them). As the student gains automaticity on targeted words, the teacher should present the word and ask, "Do you know what this word is?" If no, the teacher may say, "What do you do if you don't know the word?" and wait for the student to respond (e.g., on his AAC device). If the student does not respond or responds incorrectly, the teacher can prompt: "Sound it out in your head" or "SAM." If the student indicates that he knows the word, the teacher may skip having the student sound out the word and assess his mastery of the word by using a diagnostic distractor array (Heller & Alberto, 2010).

The NRA should be integrated into other reading activities, such as reading connected text (e.g., sentences, stories), checking for comprehension, promoting fluency, as well as spelling and writing. Often, students will need assistive technology to gain access to writing and will need augmentative communication and other adaptations to promote reading and writing skills.

Research Supporting the Nonverbal Reading Approach

The NRA is based on best practices in phonics instruction and is adapted to include inner speech and self-instruction. Owing to the paucity of researchers who investigate reading strategies with students with severe physical disabilities, the research supporting the NRA is still in its infancy, with further investigations still under way. Currently, four research articles and additional review articles and book chapters have focused on the NRA (Coleman-Martin et al., 2005; Heller & Alberto, 2010; Heller & Coleman-Martin, 2007; Heller, Fredrick, & Diggs, 1999; Heller, Fredrick, Tumlin, & Brineman, 2002; Swinehart-Jones & Heller, 2009).

Heller, Fredrick, and Diggs (1999) examined the use of the NRA in conjunction with Direct Instruction reading programs (Reading Mastery and Corrective Reading) over the course of a school year (9 months), with three students who had severe physical disabilities and anarthric or severe dysarthric speech. This pilot study used a case study format to investigate word-reading acquisition and reading gains. By the end of the study, participants showed gains in the number of words learned, with improvements ranging from 85 words to 261 words over the study (mastering 58% to 88% of the words taught). All three participants made gains in word identification on standardized achievement tests (7-month gain, 1-year gain, and a 2.5-month gain for a student who was ill 44% of the academic year). This study was considered successful due to the percentage of words learned by each student, as well as the amount of gain they had made before the study compared with the gain made after the intervention. For example, a 15-year-old participant had made only kindergarten-level gains in word recognition for all the years she was in school before the study, but she was able to make a 7-month gain in word recognition in the one academic year of this intervention. She also went from reading single words to reading paragraphs with automaticity.

Heller, Fredrick, and Diggs (1999) reported a second study that examined the importance of using diagnostic distractor arrays. This study used a reversal design (ABAB) to compare percent of correct responses for words with which students were unfamiliar using grossly dissimilar arrays (i.e., arrays in which word choices were dissimilar along multiple dimensions) (A) and diagnostic distractor arrays (B). When assessed with grossly dissimilar arrays, students had high percentages of correct responses (80% to 100%). However, when the same unknown words were presented using diagnostic distractor arrays, students were unable to guess the correct words (0% to 20% accuracy). This demonstrated that the diagnostic distractor arrays were far more accurate than grossly dissimilar arrays for assessing word identification for nonverbal individuals. It appears that students could guess the correct response on grossly dissimilar arrays by only partially decoding the word (e.g., beginning sound). This introductory study showed positive effects of using the NRA with Direct Instruction curricula and emphasized the importance of using diagnostic distractor arrays.

Heller et al. (2002) taught students words using the NRA and then examined whether the students could generalize their decoding skills to unknown words with similar phoneme sequences. A multiple-baseline probe design was used across three students with severe physical and speech disabilities. Graphic analysis and error examination indicated that the NRA was effective in teaching decoding skills with students ranging from 0% to 30% accuracy during baseline and reaching 80% to 100% accuracy for multiple sessions during intervention. These skills generalized to unknown words with little or no additional instruction (reaching 80% accuracy or higher).

The guided practice procedure of the NRA has been delivered through computer-assisted instruction (CAI) to teach word decoding to students with cerebral palsy, autism, and stroke (Coleman-Martin et al., 2005). In this study, a multiple-conditions design with drop-down baselines was used to investigate using the NRA with three students across three conditions of: (a) teacher-only instruction, (b) teacher and CAI, and (c) CAI alone. The study was not meant to determine which condition was better, but to examine if students would be able to correctly identify word sets instructed by CAI alone, after successful completion of the first two conditions (which is thought to be a typical natural progression from teacher-directed to computer-directed instruction). Baselines ranged from 0% to 20%, and all participants reached criteria in each of the three conditions (80% accuracy or above for two consecutive sessions). The results indicated that the guided practice component of the NRA can be effectively delivered through computer-assisted instruction, which has the potential to allow students time to practice decoding independently.

The most recent research article examined the effect of NRA on learning targeted words as well as the three-step decoding process as a self-instruction strategy (Swinehart-Jones & Heller, 2009). A changing-criterion design demonstrated that four students with cerebral palsy learned their targeted words as they used the decoding strategy along with motoric indicators with 0 words correct at baseline to all 10 words correct by the end of the intervention. After learning to use the three-step decoding process of the NRA with their 10 targeted words, classroom teachers used the NRA with the reading curriculum. Students were observed and evaluated for independent use of the decoding strategy, and all four students were found to use the three-step decoding process independently 6 months after initially being taught to use the strategy.

Assistive Technology to Promote Writing

Definition and Theoretical Underpinnings of Assistive Technology for Writing

Another practice that assists individuals with physical disabilities in overcoming barriers to literacy is assistive technology (AT). The Individuals with Disabilities Education Improvement Act of 2004 states, "*Assistive technology device* means any item, piece of equipment, or product system, whether acquired commercially off the shelf, modified, or customized, that is used to increase, maintain, or improve the functional capabilities of a child with a disability." Additionally, the law stipulates that the term "assistive technology" includes services that assist a child with a disability with selection, acquisition, or use of an AT device [20 U.S.C. § 1401 (1); 1401(2)]. Assistive technology opens doors to participation in a wide array of activities and settings not otherwise afforded to people with physical disabilities. Stumbo, Martin, and Hedrick (2009) found that, "appropriately chosen and implemented assistive technology" (p. 108) is imperative for adults with physical disabilities to participate on levels approaching that of peers without disabilities in education, employment, and independent living. Because AT encompasses such a wide array of devices and services, this chapter will focus on how AT devices for writing can increase access to writing and written productivity for individuals with physical disabilities.

As previously described, individuals with physical disabilities face many barriers that restrict their level of achievement in writing. Assistive technology often provides a means for individuals with disabilities to overcome such barriers. Although AT may prove beneficial for many individuals with disabilities, the presence of a physical disability often results in increased reliance on AT solutions for writing as compared to other disabilities. Parette and Peterson-Karlan (2007) defined AT as "a tool that allows a person to do a task they could not do without the tool *at the expected performance level*" (pp. 388–389). The use of AT devices and software for writing may bridge the gap between the individual's performance level and *"expected performance level"* by compensating for the functional effects of decreased motor abilities and concomitant sensory impairments as well as environmental barriers such as decreased access to writing materials and lower expectations from school personnel. Furthermore, AT can help to compensate for decreased achievement in written productivity due to differences in memory, attention, and cognition, as well as psychosocial factors such as lack of motivation and feelings of self-efficacy. The compensatory nature of AT to overcome these barriers can be associated with a theory originally developed to conceptualize human–machine interactions, Baker's Basic Ergonomic Equation (Edyburn, 2001).

Baker's Basic Ergonomic Equation was reconceptualized by T. W. King (1999) as a way to examine how human factors impact the use of AT. This theory suggests the use of AT will succeed only if the user's motivation to perform a task using the AT device is greater than the sum of the cognitive effort, physical effort, linguistic effort, and time load needed to perform the task with the device (T. W. King, 1999). When an individual has a physical disability that results in decreased ability to use writing implements or type on a standard keyboard, the physical process of writing may demand so much attention that little attention is allocated to the process of composing text. Assistive technologies such as (a) low-tech (i.e., nonelectronic, inexpensive) devices that facilitate handwriting (e.g., pencil grips, adapted paper, slant boards) or access to keyboarding (e.g., hand braces, key guards, mouth sticks) or (b) high-tech software (e.g., standard or adaptive word processors, speech recognition software) can provide an individual with a means of access less taxing physically and requiring less cognitive attention to be placed on the physical aspect of writing (Coleman & Heller, 2009). The reduced levels of attention, memory, and cognition of some individuals with physical disabilities may be aided by software that provides structure and support for written productivity such as talking word processors that support struggling writers through auditory feedback or software that provides graphic organizers to help with the organization and structure of written works. These supports may reduce the cognitive and linguistic effort required for writing, thus requiring lower levels of motivation for task completion than writing without the use of technology. However, some AT for writing requires advanced cognitive and linguistic processes for writers with physical disabilities.

Individuals with extremely limited motor abilities may need to gain access to a computer with a single switch. For writing, this involves the use of an onscreen keyboard with scanning. Scanning is the process where the computer highlights letters in sequence and the user activates his switch when the desired letter is highlighted. Usually, to make scanning faster, the sequence involves scanning each row of the keyboard until the user activates the switch indicating the desired letter is in that row and then highlighting across the row until the desired letter is reached (i.e., row–column scanning). Because this process for word processing requires multiple steps to "type" each letter, scanning poses a higher cognitive load on the user than is generally required for keyboarding. In light of Baker's Basic Ergonomic Equation, writing via scanning requires heavy cognitive

and physical effort; the AT user must have a high level of motivation to complete the writing task for this technology to be effective.

In the areas of access and written productivity, word-prediction software, which provides a list of possible words based on the first letters typed, may assist with reducing the number of keystrokes required to type a word and may improve spelling; however, it demands a shift of attention from the writing content to the word list being provided, thus increasing the cognitive load (Peterson-Karlan et al., 2008). This principle also applies to hand-held spelling checkers, or spelling checkers or dictionary features built in to word processors. If those supports are necessary for single-word production, attention is shifted and the writing process is slowed. The increased physical, cognitive, and linguistic demands placed on the task of writing by the presence of a physical disability generally slow the process. As suggested by Baker's Basic Ergonomic Equation, for an AT device to succeed in promoting writing for an individual, she must have a level of motivation that supersedes these demands.

When examined in light of Baker's Basic Ergonomic Equation, the potential impact of AT on writing for individuals with physical disabilities is evident; when motivation exceeds the additional effort required, AT can successfully enhance the communication of individuals with physical disabilities. However, the number of intervention studies addressing AT interventions for writing with this population is limited. In the following sections, the small body of research on AT for writing for students with physical disabilities is addressed along with implications for future research and practice.

Research on Assistive Technology for Writing with Students Who Have Physical Disabilities

Although ATs specifically designed for individuals with physical disabilities are available (e.g., switches, enlarged keyboards, computer input devices), technology designed for others often is equally beneficial for someone with a physical disability. For example, a word processor may be helpful to someone who physically can write with a pen or pencil (e.g., making writing faster and more legible), whereas it is assistive (i.e., necessary) for another person whose motor limitations impede handwriting. Furthermore, individuals with physical disabilities who have learning and cognitive impairments may be benefited equally by software designed to compensate for learning or intellectual disabilities. See Figure 8.2 for examples of AT for writing.

Assistive technology for writing can be categorized as providing access to writing or to promote written productivity. In some cases, the technology serves in both

Figure 8.2   Examples of assistive technology for writing for individuals with physical disabilities.

Assistive Technology for Access to Writing

Low-Tech Assistive Technology for Handwriting

Writing Implements

Felt-tip pens (require less pressure, easier to see)

Pencil grip

Larger-surface pens or pencils (commercially available or built-up with foam)

Weighted pencil or pen to decrease extraneous movements or tremors

Hand brace to provide grip and stability

Mouthstick or headstick with pencil/pen holder

Paper Adaptations or Stabilization

Paper with darker or larger lines

Paper with raised lines or use of writing guides

Stabilization of paper with tape, clipboards, or nonslip material (e.g., Dycem)

Use of a slanted surface (e.g., notebook or slant board)

Electronic Solutions for Access to Writing

Portable word processors

Word processing software

Accessibility features for typing (e.g., sticky keys, filter keys)

Hand, head, or mouth pointers used for typing

Different keyboard layouts (e.g., ABC, Dvorak)

Adaptive keyboards (e.g., smaller, larger, onscreen)

Adaptive input devices (e.g., trackball, joystick, head-controlled mouse emulators)

Switches to control scanning on onscreen keyboards

Assistive Technology to Increase Written Productivity or Written Expression

Word walls or picture dictionaries (low-tech or computerized)

Handheld spell checkers

Features in standard word processors (e.g., spell check, grammar check, dictionary, thesaurus)

Adaptive word processors (e.g., talking word processors, symbol processors)

Graphic organizer software to increase writing organization and structure

Speech recognition software

Word prediction software

Augmentative communication devices used for writing

---

capacities. Small bodies of literature examine the use of AT for access to writing and AT for increased written productivity for individuals with physical disabilities.

Assistive Technology for Access to Writing

One issue that limits research on AT for access to writing for people with physical disabilities is that there are almost as many solutions as there are individuals who need the technology. Often an individual needs a combination of technologies such as a pencil grip and slant board for documents requiring short answers and a computer with a keyguard and word processing software for more extensive writing (Coleman & Heller, 2009). In a study that examined the use of constant time delay to teach spelling to students with physical disabilities (Coleman-Martin & Heller, 2004), each of the three participants required different ATs for writing. One student used specially lined paper and a slant board to write her responses, one typed on a standard laptop keyboard, and one used a trackball to type her answers on an onscreen keyboard. These adaptations made accessing the task of spelling possible for the three students, and all three achieved criterion (i.e., 100% accuracy for three sessions) for spelling three sets of words.

Studies have explored the impact of other AT devices on writing. Lancioni et al. (2008) noted that head-controlled devices for computer access might be laborious and tiring when used for a long time. They compared the impact of a voice-detecting sensor to a pressure switch to activate an onscreen scanning keyboard for two boys with extensive physical disabilities. Both participants indicated a preference for the voice-detecting sensor, but mean writing time per letter was better with the pressure sensor for one and with the voice-detecting sensor for the other. Similar studies in the education and rehabilitation engineering literature have explored the use of various input devices for writing (e.g., tongue-activated light sensor, eye-tracking devices, acoustically controlled mouse pointer, morse code keyboard emulators, tilt sensors), often with results that show variable performance based on individual needs and abilities of the participants (e.g., Felton, Lewis, Wills, Radwin, & Williams, 2007; LoPresti, Brienza, Angelo, & Gilbertson, 2003; Yang, Chuang, Yang, & Luo, 2003). Although no single AT solution meets the needs of all individuals with physical disabilities, a couple of important points can be drawn from this research literature.

First, teachers and therapists of students with physical disabilities need to be aware of the wide array of AT available to provide access to writing for these students. The second issue is that devices should be adjustable to make them more efficient for individual students' needs. Simpson, Koester, and LoPresti (2006) proposed that,

"Because each person's disability is unique, tuning these devices to each user's strengths and limitations is critical for success in many cases" (p. 127). Advancements in AT already allow individuals with significant physical disabilities to write using movements as small as an eye blink. Researchers are working on technologies that will provide computer access through neural signals for people with severely limited physical movements (e.g., advanced amyotrophic lateral sclerosis) (Felton et al., 2007). As AT that provides access to writing for individuals with physical disabilities advances, barriers to successful literacy are torn down and doors to communication and participation open for even those with the most severe physical limitations.

Assistive Technology to Promote Written Productivity

Several types of technology can be used to increase written productivity for individuals with physical disabilities. For children who are at the emergent stages of writing, software is available that combines symbols and pictures (e.g., *Boardmaker Plus, Writing With Symbols*) to promote early sentence building and other early writing skills. Talking word processors (e.g., *Write:OutLoud, IntelliTalk*) or symbol word processors (e.g., *Writing With Symbols* 2000) provide immediate auditory feedback, visual feedback, or both, to writers who struggle with spelling and grammar. Software that provides graphic or advanced organizers (e.g., *Inspiration, Draft: Builder*) can assist students with organizing thoughts and correctly structuring their writing (Sitko, Laine, & Sitko, 2005). One type of software, word prediction, was designed to increase writing fluency for individuals with physical disabilities by decreasing keystrokes, but much of the research has shown it to be more effective in promoting spelling and only increasing writing fluency in some cases of students with severe physical disabilities who type at extremely slow rates (Mirenda, Turoldo, & McAvoy, 2006; Tumlin & Heller, 2004). One type of software that has implications for students with physical disabilities, as well as the general population, is speech recognition. Speech recognition has the ability to increase production of written material, which can be beneficial for students with physical disabilities.

Speech recognition software for individuals with physical disabilities. Speech recognition software allows users to dictate into a microphone and have their speech converted to text or to computer functions. Speech recognition software is generally marketed as a productivity tool for people without disabilities because most people speak at rates that are considerably faster than they are able to type. The average speaking rate of adults

without disabilities is approximately 125 to 160 words per minute as compared to written speed of approximately 15 to 25 words per minute (De La Paz & Graham, 1997; Feng, Karat, & Sears, 2005). Speech recognition software can be used to dictate into word processing documents, e-mail, web browsers, and other programs, and to operate basic computer functions. The use of speech recognition software requires the user to dictate the desired text, punctuation (e.g., "comma," "question mark," "end quote"), and commands (e.g., "new paragraph," "tab," "caps on," "page up") within a word processing document. If the program does not recognize words or phrases, the user can select the incorrect text through voice commands (e.g., "select *commonly misunderstood great*") and restate the correct phrase to correct the text (e.g., *"commonly misunderstood phrase"*). Additionally, some speech recognition programs offer the ability to control functions on the screen such as the mouse cursor, and opening and closing files through spoken commands (e.g., "move mouse left," "double click").

Over the years, speech recognition software has progressed from requiring the person to speak one word at a time (discrete speech recognition) to allowing the user to speak at a normal rate (continuous speech recognition). Most speech recognition programs come with templates so that, right out of the box, they can recognize some speech, but they require training by the user to increase accurate recognition of the individual's speech. Typically, this involves the user reading passages while the software creates voice files based on the user's speech. The user's voice files are integrated with the preprogrammed templates to increase the software's accuracy in recognizing the user's speech. Generally, options are available for performing additional training of the software, which will result in higher percentages of recognition accuracy. In addition to training the software to recognize the user's voice, the user needs explicit instruction for controlling the software.

Inadequate training time or inefficient training is one of the causes for AT abandonment for individuals with physical disabilities (Coleman, 2011). Training the use of speech recognition software is especially important, given that the use of speech recognition software requires users to speak differently during the dictation process than during normal speech (e.g., dictate punctuation, enunciate more clearly) and learn numerous commands. When first introducing the software to a user, it is important to discuss dictation style. Continuous speech recognition software does not require users to speak one word at a time; however, accuracy will be decreased if users speak too rapidly, run words together, drop sounds, or insert extraneous sounds (e.g., "um") as many people do in normal conversational speech. Thus, one of the first steps is to have the user practice using a dictation vocal pattern. One mother of a high school speech recognition user called it his "radio announcer's voice."

Another early step in training someone to use speech recognition software is teaching basic commands such as turning the microphone on and off (e.g., "stop listening") and the use of punctuation and capitalization (e.g., "cap that"). Having a written list of commands available for reference is useful for most new users of speech recognition software. One of the most crucial parts of training is error correction. If a user can access a keyboard and mouse, a combination of voice and physical input may be used to make corrections. Otherwise, the user will need to learn numerous commands to correct recognition errors or make changes to text. Most speech recognition software learns a user's voice as recognition errors are corrected. Excessive use of certain correction commands that are intended for replacement of recognition errors (e.g., "scratch that") instead of commands to replace text that was recognized correctly that the user wishes to change (e.g., "select . . .") may decrease the software's recognition accuracy (Koester, 2006). One final area of training is using navigation features and commands to control the program. For some users, it is faster to use the keyboard, mouse, or other input device to perform tasks such as moving the cursor and saving files; in this case, training on voice commands for those features will not be necessary. Individuals without such access methods will need to learn numerous additional commands.

Speech recognition increases the potential for independent production of written text for writers who have physical or written expression limitations. Because speech recognition does not require physical manipulation of a keyboard (physical or onscreen), it may provide a solution to writing for individuals with extremely limited motor abilities (Rosen & Yampolsky, 2000). Speaking, for most individuals, is faster, less laborious, and less fatiguing than manual text entry (Koester, 2004). For individuals with physical disabilities, the reduction of physical effort may mean successful writing experiences that cannot be achieved by handwriting or physically entering text into the computer. Additionally, the fact that speech recognition does not require the user to spell or produce words letter-by-letter makes speech recognition a viable method of writing for individuals who struggle with written expression. This has the potential to decrease cognitive and linguistic load and possibly decrease the loss of ideas that can be lost in the process of transcribing text (De La Paz, 1999).

Although speech recognition may be effectively used to promote writing, there are some considerations regarding its appropriateness for certain students. First, the software does not assist the user in learning the writing process. Writing instruction can be used in conjunction with speech recognition software so that the user learns how to spell and construct text in written rather than spoken form, if the goal is for the student to learn to read, print, and spell. Also, the differences in spoken language and more formal writing would need to be taught. A second consideration is the noise level of the classroom affecting the software program by typing extraneous noises as words. Newer versions of the software are more efficient at filtering intentional speech from extraneous noise, but background noise is a consideration when deciding the environments in which to use speech recognition software. The user's privacy and the potential of disturbing others in the environment must also be considered.

Another potential issue is that the speech recognition user must have adequate reading skills to be able to recognize whether the software is correctly transcribing his speech. Most speech recognition programs have a feature that will read the printed text to the user; however, if reading and spelling skills are not adequate, the individual may still have difficulty making corrections to his writing. Another consideration is that the process for correcting errors can be tedious and frustrating, especially for individuals who have no physical ability to gain access to the keyboard (MacArthur & Cavalier, 2004). Some speech recognition users may not see increased productivity as compared to typing due to the increased length of time required to correct errors with speech recognition compared to keyboard entry (Karat, Horn, Halverson, & Karat, 2000; Kotler & Tam, 2002). Finally, the commands and special words that the user must memorize to use speech recognition may cause an increased burden on memory (Koester, 2004).

A small but growing research base supports the use of speech recognition for increasing writing access and quality of written products for individuals with physical disabilities. Kotler and Tam (2002) investigated the impact of discrete-utterance (i.e., dictating one word at a time) speech recognition software on the speed and recognition accuracy of six adults with physical disabilities as well as disadvantages of the use of speech recognition software. While continuous speech recognition software is more commonly used, discrete-utterance speech recognition may provide more accurate recognition, and thus more efficient text generation, for individuals who have significant speech difficulties or poor breath support (e.g., individuals who use ventilators). Participants in this study were unable to effectively use a keyboard due to functional physical limitations resulting from neuromotor and degenerative conditions (e.g., cerebral palsy, muscular dystrophy, scleroderma).

Interviews indicated that speech recognition resulted in faster speeds of text generation for participants than previously used computer access methods. However, some participants reported that the recognition accuracy of the software was not acceptable. With regard to accuracy of the speech recognition software for recognition of single words, results ranged from 62.4% to 94.4%. In dictation of formatting and correction commands, the average recognition accuracy of the software ranged from 91.5% to 99.6%. It was noted that background noise, fatigue, and illnesses that affected voice quality may have played a part in decreased accuracy of speech recognition. Other disadvantages noted were voice-related problems, fatigue, and the limited confidentiality when dictating text into speech recognition software. While the results of this study generally suggest a positive impact of the use of discrete-utterance speech recognition software on writing for most of the users, Kotler and Tam (2002) cautioned that users who have the ability to type may not see the benefit of increased speed of text generation and may experience vocal or general fatigue with use of discrete-utterance software.

Through surveying 24 adults with physical disabilities who were experienced users of speech recognition technology, Koester (2004) found that most users were generally satisfied with the performance of their speech recognition systems and reported that dictation to the computer was less painful and fatiguing than using a keyboard for input. The participants in this study who typed at slow rates (<15 wpm) showed increased production of text when using speech recognition. In 2006, Koester examined 20 different factors (e.g., specific equipment, training and experience, usage techniques, user characteristics) that influence writing performance by 23 experienced speech recognition users with physical disabilities through survey and video analysis of software usage. Bivariate and multivariate analyses were used to evaluate the effect of variables on recognition accuracy and text entry rate. Of the 20 independent variables examined, results indicate that using appropriate correction strategies, the amount of time spent on the computer, manual typing speed, and the speed with which the speech recognition system recognized user's speech were the only significant indicators of better writing performance with speech recognition software. The most influential factor was participants' use of the "scratch that" feature for correction of recognition errors. As mentioned, "scratch that" is a correction strategy intended for correction of speech recognition errors, and incorrect use of this command, to have the software disregard correctly recognized speech when the user wanted to change what was written, resulted in less-accurate recognition overall because the software is designed to learn from its mistakes. Interestingly, the amount of training time was not a significant factor in better writing performance; however,

it could be argued that more appropriate training might result in more efficient use of speech recognition software if users are trained in the appropriate corrections techniques (e.g., correct use of "scratch that").

Garrett et al. (2011) compared the use of speech recognition software to word processing for creating first drafts of writing products for five high school students with physical disabilities (i.e., spina bifida, muscular dystrophy, cerebral palsy, and spinal muscular atrophy) and concomitant disabilities (e.g., Asperger's syndrome, visual impairments). They examined the areas of writing fluency, writing accuracy, type of word errors, recall of intended meaning, and length through a single-subject alternating treatments design. For all of their participants, the use of speech recognition software resulted in increased writing fluency and length of written products. However, the participants experienced varying levels of accuracy with the speech recognition software, which resulted in frustration.

For individuals with physical disabilities who also have dysarthric (i.e., motor impaired) speech, speech recognition software may not be viable. A few studies have focused on ways to increase the capability of the speech recognition software to recognize dysarthric speech. Kotler and Thomas-Stonell (1997) found that speech training for the user can increase the accuracy of speech recognition. Hux, Rankin-Erickson, Manasse, and Lauritzen (2000) found that the quality of the speech recognition software program had an impact on the accuracy of recognition for a user with dysarthric speech but did not have a substantial impact for a user without a speech impairment. Parker, Cunningham, Enderby, Hawley, and Green (2006) investigated the use of a speaker-dependent speech recognition system (i.e., every word must be trained by the user) for providing access to electronic devices such as a television, lamp, compact disc player, and radio by individuals with severely dysarthric speech. Unlike speaker-independent speech recognition that comes with user templates and does not require training of every word, this type of technology has the potential for increased accuracy because of its lack of reliance on "normal" articulation patterns. Parker et al. found positive effects for four of seven participants and mixed results for the other participants. Although this study did not address speech recognition for writing directly, accurate speech recognition is a prerequisite for individuals with physical disabilities and dysarthric speech to be able to use this software effectively to enhance writing. As this type of speech recognition system improves, individuals with physical disabilities and dysarthric speech may someday be able to use speech recognition software fluently.

As speech recognition technology continues to improve, it will continue to open doors to writing for individuals with physical disabilities. Future research should explore options for making speech recognition more effective for these users, including instruction in the use of speech recognition, writing, and features of the software that make it easier and more accurate for individual users (e.g., individuals who have motor speech impairments). Additionally, there is a crucial need for exploring writing interventions for individuals who use AAC devices. In 2004, D. C. Millar, Light, and McNaughton stated, "In fact, at present, there are no evidence-based writing instructional programs available to guide teachers in the development of instructional activities that have been appropriately modified for individuals who use AAC" (p. 165). Years later, their study, which examined the use of direct instruction and writer's workshop methods in conjunction with AAC devices for children with physical disabilities, is the only one we located that focused solely on providing an intervention for writing with the use of AAC. Because individuals who use AAC devices need to write to communicate messages that are not stored in their devices, we recommend that researchers examine how AAC users can increase their achievement in writing.

Summary

Individuals with physical disabilities face many barriers to acquisition of literacy skills including those based on the type of disability, functional impact of the disability, psychosocial impact of the disability, and environmental factors. Although the research base demonstrating effective practices for promoting literacy for individuals with physical disabilities is limited, some practices have evidentiary support for use with this population. In the area of reading, the NRA is an effective method for overcoming the barrier of limited or absent speech by teaching students to decode through inner speech and giving teachers a way to evaluate student learning. AT can overcome numerous barriers by promoting access to writing and increased written production for individuals with physical disabilities. One particularly promising AT solution is speech recognition software. This software may overcome barriers that prevent access to writing due to functional physical limitations for individuals with physical disabilities.

There is a critical need for research investigating interventions that are effective for promoting literacy for individuals with physical disabilities. Although research from other disability areas (e.g., learning disabilities) can provide some insight to teaching literacy to individuals with physical disabilities, the diversity in physical, cognitive, and academic abilities of this population makes it difficult to generalize research findings. Overall, there is a need to examine strategies that are effective in promoting reading, decoding, fluency, and comprehension for students with physical disabilities. Studies that examine the expansion strategies of the NRA are needed to investigate application of this method to reading fluency and comprehension. As in reading, there is a comprehensive need for research in the area of writing for individuals with physical disabilities. More research is needed to examine how specific features and improvements in writing software can increase writing speed and decrease fatigue during writing for individuals with limited fine motor abilities. Additionally, the impact of AT for writing (e.g., talking word processors, graphic organizer software) on the quality of writing for individuals with physical disabilities should be explored.

In summary, two practices, the NRA for reading and AT for writing, have been demonstrated to be effective for increasing literacy skills for individuals with physical disabilities. Teachers of students with physical disabilities should be instructed in the use of both of these interventions. It is especially important that teachers are educated in the individual needs of their students, which must be considered when implementing reading and writing interventions. For example, when implementing the NRA, teachers must tailor instruction to support the student's reading level and must adjust assessment procedures to incorporate the student's best means of responding. With regard to AT, teachers should consider low-tech to high-tech devices or combinations of devices and strategies that result in maximum outcomes in writing for a student with a physical disability. Future research should focus on finding additional strategies that are effective in helping students with physical disabilities overcome barriers to literacy and acquire the reading and writing abilities necessary to have more fulfilled and productive lives.

CHAPTER 9

Teaching Students Who Have Sensory Disabilities

Deborah Chen and **Rachel Friedman Narr** | *California State University, Northridge*

Diane P. Wormsley | *North Carolina Central University*

Students who have sensory disabilities belong to one of three low-incidence and heterogeneous groups: those who are deaf or hard of hearing (DHH); those who are blind, have a visual impairment (VI), or deaf-blind (DB); and those with additional intellectual, motor, or other disabilities. Lack of or limited access to comprehensible auditory or visual information influences the development of communication, language, and literacy skills; therefore, instructional practices have focused on these learning needs. In this chapter, we identify three selected practices: (a) teaching visual phonics to students who are DHH, (b) early identification of braille as the primary literacy medium for students who are blind or have a VI, and (c) the use of tangible symbols with learners who are DB. It should be noted that "person-first" language is not universally acknowledged in the fields of sensory disabilities and has been rejected by some adults with these disabilities. For example, "deaf teachers" (referring to teachers who are deaf), "deaf and hard-of-hearing students," or "blind adults" are the terms preferred by many individuals.

Visual Phonics with Deaf and Hard-of-Hearing Students

Description of Students

The Individuals with Disabilities Education Act (IDEA, 2004) differentially defines *deafness* as "a hearing impairment that is so severe that the child is impaired in processing linguistic information through hearing, with or without amplification, that adversely affects a child's educational performance," and *hearing impairment* as "an impairment in hearing, whether permanent or fluctuating, that adversely affects a child's educational performance but that is not included under the definition of deafness in this section." When DHH learners acquire a complete first language (whether spoken or signed), they can develop linguistic and academic skills commensurate with age-expected levels (Mayberry, 2010). Underachievement in reading may be related to pervasive delays in receptive and expressive language development (spoken or signed), lack of access to important elements of spoken English (phonological information), as well as the sheer difficulty of learning a second language (presumably English) through reading and writing alone. Research indicates that DHH learners struggle with all facets of the reading process including word identification, vocabulary, syntax, figurative language use in written language, and comprehension skills (Paul, 2009). However, when DHH children attain a comprehensible language, the reading process becomes more natural and more easily navigated (Chamberlain & Mayberry, 2008). DHH students may be considered English Language Learners (ELLs) or Limited English Proficient (LEP), whether they enter school with impoverished language abilities due to lack of exposure to and interaction with comprehensible input (either spoken English or in signed language) or because they have learned a signed language as their first language.

Theoretical Underpinnings

Acquisition of a natural signed language (e.g., American Sign Language [ASL]) provides the strong language base necessary for DHH students (Chamberlain & Mayberry, 2008; Mayer & Akamatsu, 2003). Because of the innate visual abilities of DHH students, even those with advanced technology such as cochlear implants or digital hearing aids, visually based instruction builds on their strengths. Understanding that text is made up of individual phonemes represented through letter combinations in print (i.e., the alphabetic principle) is at the core of learning to read text. This principle is clearly challenging for DHH students, who frequently do not internalize all the elements of spoken English. Recognizing the need to help DHH learners "crack the code," teachers have used a variety of multimodal strategies (e.g., providing speech-reading cues, making up signs or gestures to accompany phonemes, sitting close to the student to maximize auditory cues, asking the student to attempt production of phonemes or words) that provide limited amounts of information about the phonological code of spoken English. The internal representations formed are likely incomplete (Leybaert & Alegria, 2003), so these strategies remain generally problematic (Luckner, Sebald, Cooney, Young, & Muir, 2005/2006; Trezek, Wang, & Paul, 2010).

Description and Implementation of Practice

See the Sound/Visual Phonics (commonly referred to as Visual Phonics) provides a means of making phonemes of spoken English visually accessible to DHH learners. Visual Phonics is a system of hand and grapheme cues that represent the 44 to 46 phonemes in spoken English. Visual Phonics is not a communication system. Teachers use it instructionally to convey phonemic information in single words. Visual Phonics is a supplement to any reading curriculum; its hand and grapheme cues can be used to represent sound-based (typically auditory) information.

The hand cues used in Visual Phonics are manual productions of phonemic information. These hand cues were designed to imitate the speech-articulatory features of each phoneme. For example, the /t/ sound is represented by a hand cue produced by using the index finger and thumb, with the rest of the hand closed, and the index finger flicking up off the thumb. Each hand cue is distinct, making each phoneme fully perceptible by the hand cue alone. The cues are ideal for providing visually accessible phonemic information for isolated phonemes, syllables, or words. They are not appropriate for use in communicative contexts, and although speech production of the phonemes can accompany the hand cues, it is not necessary to distinguish each phoneme. For this reason, deaf teachers can also effectively use Visual Phonics because spoken production is not necessary. Some teachers and other professionals may also use Visual Phonics to enhance students' articulation skills.

A written symbol system representing each phoneme accompanies the Visual Phonics hand cues. The written symbols roughly portray the hand cues. For example, the symbol [ʃ] is used to represent the /t/ sound described above. Teachers report having mixed interest in using the written symbols, depending on the grades they are teaching and the purposes of the lessons (Narr & Cawthon, 2010). Written symbols can be helpful for making spelling patterns more transparent or for making phonic associations.

Because Visual Phonics is a supplemental system that can be used with any reading program or curriculum, its application to instruction is flexible. A teacher incorporates Visual Phonics into reading and spelling lessons where phonemic awareness and phonic concepts of English are presented. The connection between word recognition (decoding) and vocabulary (semantics) must be discretely taught to many DHH learners.

Because learning decoding skills through audition alone (sound out the word) is frequently impractical, students are taught to use other cues for decoding through Visual Phonics, such as lip movements from reading speech on other people's mouths (speech reading), sight word recognition, and structural and morphemic analysis of words (identifying affixes and word parts). The goal for DHH readers is to internalize the visual properties of written words and associate those properties with the word meaning. These supplemental word analysis cues help with word recognition and vocabulary retention and recall. Many reading curricula are structured around themes so that these skills and strategies are contextualized for the learners. DHH learners often require additional instruction in background knowledge and vocabulary due to their impoverished language development. When this instruction is infused into reading lessons, discrete instruction related to word recognition skills with the use of Visual Phonics can occur simultaneously.

Three general components are associated with the implementation of Visual Phonics:

1. *Teacher training:* To learn Visual Phonics, teachers and other professionals should attend a 10- to 14-hour training provided by a licensed International Communication Learning Institute (ICLI) trainer. Mastery is gained through practice and continued use of the system.

2. *Identify specific parts of the reading and spelling lesson with which to apply Visual Phonics:* If a specific reading curriculum or program is used, the teacher should review the content and identify how phonemic awareness, phonics, spelling, or vocabulary are to be taught.

3. *Visual Phonics instruction:* Table 9.1 demonstrates how Visual Phonics is incorporated to supplement the phonics part of a reading lesson. It also shows additional instructional strategies for DHH learners. The written symbols can be used at the discretion of the teacher to teach and reinforce spelling patterns.

Table 9.1   A Common Phonics Kindergarten Lesson with Visual Phonics Supplement

Phonics Lesson-Building Words: Segmenting and Blending Short u Words	Teacher Says/Signs and Does	Supplement with Visual Phonics	Additional Instructional Strategies for DHH Learners
Display Letter Cards *a, b, d, g, h, i, j, m, n, p, r, t, u,* and *w.* Using the Letter Cards, model how to build *hug.*	"First I'll stretch out the sounds: /h/ / u/ /g/. How many sounds do you hear? The first sound is /h/. I'll put up an *h* to spell that. The next sound is /u/. What letter spells that? The last sound is /g/. What letter should I choose for that?"	1. Say/Sign the word *hug* first. When giving the Visual Phonics cues, lean to the left to provide the "sounds" /h/ /u/ /g/ to differentiate the phoneme hand cue from a sign (Trezek, Wang, & Paul, 2010). 2. Ask "How many sounds do you hear/see?" 3. Put the *h* Letter Card on the board, and give the /h/ hand cue again. 4. Say/Sign, "The next sound is /u/." Give the hand cue. "What letter spells that?" 5. Say/Sign, "The next sound is /g/." Provide the hand cue. "What letter should I choose for that?"	Students need to know the concepts associated with each word. Preteach the vocabulary in the lesson: such as *hug, bug, rug, dug, mug.* Fingerspell 3-letter words instead of using a sign. This helps spelling and word-recognition skills.
Next remove the *h.* "Which letter should I add to build *hug?*"	Model how to read *hug* by blending /h/ with /u/ and /g/.	1. Use the hand cues for /h/ /u/ /g/, presenting each cue slowly to form the word *hug.* 2. Alternate fingerspelling the word *hug,* describing the meaning, and presenting the hand cues for the word, which helps to create a strong association between the word structure and the word meaning (Padden & Ramsey, 2000).	
Continue making and blending short *u* words by substituting *d, r, m,* and *t.*	Model several more words using these strategies.	Repeat the procedure explained above, substituting the appropriate letters and hand cues.	Encourage students to build their own words using letter blocks or letter cards. Keep the focus on word meaning.

Research Base

Research on Visual Phonics is growing. Trezek and her colleagues (Trezek & Malmgren, 2005; Trezek & Wang, 2006; Trezek, Wang, Woods, Gampp, & Paul, 2007) have published most widely in this area, documenting the effectiveness of using Visual Phonics with a variety of structured reading instructional curricula with DHH students. Narr (2008) also examined the use of Visual Phonics in reading instruction, looking specifically at decoding and rhyme judgment skills with DHH students. Narr and Cawthon (2010) conducted a national survey of 200 teachers using Visual Phonics and found that teachers overwhelmingly indicated it was easy to use, engaging to students, and beneficial for improving phonemic awareness and decoding skills. Results show that Visual Phonics is a promising tool for providing accessible information to DHH learners as they learn how to decode text.

Trezek and Malmgren (2005) demonstrated that Visual Phonics could be used effectively with 23 DHH middle school students in an urban school district in the Midwest. The 8-week intervention consisted of a daily treatment package for 45 minutes that included Direct Instruction lessons that were supplemented with Visual Phonics, Baldi (a computerized avatar that demonstrates production of phonemes; see Massaro & Light, 2004), and a pictorial glossary accompanying Baldi to facilitate vocabulary instruction within the lessons. Instruction was conducted using Total Communication (typically a combination of speech, audition, and sign language). The intervention group ($n = 12$) and comparison group ($n = 13$) were matched for hearing levels that ranged from slight to profound, grade equivalence in reading, and chronological age. Teachers for the intervention and comparison groups both held K–12 certification for DHH students, and both had more than 25 years of teaching experience. Neither teacher had prior experience with Direct Instruction, Visual Phonics, or the computer program Baldi. The teacher for the intervention group was trained by one of the researchers for a full day on the contents of the Direct Instruction lessons, Visual Phonics cues applicable within the lessons, and how to use Baldi, all as part of the treatment package for the study. A procedural reliability form and a reading instruction log sheet were used to monitor and document the fidelity of the treatment package implementation.

Teachers in the comparison group continued to use one of three district-approved reading programs in their instruction (Trezek & Malmgren, 2005). Pretest and post-test scores on a researcher-designed measure of phonemic awareness and pseudoword decoding were used to determine the effects of the treatment package. At pretest, students with better hearing in both the intervention and comparison groups scored higher than students with lower hearing levels. At post-test, students in the intervention group scored higher than students in the comparison group, regardless of hearing levels; that is, students' hearing levels did not correlate with scores on the phonemic awareness and pseudo-word decoding measure. For the comparison group, a correlation was found between hearing level and performance on the post-assessment. Although the findings do not attribute the higher assessment scores to any one part of the treatment package (Direct Instruction, Visual Phonics, or Baldi), they demonstrate that students can learn and apply phonic knowledge to reading tasks, despite being DHH.

Another study conducted by Trezek and Wang (2006) examined whether 13 kindergarten and first-grade DHH students demonstrated improvements in early reading skills after participating in a phonics-based reading curriculum with Visual Phonics as a supplement to instruction. Students had hearing levels within the severe-to-profound range, and two had cochlear implants. They were divided into three cohorts, based on their classroom placement, receiving instruction in Total Communication using Direct Instruction Reading Mastery I curriculum (Engelmann & Bruner, 1995, as cited in Trezek & Wang, 2006) for an average of 48 lessons over 8 months. Visual Phonics was used to teach the phonemic aspects of the curriculum. Three teachers of DHH students with three semesters of prior experience using Direct Instruction and Visual Phonics provided the instruction.

Subtests of the Wechsler Individual Achievement Test—II (Psychological Corporation, 2002) were used to measure reading achievement. The Word Reading subtest was administered to the four kindergarten students, and the Word Reading, Pseudoword Decoding, and Reading Comprehension subtests were administered to the nine first graders. All students demonstrated statistically significant gains as indicated by comparison of pretest and post-test performance on both the Word Reading and Pseudoword Decoding subtests. Reading Comprehension subtests scores were also characterized by large gains, although they were not statistically significant. Student achievement was not related to hearing levels, again demonstrating that both deaf and hard-of-hearing students can benefit from phonics instruction.

In a more recent investigation, Trezek and her colleagues (2007) assessed performance on early reading measures of 20 DHH students in four kindergarten and first-grade classes using a district-developed phonics-based literacy program supplemented by Visual Phonics. Students had mild-to-profound hearing losses, and half had cochlear implants. Three of the classrooms used Total

Communication, and one used an oral/aural approach. Four teachers certified to work with DHH students were trained to use Visual Phonics over a 1-month period before the study. The first author provided monitoring and consultation on the reading curriculum implementation and use of Visual Phonics. Reading instruction occurred daily for 90 minutes.

Scores on several subtests of the Dominie Reading and Writing Assessment Portfolio (DeFord, 2001) were used to measure student performance at the beginning and end of the academic year. The Sentence Writing Phoneme, Sentence Writing Spelling, and Phonemic Awareness Segmentation subtests were given to the nine kindergarten students. The same three subtests, in addition to the Phonemic Awareness Deletion, Phonics Onsets, and Phonics Rimes subtests, were given to the 11 first-grade students. Pretest scores on the reading and writing measures for all DHH students were within average ranges at the beginning of the school year, which the authors suggested may have been due to the students' participation in at least 2 years of preschool. Post-test performance showed the students significantly improved on the early reading measures, although those scores were lower than expected on several subtests when compared to the hearing normative sample for the assessments. Because all students took part in the same curriculum with the supplement of Visual Phonics, it is unclear whether participation in the phonics-based reading curriculum or the use of Visual Phonics, or a combination of the two, affected the students' performance. Taken together, Trezek's studies demonstrate the value of Visual Phonics with phonics-based reading curricula with DHH students.

Narr (2008) examined the relationships between phonological awareness, decoding using Visual Phonics symbols, reading performance, and length of time in literacy instruction with Visual Phonics for 10 DHH students in one class, grades kindergarten through third grade. Participants' hearing levels ranged from severe to profound. One teacher with over 8 years' experience using Visual Phonics delivered academic instruction through sign-supported English and American Sign Language. Reading performance was teacher reported through several curriculum-based measures and ranged between late-kindergarten and mid-second grade levels. Six of the ten students were reading at or above their grade levels. Phonological awareness skills were determined through a rhyme judgment task, and decoding abilities were determined through a picture and Visual Phonics symbols (word) matching task. Students were required to "decipher" the written word and match it with the accurate picture, demonstrating they could decode words and associate them with meaning. The students were able to make rhyme judgments and decode with greater than chance accuracy. Although no relationship was found between reading performance and rhyme judgment, or reading performance and length of time instructed with Visual Phonics, a positive relationship was found between reading ability and decoding ability. Although this study did not include a comparison group, these findings, however limited, show DHH children can use Visual Phonics to learn these skills and apply them to an accurate internal construct for vocabulary.

Summary

Research evidence related to Visual Phonics is just starting to catch up with over 20 years of use in isolated classrooms. Anecdotal evidence and word-of-mouth have propagated its dissemination and implementation. The few quasi-experimental studies that exist and are reviewed here support the efficacy of using Visual Phonics as a tool to teach early reading skills with DHH learners.

Strengths of the Research Base

Trezek's studies examined the use of Visual Phonics as a supplement to reading instruction using direct instruction. Each study demonstrated that Visual Phonics is a viable and effective tool for teaching the phonemic elements of reading to DHH learners. Two reviews of research previously acknowledged that this kind of instruction is typically omitted when teaching reading to DHH learners (Luckner et al., 2005/2006; Schirmer & McGough, 2005), primarily because of a lack of reliable and comprehensible access to phonemic information. Each of the studies reviewed previously in this discussion were conducted in self-contained classrooms where manual communication was used and the participants were functionally deaf or hard of hearing. Although this may be considered a potential limitation, it strengthens the ability to generalize across students with varying hearing levels. Each of Trezek's studies also demonstrated a high degree of social validity. The teachers who participated had not been using Visual Phonics for a long time, and although they had consultative support from the researcher, it showed that the Visual Phonics as a supplemental tool could be learned and implemented with fidelity in a reasonably short amount of time.

Limitations of the Research Base

The Trezek and Malmgren (2005) study was the only one that included a comparison group, so it is difficult to identify a causal effect on student performance within the other studies. Studies were characterized by small sample sizes, typical of research with low-incidence populations.

Possibilities of bias also existed within each study. The researchers, teachers, or both participated as examiners, allowing for the possibility of assessor bias. Both Trezek and colleagues (2005, 2006, 2007) and Narr (Narr, 2008; Narr & Cawthon, 2010) also reported they are Visual Phonics trainers, and in each of Trezek's studies, she provided the teacher training before interventions. Finally, improved overall reading achievement is the ultimate goal of these investigations; however, only Trezek and Wang (2006) included a measure of reading comprehension. The other studies measured discrete skills related to phonemic awareness and phonics/decoding. Consistent and clear gains in overall reading achievement are inconclusive from this research.

Recommendations for Future Research

A paucity of research addresses teaching phonemic awareness and phonic skills to DHH learners. With the use of Visual Phonics providing comprehensible access to phonemic information to such students, the effect of learning these skills on overall reading achievement requires further investigation. Researchers should expand investigations to include a variety of curricula and reading programs examining not only discrete skills but also how learning discrete skills (using Visual Phonics) contributes to improvements in overall reading comprehension. Longitudinal studies could demonstrate the progression of skill development, documenting when the use of Visual Phonics can be faded out. Larger sample sizes will allow further differentiation of instruction, giving insight into the characteristics of students who benefit most from acquiring these discrete skills. Finally, the use of Visual Phonics provides learners with multiple means of representation as required by the principles of Universal Design for Learning (Center for Applied Special Technology [CAST], 2008), an approach to instruction that is gaining popularity in the research literature on teaching students with special needs. Future research could examine how, using vision as an unimpaired sensory pathway, deaf *and* hard-of-hearing learners can gain access to information traditionally considered "auditory."

Professional development and implementation fidelity require further exploration. There is no research on training procedures for professionals learning Visual Phonics that subsequently investigates how training effects implementation. Furthermore, understanding how teachers integrate and implement instruction using Visual Phonics has not been examined.

Summative Recommendations for Practice

Strong language skills are a requisite for learning to read; therefore, developing those skills should be the primary focus of professionals working with young DHH children and their families. When DHH students are ready to develop the complex skills required for learning to read, Visual Phonics can be used as a tool for teaching phonemic awareness and phonic skills.

Early Identification of Braille as the Primary Reading Medium for Students with Visual Impairments

Description of Students

Approximately 1 in 1,000 school-age children has a visual impairment (VI). About 10% of this population is blind, with the remainder having various degrees of vision loss (Council for Exceptional Children [CEC], 2007). The American Printing House (APH) 2008 Federal Quota Census data (APH, 2009) includes only 58,388 legally blind students nationally. This population is very heterogeneous, varying in degree of vision, functional use of vision, and the media used for reading. Moreover, about 60% of these children have multiple disabilities (Ferrell, Shaw, & Deitz, 1998).

Learners who are blind or have severe VI need to develop fluency in reading and writing. Because fluency in reading develops over time (Pikulski, 2006), disruptions in the student's developmental process of learning to read can disrupt the eventual attainment of fluency in reading. Early identification of potential braille readers is critical to promote essential early experiences with braille that will allow these children to learn to read and write using braille as their literacy medium from kindergarten.

Description and Implementation of Practice

The IDEA requires that the individualized education program (IEP) team consider braille for a child who has a VI unless a reason is identified for not considering this literacy medium (IDEA, 2004). It is important to make the determination as early as possible if a child who has VI is likely to be a braille reader. To determine whether a child should learn to read using braille or print, or both, the teacher certified in visual impairments (TVI) should collaborate with the IEP team to conduct a learning media assessment (LMA) that includes information on the eye condition, including whether it is degenerative and likely to result in progressive vision loss; a functional vision evaluation; information on sensory functioning (i.e., visual, tactile, and auditory); and information on additional disabilities. Results of the assessment are used to determine whether the primary literacy medium would be print or braille. The TVI may need to educate the team, including the parents, as to the consequences of delaying instruction in braille. Once braille has been identified as either the primary or secondary literacy medium, it must be purposefully and systematically inserted into the child's literacy environment.

Parents and classroom teachers need assistance from the TVI to provide a braille-rich literacy environment that will facilitate learning to read braille. Exposure to braille in books, braille writing equipment, braille labels and letters, and role models of braille readers and writers should be included along with the typical language-rich activities necessary for learning to read. Beginning in kindergarten, students should have daily formal instruction in braille reading and writing. Whether the initial reading curriculum is a braille adaptation of the school's reading curriculum, or whether the TVI introduces a specialized braille curriculum for teaching reading in braille, instruction should be provided on a daily basis similar to what is provided for sighted print readers.

Theoretical Underpinnings

According to Steinman, LeJeune, and Kimbrough (2006), the development of braille reading skills follows the same developmental progression as print reading (Chall, 1983), with the exception that fluency building may extend over a longer period for braille readers until all braille contractions are introduced. Braille reading involves learning more symbols than are involved in print reading, and the number of symbols introduced each year varies according to the learner (Wall Emerson, Holbrook, & D'Andrea, 2009). Steinman and colleagues anticipate that students who are learning braille will be continually moving between Chall's Stage 1 level of reading (learning grapheme–phoneme correspondence) and subsequent stages, at least until they have learned the entire character set for braille reading. Depending on how contractions are introduced to students, this can take them up through third grade (Rex, Koenig, Wormsley, & Baker, 1994), although many students learn all contractions by the end of first or second grade (Wall Emerson, Holbrook, et al., 2009).

When all the symbols are learned, students can begin to concentrate in earnest on fluency building. Even those students with VI who begin braille reading in kindergarten are not necessarily on a par with their sighted peers in terms of their reading rates or achievement (Wall Emerson, Sitar, Erin, Wormsley, & Herlich, 2009). However, when braille instruction is not begun early, students who are braille readers fall even further behind their sighted peers in reading comprehension and fluency. In other words, the later braille is identified as the students' primary literacy medium, the later reading and writing instruction in braille will begin, and the more likely it is that the student will be hopelessly behind her peers in learning to read and write. Early identification of braille occurs most often when a highly qualified TVI is available in the school district who has experience in assessing students with VI, when TVIs have adequate instruction and experience in using the LMA to determine the literacy medium, and when TVIs are confident in their ability to teach braille and understand the importance of early, daily instruction in braille reading and writing (Spungin, 1990).

Research Base

Koenig and Holbrook (1995) developed the most commonly used LMA to be performed by a TVI with other members of the individualized family services plan (IFSP)/IEP team, including parents. Since its development, LMA has become an accepted practice in the field of blindness and VI, although tests of validity and reliability of this procedure are yet to be conducted. Other assessments of learning and literacy media have followed the Koenig and Holbrook model, with some combining functional vision assessment and LMA (Sanford & Burnett, 2008).

Sharpe, McNear, and Bosma (1995) created an inventory of items rated by a national sample of 225 TVIs, administrators, and university professors to include in their own LMA, which had many similarities to the original LMA (Koenig & Holbrook, 1995). A developmentally appropriate LMA modeled on the Koenig and Holbrook LMA has been adapted for early intervention (Anthony, 2003). Although still somewhat subjective, the LMA provides information to guide the decision about the literacy medium for a child who has VI.

Hatton and Erickson (2005) surveyed 184 adults who were blind or had VI, ages 22 to 75, who had at least a 4-year college degree and who had VI before age 6 years. When asked what would have made it easier for them to read and write, the group that used braille as their primary literacy medium ($n = 85$) listed their three most frequent responses as having more accessible resources (47.1%), having caregivers learn braille (34.1%), and having braille taught earlier (27.1%). Of those who did not use braille, the most frequent response again was having more accessible resources (39.7%) and the second was having braille taught earlier (25%). Approximately a quarter of the group surveyed, therefore, felt that having braille taught earlier would have made it easier for them to learn to read and write.

Koenig and Holbrook (2000) conducted a Delphi study with 40 professionals (university faculty, program administrators, and experienced TVIs) in the field of VI to gain consensus on the length of instruction time, the number of days per week, and the length of time overall for particular developmental phases in reading. Respondents agreed that development of early formal literacy skills ("prebraille") requires 30 to 60 minutes a day and that development of beginning braille literacy skills (first through third grade) needs 1 to 2 hours of daily instruction.

S. Millar (1974) examined tactile short-term memory in four related experiments with blind and sighted subjects. One of the conditions, delay after stimulus presentation, was shown to have detrimental effects on memory. As S. Millar stated, "the longer-term memory evolves, or is accessed, only with continual trials" (p. 262). Rex and colleagues (1994) suggested that the rapid decay of tactile memory contributes to difficulty learning and retaining braille characters. In reviewing the research on neuroscience and the impact of brain plasticity on braille reading, Hannan (2006) found neurological evidence for the brain's reorganizing itself to accommodate a tactile reading skill. "Lack of practice or reinforcement of skills causes atrophy" (p. 410). These findings support the recommendation for consistent delivery of daily braille instruction and continuous use of braille to enhance learning.

Early introduction of braille contributes to building fluency in reading. Trent and Truan (1997) interviewed 30 adolescent braille readers at the Tennessee School for the Blind, tested their reading rates, and separated them into three groups according to their rates of reading. The fastest readers were those who had learned braille from the beginning of their schooling. These researchers conclude that it is difficult, if not impossible, for students introduced to braille in the third grade or later to catch up with those who learned braille when they began school. Using a case study approach, Truan and Trent (1997) examined three adolescent males who had learned braille in late adolescence due to deteriorating eye conditions. In each case the reading rates were low, between 21 and 28 words per minute (wpm).

Wormsley (1996) reported on the reading rates of 22 elementary school braille readers (ages 6 to 12) obtained during an entire school year. The four fastest readers (highest rates 91 to 145 wpm) all began braille at ages 5 or 6 and had received 4 to 5 years of braille instruction up to the time of the study. However, these learners also were among the students with the highest IQ scores. The four slowest readers (highest rates 17 to 30 wpm) began their braille instruction at ages 6 to 9, had 1 to 2 years of braille instruction, and had lower IQ scores.

Knowlton and Wetzel (1996) reported on the reading rates of 23 braille reading adults, ages 23 to 68 years, who had learned to read from the beginning of their reading instruction at 5 to 7 years of age. These adults read

65 to 185 wpm for oral reading tasks, with a mean of 135 wpm. In contrast, Bruteig (1987) studied the reading rates of 35 adventitiously blinded adults ages 20 to 70 who learned braille after already learning to read print; Bruteig found rates of reading between 15 and 70 wpm, with a mean of 38.7 wpm.

The studies reviewed (as summarized in Appendix 9.1, at the end of this chapter) emphasize the need for early identification of potential braille readers and timely introduction of braille. When braille is ultimately to be a student's literacy medium, delaying its introduction means inhibiting the student's ability to build fluency that will enable him to gain access to the general education curriculum.

General Strengths

Although sparse, the research on reading rates of braille readers provides evidence that early identification of braille as the primary literacy medium and early introduction of braille reading and writing instruction can have beneficial effects on the development of fluent reading speeds. The combination of a Delphi study approach (Koenig & Holbrook, 2000) with the research provided by S. Millar (1974), Rex and colleagues (1994), and Hannan (2006) on tactual memory demonstrate that daily reading instruction is essential for these readers, just as it is for print readers.

General Limitations

Studies conducted have limited numbers of participants partly due to the low-incidence population. Studies with braille readers have varied in the age of subjects, degree of VI, and focus of the investigation. The limited number of researchers focusing on literacy and the lack of a concerted and unified effort to coordinate research with this population have resulted in scattered and fragmented information.

Although results of the studies reported here are fairly consistent in terms of the reading rates reported, the rates are still slow and do not approach the norms for print readers. For example, Wall Emerson, Holbrook, et al. (2009) reported on the results of the ABC Braille study, a longitudinal study of 40 young braille readers from kindergarten through fourth grade. The results showed that their overall oral reading rates did not keep pace compared with the oral reading rate norms for their sighted peers. Edmonds and Pring (2006) matched 17 children who have VI with 17 sighted children on decoding age. The groups were comparable to each other in their ability to infer, but when chronological age was compared, the children who have VI were on average a year older. These research studies suggest that even those students who were identified as braille readers and who had braille instruction from kindergarten fell behind their sighted print-reading age peers in fluency and other reading skills. These studies also seem to suggest that simply identifying braille as the literacy medium and beginning braille reading and writing instruction in kindergarten are perhaps not early enough.

Although there is a rich research base on the emergent and early literacy experiences of sighted children leading to their success in learning to read and write, there is a dearth of research on early intervention with children who are blind and potential braille readers (Erickson & Hatton, 2007; Erickson, Hatton, Roy, Fox, & Renne, 2007; Murphy, Hatton, & Erickson, 2008). No intervention studies have been conducted on the effectiveness of strategies commonly used to promote the emergent and early literacy skills of young children with visual impairments.

Recommendations for Future Research

Because children with VI are so heterogeneous, the use of well-designed, qualitative, small-group, and single-subject studies would contribute to the development of a research base. For example, a series of longitudinal case studies following students as they progress to formal learning of reading and writing through braille, print, or both as their literacy medium and through their elementary schooling would be a rich source of evidence. Research should examine the efficacy of LMA for determining the literacy media, the influence of an enriched emergent literacy environment, and the early introduction of a literacy medium to young children with VI along with daily instruction in braille reading and writing using various approaches on children's literacy skills and outcomes. Moreover, just as research has identified the significance of early literacy experiences for sighted children in their development of literacy skills, it follows that early intervention with children who are potential braille readers would also be important. To facilitate the early introduction of braille reading and writing in kindergarten, research is needed to examine the determination of literacy media in the preschool years.

Summative Recommendations for Practice

Although the research based specifically on instructional practices with young children who are potential braille readers is sparse, research-based practices support early identification of potential braille readers and early introduction to daily instruction in braille reading and writing in order for them to develop fluent reading. A concerted effort is needed to promote these practices that will support the successful literacy outcomes for students who are blind or VI.

Tangible Symbols with Students Who Are Deaf-Blind

Description of Students

The most recent report from the National Deaf-Blind Child Count (National Consortium on Deaf-Blindness [NCDB], 2009) identifies 9,200 infants, children, and young adults (between birth and 21 years) as "deaf-blind." These learners vary greatly in degree of visual impairment and hearing loss and in the nature of their additional disabilities, with the majority having some usable vision or hearing. At one extreme, some children have mild hearing loss and functional vision; and at the other, some children are totally blind and have profound hearing loss. Furthermore, more than 90% of children who are deaf-blind (DB) have additional disabilities, such as cognitive impairments (66%), orthopedic or other physical impairments (57%), complex health care needs (38%), behavior challenges (9%), and other problems (30%) (Killoran, 2007).

The combination of hearing loss with visual impairment has a severe influence on communication skills (D. Chen, 2005). As demonstrated in the memorable example of Helen Keller's first understanding of a word, "water," children who are totally DB need specific supports and experiences to develop an understanding of symbols. Although the majority of learners who are DB have some functional vision, hearing, or both, the lack of access to clear information through the visual and/or auditory senses and the additional disabilities further complicate the development of symbolic language.

Definition and Implementation of Practice

Objects, textures, and other concrete representations that facilitate memory, cognitive, and communication skills have been used with learners who are DB. These so-called "tangible symbols" are defined as three-dimensional (e.g., objects) and two-dimensional (e.g., photographs) symbols that are permanent and can be manipulated by the learner as a means of expressive communication (Rowland & Schweigert, 1989). Other terms, such as objects of reference (Aiken, Buultjens, Clark, Eyre, & Pease, 2000), object cues (D. Chen & Downing, 2006), object symbols (Bloom, 1990), and tangible cues (Trief, 2007), are also found in the literature. All these terms refer to concrete items (e.g., object, picture, textured form) that are initially used to (a) promote the learner's understanding of the daily routine, activity sequences or options, people, places, events, or things (i.e., receptive communication); and (b) provide a means by which the learner can make requests, refusals, or choices (i.e., expressive communication). Tangible symbols provide a means of communicative exchange for a child who does not understand abstract symbols and should be used to supplement spoken and signed communication (D. Chen & Downing, 2006).

Effective intervention with learners who are DB requires a systematic approach to (a) select an appropriate mode of communication and instructional procedures that will overcome the limitations of combined visual impairments and hearing loss and (b) promote use of the selected mode (Sigafoos, Didden, Schlosser, Green, O'Reilly, & Lancioni, 2008). A literature review suggests the following sequence of planning and implementation of tangible symbols (D. Chen & Downing, 2006; Murray-Branch, Udvari-Solner, & Bailey, 1991; Rowland & Schweigert, 1989, 2000; Turnell & Carter, 1994):

1. Conduct an authentic interdisciplinary assessment of the learner's communication skills, preferences, and interests. Provide an interdisciplinary team to address considerations related to the child's vision, hearing, cognitive, and motor skills in developing an individualized tangible symbol communication system. Use ecological and preference inventories to identify opportunities that are likely to motivate the learner's communication interactions.

2. Draw on assessment results to develop an individualized intervention plan and materials to support the learner's communication skills. Results should reveal (a) high-frequency vocabulary that the learner will be motivated to use, (b) types of materials that the learner is likely to touch and manipulate, and (c) the starting point for the appropriate level of representation based on perceptual features from the learner's perspective. For example, if a child enjoys the playground swing and holds on to the chain attached on each side of the swing, then an appropriate tangible symbol to represent "swing" would be a 3-inch piece of chain.

3. Begin with a limited number of selected tangible symbols to represent frequently occurring and motivating activities, and teach the learner to indicate choices, express desires, or initiate conversations. Selected items should be tactilely salient and distinctive from each other. Increase the array of tangible symbols to represent different referents as the learner demonstrates recognition and understanding of selected symbols.

4. Gradually increase the use of abstract symbolic representations. At first, objects selected as tangible symbols must be those that are used in the actual activity in order for the child to understand what they represent. For example, a lunch ticket that is required to purchase lunch may be used as a referent for the upcoming activity. Once the learner associates the selected object (tangible symbol) with its referent, fade the use of concrete objects, and introduce more abstract tangible symbols to increase the distance between the "tangible symbol" and its referent.

5. Select tangible symbols that are easy for the child to discriminate and small enough to be portable. Avoid the use of miniatures whose similarities to their referents are purely visual (e.g., plastic dog to refer to a pet).

6. Organize the learner's tangible symbols to be accessible to the student and to be used consistently across activities, people, and environments (e.g., a partitioned box for an activity schedule, a binder separated by categories, a communication board). Write the intended message on the tangible symbol or on the material that holds the tangible symbol.

7. Implement use of the tangible-symbol communication system consistently in daily activities through systematic and direct instruction using behavioral strategies (e.g., reinforcement, prompting, fading). Once the learner understands its meaning, include the tangible symbol with others to offer a choice. Present the tangible symbol for the preferred referent with a foil (i.e., symbol without a referent) or a tangible symbol that represents a disliked referent.

8. Collect trial-by-trial data on the learner's expressive use of tangible symbols, and analyze these data at least weekly to identify any need for changing instruction.

9. Implement opportunities for generalization of tangible symbols across settings and people. Learners should have consistent access to their communication systems wherever they are. Further, communication partners need to be trained to engage the learner in communication using her preferred system.

Theoretical Underpinnings

The use of tangible symbols in the field of deaf-blindness is derived from theories of early symbolic communication. According to Werner and Kaplan (1963), children develop symbols first by associating objects or topics with concrete representations and gradually making abstract or distant (i.e., not intrinsic) associations (i.e., words) through "distancing" processes termed *denaturalization* and *decontextualization.* Denaturalization is the decreasing need for similarity between the communicative act and that which it represents. The continuum ranges from expressions in which the communicative act and its meaning are the same (e.g., the student puts the teacher's hand on the cookie jar to request a cookie), to the most denaturalized or abstract communicative act, using speech or sign to make a request. Decontextualization is the process through which the meaning of the communicative act becomes constant regardless of where it appears and who uses it. For example, an identical object (e.g., cup) used in and to represent the activity (e.g., snack) is a concrete and proximal representation that is understood within a specific context; whereas an arbitrary symbol (e.g., the printed or spoken word *snack*) is an abstract and distal representation whose meaning is understood no matter where it is used.

Decades ago, van Dijk (1967) introduced the systematic use of objects to facilitate communication with children who are DB. He drew on the work of Werner and Kaplan's (1963) concept of distancing to help children learn ways to characterize and recognize people, objects, animals, and events. These characteristics are used to help the child develop concepts of time, for example, by using objects to depict a tangible sequence of daily activities, as well as events and activities (e.g., going to the beach), by using a "memory" book or box that contains artifacts related to the experience.

Pierce (1932, as cited in E. Bates, Benigni, Bretherton, Camaioni, & Volterra, 1979) identified three types of signs or symbolic means (e.g., words or pictures): index, icon, and symbol. An index is a sign that is part of or participates in the object or event that it represents (e.g., a lunch ticket to indicate "lunch time"). An icon is a sign that is related to its referent through some physical, visual, or tactile resemblance; but unlike an index, an icon is not a component of the activity (e.g., a toy cup to indicate "lunch time"). A symbol is a sign related to its referent only through conventions agreed upon by its users (e.g., a textured shape to indicate lunch time that is a match to the one attached to the door of the cafeteria, the label "lunch time" in braille or print). Tangible symbols are thought to be effective with learners who are DB because they are concrete indices or icons whose representations are easy to understand and perceive. Further, they provide a scaffold to the development of symbols because "distancing" can be encouraged through use of progressively more varied and abstract objects and symbols (Bruce, 2005).

Research Base

Although tangible symbols (objects and other concrete representations) have been used for decades both nationally and internationally with learners who are DB (Aiken et al., 2000; Bloom, 1990; Rowland & Schweigert, 1989; van Dijk, 1967), research on this practice is limited. Appendix 9.2, at the end of this chapter, identifies studies, sample size, age range, characteristics, research design, and key findings of available studies. The majority

of participants had sensory impairments, intellectual disabilities, physical disabilities, and medical problems.

Murray-Branch and colleagues (1991) evaluated the use of textured symbols with two high-school-aged girls who were DB and had additional disabilities. Although one learner understood 28 receptive tactile signs, she used only four signs, infrequently and often incorrectly; the other learner communicated through facial expressions and vocalizations. Textured symbols were selected as a communication means because they motivated manual searching, were portable, and were easy to discriminate. After 3 months of systematic direct individual instruction (three to four times a day) in daily, naturally occurring activities (at least 10 opportunities in each activity), both learners demonstrated use of multiple textured symbols to make requests and indicate choices for preferred items and activities. One girl learned to use 3 and the other used 20 symbols. The intervention included generalization of textured symbols use across environments and people. No reliability data were reported.

Rowland and Schweigert (1989) examined the use of tangible symbols with nine school-age participants with severe intellectual impairments, visual impairments, and hearing loss. Case studies are reported for two children (a 6-year-old girl and a 4.5-year-old boy) with severe-to-profound hearing loss, VI or blindness, and severe intellectual disabilities. Training involved offering a high-preference item to the learner and prompting the learner to select its tangible symbol representation (from an array of one to three symbols) and give it to the teacher. Correct selection was reinforced by the preferred activity or item. Findings revealed that all nine learners acquired 16 to 98 symbols (mean of 43) in 10 to 19 months of training (mean of 14.5 months). On average, participants required 13.4 training sessions to acquire the first three symbols, which decreased to an average of 6.5 training sessions for the last three symbols across home and school settings. Some learners also acquired two-dimensional symbols (line drawings) and manual signs. Learners demonstrated increased communication development as measured by the Wisconsin Behavior Rating Scale (Song et al., 1980) and the Callier Azusa Scale-H (Stillman & Battle, 1986). The majority used tangible symbols in typical classroom activities as measured by observational data during three 1-hour observations per month. Communicative behavior (presymbolic and symbolic) was scored for each 30-second interval, and reliability was calculated on 20% of the observations. This study used a pre and post-test design and lacked a control group.

Rowland and Schweigert (2000) implemented the use of tangible symbols (i.e., objects, textures, and pictures) with 41 learners (3 to 18 years, mean of 6 years; 24 males and 17 females) who had severe and multiple disabilities. Most did not understand speech, signs, or printed words.

Some communicated through gestures, and seven had a few spoken words and used a few (one to eight) tangible symbols. Seven had both visual impairment and hearing loss. The Communication Matrix (Rowland, 1996) and Levels of Representation Pretest (Rowland & Schweigert, 1990) were administered to determine the learner's expressive communication level and what level of symbolic representation, if any, would be meaningful to that individual. Learners without intentional communicative behaviors were first taught to use presymbolic communication behaviors (e.g., hand movements, vocalizations) for intentional communication (e.g., make requests, gain attention, establish joint attention). Once these were accomplished, then tangible symbols were introduced.

Intervention began with one-symbol arrays and increased quickly to two- and three-symbol arrays, with some learners making selections from a book of symbols. The initial communication function was requesting, with some learners moving to comments and labels. Learners were required to point to or touch a symbol while looking at the communication partner or give it to the communication partner before obtaining the motivating referent. Intervention involved direct individual instruction by project staff for approximately 15 minutes during each school day for an average of 6.5 months. Results indicate that 35 of the 41 children acquired the use of tangible symbols (average of 12 to 22 symbols) for expressive communication, and some progressed to using abstract symbols including speech. Two of the seven learners who were DB failed to acquire any tangible symbols. Learners were considered to have acquired a new symbol when they independently made the correct selection from an array of at least three symbols for at least 80% of the trials over two consecutive sessions. A reliability probe conducted by the project coordinator during observation of 40% of all direct intervention sessions during 5 consecutive days resulted in a mean of 92% agreement. Data from monthly videotapes were compared to data collected during the intervention session. Mean interobserver agreement on direct observation sessions was 90%. Reliability checks obtained on 20% of the monthly videotapes of intervention sessions resulted in a mean kappa coefficient of 0.89. This study used a pre–post-test design but did not include baseline data, control group, or sufficient detail to enable replication.

Trief (2007) implemented the use of tangible symbols with 25 learners (4 to 16 years) who were blind or VI with additional disabilities. Ten were totally blind, and 15 had low vision. A total of 28 tangible symbols that consisted of whole or parts of objects embedded in a cardboard card represented daily activities and places in the school. Learners were asked to select the corresponding symbol from an array of two cues and hand it to the communication partner for the activity to begin.

They were introduced to different symbols depending on their daily activities. Data were collected and compared from the beginning (September) to the end of the school year (June). Five learners learned the referents of all 28 symbols, 10 learners identified 1 to 20 symbols, and 10 students (who had the most severe cognitive, physical, and visual disabilities) failed to learn any symbols. This study is an intervention study that does not provide baseline information or sufficient detail for replication. Although this sample did not include learners who are DB, they had similar additional disabilities and communication difficulties. This study was also included as the most recent of those investigating the use of tangible symbols and focused on the daily school schedule rather than targeting high-preference objects or activities.

Turnell and Carter (1994) found that an 8-year-old boy who had a VI, hearing loss, and other severe and multiple disabilities learned to use three tangible symbols to make requests. These tangible symbols represented high-preference activities and items: a bike, a spinning toy, and a walking frame. Instruction involved three sessions a day each, with five trials, for a total of 15 trials a day over 9 school weeks. This study used a multiple-probe design across symbols.

Summary

The few available studies on the use of tangible symbols with learners who are DB or VI with significant multiple disabilities highlight the diversity of these students in terms of sensory status, abilities, and learning needs. These characteristics contribute to the challenges of building an evidence base on effective practices.

General Strengths

All studies included an interdisciplinary team (e.g., special education teacher, speech and language pathologist, occupational or physical therapist) approach in the development of selected symbols and used ecological inventories to identify frequently occurring activities. With the exception of Trief (2007), studies focused on high-preference activities and used systematic and direct instruction. The majority of learners acquired the use of tangible symbols for making requests and choices. Tangible symbols appeared to serve as a scaffold to symbolic communication (manual signs or speech) for a few learners.

General Limitations

The extremely heterogeneous and low-incidence nature of school-age children labeled as "deaf-blind" is reflected in the various descriptions used by researchers and presents a challenge to rigorous research designs (e.g., matched intervention and control groups). Thus, evidence on the use of tangible symbols causing improved communication outcomes is inconclusive. Moreover, available studies of tangible symbols with learners who are DB were conducted more than 9 to 20 years ago, with a majority of learners in segregated classrooms. Another limitation is the general lack of emphasis on family involvement in the development and implementation of the communication intervention. Further, available research findings do not provide evidence by which to determine selection of a specific type of tangible symbol (index, icon, or symbol) that is likely to be easily understood and acquired by a particular learner.

Recommendations for Future Research

The evidence base for use of tangible symbols with learners who are DB should be expanded through a series of carefully designed single-subject studies that target learners with specific characteristics. This way, participants could be selected according to age, educational experience, degree of visual impairment and hearing loss, other disabilities, and communication level; and these studies could be replicated. Investigations could examine whether different types of tangible symbols (index, icon, or symbol) differ in their ease and rate of acquisition to guide the decision-making process for individual learners. Further, instruction and generalization could be implemented across environments and people. Participants should also include learners who are fully included in general education settings to identify ways to support communication with peers. Another source of evidence should be to examine communication intervention studies with learners who have a VI, hearing loss, and significant additional disabilities to identify potential interventions that may be appropriate for learners who are DB.

Summative Recommendations for Practice

To address the diverse abilities and needs of learners who are DB, an interdisciplinary team approach and family–professional collaboration are essential. Ecological and preference inventories are required to identify the initial vocabulary that should be translated into tangible symbols. Moreover, carefully planned and sequenced direct and individualized instruction with behavioral strategies and data collection are required to support the learner's acquisition of these symbols.

Conclusion

Clearly, research on instructional practices with students who have sensory disabilities is urgently needed. The promise of using Visual Phonics with DHH students should continue to be evaluated as the research base grows through extending the instructional settings and further defining the characteristics of DHH students for whom this practice is most beneficial. Similarly, the effects of early identification of students with VI who require braille as their primary reading medium will continue to be examined. Further research on tangible symbols is needed to reveal how they may scaffold the development of symbolic communication (i.e., expressive speech or sign production).

Access to participants with low-incidence disabilities and research could be increased through the development of national collaborative efforts among researchers with similar interests. Further, practitioners should be encouraged to contribute to the evidence base through systematic implementation of instruction and careful documentation, which could lead to publication of their instructional practices with learners who are DHH or DB, have a VI, or are blind.

Appendix 9.1

Available Studies on Braille Reading

Study	Sample Size	Age (Years)	Characteristics	Research Design	Findings
Trent & Truan (1997)	30	Adolescents	Scored at sixth-grade level of Gilmore Oral Reading Test. Grouped according to reading speed as well as age at which they lost vision.	Interview plus collection of data on Gilmore Oral Reading	Fastest readers were all in congenital/preschool group for onset; late-blinded group included students from middle and lowest reading groups.
Truan & Trent (1997)	3	17, 14, 18	Progressive vision loss resulting in severe visual impairment and learning braille in late adolescence.	Case study	Reading rates of 26, 28, and 21 wpm, respectively.
Wormsley (1996)	22	6–12	Braille as primary reading medium.	Time Series Design/ Case studies	Four fastest readers all began braille at age 5 or 6; had received 4–5 years of instruction; had high IQ scores. Four slowest readers began braille at ages 6–9; had 1–2 years of instruction; had lower IQ scores.
Knowlton & Wetzel (1996)	23	23–68	Braille reading as primary mode from ages 5–7.	4 x 3 factorial design: reading task with four levels, and presentation task with three levels.	Oral reading speeds ranged from 65–185 wpm (Mean = 135 wpm).
Bruteig (1987)	35	20–71	Late-blinded adults	Reading rate data on narrative texts in both contracted and uncontracted to compare speeds.	Silent reading rates of 15–70 wpm (Mean = 38.7 wpm).

Appendix 9.2

Available Studies on Tangible Symbols

Study	Sample Size	Age (Years)	Characteristics	Research Design	Findings
Murray-Branch et al. (1991)	2	15–19	Blind, HL, cerebral palsy, severe–profound intellectual disability, microcephaly medical problems	Case study Intervention study	3–20 symbols used for requests and choices
Rowland & Schweigert (1989)	9	"school age"	VI, severe–profound HL intellectual disability	Pre–post (Case study for 2)	16–98 symbols used for requests and choices
Rowland & Schweigert (2000)	41 (7 DB)	3–18	VI, HL, physical disabilities, seizure disorders, autism, intellectual disability	Pre–post	35 acquired 3–35 symbols for requests and choices
Trief (2007)	25	4–16	VI, moderate–severe intellectual disabilities, physical disabilities, seizure disorders	Intervention study	15 acquired 1–28 symbols to label activity
Turnell & Carter (1994)	1	8	Moderate HL, VI, athetoid quadriplegia, intellectual disability seizures	Multiple probe across symbols	3 symbols used for requests

Note: DB = deaf-blind; HL = hearing loss; VI = visual impairment including blindness.

CHAPTER 10

Teaching for Transition to Adulthood

David W. Test, Kelly R. Kelley, and **Dawn A. Rowe** | *University of North Carolina at Charlotte*

T hroughout all stages of life, individuals experience many transitions. Graduating from high school and pursuing a productive adulthood is one of the more significant transitions that adolescents face with long-term outcomes. Many changes take place for individuals with and without disabilities as they complete high school and move into adulthood, specifically in the areas of employment, education, and independent living. Halpern (1992) defined this transition as "a period of floundering that occurs for at least the first several years after leaving school as adolescents attempt to assume a variety of adult roles in their communities" (p. 203). For individuals with disabilities, this transition period is critical because the choices and actions made can affect them for a lifetime.

Numerous postschool outcome data continue to illustrate that individuals with disabilities have poor postschool outcomes compared to individuals without disabilities in education, employment, and independent living. Although reports of postschool outcomes for students with disabilities have shown some improvement since the first National Longitudinal Transition Study (NLTS), conducted from 1985 to 1993, they continue to remain dismal when compared to their peers without disabilities (Blackorby & Wagner, 1996; Wagner, Newman, Cameto, Garza, & Levine, 2005). Young adults with disabilities are performing much lower than their peers in postschool life skill areas essential to becoming productive members of society (i.e., education, employment,

independent living, and community living). In evaluating data across disability categories such as specific learning disabilities, emotional disturbances, and mental retardation based on the most recent National Longitudinal Transition Study (NLTS2) results, outcomes across disability categories also show variation (Newman, Wagner, Cameto, & Knokey, 2009).

For example, comparisons of postsecondary program enrollment results vary widely. In terms of education, Newman et al. (2009) reported 45% of youth with disabilities had pursued postsecondary education within 4 years of leaving high school compared to 53% of youth in the general population. In terms of education, students with disabilities who completed high school were three times more likely to be enrolled in postsecondary education than were students who did not complete high school (Newman et al., 2009). Postsecondary attendance up to 4 years after leaving high school ranged from 27% to 78% across all students with disabilities. In comparing disability categories, 47% of students with learning disabilities, 34% of students with emotional disturbances, and 27% of individuals with mental retardation reported participation in postsecondary programs (i.e., vocational, technical, community, and university). Despite the reported 89% of youth with disabilities intending to finish their degree or certificate programs, only 29% of the students reported completion of the programs, with the remaining 71% of participants with disabilities not graduating or completing their postsecondary programs.

In terms of employment, 57% of youth with disabilities leaving high school were employed outside of the home compared to 67% of the general population (Newman et al., 2009). Employment status fluctuated greatly in comparison to the NLTS2 (Wagner, Newman, Cameto, Levine, & Garza, 2006) data. Again, employment rates varied across disability categories. For example, 64% of students with learning disabilities, 42% of students with emotional disturbances, and 31% of individuals with mental retardation were currently working at the time of the interviews (Newman et al., 2009).

Twenty-five percent of youth with disabilities as compared to 28% of the general population reported living independently (Newman et al., 2009). Across disability categories, 29% of individuals with learning disabilities, 22% with emotional disturbances, and 14% with mental retardation reported living independently. Although at least 56% of youth with disabilities reported having savings accounts and 28% reported having credit cards in their name, few could live independently or provide for additional family members because 89% had annual incomes of $25,000 or less, and more than half of these youth earned less than $5,000 per year. Although these results have changed for the better over time, there continues to be room for improvement.

One way to help improve postschool outcomes is to use research-based practices and predictors to guide educational practices in secondary education settings. Test, Fowler, et al. (2009) conducted a literature review to identify research-based practices (i.e., practices supported by high-quality studies that use experimental research designs) in secondary transition. Overall, 32 secondary-transition research-based practices were identified. The majority of practices (*n* = 25; 78.1%) involved teaching students specific transition skills, such as self-determination skills and daily living skills. In addition, community-based instruction (CBI) was identified as a research-based practice.

Although these research-based practices were designed to teach students specific transition-related skills, to date, experimental studies have not measured the impact of these skills on postschool outcomes. As a result, Test, Mazzotti, et al. (2009) conducted a second literature review that included rigorous correlational research in secondary transition to identify the research-based predictors that correlated with improved postschool outcomes in education, employment, or independent living. Based on results of this review, 16 research-based, in-school predictors of postschool outcomes were identified. The three research-based practices most closely associated with positive postschool outcomes were: (a) self-advocacy/self-determination skills were

related to higher postschool education and employment outcomes; (b) self-care/independent living skills were related to higher postschool education, employment, and independent living outcomes; and (c) community experiences and paid employment/work experience were related to higher postschool outcomes in education, employment, and independent living.

In conclusion, based on high-quality experimental and correlational research, both self-determination skills and CBI have been identified as research-based instructional practices and predictors of postschool success. As a result, the remainder of this chapter provides more detail on each of these practices by first defining each one, providing a brief overview of the research base for each practice, and then describing examples of how to implement each practice.

Self-Determination
What Is Self-Determination?

One area that is currently receiving much attention in the research literature is self-determination. Self-determination is a construct based primarily on social psychology theories (Wehmeyer, 1992). For example, Deci and Ryan (1985) theorized that self-determination represents an innate human need to control one's life. Next, behavioral theory describes self-determination in terms of self-control, as individuals directing their own behavior. Finally, social learning theorists view self-determination as closely related to self-efficacy, individuals' belief that they can perform a certain behavior. As a result, Wehmeyer (1992) suggested

> Self-determination refers to the attitudes and abilities required to act as the primary causal agent in one's life and to make choices regarding one's actions free from undue external influence or interference. It involves autonomy (acting according to one's own priorities or principals [sic]), self-actualization (the full development of one's unique talents and potentials) and self-regulation (cognitive or self-controlled medication of one's behavior). (p. 304)

For teachers to promote self-determination in their classrooms more easily, the concept of self-determination has been divided into a number of teachable components (e.g., Field & Hoffman, 1994; Ward, 1988; Wehmeyer, 1996) including choice/decision making, goal setting/attainment, problem solving, self-evaluation/management, self-advocacy, person-centered individualized education program (IEP) planning, relationships with others, and self-awareness. Two specific strategies, the Self-Advocacy Strategy and the Self-Directed IEP, are examined in following sections in this chapter.

What Does Research Say About Self-Determination Skills?

Cobb, Lehmann, Newman-Gonchar, and Alwell (2009) identified seven narrative and systematic reviews published since 2000 on self-determination that concluded that self-determination interventions were effective. Furthermore, self-determination skills have been identified as a research-based predictor of postschool success (Test, Mazzotti, et al., 2009). For example, Benitez, Lattimore, and Wehmeyer (2005) found that teaching self-determination skills in high school was positively correlated with improved postschool outcomes for students with disabilities. Wehmeyer and Palmer (2003) found that self-determination skills in high school were significant predictors of postschool education and independent living success. When used in combination with Direct Instruction strategies, self-determination strategies have resulted in improved academic performance by both students with learning disabilities (Konrad, Fowler, Walker, Test, & Wood, 2007) and developmental disabilities (Fowler, Konrad, Walker, Test, & Wood, 2007).

Finally, Test, Fowler, et al. (2009) identified teaching self-determination skills as a research-based instructional practice based on their literature review of high-quality experimental research (using both group and single-subject designs). Similarly, Test and colleagues' (2004) review of the literature on interventions designed to increase students' involvement in their IEP process found that using the IEP process is an excellent way to increase student self-determination skills. Test et al. (2004) found that students with widely varying disabilities can be actively involved in the IEP process and that both published curricula designed to teach students skills to enhance their participation before IEP meetings and person-centered planning strategies were effective in increasing students' involvement in their IEP meetings. Two research-based practices that teach self-determination strategies via the IEP process are the Self-Advocacy Strategy (Van Reusen & Bos, 1994; Test & Neale, 2004) and the Self-Directed IEP (Allen, Smith, Test, Flowers, & Wood, 2001; Arndt, Konrad, & Test, 2006; Martin, Van Dycke, Christensen, et al., 2006).

The Self-Advocacy Strategy

The Self-Advocacy Strategy is a motivation strategy designed to prepare students to participate in any education or transition-planning meeting. Prerequisites include a willingness to learn the strategy and the ability to communicate (i.e., through gestures or words). The Self-Advocacy Strategy consists of five steps that can be taught over a series of seven lessons. The five steps are presented using the acronym "I PLAN" to help students remember the steps in the strategy:

1. *I*nventory your strengths, areas to improve or to learn, goals, and choices for learning or accommodations. In this first step, students complete an inventory sheet that they can use at their meetings. This inventory identifies strengths, areas to improve or to learn, goals, and choices for learning or accommodations.

2. *P*rovide your inventory information. In the second step, students use their inventory sheet during discussion in the IEP meeting.

3. *L*isten and respond. The third step involves students' learning the proper times to listen (e.g., when someone is making a statement, when someone is asking a question) and respond (e.g., when someone asks a question, when you have information to add).

4. *A*sk questions. The fourth step involves teaching students how to ask questions when they don't understand what people are saying.

5. *N*ame your goals. The last step teaches students to name the goals they would like included in their IEP.

Based on criteria used by Test, Fowler, et al. (2009), the Self-Advocacy Strategy was identified as having a moderate level of evidence based on one high-quality group experimental study (Van Reusen & Bos, 1994) and four acceptable-quality single-subject studies (Hammer, 2004; Lancaster, Schumaker, & Deshler, 2002; Test & Neale, 2004; Van Reusen, Deshler, & Schumaker, 1989). Research studies documenting the positive effects of the Self-Advocacy Strategy have involved both males and females, aged 12 to 17, identified as having mild-to-moderate disabilities to participate in their IEP meeting. In addition, students who served as participants in these studies were identified as Caucasian, Hispanic, African American, Native American, or Asian Pacific Islander. The Self-Advocacy Strategy has been taught using both teacher-led instruction and technology-guided instruction using hypermedia and CD-ROM. For example, Test and Neale (2004) taught the Self-Advocacy Strategy in ten 20- to 45-minute tutoring sessions over 2 weeks to four students with mild disabilities. Figure 10.1 is the research-to-practice lesson plan for using the Self-Advocacy Strategy. Research-to-practice lessons provide teachers with basic information needed to develop a lesson plan including an objective, setting and materials, content to be taught, teaching procedures, and an evaluation strategy. All material in a research-to-practice lesson plan starter is taken directly from one of the published articles used by Test, Fowler, et al. (2009) to establish the research base for the practice.

Figure 10.1 Research-to-practice lesson plan starter for using the Self-Advocacy Strategy.

Objective: To teach students to enhance the quality of their verbal contributions and self-determination skills using the Self-Advocacy Strategy

Setting and Materials:

Setting: Classroom

Materials:

1. The Self-Advocacy Strategy for Education and Transition Planning Manual
2. Tape recorder or video camera (optional for recording student responses)

Content Taught:

The Self-Advocacy Strategy is a motivation and self-determination strategy designed to prepare students to participate in education or transition-planning conferences. The strategy consists of five steps using the acronym "I PLAN" to help cue students to remember the steps for using this strategy.

   Step 1: I = "Inventory." Students list their strengths, areas to improve or to learn, education and transition goals, accommodations needed, and choices for learning on an inventory sheet.

   Step 2: P = "Provide Your Inventory Information." Focuses on teaching students how to provide input during the meeting.

   Step 3: L = "Listen and Respond." Relates to listening to others' statements or questions and responding appropriately.

   Step 4: A = "Ask Questions." Involves asking appropriate questions to gather needed information.

   Step 5: N = "Name your Goals." Communicates personal goals and ideas on actions to be taken.

Ten lessons are taught to the students one-on-one, with lessons ranging from 20 to 45 minutes each. The entire curriculum can be taught in approximately 2 weeks.

Teaching Procedures:

1. Give the pretest by asking the students the 10 questions listed below before beginning instruction, and record or score their responses based on a 4-point scale (see evaluation).

2. Teach the lessons and specific instructional phases as outlined in the teacher's handbook of the Self-Advocacy Strategy.

3. Ask students the 10 questions again, and record their responses after phase three (model and prepare), four (verbal practice), five (practice and feedback), and six (practice and feedback), which also mark specific mastery points of the Self-Advocacy Strategy.

4. When possible, ask the students the 10 questions during their actual IEP meeting to see if the skills are generalized to other settings and conditions.

Evaluation:

   a. (Student's Name), what do you think are your strongest study or learning skills?

   b. Can you tell me what you think are your weakest study or learning skills?

   c. What skills do you want to improve or learn over this next year that will help you to do better in school or get along better with other people?

   d. Can you tell me about any activities or materials that teachers have shared with you in the past that have helped you learn your school subjects?

   e. Are there any after-school activities, such as sports, jobs, or clubs, in which you want to become involved?

   f. Many students at your age have begun to think about careers or jobs they might like after they finish high school. Upon graduating from school, what kind of job or career would you like to pursue?

   g. What types of study or learning activities work best for you?

   h. What size learning or study group works best for you?

   i. I'm sure you've taken a lot of tests during your years in school. Can you name or describe the type of test items on which you do best when taking tests over material you have learned?

   j. Is there anything we've overlooked or something you'd like to say about school, or any other area you are concerned about?

Score the student responses to pretest/post-test questions using a 4-point scale:

   0 = student does not respond or does not know the answer

   1 = student response is not related to the specific question asked

   2 = student response is related to the question, but is not specific enough

   3 = student responds to the question appropriately and with specific details

Note: Lesson plan based on: Test, D. W., & Neale, M. (2004). Using the *Self-Advocacy Strategy* to increase middle graders' IEP participation. *Journal of Behavioral Education, 13,* 135–145.

Source: Based on National Secondary Transition Technical Assistance Center (NSTTAC) Lesson Plan Starters. National Secondary Transition Technical Assistance Center. (2008). *IEP meeting participation using the Self-Advocacy Strategy (2).* Charlotte, NC: NSTTAC. Retrieved from http://nsttac.appstate.edu/sites/default/files/assets/pdf/5.pdf.

The Self-Directed IEP

The Self-Directed IEP (Martin, Marshall, Maxson, & Jerman, 1997) consists of 11 steps students can follow to lead their own IEP meeting. Steps are organized across 11 lessons taught in six to ten 45-minute sessions. The Self-Directed IEP package also includes assessments, videotape, and student workbook. The 11 steps are:

1. *Begin meeting by stating the purpose:* Students learn how to explicitly state the purpose of the meeting (e.g., review goals).

2. *Introduce everyone:* Students learn who is required to be at an IEP meeting and who else they would like to invite, as well as practice introducing these individuals.

3. *Review past goals and performance:* Students state their goals and learn which actions can be taken to help meet their goals.

4. *Ask for others' feedback:* Students learn what feedback is and the different ways they can receive feedback on their goals.

5. *State your school and transition goals:* Students identify their interests, skills, and needs, and the goals they would like to achieve in school.

6. *Ask questions if you don't understand:* Students learn how to ask questions for clarification.

7. *Deal with differences in opinion:* Students learn the LUCK strategy (Listening to other person's opinion, Using a respectful tone of voice, Compromising or Changing your opinion if necessary, and Knowing and stating the reasons for your opinion).

8. *State the support you will need to reach your goal:* Students learn about the supports that will help them in achieving their goals.

9. *Summarize your current goals:* Students restate their goals and the actions they will take to meet those goals as well as state how they would receive feedback in meeting those goals.

10. *Close meeting by thanking everyone:* Students learn how to bring closure to the meeting by using closing statements and thanking everyone for attending.

11. *Work on IEP goals all year:* Students are reminded to work on their goals all year by taking actions, receiving feedback, and gaining support to accomplish these goals.

The Self-Directed IEP can be easily implemented by following the guidelines in the teacher's workbook. Each lesson follows the format listed in the research-to-practice lesson plan starter in Figure 10.2, under "Teaching Procedures."

Based on criteria used by Test, Fowler, et al. (2009), the Self-Directed IEP has a moderate level of evidence based on one high-quality group experimental study (Martin, Van Dycke, Christensen, et al., 2006) and has been used to teach both males and females, aged 12 to 21, identified as having mild-to-moderate disabilities to participate in their IEP meeting. In addition, students who served as participants in this study were identified as Caucasian, Hispanic, African American, and Native American.

Community-Based Instruction

What Is Community-Based Instruction?

CBI (sometimes referred to as *in vivo training*) is defined as instruction of functional skills that takes place in the community where target skills would naturally occur (L. Brown et al., 1983). It is a reality-based training program in which a student works and trains at selected community businesses, services, and other places, with desired outcomes being competitive employment and independent performance of living skills (Wehman & Kregel, 2003). The primary theory underlying CBI is that more naturalistic instructional arrangements allow students opportunities to respond to actual stimuli rather than simulations, thereby alleviating problems with generalizing skills taught (P. E. Bates, Cuvo, Miner, & Korabek, 2001; L. Brown et al., 1983). CBI provides opportunities for students to generalize newly learned skills to community settings in addition to opportunities for students with disabilities to be included in society with individuals without disabilities (Wolfe, 1994). This section describes CBI as a practice for teaching functional skills, including two examples of such skills.

What Does Research Say About CBI?

Research has shown that using CBI results in increased acquisition and generalization of employment and life skills for students with disabilities (P. E. Bates et al., 2001; Branham, Collins, Schuster, & Kleinert, 1999; Cihak, Alberto, Kessler, & Taber, 2004; Westling & Fox, 2009). Many skills that have been taught using CBI include laundry skills (P. E. Bates et al., 2001; Taylor, Collins, Schuster, & Kleinert, 2002), grocery shopping (Alcantara, 1994; P. E. Bates et al., 2001; Morse & Schuster, 2000), vocational skills, initiating requests, job training (P. E. Bates et al., 2001), leisure skills (Schloss et al., 1995), and safety skills (Taber, Alberto, Hughes, & Seltzer, 2002). When used in combination with appropriate

Figure 10.2 Research-to-practice lesson plan starter for using the Self-Directed IEP.

Objective: To teach students to participate in IEP meetings through the use of the Self-Directed IEP multimedia package modified for nonreaders.

Setting/Materials:

Setting: High school classroom

Materials: Self-Directed IEP Multimedia Package (includes teacher's manual, student workbook, two videos)

Content Taught: (Note: Not all steps were included in this study)

Instructional Unit 1: Leading Meeting

Step 1: Begin Meeting by Stating a Purpose

Step 2: Introduce Everyone

Step 3: Review Past Goals and Performance

Step 10: Close Meeting by Thanking Everyone

Instructional Unit 2: Reporting Interests

Step 5: State Your School and Transition Goals

Instructional Unit 3: Reporting Skills

Step 5: State Your School and Transition Goals

Instructional Unit 4: Reporting Options

Step 9: Summarize Your Goals

Teaching Procedures:

Within each step a similar format is followed:

    a. Review of prior steps, as needed.

    b. Preview lesson content and instruction on new vocabulary used.

    c. Videotape material provides model and sample situations used for guided practice.

    d. Workbook activities (e.g., teacher reads aloud, writes on overhead, and leads class discussion in place of workbook activities when needed) used to practice each step.

    e. Teacher demonstrates and students practice for real IEP meetings.

    f. Brief student skill evaluation.

    g. Ask students to relate skills to other situations, wrap up.

    h. Picture prompts are used for students with limited reading, writing, and cognitive skills.

Evaluation:

1. **Five Mock IEP Meetings.** After each instructional unit is completed, a mock IEP meeting is held using the following format:

    a. **State the Purpose of the Meeting:** (Name of Student), why are we having this meeting today?

    b. **Introduce Everyone:** (Name of Student), who is attending this meeting? (May point to self and other members of the meeting and say, "Who is that?/Who am I?")

    c. **Review Past Performance and Goals:** (Name of Student), do you think you have worked hard in school so far? What have you been working on?

    d. **Student Interests:** Great, (Name of Student). Before we look at new goals, let's talk about your interests. This discussion will help determine your new goals.

        – What do you want to learn about in school?

        – We have visited several job sites. What do you think you want to do after you graduate from high school?

        – What are some of your personal interests? What sports do you like to play or activities do you like to participate in? (Probe if necessary by providing examples of sports, activities, etc.)

- If you were going to live on your own or with a roommate, what daily living skills would you be interested in learning about?

- After you graduate from high school, where do you want to live?

- What community activities would you like to participate in?

e. **Skills and Limits:** For each area, which skills are you strong in and what skills do you need?

f. **Options and Goals:** OK, now we are going to write down several options for education (replace *education* with each of the areas). From these options, we are going to write goals for each of the transition areas.

- You have mentioned several school subjects that you are interested in. What other school subjects would you like to learn about? Repeat this format for all areas (use pictorial representations of the student's options if needed).

- Now, from your options, we are going to determine goals for you to work on. Talk to student about reasonable goals.

g. **Closing the Meeting:** Now that we have finished determining your goals, it's time to end the meeting. Let's review.

- (Name of Student), what are your new goals? Great job!

- (Name of Student), would you please bring our meeting to a close? (Cue for student to shake hands and say thank you.)

2. **Student Performance in Mock and Real IEP Meetings Is Measured Using Choicemaker Curriculum Checklist:**

Students are assessed on expressing both skills and limits in the areas of education, employment, personal, daily skills, housing, and community participation.

3. **Real IEP Meetings:**

The first real IEP meeting is held before any instruction begins. The second IEP meeting is held after all instruction and mock IEP meetings are completed.

a. (Name of Student), do you know why we are here today? Please tell us.

b. (Name of Student), please introduce the people attending your meeting.

c. Let's look at past goals and your progress toward them. (Cue for student to tell how well student did meeting past goals.)

d. OK, before we get started, let's talk about your interests, (Name of Student). Is there anything you would like to learn about in school?

e. What do you want to do after you graduate?

f. What are some skills that you would need to have to learn, live, or work on your own?

g. What are some skills limits?

h. I see you have some options for each transition area (referring to list of options created prior to the meeting). Please tell us a few.

i. Great. Now, let's decide on a goal for you to work toward. (Cue for student to state goal in each transition area.)

j. Nice job. Let's finish signing all of the paperwork, and then we will end this meeting.

k. What are some goals you are going to work toward? Thank you. (Cue for student to say thanks and shake hands.)

Note: Lesson plan based on: Allen, S., Smith, A., Test, D., Flowers, C., & Wood, W. (2001). The effects of *Self-Directed IEP* on student participation in IEP meetings. *Career Development for Exceptional Individuals, 24,* 107–120.

Source: Based on National Secondary Transition Technical Assistance Center (NSTTAC) Lesson Plan Starters. National Secondary Transition Technical Assistance Center. (2008). *IEP meeting participation: Using Choicemaker Self-Directed IEP.* Charlotte, NC: NSTTAC. Retrived from http://nsttac.appstate.edu/sites/default/files/assets/pdf/1_and_8.pdf.

nonintrusive instructional techniques—such as least-to-most prompts, nonexclusionary time-out, and data collection using a notepad or stopwatch—CBI has been found to be a socially valid teaching method (Wolfe, 1994). In a recent literature review on CBI, Walker, Uphold, Richter, and Test (2010) identified 23 studies that taught functional skills using CBI in one of four domains: vocational, daily living, community, and recreation. The two most common skills taught using CBI in these studies were grocery shopping ($n = 6$; 26.1%) and employment skills ($n = 4$; 17.4%). Overall, studies reviewed showed increases in target skill acquisition for participants.

Because CBI is an essential component of transition programming and has been identified as a research-based practice leading to improved postschool outcomes (Test, Fowler, et al., 2009), it is important to include CBI in the educational programming of students with disabilities at all grade levels and across functional content areas such as grocery shopping and employment skills.

Teaching Grocery Shopping

Teaching grocery shopping skills includes instruction on making a shopping list, locating items in a grocery store, locating and then purchasing items from a shopping list, and choosing items that are more economical or the better buy. The instructional practices associated with teaching grocery shopping include various levels and orders of prompting (e.g., least-to-most, most-to-least), picture or written task analysis, computer assisted, simulated, and CBI. Based on criteria used by Test, Fowler, et al.

(2009), using CBI to teach grocery shopping has been identified as having a moderate level of evidence based on one high-quality quasi-experimental group study (P. E. Bates et al., 2001) and on two acceptable single-subject studies (Ferguson & McDonnell, 1991; Gaule, Nietupski, & Certo, 1985). Research studies using CBI to teach grocery shopping involved both male and female participants, ages 17 to 20, identified as having mild-to-severe intellectual disabilities. None of the studies provided information on ethnicity.

Grocery shopping skills have been taught using CBI in a variety of ways. For example, Gaule et al. (1985) taught students how to prepare a shopping list using a picture recipe in the classroom and then taught locating and purchasing items using an adapted picture shopping list in a grocery store (see Figure 10.3 for the

Figure 10.3   Research-to-practice lesson plan starter for grocery shopping.

Objective: To teach students to prepare a shopping list, locate and obtain items from the supermarket, and purchase obtained items.

Setting/Materials:

Settings: Community grocery store and high school classroom

Materials:

1. Pictorial Meal Preparation Manual:

    a. The manual contains picture recipes and is used to generate shopping lists for supermarket items.

    b. The first page contains pictures of necessary food items, as well as utensils needed in preparing the meal.

    c. To simplify the development of the shopping list, as appropriate, the teacher may circle all of the food items on the page so students do not have to discriminate between food and nonfood items.

2. Adaptive shopping list:

    a. An adaptive shopping aid is placed in a three-ring binder that can be opened and put in the seat section of a shopping cart.

    b. The shopping aid contains pictures of all of the items for each student's recipe.

    c. Adjacent to each picture is a square that denotes the approximate cost. Each square represents a 50-cent interval. Thus, a quart of milk that costs $1.49 has three squares.

    d. Another feature of the shopping aid is the money line on which students mark off the number of squares to determine approximate cost. Students count number of dollars available for shopping and use a marking pen to indicate available funds for shopping.

Content Taught:

1. Shopping list preparation (taught in classroom)

    a. Obtain the adaptive shopping list from its storage area.

    b. Check off each food item depicted in the recipe on the shopping list.

    c. Erase checks from pictures of grocery items on hand.

    d. Count the number of $1.00 bills available for shopping.

    e. Mark a line designating the number of dollars available on the money line found on the shopping aid.

2. Locating and obtaining items from the supermarket (taught in community)

    a. Enter the store.

    b. Obtain a cart.

  c. Place the open shopping aid in the seat of the cart.

  d. Obtain the needed supermarket items within 30 minutes.

  e. Cross out each item depicted on the shopping aid as it is obtained.

  f. Check off the appropriate number of squares for each item on the money line when the item is obtained.

3. Purchasing obtained items (taught in community)

  a. Enter the checkout lane with the cart.

  b. Give the appropriate number of dollars to the clerk.

  c. Receive and put away any change.

  d. Pick up the sack of items.

  e. Exit store.

Teaching Procedures:

1. Shopping list preparation

  a. At the beginning of each instructional session, the teacher demonstrates the steps in the task sequence.

  b. Three to five individual instructional trials are given to the student with the number of trials given dependent on the available time.

  c. Each trial consists of presentation cues and materials indicated on task analysis.

  d. The student is allowed to perform the task steps until the sequence is completed correctly or until an error is made.

  e. Verbal praise is used to reinforce correct performance.

  f. Incorrect responses are followed by: (a) verbal prompt, (b) teacher modeling correct response and required imitation by student, and (c) verbal cues to perform task step and physical guidance.

  g. Following error correction, student is allowed to proceed to next step.

  h. After percentage of correctly performed task steps on initial instructional trial reaches 50% on 3 consecutive days, teacher demonstration at the beginning of the session is discontinued.

2. Locating and obtaining items from the supermarket

  a. The reinforcement and correction procedures are identical to shopping list preparation, with the exception that no teacher model is provided on arrival at the supermarket.

3. Purchasing obtained items

  a. The reinforcement and correction procedures are identical to locating and obtaining items from the supermarket.

Evaluation:

Evaluate the student's performance by collecting data on the percentage of steps correct on the task analyses.

Note: Lesson plan based on: Gaule, K., Nietupski, J., & Certo, N. (1985). Teaching supermarket shopping skills using an adaptive shopping list. *Education and Training of the Mentally Retarded, 20,* 53–59.

Source: From National Secondary Transition Technical Assistance Center (NSTTAC) Lesson Plan Starters. National Secondary Transition Technical Assistance Center. (2008). *Grocery shopping.* Charlotte, NC: NSTTAC. Retrieved from http://nsttac.appstate.edu/sites/default/files/assets/pdf/49.pdf.

research-to-practice lesson plan starter). Locating and purchasing items at the grocery store have been taught using prompting systems, written and picture task analyses, and combinations of prompting and task analyses (Alcantara, 1994; P. E. Bates et al., 2001; Ferguson & McDonnell, 1991; McDonnell, Horner, & Williams, 1984; Mechling, 2004; Morse & Schuster, 2000). Purchasing has also been taught in the community using the dollar-more strategy and an adapted number line (McDonnell et al., 1984; Sandknop, Schuster, Wolery, & Cross, 1992). Finally, Nietupski, Welch, and Wacker

(1983) taught students to acquire, maintain, and transfer purchasing skills at community grocery stores using a calculator.

Teaching Employment Skills

Teaching employment skills includes a range of instructional topics including time management and self-monitoring for completing vocational tasks, cleaning public restrooms, and performing clerical tasks such as operating a copying machine. The instructional practices associated with employment skills include various levels and orders of prompting (e.g., least-to-most, most-to-least), picture or written task analysis, constant time delay, CBI, and simulated instruction paired with CBI. Based on criteria used by Test, Fowler, et al. (2009), using CBI to teach employment skills has been identified as having a moderate level of evidence based on one acceptable-quality group-design experimental study (P. E. Bates et al., 2001), one high-quality single-subject study (DiPipi-Hoy, Jitendra, & Kern, 2009), and one acceptable-quality single-subject study (Cihak et al., 2004). Research that successfully used CBI to teach employment skills has involved both

male (*n* = 36) and female participants (*n* = 13), ages 16 to 20, identified as having mild-to-moderate intellectual disabilities. None of the studies provided information on ethnicity.

Employment skills have been taught using CBI in a variety of ways. More specifically, P. E. Bates et al. (2001) taught students how to clean a public restroom using a 43-step task analysis. Next, Cihak et al. (2004) taught students how to operate a copying machine using 3-second time delay and least-to-most prompting (see Figure 10.4 for the research-to-practice lesson plan starter). Finally, DiPipi-Hoy et al. (2009) taught students to use digital

Figure 10.4   Research-to-practice lesson plan starter for employment skills.

Objective: To teach students to make collated photocopies using simulated and community-based instruction on the same day

Setting/Materials:

Setting: Local print shop and classroom

Materials:

1. Copy machine with top feeder tray and key pad

2. Camera to take photographs of photocopy machine

3. Photo album

    a. For each of 12 steps in the task analysis, create 4 photographs that correspond to the step

        (i.e., a total of 128 photographs) including:

        i. photograph depicting correct action being performed in the relevant setting.

        ii. photograph depicting correct materials, but wrong manipulation.

        iii. photograph depicting an out-of-sequence action.

        iv. photograph depicting an action associated with the task, but not included in the training sequence.

Content Taught:

Task Analysis:

1. Place the original newsletter on the feeder tray.

2. Enter a four-digit PIN code.

3. Press the ID button.

4. Press the number 5 for the number of copies.

5. Press the collate button.

6. Press the OK button.

7. Press the start button.

8. Remove the original from the upper tray.

9. Remove the copies from the bottom tray.

Teaching Procedures:

1. On the same day, provide training in the classroom before community-based instruction. For example, provide instruction using the simulated procedures on Monday morning, and provide community-based instruction on Monday afternoon.

2. During classroom instruction, use the photo album to provide instruction.

    a. Tell students to pretend they are going to make copies using a photocopy machine.

    b. Present the photo album to the student.

---

c. Tell students to visually scan the photos on the album cover and point to the picture indicating the task they would complete.

d. Present task materials to the student.

e. Open the album and ask, "What is the first thing you do?"

f. Tell students to put a finger on the photo that depicts what is next on each photo page.

g. Use a system of least prompts with a 3-second interval between each prompt level. To assist a student in successfully identifying the photos depicting steps to complete the task, prompts should be provided in the following order:

   i. Verbal prompt (e.g., "Do you see where the writing is"?)

   ii. Gesture (e.g., pointing to discriminative stimulus on page opposite the 4 photos)

   iii. Gesture plus verbal explanation (e.g., pointing to the discriminative stimulus on page opposite the 4 photos and providing a verbal explanation)

   iv. Modeling plus verbal explanation (e.g., pointing to correct picture and plus providing verbal explanation)

   v. Physical assistance plus verbal explanation (e.g., holding the student's wrist, guiding the correct response, and providing an explanation)

3. Provide training at a photocopy machine in a community print shop.

   a. Tell students that they are going to make copies using a photocopy machine.

   b. Use a system of least prompts with a 3-second interval between each prompt level.

   c. To assist a student in successfully completing the task, prompts should be provided in the following order:

      i. Verbal prompt (e.g., "Do you see where the writing is"?)

      ii. Gesture (e.g., pointing to discriminative stimulus on the machine)

      iii. Gesture plus verbal explanation (e.g., pointing to the discriminative stimulus and providing a verbal explanation)

      iv. Modeling plus verbal explanation (e.g., demonstrating appropriate actions plus verbal explanation)

      v. Physical assistance plus verbal explanation (e.g., holding the student's wrist, guiding the correct response, and providing an explanation)

Evaluation:

Collect student performance data on the number of steps completed independently and correctly.

Note: Lesson plan based on: Cihak, D. F., Alberto, P. A., Kessler, K., & Taber, T. A. (2004). An investigation of instructional scheduling arrangements for community based instruction. *Research in Developmental Disabilities, 25,* 67–88.

Source: From National Secondary Transition Technical Assistance Center (NSTTAC) Lesson Plan Starters. National Secondary Transition Technical Assistance Center. (2008). *Grocery shopping.* Charlotte, NC: NSTTAC. Retrieved from http://nsttac.appstate.edu/sites/default/files/assets/pdf/49.pdf.

watches in the classroom and community employment settings to manage their time and monitor work tasks. A majority of the research base with employment paired simulated instruction with CBI. However, when instruction took place immediately after simulation within community settings, employment skills were taught within settings such as a florist, print shop, public restroom, recreational camp, and veterinarian's office (P. E. Bates et al., 2001; Cihak et al., 2004; DiPipi-Hoy et al., 2009).

Instructional Approaches

The instructional approaches often used in teaching self-determination skills and when using CBI to teach grocery shopping and employment skills are based on a behavioral framework. Based on the principles of applied behavior analysis (see J. O. Cooper, Heron, & Heward, 2007), Heward and Orlansky (1984) identified seven characteristics common to using a behavioral approach to instruction: (a) specifying the skill or behavior to be learned (often using task analysis); (b) using direct and continuous measurement; (c) using techniques that can be replicated by others; (d) requiring learners to repeatedly perform the target skill during each instructional session; (e) providing immediate feedback (usually in the form of positive reinforcement or specific corrective feedback); (f) systematically using and withdrawing cues and prompts (e.g., modeling, physical guidance, time-delay, least-to-most prompting); and (g) designing instruction to help learners generalize newly acquired skills to new, untrained settings. The lesson plan starters included in this chapter incorporate many of these seven characteristics of a behavior approach to teaching, because all have specific objectives and specify content to be taught (often in the form of a task analysis), have specific instructional strategies that include both prompting and feedback strategies, and incorporate a method that can be used to directly and continuously evaluate the effects of instruction.

Analysis of the Research Base

The practices described in this chapter were taken from the literature review conducted by the National Secondary Transition Technical Assistance Center and reported by Test, Fowler, et al. (2009). As part of their systematic review, published research studies were reviewed using the quality indicators for group and quasi-experimental research proposed by Gersten et al. (2005) or the quality indicators for single-subject research proposed by R. H. Horner et al. (2005). As a result, the research base used in this chapter consisted of studies that were of acceptable or high quality as defined by Gersten et al. or Horner et al. However, the review of the literature was not comprehensive; that is, once the number of studies needed to establish a practice had reached a "strong" level of evidence, further articles on that practice were not reviewed. Given this background, the remainder of this section summarizes the general strengths and limitations of the research base reviewed for self-determination (specifically, for the Self-Advocacy Strategy and the Self-Directed IEP) and CBI, and it provides recommendations for future research and practice in relation to these practices.

Strengths of the Research Base

In general, the research reviewed (in previous sections) for self-determination, including the Self-Advocacy Strategy and the Self-Directed IEP, and CBI, including grocery shopping and employment skills, had many strengths. Specific to their methodology, the researchers described (a) participants, the process for selecting participants, and setting; (b) dependent variables with operational precision and measured them over time with a quantifiable index; and (c) independent variables with operational precision and measures of treatment fidelity. By supplying this level of detail, these studies provide practitioners with the specificity needed to use their professional judgment to decide not only if the practice might be successful with their students in their settings, but also how to teach each skill.

The single-subject studies reviewed included a baseline phase and repeated measures of the dependent variable over time; provided at least three demonstrations of experimental effect at different points in time to control for common threats to internal validity; and

replicated experimental effects across participants, settings, or materials to establish external validity. In addition, they included measures of interrater reliability. The use of high-quality experimental designs (i.e., valid, single-subject research designs such as multiple baseline and reversal designs, and group experimental and quasi-experimental designs) ensures practitioners that a functional relationship existed between the intervention used in the studies and changes in student behavior; that is, self-determination and CBI resulted in improved student outcomes. Given these strengths of the literature base on self-determination and CBI, practitioners can be confident that these interventions should result in similar changes in their students' behavior if implemented with integrity.

Weaknesses of Research Base

In general, the research for self-determination (as reviewed in previous sections), including the Self-Advocacy Strategy, the Self-Directed IEP, and using CBI to teach grocery shopping and employment skills, also had several weaknesses. Most studies lacked formal measures of social validity. In secondary transition, social validity data are typically gathered by collecting consumer satisfaction on the goals, procedures, or outcomes of an intervention from students, teachers, or parents. Although it is important to know that an intervention works, if consumers do not value the goals, if they believe the procedures are too difficult to implement, or if they are not satisfied with the outcomes, the specific interventions will probably not be used in a classroom. In these cases, potentially effective practices may go unused by many teachers. Therefore, it is important to have interventions that are effective but also socially valid. Group studies also lacked descriptions of fidelity of implementation and evidence of adequate reliability for outcome measures. Without evidence that the intervention was implemented as designed and data collected were reliable, research consumers should be cautious about placing their full confidence in study findings. As a result, practitioners should be cautious about using practices that do not have such evidence and even more diligent than usual in planning for and evaluating the generalization of these skills.

Although the research-based practices identified by this review do provide practitioners with strategies for teaching specific skills, the experimental literature reviewed did not correlate student skill development with improved postschool outcomes. The limitations in the experimental research base point to the ongoing need for research but also highlight the fact that as special educators use research to guide practice, they need to remain steadfast in connecting individual student outcomes with practices used. Especially until experimental studies begin to measure the longitudinal impact of interventions, practitioners should collect their own data to link their instructional practices to development of student skills that predict postschool success (Test, Fowler, et al., 2009).

Suggestions for Future Research

The limitations of the current research base provide direction for next steps in examining the effectiveness of self-determination, including the Self-Advocacy Strategy, the Self-Directed IEP, and using CBI to teach grocery shopping and employment skills. First, it is important that future research examine maintenance and generalization of all skills taught. Maintenance (i.e., the student's ability to demonstrate the skill over time) and generalization (i.e., the students' ability to demonstrate the skill in settings beyond those in which the skills were taught) are critical elements for using skills that have been learned and are, therefore, important outcomes to intervention research. For practitioners to have the best information to use when selecting possible practices for use in their classrooms, researchers need to expand their examinations of the maintenance and generalization of self-determination and CBI.

Future research also needs to measure the social validity of the goals, procedures, and outcomes of transition skills instruction from the viewpoints of parents, teachers, and students to determine if skills taught are relevant for everyday living. Moreover, given that self-determination focuses on helping individuals gain greater control over their lives, it would seem that, at a minimum, social validity data would always be collected from students. In addition to adding measures of social validity, future research should also investigate the use of new and innovative technologies. The use of technology can also help build in strategies to ensure generalization and maintenance of newly learned skills. For example, using a handheld media device to list the steps in a task analysis will allow students to have the directions on how to perform the task wherever they go.

Over and above improving specific aspects of research design (e.g., social validity, implementation fidelity) and examining critical aspects of the practices (e.g., generalization, use of technology), it is important that researchers systematically study the effects of self-determination and CBI through more research and replication of findings. Many of the secondary-transition related skills that could be taught using CBI (e.g., managing finances, physical fitness, travel, healthy living, engaging in civic activities, maintaining employment) do not appear to have a substantial research base. Future research studies in these areas must be designed to meet the quality indicators for group or single-subject designs, conducted with measured and reported integrity, and have their results linked with postschool outcomes such as employment, education/training, and quality of life.

Recommendations for Practice

Although much remains to do in relation to bolstering the research base, the practices highlighted in this chapter for self-determination and CBI are research-based approaches that focus on modifiable predictors of critical postschool outcomes (e.g., Test, Fowler, et al., 2009). To maximize effectiveness of the practices, practitioners should consider a few implications for implementing them. The primary argument for using CBI as a teaching strategy is to maximize the potential for skill generalization (P. E. Bates et al., 2001). To maximize instructional time while in the community, it may be necessary to develop simulated training opportunities in addition to CBI. For example, simulated classroom training might be used to provide students with repeated opportunities to practice the skill of paying for groceries if they are having trouble mastering the skill at the grocery store. In this case, a teacher could provide students with multiple opportunities to practice paying for items in the classroom, whereas at the grocery store only one opportunity to respond would occur per day. Not surprisingly, researchers recommend that any simulated instructional opportunities should share as many characteristics as possible with the natural environment where the new behavior is expected to be performed, to ensure generalization to the community (P. E. Bates et al., 2001; Nietupski, Hamre-Nietupski, Clancy, & Veerhusen, 1986).

In relation to self-determination skills, consider having students with limited verbal skills develop Power-Point slides to use to guide their IEP meetings (Parent & Wehman, 2011). Both of the research-based practices for enhancing self-determination skills described in this chapter, the Self-Advocacy Strategy and the Self-Directed IEP, provide a framework for developing the content to be used. In addition, student voices can be added to PowerPoint presentations for individuals who may be too shy to speak in front of the IEP team.

Conclusion

In conclusion, this chapter provides practitioners with a starting point for implementing several research-based practices in the area of secondary transition. Are they guaranteed to work? Not always and not for every individual. But practitioners can be confident that the practices described in this chapter will produce the positive effects described in the review of research with most of their students when implemented as designed. Teachers should, then, use these strategies first when teaching self-determination skills to involve students in the IEP process and should use CBI to teach functional skills such as grocery shopping or employment skills.

References

Abedi, J. (2006). Psychometric issues in the ELL assessment and special education eligibility. *Teachers College Record, 108,* 2282–2303.

Ada, A. F., & Campoy, I. (2003). *Authors in the classroom: A transformative education process.* Boston, MA: Allyn & Bacon.

Adams, M. J., Bereiter, C., McKeough, A., Case, R., Roit, M., Hirschberg, J., et al. (2002). *Open court reading.* Columbus, OH: McGraw-Hill.

Adams, M. J., Foorman, B. R., Lundberg, I., & Beeler, T. (1998). *Phonemic awareness in young children: A classroom curriculum.* Baltimore: Brookes.

Agran, M., Alper, S., Cavin, M., Sinclair, T., Wehmeyer, M., & Hughes, C. (2005). Using self-monitoring to increase following-direction skills of students with moderate to severe disabilities in general education. *Education & Training in Developmental Disabilities, 40,* 3–13.

Agran, M., King-Sears, M. E., Wehmeyer, M. L., & Copeland, S. R. (2003). *Teachers' guides to inclusive practices: Student-directed learning strategies.* Baltimore: Brookes.

Aiken, S., Buultjens, M., Clark, C., Eyre, J. T., & Pease, L. (2000). *Teaching children who are deaf-blind: Contact, communication and learning.* London, UK: David Fulton.

Alberto, P. A., & Troutman, A. C. (2009). *Applied behavior analysis for teachers* (8th ed.). Upper Saddle River, NJ: Pearson.

Alcantara, P. R. (1994). Effects of videotape instructional package on purchasing skills of children with autism. *Exceptional Children, 61,* 40–55.

Alexander, R. (1996). In search of good primary practice. In P. Woods (Ed.), *Contemporary issues in teaching and learning* (pp. 57–72). New York: Routledge.

Allen, S., Smith, A., Test, D. W., Flowers, C., & Wood, W. M. (2001). The effects of *Self-Directed IEP* on student participation in IEP meetings. *Career Development for Exceptional Individuals, 24,* 107–120.

Alpert, C. L., & Kaiser, A. (1992). Training parents as milieu language teachers. *Journal of Early Intervention, 16,* 31–52.

Alpert, C. L., & Rogers-Warren, A. K. (1984). *Mothers as incidental language trainers of their language-disordered children.* Unpublished manuscript, University of Kansas, Lawrence.

American Printing House for the Blind (APH). (2009). Distribution of eligible students based on the federal quota census of January 2, 2009 (fiscal year 2008). Retrieved from http://www.aph.org/about/ar2008.pdf

American Psychiatric Association. (1994). *Diagnostic and statistical manual of mental disorders* (4th ed). Washington, DC: American Psychiatric Association.

Americans with Disabilities Act of 1990, 42 U.S.C. § 12101.

Anthony, T. L. (2003). *Individual Sensory Learning Profile Interview (ISLPI).* Chapel Hill, NC: Early Intervention Training Center for Infants and Toddlers with Visual Impairments, FPG Child Development Institute, UNC-CH. Retrieved from http://www.fpg.unc.edu/~edin/Resources/modules/VCM/4/session_files/handouts/VCM4_HandoutK_ISLP.pdf

Arndt, S. A., Konrad, M., & Test, D. W. (2006). Effects of *Self-Directed IEP* on student participation in planning meetings. *Remedial and Special Education, 27,* 194–207.

Arntzen, E., Halstadtro, A., & Halstadtro, M. (2003). Training play behavior in a 5-year-old boy with developmental disabilities. *Journal of Applied Behavior Analysis, 36,* 367–370.

Artiles, A. J., & Klingner, J. K. (2006). Forging a knowledge base on English language learners with special needs: Theoretical, population, and technical issues. *Teachers College Record, 108,* 2187–2194.

Artiles, A. J., Klingner, J., Sullivan, A., & Fierros, E. (2010). Shifting landscapes of professional practices: English learner special education placement in English-only states. In P. Gándara & M. Hopkins (Eds.), *Forbidden language: English learners and restrictive language policies* (pp. 102–117). New York: Teachers College Press.

Artiles, A. J., Rueda, R., Salazar, J. J., & Higareda, I. (2005). Within-group diversity in minority disproportionate representation: English language learners in urban school districts. *Exceptional Children, 71,* 283-300.

Artiles, A. J., Trent, S. C., & Palmer, J. (2004). Culturally diverse students in special education. In J. A. Banks & C. M. Banks (Eds.), *Handbook of research on multicultural education* (2nd ed., pp. 716–735). San Francisco: Jossey-Bass.

Arunachalam, V. (2001). The science behind tradition. *Current Science, 80,* 1272–1275.

Atkinson, R. (1975). Mnemotechnics in second language learning. *American Psychologist, 30,* 821–828.

Au, K. H. (1998). Social constructivism and the school literacy learning of students of diverse backgrounds. *The Journal of Literacy Research, 30,* 297–319.

Au, K., & Raphael, T. (2000). Equity and literacy in the next millennium. *Reading Research Quarterly, 35,* 170–188.

August, D., & Hakuta, K. (Eds.). (1997). *Improving schooling for language minority children: A research agenda.* Washington, DC: National Academy Press.

August, D. L., & Shanahan, T. (2006). Synthesis: Instruction and professional development. In D. L. August & T. Shanahan (Eds.), *Developing literacy in a second language: Report of the National Literacy Panel.* Mahwah, NJ: Erlbaum.

Ault, M. J., Wolery, M., Doyle, P. M., & Gast, D. L. (1989). Review of comparative studies in the instruction of students with moderate and severe handicaps. *Exceptional Children, 55,* 346–356.

Baddeley, A., & Wilson, B. (1985). Phonological coding and short term memory in patients without speech. *Journal of Memory and Language, 24,* 490–502.

Bailey, E. & Bricker, D. (1985). Evaluation of a three-year early intervention demonstration project. *Topics in Early Childhood Special Education, 5*(2), 52–65.

Bakkaloglu, H. (2008). The effectiveness of activity-based intervention program on the transition skills of children with developmental disabilities aged between 3 and 6 years. *Educational Sciences: Theory and Practice, 8,* 393–406.

Bambara, L. M., & Ager, C. (1992). Using self-scheduling to prompt self-directed leisure activity in home and community settings. *Journal of the Association for Persons with Severe Handicaps, 17,* 67–76.

Barone, D., & Wright, T. E. (2008). Literacy instruction with digital and media technologies. *Reading Teacher, 62,* 292–302.

Bartsch, K., & Wellman, H. M. (1995). *Children talk about the mind.* New York: Oxford University Press.

Bates, E., Benigni, L., Bretherton, I., Camaioni, L., & Volterra, V. (1979). *The emergence of symbols. Cognition and communication in infancy.* New York: Academic Press.

Bates, P. E., Cuvo, T., Miner, C. A., & Korabek, C. A. (2001). Simulated and community-based instruction involving persons with mild and moderate mental retardation. *Research in Developmental Disabilities, 22,* 95–115.

Bauer, R. (1977). Short-term memory in learning disabled and nondisabled children. *Bulletin of the Psychonomic Society, 10,* 128–130.

Baumwell, L., Tamis-LeMonda, C. S., & Bornstein, M. H. (1997). Maternal verbal sensitivity and child language comprehension. *Infant Behavior and Development, 20,* 247–258.

Beck, I., & McKeown, M. (1981). Developing questions that promote comprehension: The story map. *Language Arts, 58,* 913–918.

Beirne-Smith, M., Patton, J. R., & Kim, S. H. (2006). *Mental retardation* (7th ed.). Upper Saddle River, NJ: Merrill/Pearson.

Benitez, D. T., Lattimore, J., & Wehmeyer, M. L. (2005). Promoting the involvement of students with emotional and behavioral disorders in career and vocational planning and decision making: The self-determined career development model. *Behavioral Disorders, 30,* 431–447.

Berkeley, T. R., & Ludlow, B. L. (1989). Toward a reconceptualization of the developmental model. *Topics in Early Childhood Special Education, 9,* 51–66.

Bernhard, J. K., Cummins, J., Campoy, F. I., Ada, A. F., Winsler, A., & Bleiker, C. (2006). Identity texts and literacy development among preschool English language learners: Enhancing learning opportunities for children at risk for learning disabilities. *Teachers College Record, 108,* 2380–2405.

Bernhard, J. K., Winsler, A., Bleiker, C., Ginieniewicz, J., & Madigan, A. (2008). Read my story: Promoting early literacy among diverse, urban, preschool children in poverty with the Early Authors Program. *Journal of Education for Students Placed at Risk, 13*(1), 76–105.

Bishop, D., & Robson, J. (1989). Unimpaired short-term memory and rhyme judgment in congenitally speechless individuals: Implications for the notion of "articulatory coding." *Quarterly Journal of Experimental Psychology, 41,* 123–140.

Blackorby, J., & Wagner, M. (1996). Longitudinal postschool outcomes of youth with disabilities: Findings from the National Longitudinal Transition Study. *Exceptional Children, 62,* 399–413.

Blauvelt-Harper, C., Symon, J. B. G., & Frea, W. D. (2008). Recess is time-in: Using peers to improve social skills of children with autism. *Journal of Autism and Developmental Disabilities, 28,* 815–826. doi: 10.1007s10803-007-0449-2

Bloom, Y. (1990). *Object symbols: A communication option.* Sydney, Australia: North Rocks Press.

Boardman, A. G., Arguelles, M. E., Vaughn, S., Hughes, M. T., & Klingner, J. (2005). Special education teachers' views of research-based practices. *Journal of Special Education, 39,* 168–180.

Bopp, K. D., Brown, K. E., & Mirenda, P. (2004). Speech-language pathologists' roles in the delivery of positive behavior support for individual with developmental disabilities. *American Journal of Speech-Language Pathology, 13,* 5–10.

Boulinea, T., Fore, C., Hagan-Burke, S., & Burke, M. (2004). Use of story-mapping to increase the story-grammar text comprehension of elementary students with learning disabilities. *Learning Disability Quarterly, 27,* 105–121.

Brainerd, C., Kingma, J., & Howe, M. (1986). Long-term memory development and learning disability: Storage and retrieval loci of disabled/nondisabled differences. In S. Ceci (Ed.), *Handbook of cognitive, social, and neuropsychological aspects* of learning disabilities (vol. 1, pp. 161–184). Hillsdale, NJ: Erlbaum.

Branham, R. S., Collins, B. C., Schuster, J. W., & Kleinert, H. (1999). Teaching community skills to students with moderate disabilities: Comparing combined techniques of classroom simulation, videotape modeling, and community-based instruction. *Education and Training in Mental Retardation and Developmental Disabilities, 2,* 170–181.

Bransford, J., Brown, A., & Cocking, R. (Eds.). (2000). *How people learn.* Washington, DC: National Academies Press.

Bredekamp, S. (Ed.). (1987). *Developmentally appropriate practice in early childhood programs serving children from birth through age 8.* Washington, DC: National Association for Education of Young Children.

Bredekamp, S., & Rosegrant, T. (1992). *Reaching potentials: Appropriate curriculum and assessment for young children* (Vol. 1). Washington, DC: National Association for Education of Young Children.

Bricker, D. (1986). *Early education of at-risk and handicapped infants, toddlers, and preschool children.* Glenview, IL: Scott, Foresman.

Bricker, D., & Bricker, W. (1971). *Toddler research and intervention project report: Year 1 (IMRID Behavioral Sciences Monograph No. 20).* Nashville, TN: George Peabody College, Institute of Mental Retardation & Intellectual Development.

Bricker, D., Bricker, W., Iacino, R., & Dennison, L. (1976). *Intervention strategies for the severely and profoundly handicapped child.* (Vol. 1). New York: Grune & Stratton.

Bricker, D., Bruder, M., & Bailey, E. (1982). Developmental integration of preschool children. *Analysis and Intervention in Developmental Disabilities, 2,* 207–222.

Bricker, D., & Cripe, J. J. (1989). Activity-based intervention. In D. Bricker (Ed.), *Early education of at risk handicapped infants, toddlers, and preschoolers* (pp. 251–274). Palo Alto, CA: VORT Corp.

Bricker, D., & Cripe, J. (1992). *An activity-based approach to early intervention.* Baltimore: Brookes.

Bricker, D., & Gumerlock, S. (1988). Application of a three-level evaluation plan for monitoring child progress and program effects. *Journal of Special Education, 22,* 66–81.

Bricker, D., & Sheehan, R. (1981). Effectiveness of an early intervention program as indexed by child change. *Journal of the Division for Early Childhood, 4,* 11–27.

Bricker, W. A., & Bricker, D. (1974). An early language training strategy. In R. L. Schieflelbush & L. L. Lloyd (Eds.), *Language perspective: Acquisition, retardation, and intervention.* Baltimore: University Park Press.

Bricker, W. A., & Bricker, D. (1976). The infant, toddler, and preschool research and intervention project. In T. Tjossem (Ed.), *Intervention strategies for high risk infants and young children* (pp. 545–572). Baltimore: University Park Press.

Brophy, J., & Good, T. L. (1986). Teacher behavior and student achievement. In M. C. Wittrock (Ed.), *Handbook of research on teaching* (3rd ed., pp. 328–375). New York: Macmillan.

Browder, D. (2001). *Curriculum and assessment for students with moderate and severe disabilities.* New York: Guilford Press.

Browder, D. M., Ahlgrim-Delzell, L., Spooner, F., Mims, P. J., & Baker, J. N. (2009). Using time delay to teach literacy to students with severe disabilities. *Exceptional Children, 75,* 343–364.

Browder, D. M., Spooner, F., Wakeman, S., Trela, K., & Baker, J. N. (2006). Aligning instruction with academic content standards: Finding the link. *Research & Practice for Persons with Severe Disabilities, 31,* 309–321.

Brown, F., & Snell, M. E. (2006). Meaningful assessment. In M. E. Snell & F. Brown (Eds.), *Instruction of students with severe disabilities* (6th ed., pp. 67–110). Upper Saddle River, NJ: Merrill/Pearson.

Brown, F., Lehr, D., & Snell, M. (2011). Conducting and using student assessment. In M. E. Snell & F. Brown (Eds.), *Instruction of students with severe disabilities* (7th ed.). Upper Saddle River, NJ: Pearson.

Brown, L., Nisbet, J., Ford, A., Sweet, M., Shiraga, B., York, J., & Loomis, R. (1983). The critical need for nonschool instruction in educational programs for severely handicapped students. *Journal of the Association for the Severely Handicapped, 8,* 71–77.

Browning, N. (2002). Literacy of children with physical disabilities: A literature review. *Canadian Journal of Occupational Therapy, 69,* 176–182.

Bruce, S. M. (2005). The application of Werner and Kaplan's concept of "distancing" to children who are deaf-blind. *Journal of Visual Impairment & Blindness, 99,* 464–477.

Bruder, M. B. (2001). Infants and toddlers: Outcomes and ecology. In M. J. Guralnick (Ed.), *Early childhood inclusion: Focus on change* (pp. 203–228). Baltimore: Brookes.

Bruner, J. S. (1975). The ontogenesis of speech acts. *Journal of Child Language, 2,* 1–19.

Bruner, J. (1983). *Child's talk.* New York: Norton.

Bruteig, J. M. (1987). The reading rates for contracted and uncontracted braille of blind Norwegian adults. *Journal of Visual Impairment and Blindness, 81,* 19–23.

Bulgren, J. A., Schumaker, J. B., & Deshler, D. D. (1994). The effects of a recall enhancement routine on the test performance of secondary students with and without learning disabilities. *Learning Disabilities Research and Practice, 9*(1), 2–11.

Burns, M. K., & Ysseldyke, J. E. (2009). Reported prevalence of evidence-based instructional practices in special education. *Journal of Special Education, 43,* 3–11.

Butler, L. R., & Luiselli, J. K. (2007). Escape-maintained problem behavior in a child with autism: Antecedent functional analysis and intervention evaluation of noncontingent escape and instructional fading. *Journal of Positive Behavior Interventions, 9,* 195–202.

Cable, A. (2007). *An oral narrative intervention for second graders with poor oral narrative ability.* Unpublished doctoral dissertation. University of Texas-Austin.

Campbell, P. H. (2004). Participation-based services: Promoting children's participation in natural settings. *Young Exceptional Children, 8,* 20–29.

Carnine, D. (1997). Bridging the research-to-practice gap. *Exceptional Children, 63,* 513–521.

Carr, E. G. (1988). Functional equivalence as a mechanism of response generalization. In R. H. Horner, G. Dunlap, & K. L. Koegel (Eds.), *Generalization and maintenance: Life-style changes in applied settings* (pp. 221–241). Baltimore: Brookes.

Carr, E. G., Dunlap, G., Horner, R. H., Koegel, R. L., Turnbull, A. P., Sailor, W., et al. (2002). Positive behavior support: Evolution of an applied science. *Journal of Positive Behavior Interventions, 4,* 4–16, 20.

Carta, J. J., Schwartz, I. S., Atwater, J. B., & McConnell, S. R. (1991). Developmentally appropriate practice: Appraising its usefulness for young children with disabilities. *Topics in Early Childhood Special Education, 11,* 1–20.

Carter, E. W., & Kennedy, C. H. (2006). Promoting access to the general curriculum using peer support strategies. *Research and Practice for Persons with Severe Disabilities, 32,* 284–292.

Carter, M., & Kemp, C. R. (1996). Strategies for task analysis in special education. *Educational Psychology, 16,* 155–176.

Case, R. E., & Taylor, S. S. (2005). Language difference or learning disability? Answers from a linguistic perspective. *The Clearinghouse, 78*(3), 127–130.

Casey, A. M., & McWilliam, R. A. (2008). Graphical feedback to increase teachers' use of incidental teaching. *Journal of Early Intervention, 30,* 251–268.

Cavallaro, C. C., & Bambara, L. (1982). Two strategies for teaching language during free play. *Journal of the Association for the Severely Handicapped, 7,* 80–93.

Cavallaro, C. C., Haney, M., & Cabello, B. (1993). Developmentally appropriate strategies for promoting full participation in early childhood settings. *Topics in Early Childhood Special Education, 13,* 293–307.

Ceci, S. (1984). A developmental study of learning disabilities and memory.

Journal of Experimental Child Psychology, 38, 352–371.

Center for Applied Special Technology (CAST). (2008). *Universal design for learning (UDL) guidelines-Version 1.0.* Retrieved from http://www.cast.org/publications/UDLguidelines/version1.html

Centers for Disease Control and Prevention. (2010). *CDC study: An average of 1 in 110 children have an ASD.* Retrieved from http://www.cdc.gov/Features/CountingAutism

Chabris, C., & Simons, D. (2010). *The invisible gorilla: And other ways our intuitions deceive us.* New York: Crown.

Chafouleas, S. M., Riley-Tillman, T. C., & Christ, T. J. (2009). Direct behavior rating (DBR): An emerging method for assessing social behavior within a tiered intervention system. *Assessment for Effective Intervention, 34,* 195–200.

Chall, J. (1983). *Stages of reading development.* New York: McGraw Hill.

Chamberlain, C., & Mayberry, R. (2008). American sign language syntactic and narrative comprehension in skilled and less skilled readers: Bilingual and bimodal evidence for the linguistic basis for reading. *Applied Psycholinguistics, 29,* 367–388.

Chambers, J., Parrish, T., & Harr, J. (2004). *What are we spending on special education services in the United States, 1999–2000?* Palo Alto, CA: American Institutes for Research, Center for Special Education Finance.

Chandler, W., Schuster, J. W., & Stevens, K. B. (1993). Teaching employment skills to adolescents with mild to moderate disabilities using a constant time delay procedure. *Education and Training in Mental Retardation and Developmental Disabilities, 28,* 155–168.

Chapman, R. (2000). Children's language learning: An interactionist perspective. *Journal of Child Psychology and Psychiatry, 41,* 33–54.

Chard, D. J., Cook, B. G., & Tankersley, M. (Eds.). (2013). *Research-based strategies for improving outcomes in academics.* Columbus, OH: Pearson.

Charlier, B. L., & Leybaert, J. (2000). The rhyming skills of deaf children educated with phonetically augmented

speechreading. *Quarterly Journal of Experimental Psychology, 53A,* 349–375.

Charlop-Christy, M. H., & Carpenter, M. H. (2000). Modified incidental teaching sessions: A procedure for parents to increase spontaneous speech in their children with autism. *Journal of Positive Behavior Interventions, 2,* 98–112.

Chávez, L. (2008). *The Latino threat: Constructing immigrants, citizens and the nation.* Stanford, CA: Stanford University Press.

Chen, D. (2005). Young children who are deaf-blind: Implications for professionals in deaf and hard of hearing services. *Volta Review, 104,* 273–287.

Chen, D., & Downing, J. E. (2006). *Tactile strategies for children with visual impairments and multiple disabilities: Promoting communication and learning skills.* New York: AFB Press.

Chen, S., Zhang, J., Lange, E., Miko, P., & Joseph, D. (2001). Progressive time delay procedure for teaching motor skills to adults with severe mental retardation. *Adapted Physical Activity Quarterly, 18,* 35–48.

Christensen, T. J., Ringdahl, J. E., Bosch, J. J., Falcomata, T. S., Luke, J. R., & Andelman, M. S. (2009). Constipation associated with self-injurious and aggressive behavior exhibited by a child diagnosed with autism. *Education and Treatment of Children, 32,* 89–103.

Chung, K. M., Reavis, S., Mosconi, M., Drewry, J., Matthews, T., & Tasse, M. J. (2007). Peer-mediated social skills training program for young children with high-functioning autism. *Research in Developmental Disabilities, 28,* 423–436.

Cihak, D. F., Alberto, P. A., Kessler, K., & Taber, T. A. (2004). An investigation of instructional scheduling arrangements for community-based instruction. *Research in Developmental Disabilities, 25,* 67–88.

Cihak, D. F., Kessler, K. B., & Alberto, P. A. (2006). Generalized use of a handheld prompting system. *Research in Developmental Disabilities, 28,* 397–408.

Cleave, P. L., & Fey, M. E. (1997). Two approaches to the facilitation of grammar in children with language impairments: Rationale and description. *American Journal of Speech-Language Pathology, 6*, 22–32.

Clifford, S. M., & Dissanayake, C. (2008). The early development of joint attention in infants with autistic disorder using home video observations and parental interview. *Journal of Autism and Developmental Disorders, 38*, 791–805.

Cobb, B., Lehmann, J., Newman-Gonchar, R., & Alwell, M. (2009). Self-determination for students with disabilities: A narrative metasynthesis. *Career Development for Exceptional Individuals, 32*, 108–114.

Cohen, J. (2007). A case study of a high school English-language learner and his reading. *Journal of Adolescent & Adult Literacy, 51*, 164–176.

Cole, K., Dale, P., & Mills, P. (1991). Individual differences in language delayed children's responses to direct and interactive preschool instruction. *Topics in Early Childhood Special Education, 11*, 99–124.

Coleman, M. B. (2011). Successful implementation of assistive technology to promote access to curriculum and instruction for students with physical disabilities. *Physical Disabilities: Education and Related Services, 30*(2), 2–22.

Coleman, M. B., & Heller, K. W. (2009). Assistive technology considerations. In K. W. Heller, P. E. Forney, P. A. Alberto, S. J. Best, & M. N. Swartzman (Eds.), *Understanding physical, health, and multiple disabilities* (2nd ed., pp. 139–153). Upper Saddle River, NJ: Pearson Education.

Coleman-Martin, M. B., & Heller, K. W. (2004). Using a modified constant prompt-delay procedure to teach spelling to students with physical disabilities. *Journal of Applied Behavior Analysis, 37*, 469–480.

Coleman-Martin, M. B., Heller, K. W., Cihak, D. F., & Irvine, K. L. (2005). Using computer-assisted instruction and the nonverbal reasing approach to teach work identification. *Focus on Autism and Other Developmental Disabilities, 20*, 80–90.

Collins, B. C., Branson, T., A., & Hall, M. (1995). Teaching generalized reading of cooking product labels to adolescents with mental disabilities through the use of key words taught by peer tutors. *Education and Training in Mental Retardation and Developmental Disabilities, 30*, 64–75.

Collins, B. C., Stinson, D. M., & Land, L. (1993). A comparison of in vivo and simulation prior to in vivo instruction in teaching generalized safety skills. *Education and Training in Mental Retardation, 28*, 128–142.

Conti-Ramsden, G., & Jones, M. (1997). Verb use in specific language impairment. *Journal of Speech, Language, and Hearing Research, 40*, 1298–1313.

Cook, B. G., Landrum, T. J., Tankersley, M., & Kauffman, J. M. (2003). Bringing research to bear on practice: Effecting evidence-based instruction for students with emotional or behavioral disorders. *Education and Treatment of Children, 26*, 325–361.

Cook, B. G., & Schirmer, B. R. (2006). An overview and analysis of the role of evidence-based practices in special education. In B. G. Cook & B. R. Schirmer (Eds.), *What is special about special education: The role of evidence-based practices* (pp. 175–185). Austin, TX: Pro-Ed.

Cook, B. G., & Smith, G. J. (2012). Leadership and instruction: Evidence-based practices in special education. In J. B. Crockett, B. S. Billingsley, & M. L. Boscardin (Eds.), *Handbook of leadership and administration for special education.* London: Routledge.

Cook, B. G., & Tankersley, M. (2013). *Research-based practices in special education.* Columbus, OH: Pearson.

Cook, B. G., Tankersley, M., Cook, L., & Landrum, T. J. (2008). Evidence-based practices in special education: Some practical considerations. *Intervention in School & Clinic, 44*(2), 69–75.

Cook, B. G., Tankersley, M., & Harjusola-Webb, S. (2008). Evidence-based special education and professional wisdom: Putting it all together. *Intervention in School and Clinic, 44*, 105–111.

Cook, L., Cook, B. G., Landrum, T. J., & Tankersley, M. (2008). Examining the role of group experimental research in establishing evidenced-based practices. *Intervention in School & Clinic, 44*(2), 76–82.

Cook, S., Scruggs, T. E., Mastropieri, M. A., & Casto, G. C. (1985–1986). Handicapped students as tutors. *Journal of Special Education, 19*, 483–492.

Cooney, J., & Swanson, H. (1987). Memory and learning disabilities: An overview. In H. L. Swanson (Ed.), *Advances in learning and behavioral disabilities: Memory and learning disabilities* (Suppl. 2, pp. 1–40). Greenwich, CT: JAI Press.

Cooper, J. D., & Pikulski, J. J. (2003). *A world of animals.* California Teacher's Edition. Kindergarten. Boston, MA: Houghton Mifflin.

Cooper, J. O., Heron, T. E., & Heward, W. L. (2007). *Applied behavior analysis* (2nd Edition). Upper Saddle River, NJ: Pearson.

Cooper, K. J., & Browder, D. M. (1998). Enhancing choice and participation for adults with severe disabilities in community-based instruction. *Journal of the Association for Persons with Severe Handicaps, 23*, 252–260.

Copeland, S. R., & Hughes, C. (2000). Acquisition of a picture prompt strategy to increase independent performance. *Education & Training in Mental Retardation & Developmental Disabilities, 35*, 294–305.

Copeland, S. R., Hughes, C., Agran, M., Wehmeyer, M., & Fowler, S. E. (2002). An intervention package to support high school students with mental retardation in general education classrooms. *American Journal on Mental Retardation, 107*, 32–45.

Copple, C., & Bredekamp, S. (Eds.). (2009). *Developmentally appropriate practice in early childhood programs serving children from birth through age 8* (3rd ed.). Washington, DC: National Association for Education of Young Children.

Cornwall, A. (1992). The relationship of phonological awareness, rapid naming, and verbal memory to severe reading and spelling disability. *Journal of Learning Disabilities, 25*, 532–538.

Council for Exceptional Children. (2007). *Blindness and visual impairment.* Retrieved from http://www.cec.sped.org/AM/Template.cfm?Section=Home&CONTENTID=7568&TEMPLATE=/CM/ContentDisplay.cfm

Council for Exceptional Children. (2009). *What every special educator must know: Ethics, standards, and guidelines* (6th ed.). Arlington, VA: Council for Exceptional Children.

Cummins, J. (2000). *Language, power and pedagogy: Bilingual children in the crossfire.* Clevedon, England: Multilingual Matters Ltd.

Dacy, B. J. S., Nihalani, P. K., Cestone, C. M., & Robinson, D. H. (2011). (Lack of) support for prescriptive statements in teacher education textbooks. *The Journal of Educational Research, 104,* 1–6.

Dammann, J. E., & Vaughn, S. (2001). Science and sanity in special education. *Behavioral Disorders, 27,* 21–29.

Daugherty, S., Grisham-Brown, J., & Hemmeter, M. L. (2001). The effects of embedded skill instruction on the acquisition of target and nontarget skills in preschoolers with developmental delays. *Topics in Early Childhood Special Education, 21,* 213–221.

Davies, D. K., Stock, S. E., & Wehmeyer, M. L. (2003). A palmtop computer-based intelligent aid for individuals with intellectual disabilities to increase independent decision making. *Research & Practice for Persons with Severe Disabilities, 28,* 182–193.

Davis, C. A., Brady, M. P., Williams, R. E., & Burta, M. (1992). The effects of self-operated auditory prompting tapes on the performance fluency of persons with severe mental retardation. *Education and Training in Mental Retardation, 27,* 39–50.

Davis, Z. T. (1994). Effects of prereading story-mapping on elementary readers' comprehension. *Journal of Educational Research, 7,* 353–360.

Dawson, G., & Osterling, J. (1997). Early intervention in autism. In M. Guralnick (ed.) *The effectiveness of early intervention* (pp. 307–326). Baltimore: Brookes.

De La Paz, S. (1999). Composing via dictation and speech recognition systems: Compensatory technology for students with learning disabilities. *Learning Disabilities Quarterly, 22,* 173–182.

De La Paz, S., & Graham, S. (1997). Effects of dictation and advanced planning instruction on the composing of students with writing and learning problems. *Journal of Educational Psychology, 89,* 203–222.

De Valenzuela, J., Copeland, S., Qi, C., & Park, M. (2006). Examining educational equity: Revisiting the disproportionate representation of minority students in special education. *Exceptional Children, 72,* 425–441.

DEC/NAEYC. (2009). *Early childhood inclusion: A joint position statement of the Division for Early Childhood (DEC) and the National Association for the Education of Young Children (NAEYC).* Chapel Hill, NC: The University of North Carolina, FPG Child Development Institute.

Deci, E. L., & Ryan, R. H. (1985). *Intrinsic motivation and self-determination in human behavior.* New York: Plenum.

DeFord, D. (2001). *Dominie reading and writing assessment portfolio* (3rd ed.). Carlsbad, CA: Dominie Press.

Delpit, L. (1986). Skills and other dilemmas of a progressive Black educator. *Harvard Educational Review, 56,* 379–385.

Delpit, L. (1988). The silenced dialogue: Power and pedagogy in educating other people's children. *Harvard Educational Review, 58,* 280–298.

Demchak, M. (1990). Response prompting and fading methods: A review. *American Journal on Mental Retardation, 94,* 603–615.

Denny, M., Martella-Marchand, N., Martella, R. C., Reilly, J. R., Reilly, J. F., & Cleanthous, C. C. (2000). Using parent-delivered graduated guidance to teach functional living skills to a child with Cri du Chat syndrome. *Education and Treatment of Children, 23,* 441–454.

Deno, S. L. (2006). Developments in curriculum-based measurement. In B. G. Cook & B. R. Schirmer (Eds.), *What is special about special education: The role of evidence-based practices* (pp. 100–112). Austin, TX: Pro-Ed.

Denton, C. A., Wexler, J., Vaughn, S., & Bryan, D. (2008). Intervention provided to linguistically diverse middle school students with severe reading difficulties. *Learning Disabilities Research & Practice, 23,* 79–89.

Detrich, R. (2008). Evidence-based, empirically supported, or best practice? A guide for the scientist-practitioner. In J. K. Luiselli, D. C. Russo, W. P. Christian, & S. M. Wilczynski (Eds.), *Effective practices for children with autism: Educational and behavioral support interventions that work* (pp. 3–26). New York: Oxford.

Dewey, J. (1916). *Democracy and education: An introduction to the philosophy of education.* New York: Macmillan.

Diaz, R. M., Neal, C. J., & Amaya-Williams, M. (1990). The social origin of self-regulation. In L. C. Moll (Ed.), *Vygotsky and education: Instructional implications and applications of sociohistorical psychology* (pp. 127–154). New York: Cambridge University Press.

Dickson, D. (2003). Let's not get too romantic about traditional knowledge. *Science Development Network.* Retrieved from http://www.scidev.net/en/editorials/lets-not-get-too-romantic-about-traditional-knowl.html

DiPipi-Hoy, C., Jitendra, A. K., & Kern, L. (2009). Effects of time management instruction on adolescents' ability to self-manage time in a vocational setting. *Journal of Special Education, 43,* 145–159.

Dogoe, M., & Banda, D. R. (2009). Review of recent research using constant time delay to teach chained tasks to persons with developmental disabilities. *Education and Training in Developmental Disabilities, 44,* 177–186.

Donovan, M. S., & Cross, C. T. (Eds.). (2002). *Minority students in special and gifted education.* Washington, DC: National Academies Press.

Doyle, P. M., Wolery, M., Ault, M. J., & Gast, D. L. (1988). System of least prompts: A literature review of procedural parameters. *Journal of the Association for Persons with Severe Handicaps, 13,* 28–40.

Doyle, W. (1986). Classroom organization and management. In M. C. Wittrock (Ed.), *Handbook of research on teaching* (3rd ed., pp. 392–431). New York: Macmillan.

Duda, M. A., Dunlap, G., Fox, L., Lentini, R., & Clarke, S. (2004). An experimental evaluation of positive behavior support in a community preschool program. *Topics in*

Early Childhood Special Education, 24, 143–155.

Dunlap, G., & Fox, L. (1999). A demonstration of behavioral support for young children with autism. *Journal of Positive Behavior Interventions, 1,* 77–87.

Dunlap, G., & Iovannone, R. (2008). Essential components for effective autism educational programs. In J. K. Luiselli, D. C. Russo, W. P. Christian, & S. M. Wilczynski (Eds.), *Effective practices for children with autism: Educational and behavioral support interventions that work* (pp. 111–136). New York: Oxford.

Dunlap, G., Iovannone, R., Kincaid, D., Wilson, K., Christiansen, K., Strain, P., & English, C. (2010). *Prevent-Teach-Reinforce: A school-based model of individualized positive behavior support.* Baltimore: Brookes.

Dunlap, G., Iovannone, R., Wilson, K., Strain, P., & Kincaid, D. (2010). Prevent-Teach-Reinforce: A standardized model of school-based behavioral intervention. *Journal of Positive Behavior Interventions, 12,* 9–22.

Dunlap, G., & Robbins, F. R. (1991). Current perspectives in service delivery for young children with autism. *Comprehensive Mental Health Care, 1,* 177–194.

Dunst, C. J., & Bruder, M. B. (2006). Early intervention service coordination models and service coordinator practices. *Journal of Early Intervention, 28,* 155–165.

Dunst, C. J., Bruder, M. B., Trivette, C. M., Hamby, D., Raab, M., & McLean, M. (2001). Characteristics and consequences of everyday natural learning opportunities. *Topics in Early Childhood Special Education, 21,* 68–92.

Dunst, C. J., Hamby, D., Trivette, C. M., Raab, M., & Bruder, M. B. (2000). Everyday family and community life and children's naturally occurring learning opportunities. *Journal of Early Intervention, 23,* 151–164.

Durán, R. P. (2008). Assessing English-language learners' achievement. *Review of Research in Education, 32,* 292–327.

Economic Opportunity Amendments of 1972, Pub. L. No. 92-424.

Edmonds, C. J., & Pring, L. (2006). Generating inferences from written and spoken language: A comparison of children with visual impairment and children with sight. *British Journal of Developmental Psychology, 24,* 337–351.

Education for All Handicapped Children Act Amendments of 1986, Pub. L. No. 99-457, 20 U.S.C. 1400 *et seq.*

Education for All Handicapped Children Act of 1979, Pub. L. No. 94-142, 20 U.S.C. 1400 *et seq.*

Education Trust. (2009). *Education Watch National Report.* Washington, DC: Author.

Edyburn, D. L. (2001). Models, theories, and frameworks: Contributions to understanding special education technology. *Special Education Technology Practice, 4*(2), 16–24.

Ellis, D. N., Cress, P. J., & Spellman, C. R. (1992). Using timers and lap counters to promote self-management of independent exercise in adolescents with mental retardation. *Education and Training in Mental Retardation, 27,* 51–59.

Engelmann, S., & Bruner, E. C. (1995). *SRA reading mastery rainbow edition.* Chicago, IL: SRA/McGraw-Hill.

Erickson, K. A., & Hatton, D. (2007). Expanding understanding of emergent literacy: Empirical support for a new framework. *Journal of Visual Impairment and Blindness, 101,* 261–277.

Erickson, K. A., Hatton, D., Roy, V., Fox, D., & Renne, D. (2007). Literacy in early intervention for children with visual impairments: Insights from individual cases. *Journal of Visual Impairment and Blindness, 101,* 80–95.

Fantuzzo, J. W., Polite, K., Cook, D. M., & Quinn, G. (1988). An evaluation of the effectiveness of teacher- vs.-student-management classroom interventions. *Psychology in the Schools, 25,* 154–163.

Farlow, L. J., & Snell, M. E. (2006). Teaching self-care skills. In M. E. Snell & F. Brown (Eds.), *Instruction of students with severe disabilities* (6th ed., pp. 328–374). Upper Saddle River, NJ: Pearson.

Felton, E. A., Lewis, N. L., Wills, S. A., Radwin, R. G., & Williams, J. C. (2007). *Neural signal based control of the Dasher Writing System.* Paper presented at the 3rd International IEEE EMBS Conference on Neural Engineering, Kohala Coast, Hawaii.

Feng, J., Karat, C. M., & Sears, A. (2005). How productivity improves in hands-free continuous dictation tasks: Lessons learned from a longitudinal study. *Interacting with Computers, 17,* 265–289.

Ferguson, B., & McDonnell, J. (1991). A comparison of serial and concurrent sequencing strategies in teaching generalized grocery item location to students with moderate handicaps. *Education and Training in Mental Retardation, 26,* 292–304.

Ferreira, J., Rönnberg, J., Gustafson, S., & Wengelin, Å. (2007). Reading, why not?: Literacy skills in children with motor and speech impairments. *Communication Disorders Quarterly, 28,* 236–251.

Ferrell, K. A., Shaw, A. R., & Deitz, S. J. (1998). *Project PRISM: A longitudinal study of developmental patterns of children who are visually impaired. (Final Report, CFDA 84-023C, Grant H023C10188).* Greeley: University of Northern Colorado, Division of Special Education.

Ferretti, R. P., Cavalier, A. R., Murphy, M. J., & Murphy, R. (1993). The self-management of skills by persons with mental retardation. *Research in Developmental Disabilities, 14,* 189–205.

Fey, M. E. (1986). *Language intervention with young children.* Newton, MA: Allyn & Bacon.

Fey, M. E., Cleave, P. L., & Long, S. H. (1997). Two models of grammar facilitation in children with language impairments. *Journal of Speech, Language, and Hearing Research, 40,* 5–19.

Fey, M. E., Cleave, P. L., Long, S. H., & Hughes, D. L. (1993). Two approaches to the facilitation of grammar in children with language impairment: An experimental evaluation. *Journal of Speech and Hearing Research, 36,* 141–157.

Fey, M. E., Krulik, T. E., Loeb, D. F., & Proctor-Williams, K. (1999). Sentence recast use by parents of children with typical language and children with specific language impairment. *American Journal of Speech-Language Pathology, 8,* 273–286.

Fey, M. E., & Loeb, D. F. (2002). An evaluation of the facilitative effects of inverted yes–no questions on the acquisition of auxiliary verbs. *Journal of Speech, Language, and Hearing Research, 45,* 160–174.

Fey, M. E., Long, S. H., & Finestack, L. H. (2003). Ten principles of grammar facilitation for children with specific language impairments. *American Journal of Speech-Language Pathology, 12,* 3–15.

Fickel, K. M., Schuster, J., & Collins, B. C. (1998). Teaching different tasks using different stimuli in a heterogeneous small group. *Journal of Behavioral Education, 8,* 219–244.

Field, S., & Hoffman, A. (1994). Development of a model for self-determination. *Career Development for Exceptional Individuals, 17,* 159–169.

Field, S., Martin, J., Miller, R., Ward, M., & Wehmeyer, M. (1998). *A practical guide to teaching self-determination.* Reston, VA: Council for Exceptional Children.

Fitzgerald, J., & Spiegel, D. L. (1983). Enhancing children's reading comprehension through instruction in narrative structure. *Journal of Reading Behavior, 15,* 1–17.

Fleming, J. L., Sawyer, L. B., & Campbell, P. H. (2011). Early intervention providers' perspectives about implementing participation-based practices. *Topics in Early Childhood Special Education, 30,* 233–244.

Flood, J., Heath, S. B., & Lapp, D. (Eds.). (2008). *Handbook of research on teaching literacy through the communicative and visual arts.* New York: Routledge.

Foley, B. E., & Pollatsek, A. (1999). Phonological processing and reading abilities in adolescents and adults with severe congenital speech impairments. *Augmentative and Alternative Communication, 15,* 156–173.

Fontana, J., Scruggs, T.E., & Mastropieri, M. A. (2007). Mnemonic strategy instruction in inclusive secondary social studies classes. *Remedial and Special Education, 28,* 345–355.

Ford, J., & Milosky, L. (2003). Inferring emotional reactions in social situations: Differences in children with language impairment. *Journal of Speech, Language, and Hearing Research, 46,* 21–30.

Forness, S. R. (2001). Special education and related services: What have we learned from meta-analysis? *Exceptionality, 9,* 185–197.

Fowler, C. H., Konrad, M., Walker, A. R., Test, D. W., & Wood, W. M. (2007). Self-determination interventions' effects on the academic performance of students with developmental disabilities. *Education and Training in Developmental Disabilities, 42,* 270–285.

Fox, L. (1989). Stimulus generalization of skills and persons with profound mental handicaps. *Education and Training in Mental Retardation, 24,* 219–229.

Fox, L., & Hanline, M. F. (1993). A preliminary evaluation of learning within developmentally appropriate early childhood settings. *Topics in Early Childhood Special Education, 13,* 308–327.

Francis, D., Rivera, M., Lesaux, N., Kieffer, M., & Rivera, H. (2006). *Practical guidelines for the education of English language learners: Research-based recommendations for instruction and academic interventions.* Portsmouth, NH: RMC Research Corporation, Center on Instruction.

Frederick-Dugan, A., Test, D. W., & Varn, L. (1991). Acquisition and generalization of purchasing skills using a calculator by students who are mentally retarded. *Education and Training in Mental Retardation, 26,* 381–387.

Freedman, D. H. (2010). *Wrong: Why experts keep failing us—and how to know when not to trust them.* New York: Little, Brown.

Freire, P. (1970). *Pedagogy of the oppressed.* New York: Herder and Herder.

Gambrell, L. B., & Jawitz, P. B. (1993). Mental imagery, text illustrations, and children's story comprehension and recall. *Reading Research Quarterly, 28,* 264–276.

Gándara, P., Maxwell-Jolly, J., & Driscoll, A. (2005). *Listening to teachers of English language learners: A survey of California's teachers' challenges, experiences, and professional development needs.* Santa Barbara, CA: UC Linguistic Minority Research Institute.

Ganger, J., & Brent, M. R. (2004). Reexamining the vocabulary spurt. *Developmental Psychology, 40,* 621–632.

Ganz, J. B. (2008). Self-monitoring across age and ability levels: Teaching students to implement their own positive behavioral interventions. *Preventing School Failure, 53,* 39–48.

Ganz, J. B., & Sigafoos, J. (2005). Self-monitoring: Are young adults with MR and autism able to utilize cognitive strategies independently? *Education and Training in Developmental Disabilities, 40,* 24–33.

Gardill, M. C., & Jitendra, A. K. (1999). Advanced story-map instruction: Effects on the reading comprehension of students with learning disabilities. *The Journal of Special Education, 33,* 2–17.

Garrett, J., Heller, K., Fowler, L., Alberto, P., Fredrick, L., & O'Rourke, C. (2011). Using speech recognition software to increase writing fluency for individuals with physical disabilities. *Journal of Special Education Technology, 26(1),* 25–41.

Gaule, K., Nietupski, J., & Certo, N. (1985). Teaching supermarket shopping skills using an adaptive shopping list. *Education and Training of the Mentally Retarded, 20,* 53–59.

Gay, G. (2000). *Culturally responsive teaching: Theory, research, and practice.* New York: Teachers College Press.

Gee, J. P. (1996). *Social linguistics and literacies: Ideology in discourses.* London/ Bristol, PA: Taylor & Francis.

Gee, J. P. (2000). The limits of reframing: A response to Professor Snow. *Journal of Reading Behavior, 32,* 121–128.

Genesee, F., Lindholm-Leary, K., Saunders, W., & Christian, D. (2005). English language learners in U.S. schools: An overview of research findings. *Journal of*

Education for Students Placed at Risk, 10, 363–385.

Gerber, M. M., Jimenez, T., Leafstedt, J., Villaruz, J., Richards, C., & English, J. (2004). English reading effects of small-group intensive intervention in Spanish for K-1 English learners. *Learning Disabilities Research & Practice, 19*, 239–251.

Gersten, R., Baker, S. K., Shanahan, T., Linan-Thompson, S., Collins, P., & Scarcella, R. (2007). *Effective literacy and English language instruction for English learners in the elementary grades: A practical guide.* Washington, DC: National Center for Education Evaluation and Regional Assistance, Institute of Education Sciences, U.S. Department of Education.

Gersten, R., Fuchs, L. S., Compton, D., Coyne, M., Greenwood, C., & Innocenti, M. S. (2005). Quality indicators for group experimental and quasi-experimental research in special education. *Exceptional Children, 71*, 149–164.

Gilberts, G. H., Agran, M., Hughes, C., & Wehmeyer, M. (2001). The effects of peer delivered self-monitoring strategies on the participation of students with severe disabilities in general education classrooms. *Journal of the Association for Persons with Severe Handicaps, 26*, 25–36.

Gillam, R. B., & Pearson, N. A. (2004). *Test of Narrative Language.* Austin, TX: Pro-Ed.

Gillam, S., Gillam, R., Petersen, D., & Bingham, C. (2008). *Narrative language intervention program: Promoting oral language development.* Technical session presented at The Annual Convention of the American Speech Language and Hearing Association, Chicago, IL.

Girolametto, L., Pearce, P. S., & Weitzman, E. (1996). Interactive focused stimulation for toddlers with expressive vocabulary delays. *Journal of Speech and Hearing Research, 39*, 1275.

Girolametto, L., & Weitzman, E. (2002). Responsiveness of child care providers in interactions with toddlers and preschoolers. *Language, Speech, and Hearing Services in Schools, 33*, 268–281.

Gitlin, A., Buendía, E., Crosland, K., & Doumbia, F. (2003). The production of margin and center: Welcoming–unwelcoming of immigrant students. *American Educational Research Journal, 40*, 91–122.

Giumento, A. (1990). *The effectiveness of two intervention procedures on the acquisition and generalization of object labels by young children who are at-risk or have developmental delays.* Unpublished doctoral dissertation, University of Oregon, Eugene.

Goldenberg, C., Rueda, R., & August, D. (2006). Synthesis: Sociocultural contexts and literacy development. In D. August & T. Shanahan (Eds.), *Report of the national literacy panel on language minority youth and children* (pp. 249–267). Mahwah, NJ: Erlbaum.

Goldman, S., & Varnhagen, C. K. (1986). Memory for embedded and sequential story structures. *Journal of Memory and Language, 25*, 401–418.

Gordon, C. J., & Pearson, P. D. (1983). *The effects of instruction in metacomprehension and inferencing on children's comprehension abilities* (Tech. Rep. No. 277). Urbana, IL: University of Illinois, Center for the Study of Reading.

Graesser, A. C., Singer, M., & Trabasso, T. (1994). Constructing inferences during narrative text comprehension. *Psychological Review, 101*, 371–395.

Graff, R. B., & Green, G. (2004). Two methods for teaching simple visual discriminations to learners with severe disabilities. *Research in Developmental Disabilities, 25*, 295–307.

Greenwood, C. (1997). Classwide peer tutoring. *Behavior and Social Issues, 7*, 53–57.

Greenwood, C. R., & Abbott, M. (2001). The research-to-practice gap in special education. *Teacher Education and Special Education, 24*, 276–289.

Griffen, A. K., Wolery, M., & Schuster, J. W. (1992). Triadic instruction of chained food preparation responses: Acquisition and observational learning. *Journal of Applied Behavior Analysis, 25*, 193–204.

Grisham-Brown, J. L., Schuster, J. W., Hemmeter, M. L., & Collins, B. C. (2000). Using embedded strategies to teach preschoolers with significant disabilities. *Journal of Behavior Education, 10*, 139–162.

Grossi, T. A. (1998). Using a self-operated auditory prompting system to improve the work performance of two employees with severe disabilities. *Journal of the Association for the Severely Handicapped, 23*, 149–154.

Gunn, B., Biglan, A., Smolkowski, K., & Ary, D. (2005). The efficacy of supplemental instruction in decoding skills for Hispanic and non-Hispanic students in early elementary school. *Journal of Special Education, 34*, 90–113.

Günther, T., Holtkamp, K., Jolles, J., Herpertz-Dahlmann, B., & Konrad, K. (2004). Verbal memory and aspects of attentional control in children and adolescents with anxiety disorders or depressive disorders. *Journal of Affective Disorders, 82*, 265–269.

Guralnick, M. J. (2001). *Early childhood inclusion: Focus on change.* Baltimore: Brookes.

Hagopian, L. P., Farrell, D. A., & Amari, A. (1996). Treating total liquid refusal with backward chaining and fading. *Journal of Applied Behavior Analysis, 29*, 573–575.

Halle, J. W., Baer, D. M., & Spradlin, J. E. (1981). Teachers' generalized use of delay as a stimulus control procedure to increase language use in handicapped children. *Journal of Applied Behavior Analysis, 14*, 387–400.

Halle, J. W., Marshall, A. M., & Spradlin, J. E. (1979). Time delay: A technique to increase language use and facilitate generalization in retarded children. *Journal of Applied Behavior Analysis, 12*, 431–440.

Halpern, A. S. (1992). Transition: Old wine in new bottles. *Exceptional Children, 58*, 202–211.

Hammer, M. R. (2004). Using the Self-Advocacy Strategy to increase student participation in IEP conferences. *Intervention in School and Clinic, 39*, 295–300.

Hancock, T. B., & Kaiser, A. P. (1996). Siblings' use of milieu teaching at home. *Topics in Early Childhood Special Education, 16*, 168–190.

Hancock, T. B., & Kaiser, A. P. (2002). The effects of trainer-implemented enhanced milieu teaching on the social communication of children with autism. *Topics in Early Childhood Special Education, 22,* 39–54.

Hancock, T. B., & Kaiser, A. P. (2006). Enhanced milieu teaching. In R. J. McCauley & M. E. Fey (Eds.), *Treatment of language disorders in children.* Baltimore, MD: Paul H. Brookes.

Hannan, C. K. (2006). Review of research: Neuroscience and the impact of brain plasticity on braille reading. *Journal of Visual Impairment and Blindness, 100,* 397–413.

Hansford, D., & Adlington, R. (2009). Digital spaces and young people's online authoring: Challenges for teachers. *Australian Journal of Language & Literacy, 32*(1), 55–68.

Harper, C. B., Symon, J. B. G., & Frea, W. D. (2008). Recess is time-in: Using peers to improve social skills of children with autism. *Journal of Autism and Developmental Disorders, 38,* 815–826.

Harrower, J. D., Fox, L., Dunlap, G., & Kincaid, D. (2000). Functional assessment and comprehensive early intervention. *Exceptionality, 8,* 189–204.

Hart, B., & Risley, T. R. (1968). Establishing use of descriptive adjectives in the spontaneous speech of disadvantaged preschool children. *Journal of Applied Behavior Analysis, 1,* 109–120.

Hart, B., & Risley, T. R. (1974). Using preschool materials to modify the language of disadvantaged children. *Journal of Applied Behavior Analysis, 7,* 243–256.

Hart, B., & Risley, T. R. (1975). Incidental teaching of language in the preschool. *Journal of Applied Behavior Analysis, 8,* 411–420.

Hart, B., & Risley, T. R. (1980). In vivo language interventions: Unanticipated general effects. *Journal of Applied Behavior Analysis, 13,* 407–432.

Hart, B., & Risley, T. R. (1995). *Meaningful differences in the everyday experience of young American children.* Baltimore: Brookes.

Hart, B., & Rogers-Warren, A. K. (1978). A milieu approach to teaching language. In R. L. Schiefelbusch (Ed.), *Language intervention strategies* (pp. 193–235). Baltimore: University Park Press.

Hatton, D. D., & Erickson, K. (2005, November). *Highly literate individuals with visual impairments: Practical applications from research.* Paper presented at the Seventh Biennial Getting in Touch with Literacy Conference, Denver, CO.

Hayward, D., & Schnieder, P. (2000). Effectiveness of teaching story grammar knowledge to pre-school children with language impairment. An exploratory study. *Child Language Teaching and Therapy, 30,* 255–284.

Heal, L. W., Borthwick-Duffy, S. A., & Saunders, R. R. (1996). Assessment of quality of life. In J. W. Mulick & J. Anton (Eds.), *Manual of diagnosis and professional practice in mental retardation* (pp. 199–209). Washington, DC: American Psychological Association.

Heller, K. W. (2009a). Learning and behavioral characteristics of students with physical, health, or multiple disabilities. In K. W. Heller, P. E. Forney, P. A. Alberto, S. J. Best & M. N. Swartzman (Eds.), *Understanding physical, health, and multiple disabilities* (2nd ed., pp. 18–34). Upper Saddle River, NJ: Pearson Education, Inc.

Heller, K. W. (2009b). Understanding disabilities and effective teaming. In K. W. Heller, P. E. Forney, P. Alberto, S. J. Best, & M. N. Schwartzman (Eds.), *Understanding physical, health, and multiple disabilities* (2nd ed., pp. 3-17). Upper Saddle River, NJ: Pearson Education Inc.

Heller, K. W. (2010). Writing instruction and adaptations. In S. Best, K. W. Heller, & J. Bigge (Eds.), *Teaching individuals with physical, health, or multiple disabilities* (6th ed., pp. 407–431). Upper Saddle River, NJ: Merrill/Pearson Education.

Heller, K. W., & Alberto, P. A. (2010). Reading instruction and adaptations. In S. Best, K.W. Heller, J. Bigge (Eds.), *Teaching individuals with physical, health, or multiple disabilities* (6th ed., pp. 375–406). Upper Saddle River, NJ: Pearson.

Heller, K. W., & Coleman-Martin, M. B. (2007). Strategies for promoting literacy for students who have physical disabilities. *Communication Disorders Quarterly, 28,* 69–72.

Heller, K. W., Coleman-Martin, M. B., & Swinehart-Jones, D. (2006). *Strategies for promoting literacy with students who have physical disabilities* (3rd ed.). Atlanta, Georgia: Georgia Bureau for Students with Physical and Health Impairments.

Heller, K. W., Forney, P. E., Alberto, P. A., Best, S. J., & Schwartzman, M. N. (2009). *Understanding physical, health, and multiple disabilities* (2nd ed.). Upper Saddle River, NJ: Pearson.

Heller, K. W., Fredrick, L. D., & Diggs, C. A. (1999). Teaching reading to students with severe speech and physical impairments using the nonverbal reading approach. *Physical Disabilities: Education and Related Services, 18,* 3–34.

Heller, K. W., Fredrick, L. D., Dykes, M. K., Best, S. J., & Cohen, E. T. (1999). A national perspective of competencies for teachers of individuals with physical and health disabilities. *Exceptional Children, 65,* 219–234.

Heller, K. W., Fredrick, L. D., Tumlin, J., & Brineman, D. G. (2002). Teaching decoding for generalization using the Nonverbal Reading Approach. *Journal of Developmental and Physcial Disabilities, 14,* 19–35.

Heller, K. W., Mezei, P., & Schwartzman, M. N. (2009). Muscular dystrophies. In K. W. Heller, P. E. Forney, P. Alberto, S. J. Best & M. N. Schwartzman (Eds.), *Understanding physical, health, and multiple disabilities* (2nd ed., pp. 232–247). Upper Saddle River, NJ: Pearson, Inc.

Heller, K. W., & Swinehart-Jones, D. (2003). Supporting the educational needs of students with orthopedic impairments. *Physical Disabilities: Education and Related Services, 22,* 3–24.

Hemmeter, M. L. (2000). Classroom-based interventions: Evaluating the past and looking toward the future. *Topics in Early Childhood Special Education, 20,* 56–61.

Hemmingson, H., & Borell, L. (2002). Environmental barriers in mainstream schools. *Child: Care, Health & Development, 28*(1), 57–63.

Henry, L. (2008). Short-term memory coding in children with intellectual disabilities. *American Journal on Mental Retardation, 113,* 187–200.

Hess, F., & Petrilli, M. (2006). *No Child Left Behind primer*. New York: Peter Lang.

Heward, W. L., & Orlansky, M. D. (1984). *Exceptional children* (2nd ed.). Columbus, OH: Merrill.

Hoffman, P. R., Norris, J. A., & Monjure, J. (1990). Comparison of process targeting and whole language treatments for phonologically delayed preschool children. *Language, Speech, and Hearing Services in Schools, 21,* 102–109.

Hoggan, K., & Strong, C. (1994). The magic of "Once upon a time": Narrative teaching strategies. *Language, Speech, and Hearing Services in Schools, 25,* 76–89.

Hogue, A., Henderson, C. E., Dauber, S., Barajas, P. C., Fried, A., & Liddle, H. A. (2008). Treatment adherence, competence, and outcome in individual and family therapy for adolescent behavior problems. *Journal of Consulting and Clinical Psychology, 76,* 544–555.

Horn, E., Lieber, J., Li, S., Sandall, S., & Schwartz, I. (2000). Supporting young children's IEP goals in inclusive settings through embedded learning opportunities. *Topics in Early Childhood Special Education, 20,* 208–223.

Horner, R. D., & Keilitz, I. (1975). Training mentally retarded adolescents to brush their teeth. *Journal of Applied Behavior Analysis, 8,* 301–309.

Horner, R. H., Carr, E. G., Halle, J., McGee, G., Odom, S., & Wolery, M. (2005). The use of single-subject research to identify evidence-based practice in special education. *Exceptional Children, 71,* 165–179.

Horner, R. H., Diemer, S. M., & Brazeau, K. C. (1992). Educational support for students with severe problem behaviors in Oregon: A descriptive analysis from the 1987–88 school year. *Journal of the Association for Persons with Severe Handicaps, 17,* 154–169.

Horner, R. H., Sprague, J., & Wilcox, B. (1982). General case programming for community activities. In B. Wilcox & G. T. Bellamy (Eds.), *Design of high school programs for severely handicapped students* (pp. 61–98). Baltimore: Brookes.

Hoyson, M., Jamieson, B., & Strain, P. S. (1984). Individualized group instruction of normally developing and autistic-like children: The LEAP curriculum model. *Journal of Educational Psychology, 55,* 95–41.

Hughes, C., Copeland, S. R., Agran, M., Wehmeyer, M. L., Rodi, M. S., & Presley, J. A. (2002). Using self-monitoring to improve performance in general education high school classes. *Education and Training in Mental Retardation and Developmental Disabilities, 37,* 262–272.

Hughes, C., Fowler, S. E., Copeland, S. R., Agran, M., Wehmeyer, M. L., & Church-Pupke, P. (2004). Supporting high school students to engage in recreational activities with peers. *Behavior Modification, 28,* 3–27.

Hughes, C., Rung, L. L., Wehmeyer, M., L., Agran, M., Copeland, S. R., & Bogseon, H. (2000). Self-prompted communication book use to increase social interaction among high school students. *Journal of the Association for Persons with Severe Handicaps, 25,* 153–166.

Hughes, D., McGillivray, L., & Schmidek, M. (1997). *Guide to narrative language: Procedures for assessment*. Eau Claire, WI: Thinking Publications.

Hurth, J., Shaw, E., Izeman, S. G., Whaley, K., & Rogers, S. J. (1999). Areas of agreement about effective practices among programs serving young children with autism spectrum disorder. *Infants and Young Children, 12,* 17–26.

Hux, K., Rankin-Erickson, J., Manasse, N., & Lauritzen, E. (2000). Accuracy of three speech recognition systems: Case study of dysarthric speech. *Augmentative and Alternative Communication, 16,* 186–196.

Iddon, J. L., Morgan, D. J. R., Loveday, C., Sahakian, B. J., & Pickard, J. D. (2004). Neuropsychological profile of young adults with spina bifida with or without hydrocephalus. *Journal of Neurology Neurosurgery and Psychiatry, 75,* 1112–1118.

Idol, L. (1987). Group story mapping: A comprehension strategy for both skilled and unskilled readers. *Journal of Learning Disabilities, 20*(4), 196–205.

Ihnot, C. (1991). *Read Naturally*. St. Paul, MN: Read naturally.

Individuals with Disabilities Education Act of 1990, Pub. L. No. 101-476,104 Stat. 1142.

Individuals with Disabilities Education Act of 1991, Pub. L. No. 102-119, 105 Stat. 587.

Individuals with Disabilities Education Act of 1997, Pub. L. No. 105-17, 105 Stat. 37.

Individuals with Disabilities Education Improvement Act of 2004, Pub. L. No. 108-446, 118 Stat. 2647.

Iovannone, R., Dunlap, G., Huber, H., & Kincaid, D. (2003). Effective educational practices for students with autism spectrum disorders. *Focus on Autism and Other Developmental Disabilities, 18,* 150–165.

Iovannone, R., Greenbaum, P., Wei, W., Kincaid, D., Dunlap, G., & Strain, P. (2009). Randomized controlled trial of a tertiary behavior intervention for students with problem behaviors: Preliminary outcomes. *Journal of Emotional and Behavioral Disorders, 17,* 213–225.

Irvine, A. B., Erickson, A. M., Singer, G. H. S., & Stahlberg, D. (1992). A coordinated program to transfer self-management skills from school to home. *Education and Training in Mental Retardation, 27,* 241–254.

Jameson, J. M., McDonnell, J., Johnson, J. W., Riesen, T., & Polychronis, S. (2007). A comparison of one-to-one embedded instruction in the general education classroom and one-to-one massed practice instruction in the special education classroom. *Education and Treatment of Children, 30,* 23–44.

Jensen, T., Orquiz, P., & Gillam, S. (April, 2009). Narrative language intervention for English language learners. *National Conference on Undergraduate Research*. LaCrosse, Wisconsin (poster session).

Johnson, J. E., & Johnson, K. M. (1992). Clarifying the developmental perspective in response to Carta, Schwartz, Atwater, & McConnell. *Topics in Early Childhood Special Education, 12,* 439–457.

Jones, C. D., & Schwartz, I. S. (2004). Siblings, peers, and adults: Differential affects of models for children with autism. *Topics in Early Childhood Special Education, 24,* 187–198.

Jones, M. L. (2009). A study of novice special educators' views of evidence-based practices. *Teacher*

Education and Special Education, 32(2), 101–120.

Junkala, J., & Talbot, M. L. (1982). Cognitive styles of students with cerebral palsy. *Perceptual and Motor Skills, 55*, 403–410.

Justice, L. M. (2010). *Communication sciences and disorders: A contemporary perspective* (2nd ed.). Upper Saddle River, NJ: Pearson.

Justice, L. M., & Ezell, H. K. (1999). Vygotskian theory and its application to assessment: An overview for speech-language pathologists. *Contemporary Issues in Communication Science and Disorders, 26*, 111–118.

Kaiser, A. P. (1993). Parent-implemented language intervention: An environmental systems perspective. In A. P. Kaiser & D. B. Gray (Eds.), *Enhancing children's communication: Research foundations for intervention* (Vol. 2, pp. 63–84). Baltimore: Brookes.

Kaiser, A. P. (2000). Teaching functional communication skills. In M. E. Snell & F. Brown (Eds.), *Instruction of students with severe disabilities* (4th ed., pp. 347–370). Upper Saddle River, NJ: Merrill/Pearson.

Kaiser, A. P., & Hancock, T. B. (2003). Teaching parents new skills to support their young children's development. *Infants and Young Children, 16*(1), 9–21.

Kaiser, A. P., Hancock, T. B., & Hester, P. P. (1998). Parents as cointerventionists: Research on applications of naturalistic language teaching procedures. *Infants and Young Children, 10*(4), 46–55.

Kaiser, A. P., Hemmeter, M. L., & Hester, P. P. (1997). The facilitative effects of input on children's language development: Contributions from studies on enhanced milieu teaching. In L. B. Adamson & M. A. Romski (Eds.), *Communication and language acquisition: Discoveries from atypical development* (pp. 267–294). Baltimore: Brookes.

Kaiser, A. P., & Hester, P. P. (1994). Generalized effects of enhanced milieu teaching. *Journal of Speech & Hearing Research, 37*, 1320–1341.

Kaiser, A. P., Ostrosky, M. M., & Alpert, C. L. (1993). Training teachers to use environmental arrangement and milieu teaching with nonvocal preschool children. *Journal of the Association for Persons with Severe Handicaps, 18*, 188–199.

Kaiser, A., Yoder, P., & Keetz, A. (1992). Evaluating milieu teaching. In S. F. Warren & J. Reichle (Eds.), *Causes and effects in communication and language intervention* (pp. 9–47). Baltimore: Brookes.

Kamps, D., Abbott, M., Greenwood, C., Arreaga-Mayer, C., Wills, H., Longstaff, J., . . . Walton, C. (2007). Use of evidence-based, small group reading instruction for English language learners in elementary grades: Second tier intervention. *Learning Disabilities Quarterly, 30*, 153–168.

Kamps, D. M., Leonard, B. R., Vernon, S., Dugan, E. P., Delquadri, J. C., Gershon, B., Wade, L., & Folk, L. (1992). Teaching social skills to students with autism to increase peer interactions in an integrated first-grade classroom. *Journal of Applied Behavior Analysis, 25*, 281–288.

Karat, J., Horn, D. B., Halverson, C. A., & Karat, C. M. (2000, April). *Overcoming unusabilty: Developing efficient strategies in speech recognition systems*. Paper presented at the CHI 2000, AMC Conference on Human Factors in Computer Systems, The Hague, Netherlands.

Kauffman, J. M. (1996). Research to practice issues. *Behavioral Disorders, 22*, 55–60.

Kavale, K. A., & Forness, S. R. (1992). Learning difficulties and memory problems in mental retardation: A meta-analysis of theoretical perspectives. In T. E. Scruggs & M. A. Mastropieri (Eds.), *Advances in learning and behavioral disabilities* (vol. 7, pp. 177–222). Greenwich, CT: JAI Press.

Keller-Allen, C. (2006). *English language learners with disabilities: Identification and other state policies and issues*. Alexandria, VA: Project Forum.

Kelly, P. R., Gomez-Bellenge, F. X., Chen, J., & Schulz, M. M. (2008). Learner outcomes for English language learner low readers in an early intervention. *TESOL Quarterly, 42*, 235–260.

Killoran, J. (2007). *The national deaf-blind child count 1998-2005 in review*. The National Technical Assistance Consortium for Children and Young Adults Who Are Deaf-Blind. Retrieved from http://nationaldb.org/documents/products/Childcountreview0607Final.pdf

King, G. A., Schultz, I. Z., Steel, K., Gilpin, M., & Cathers, T. (1993). Self-evaluation and self-concept of adolescents with physical disabilities. *The American Journal of Occupational Therapy, 47*, 132–140.

King, T. W. (1999). *Assistive technology: Essential human factors*. Boston: Allyn & Bacon.

King-Sears, M. E., Mercer, C. D., & Sindelar, P. (1992). Toward independence with keyword mnemonics: A strategy for science vocabulary instruction. *Remedial and Special Education, 13*, 22–33.

Kintsch, W., & van Dijk, T. A. (1978). Toward a model of text comprehension and production. *Psychological Review, 85*, 363–394.

Klecan-Aker, J., Flahive, L.K. & Fleming, S. (1997). Teaching storytelling to a group of children with learning disabilities: A look at treatment outcomes. *Contemporary Issues in Communication Science and Disorders, 24*, 23–32.

Kleinert, H. L., & Kearns, J. F. (2001). *Measuring outcomes and supports for students with disabilities*. Baltimore: Brookes.

Knowlton, M., & Wetzel, R. (1996). Braille reading rates as a function of reading tasks. *Journal of Visual Impairment and Blindness, 90*, 227–236.

Koegel, L. K., Koegel, R. L., Harrower, J. K., & Carter, C. M. (1999). Pivotal response intervention I: Overview of approach. *Journal of the Association for Persons with Severe Handicaps, 24*, 174–185.

Koegel, R. L., & Koegel, L. K. (2006). *Pivotal response treatments for autism: Communication, social, & academic development*. Baltimore: Brookes.

Koegel, R. L., Koegel, L. K., & Surratt, A. (1992). Language intervention and disruptive behavior in pre-school children with autism. *Journal of Autism and Developmental Disabilities, 22*, 141–153.

Koenig, A. J., & Holbrook, M. C. (1995). *Learning media assessment of students with visual impairments: A resource guide for teachers. Second Edition.* Austin, TX: Texas School for the Blind and Visually Impaired.

Koenig, A. J., & Holbrook, M. C. (2000). Ensuring high-quality instruction for students in braille literacy programs. *Journal of Visual Impairment & Blindness, 94,* 677–694.

Koester, H. H. (2004). Usage, performance, and satisfaction outcomes for experienced users of automatic speech recognition. *Journal of Rehabilitation Research & Development, 41,* 739–754.

Koester, H. H. (2006). Factors that influence the performance of experienced speech recognition users. *Assistive Technology, 18,* 56–76.

Kohl, F. L., & Stettner-Eaton, B. A. (1985). Fourth graders as trainers of cafeteria skills to severely handicapped students. *Education and Training of the Mentally Retarded, 20,* 60–68.

Kohler, F. W., Greteman, C., Raschke, D., & Highnam, C. (2007). Using a buddy skills package to increase the social interactions between a preschooler with autism and her peers. *Topics in Early Childhood Special Education, 27,* 155–163. doi: 10.1177/02711214070270030601

Kohler, F. W., & Strain, P. S. (1990). Peer-assisted interventions: Early promises, notable achievements, and future aspirations. *Child Psychology Review, 10,* 441–452.

Kohler, F. W., Strain, P. S., Hoyson, M., & Jamieson, B. (1997). Merging naturalistic teaching and peer-based strategies to address the IEP objectives of preschoolers with autism: An examination of structural and child behavior outcomes. *Focus on Autism and Other Developmental Disabilities, 12,* 196–206.

Konrad, M., Fowler, C. H., Walker, A. R., Test, D. W., & Wood, W. M. (2007). Effects of self-determination interventions on the academic skills of students with learning disabilities. *Learning Disabilities Quarterly, 30,* 89–113.

Koppenhaver, D. A., Hendrix, M. P., & Williams, A. R. (2007). Toward evidence-based literacy interventions for children with severe and multiple disabilities. *Seminars in Speech & Language, 28*(1), 79–89.

Kotler, A. L., & Tam, C. (2002). Effectiveness of using discreet utterance speech recognition software. *Augmentative and Alternative Communication, 18,* 137–146.

Kotler, A. L., & Thomas-Stonell, N. (1997). Effects of speech training on the accuracy of speech recognition for an individual with a speech impairment. *Augmentative and Alternative Communication, 13,* 71–80.

Labov, W. (1972). *Language in the inner city.* Philadelphia: University of Pennsylvania Press.

Ladson-Billings, G. (1992). Reading between the lines and beyond the pages: A culturally relevant approach to literacy teaching. *Theory into Practice, 31,* 312–320.

Lancaster, P. E., Schumaker, J. B., & Deshler, D. D. (2002). The development and validation of an interactive hypermedia program for teaching a self-advocacy strategy to students with disabilities. *Learning Disability Quarterly, 25,* 277–302.

Lancioni, G. E., Klaase, M., & Goossens, A. (1995). Brief report: Pictorial vs. auditory prompt systems for promoting independent task performance in adolescents with multiple handicaps. *Behavioral Interventions, 10,* 237–244.

Lancioni, G. E., & O'Reilly, M. F. (2001). Self-management of instruction cues for occupation: Review of studies with people with severe and profound developmental disabilities. *Research in Developmental Disabilities, 22,* 41–65.

Lancioni, G. E., Singh, N. N., O'Reilly, M. F., Sigafoos, J., Green, V., Chiapparino, C., & Oliva, D. (2008). A voice-detecting sensor and a scanning keyboard emulator to support word writing by two boys with extensive motor disabilities. *Research in Developmental Disabilities, 30,* 203–209.

Landrum, T. J., Cook, B. G., Tankersley, M. T., & Fitzgerald, S. (2002). Teachers' perceptions of the trustworthiness, useability, and accessibility of information from different sources. *Remedial and Special Education, 23*(1), 42–48.

Landrum, T. J., Cook, B. G., Tankersley, M., & Fitzgerald, S. (2007). Teacher perceptions of the usability of intervention

information from personal versus data-based sources. *Education and Treatment of Children, 30,* 27–42.

Landrum, T. J., & McDuffie, K. A. (2010). Learning styles in the age of differentiated instruction. *Exceptionality, 18,* 6–17.

Landrum, T. J., & Tankersley, M. (2004). Science at the schoolhouse: An uninvited guest. *Journal of Learning Disabilities, 37,* 207–212.

Lane, K. L., Cook, B. G., & Tankersley, M. (Eds.). (2013). *Research-based strategies for improving outcomes in behavior.* Columbus, OH: Pearson.

Lang, R., O'Reilly, M., Machalicek, W., Lancioni, G., Rispoli, M., & Chan, J. M. (2008). A preliminary comparison of functional analysis results when conducted in contrived versus natural settings. *Journal of Applied Behavior Analysis, 41,* 441–445.

Law, J., Garrett, Z. & Nye, C. (2004). The efficacy of treatment for children with developmental speech and language delay/disorder. *Journal of Speech, Language, and Hearing Research, 47,* 924–943.

Law, S. G., & Lane, D. S. (1987). Multicultural acceptance by teacher education students. *Journal of Instructional Psychology, 14,* 3–9.

Leafstedt, J. M., Richards, C. R., & Gerber, M. M. (2004). Effectiveness of explicit phonological-awareness instruction for at-risk English learners. *Learning Disabilities Research & Practice, 19,* 252–261.

Lee, C., & Smagorinsky, P. (Eds.). (1999). *Vygotskian perspectives on literacy research: Constructing meaning through collaborative inquiry.* New York: Cambridge University Press.

Lee, S., Odom, S. I., & Loftin, R. (2007). Social engagement with peers and stereotypic behavior of children with autism. *Journal of Positive Behavior Interventions, 9,* 67–79. doi: 10.1177/10983007070090020401

Leonard, L. B. (2000). *Children with specific language impairment.* Cambridge, MA: MIT Press.

Leslie, L., & Caldwell, J. (2001). *Qualitative Reading Inventory-3.* Boston, MA: Allyn & Bacon.

Levin, J., Anglin, G., & Carney, R. (1987). On empirically validating functions of pictures in prose. In D. Willows & H. Houghton (Eds.), *The psychology of illustration, volume 1: Instructional issues* (pp. 51–85). New York: Springer-Verlag.

Leybaert, J., & Alegria, J. (2003). The role of cued speech in language development of deaf children. In M. Marschark & P. E. Spencer (Eds.), *Oxford handbook of deaf studies, language, and education.* New York: Oxford University Press.

Limbos, M. M., & Geva, E. (2001). Accuracy of teacher assessments of second-language students at risk for reading disability. *Journal of Learning Disabilities, 34,* 136–151.

Linan-Thompson, S., Vaughn, S., Hickman-Davis, P., & Kouzekanani, K. (2003). Effectiveness of supplemental reading instruction for second-grade English language learners with reading difficulties. *Elementary School Journal, 103,* 221–238.

Lloyd, J. W., Pullen, P. C., Tankersley, M., & Lloyd, P. A. (2006). Critical dimensions of experimental studies and research syntheses that help define effective practice. In B. G. Cook & B. R. Schirmer (Eds.), *What is special about special education? Examining the role of evidence-based practices* (pp. 136–153). Austin, TX: Pro-Ed.

LoPresti, E. F., Brienza, D. M., & Angelo, J. (2002). Head-operated computer controls: Effect of control method on performance for subjects with and without disability. *Interacting with Computers, 14,* 359–377.

LoPresti, E. F., Brienza, D. M., Angelo, J., & Gilbertson, L. (2003). Neck range of motion and use of computer head controls. *Journal of Rehabilitation Research & Development, 40,* 199–212.

Losardo, A., & Bricker, D. (1994). Activity-based intervention and direct instruction: A comparison study. *American Journal on Mental Retardation, 98,* 744–765.

Losen, D. J., & Orfield, G. (2002). *Racial inequity in special education.* Cambridge, MA: Harvard Education Press.

Lovett, M. V., De Palma, M., Steinbach, K., Temple, M., Benson, N., & Lacerenza, L. (2008). Interventions for reading difficulties: A comparison of response to intervention by ELL and EFL struggling readers.

Journal of Learning Disabilities, 41, 333–352.

Luckner, J. L., Sebald, A. M., Cooney, J., Young, J., & Muir, S. G. (2005/2006). An examination of the evidence-based literacy research in deaf education. *American Annals of the Deaf, 150,* 443–456.

Lucyshyn, J. M., Albin, R. W., Horner, R. H., Mann, J. C., Mann, J. A., & Wadsworth, G. (2007). Family implementation of positive behavior support for a child with autism: Longitudinal, single-case, experimental, and descriptive replication and extension. *Journal of Positive Behavior Interventions, 5,* 131–150.

Lynch, J., van den Broek, P., Kremer, K., Kendeou, P., White, M., & Lorch, E. (2008). The development of narrative comprehension and its relation to other early reading skills. *Reading Psychology, 29,* 327–333.

Lyon, G. R. (1998). Why reading is not a natural process. *Educational Leadership, 55*(6), 14–18.

MacArthur, C. A., & Cavalier, A. R. (2004). Dictation and speech recognition technology as test accommodations. *Exceptional Children, 71,* 43–58.

Macy, M. G., & Bricker, D. D. (2007). Embedding individualized social goals into routine activities in inclusive early childhood classrooms. *Early Childhood Development and Care, 177,* 107–120.

Madelaine, A., & Wheldall, K. (2005). Identifying low-progress readers: Comparing teacher judgment with a curriculum-based measurement procedure. *International Journal of Disability, Development and Education, 52,* 33–42.

Magill-Evans, J. E., & Restall, G. (1991). Self-esteem of persons with cerebral palsy: From adolescence to adulthood. *The American Journal of Occupational Therapy, 45,* 819–825.

Malouf, D. B., & Schiller, E. P. (1995). Practice and research in special education. *Exceptional Children, 61,* 414–424.

Marshak, L. (2008). *Curriculum enhancements in inclusive social studies classrooms: Effects on students with and without disabilities.* Unpublished doctoral dissertation, Fairfax, VA: George Mason University,

College of Education and Human Development.

Marshak, L., Mastropieri, M. A., & Scruggs, T. E. (April, 2009). *Peer tutoring with strategic mnemonic instruction in inclusive history classes: Effects for middle school students with and without disabilities.* Paper presented at the annual meeting of the American Educational Research Association, San Diego.

Martin, J. E., Marshall, L. H., Maxson, L., & Jerman, P. (1997). *Self-Directed IEP.* Longmont, CO: Sopris West.

Martin, J. E., Van Dycke, J. L., Christensen, W. R., Greene, B. A., Gardner, J. E., & Lovett, D. L. (2006). Increasing student participation in their transition IEP meetings: Establishing the *Self-Directed IEP* as an evidenced-based practice. *Exceptional Children, 72,* 299–316.

Massaro, D. W., & Light, J. (2004). Using visible speech to train perception and production of speech for individuals with hearing loss. *Journal of Speech, Language, and Hearing Research, 47,* 304–320.

Mastropieri, M. A., Emerick, K., & Scruggs, T. E. (1988). Mnemonic instruction of science concepts. *Behavioral Disorders, 14,* 48–56.

Mastropieri, M. A., Jenkins, V., & Scruggs, T. E. (1985). Academic and intellectual characteristics of behaviorally disordered children and youth. *Severe Behavior Disorders Monographs, 8,* 86–104.

Mastropieri, M. A., & Scruggs, T. E. (1988). Increasing the content area learning of learning disabled students: Research implementation. *Learning Disabilities Research, 4,* 17–25.

Mastropieri, M. A., & Scruggs, T. E. (1989a). Constructing more meaningful relationships: Mnemonic instruction for special populations. *Educational Psychology Review, 1,* 83–111.

Mastropieri, M. A., & Scruggs, T. E. (1989b). Mnemonic social studies instruction: Classroom applications. *Remedial and Special Education, 10*(3), 40–46.

Mastropieri, M. A., & Scruggs, T. E. (1989c). Reconstructive elaborations: Strategies that facilitate content learning. *Learning Disabilities Focus, 4,* 73–77.

Mastropieri, M. A., & Scruggs, T. E. (2004). Effective classroom instruction. In C. Spielberger (Ed.), *Encyclopedia of applied psychology* (pp. 687–691). Oxford, UK: Elsevier.

Mastropieri, M. A., & Scruggs, T. E. (2009). *The inclusive classroom: Strategies for effective differentiated instruction* (4th ed.). Upper Saddle River, NJ: Prentice Hall.

Mastropieri, M. A., Scruggs, T. E., Bakken, J. P., & Whedon, C. (1997). Using mnemonic strategies to teach information about U.S. presidents: A classroom-based investigation. *Learning Disability Quarterly, 20,* 13–21.

Mastropieri, M. A., Scruggs, T. E., & Fulk, B. J. M. (1990). Teaching abstract vocabulary with the keyword method: Effects on recall and comprehension. *Journal of Learning Disabilities, 23,* 92–96.

Mastropieri, M. A., Scruggs, T. E., & Graetz, J. (2005). Cognition and learning in inclusive high school chemistry classes. In T. E. Scruggs & M. A. Mastropieri (Eds.), *Cognition and learning in diverse settings: Advances in learning and behavioral disabilities* (vol. 18, pp. 107–118). Oxford, UK: Elsevier.

Mastropieri, M. A., Scruggs, T. E., & Levin, J. R. (1985). Maximizing what exceptional students can learn: A review of research on the keyword method and related mnemonic techniques. *Remedial and Special Education, 6*(2), 39–45.

Mastropieri, M. A., Scruggs, T. E., & Levin, J. R. (1986). Direct vs. mnemonic instruction: Relative benefits for exceptional learners. *Journal of Special Education, 20,* 299–308.

Mastropieri, M. A., Scruggs, T. E., Levin, J. R., Gaffney, J., & McLoone, B. (1985). Mnemonic vocabulary instruction for learning disabled students. *Learning Disability Quarterly, 8,* 57–63.

Mastropieri, M. A., Scruggs, T. E., Mantzicopoulos, P. Y., Sturgeon, A., Goodwin, L., & Chung, S. (1998). "A place where living things affect and depend on each other": Qualitative and quantitative outcomes associated with inclusive science teaching. *Science Education, 82,* 163–179.

Mastropieri, M. A., Scruggs, T. E., & Marshak, L. (2008). Training teachers, parents, and peers to implement effective teaching strategies for content area learning. In T. E. Scruggs & M. A. Mastropieri (Eds.), *Personnel preparation: Advances in learning and behavioral disabilities* (vol. 21, pp. 311–329). Bingley, UK: Emerald.

Mastropieri, M. A., Scruggs, T. E., Norland, J., Berkeley, S., McDuffie, K., Tornquist, E. H., & Conners, N. (2006). Differentiated curriculum enhancement in inclusive middle school science: Effects on classroom and high-stakes tests. *Journal of Special Education, 40,* 130–137.

Mastropieri, M. A., Scruggs, T. E., Whittaker, M. E. S., & Bakken, J. P. (1994). Applications of mnemonic strategies with students with mental disabilities. *Remedial and Special Education, 15*(1), 34–43.

Mastropieri, M. A., Sweda, J., & Scruggs, T. E. (2000). Putting mnemonic strategies to work in an inclusive classroom. *Learning Disabilities Research & Practice, 15,* 69–74.

Mathes, P., & Torgesen, J. (2005). *Early interventions in reading.* New York: McGraw Hill/SRA.

Mayberry, R. (2010). Early language acquisition and adult language ability: What sign language reveals about the critical period for language. In M. Marschark & P. Spencer (Eds.), *The Oxford handbook of deaf studies, language, and education, Volume 2.* New York: Oxford University Press.

Mayer, C., & Akamatsu, C. (2003). Bilingualism and literacy. In M. Marschark & P. Spencer (Eds.), *The Oxford handbook of deaf studies, language, and education.* New York: Oxford University Press.

McBride, B. J., & Schwartz, I. S. (2003). Effects of teaching early interventionists to use discrete trials during ongoing classroom activities. *Topics in Early Childhood Special Education, 23,* 5–18.

McCormick, L. (2003). Introduction to language acquisition. In L. McCormick, D. F. Loeb & R. L. Schiefelbusch (Eds.), *Supporting children with communication difficulties in inclusive settings: School-based language intervention* (2nd ed., pp. 1–42). Boston: Allyn & Bacon.

McDonnell, J. (1998). Instruction for students with severe disabilities in general education settings. *Education and Training in Mental Retardation and Developmental Disabilities, 33,* 199–215.

McDonnell, J., & Ferguson, B. (1989). A comparison of time delay and decreasing prompt hierarchy strategies in teaching baking skills to students with moderate handicaps. *Journal of Applied Behavior Analysis, 22,* 85–91.

McDonnell, J., Horner, R. H., & Williams, J. A. (1984). Comparison of three strategies for teaching generalized grocery purchasing to high school students with severe handicaps. *The Journal of the Association for Persons with Severe Handicaps, 9,* 123–133.

McDonnell, J., & Laughlin, B. (1989). A comparison of backward ad concurrent chaining strategies in teaching community skills. *Education and Training in Mental Retardation, 24,* 230–238.

McDonnell, J., & McFarland, S. (1988). A comparison of forward and concurrent chaining strategies in teaching Laundromat skills to students with severe handicaps. *Research in Developmental Disabilities, 9,* 177–194.

McDuffie, K. A., Mastropieri, M. A., & Scruggs, T. E. (2009). Differential effects of co-teaching and peer-mediated instruction: Results for content learning and student-teacher interactions. *Exceptional Children, 75,* 493–510.

McGee, G. G., Krantz, P. J., Mason, D., & McClannahan, L. E. (1983). A modified incidental-teaching procedure for autistic youth: Acquisition and generalization of receptive object labels. *Journal of Applied Behavior Analysis, 16,* 329–338.

McGee, G. G., Krantz, P. J., & McClannahan, L. E. (1985). The facilitative effects of incidental teaching on preposition use by autistic children. *Journal of Applied Behavior Analysis, 18,* 17–31.

McGee, G. G., & McCoy, J. F. (1981). Training procedures for acquisition and retention of reading in retarded youth. *Applied Research in Mental Retardation, 2*(3), 263–276.

McGregor, K., & Leonard, L. B. (1995). Intervention for word-finding deficits in children. In M. Fey, J. Windsor, & S. Warren (Eds.), *Language intervention: Preschool through the elementary years* (pp. 85–105). Baltimore: Brookes.

McLoone, B. B., Scruggs, T. E., Mastropieri, M. A., & Zucker, S. F. (1986). Memory strategy instruction and training with LD adolescents. *Learning Disabilities Research, 2*, 45–53.

McMaster, K. L., Fuchs, D., & Fuchs, L. S. (2006). Research on peer-assisted learning strategies: The promise and limitations of peer-mediated instruction. *Reading and Writing Quarterly: Overcoming Learning Difficulties, 22*, 5–25.

McMaster, K. L., Fuchs, D., Saenz, L., Lemons, C., Kearns, D., Yen, L., . . . Fuchs, L. S. (2010). Scaling up PALS: The importance of implementing evidence-based practice with fidelity and flexibility. *New Times for DLD, 28*(1), 1–3. Retrieved from http://www.teachingld.org/pdf/NewTimes_ScalingUpPals2010.pdf

McWilliam, R. A. & Casey, A. M., (2008). *Engagement of every child in the preschool classroom.* Baltimore: Brookes.

Mechling, L. C. (2004). Effects of multimedia, computer-based instruction on grocery shopping fluency. *Journal of Special Education Technology, 19*, 23–34.

Mechling, L. C. (2007). Assistive technology as a self-management tool for prompting students with intellectual disabilities to initiate and complete daily tasks: A literature review. *Education and Training in Developmental Disabilities, 42*, 252–269.

Mechling, L. C., & Gast, D. L. (1997). Combination audio-visual self-prompting system for teaching chained tasks to students with intellectual disabilities. *Education and Training in Mental Retardation and Developmental Disabilities, 32*, 138–153.

Mike, D. G. (1995). Literacy and cerebral palsy: Factors influencing literacy learning in a self-contained setting. *Journal of Reading Behavior, 27*, 627–642.

Millar, D. C., Light, J. C., & Mcnaughton, D. B. (2004). The effect of direct instruction and writer's workshop on the early writing skills of children who use augmentative and alternative communication. *Augmentative and Alternative Communication, 20*, 164–178.

Millar, S. (1974). Tactile short-term memory by blind and sighted children. *British Journal of Psychology, 65*, 253–263.

Miller, U. C., & Test, D. W. (1989). A comparison of constant time delay and most-to-least prompting in teaching laundry skills to students with moderate mental retardation. *Education and Training in Mental Retardation, 24*, 363–370

Mirenda, P., Turoldo, K., & McAvoy, C. (2006). The impact of word prediction software on the written output of students with physical disabilities. *Journal of Special Education Technology, 21*(3), 5–12.

Montgomery, J., & Kahn, N. (2003). You are going to be an author: Adolescent narratives as intervention. *Communication Disorders Quarterly, 24*, 143–152.

Moore, S. C., Agran, M., & Fodor-Davis, J. (1989). Using self-management strategies to increase the production rates of workers with severe handicaps. *Education and Training in Mental Retardation, 24*, 324–332.

Moreau, M., & Fidrych-Puzzo, H. (1994). *The story grammar marker.* Easthampton, MA: Discourse Skills Productions.

Morrison, L., Kamps, D., Garcia, J., & Parker, D. (2001). Peer mediation and monitoring strategies to improve initiations and social skills for students with autism. *Journal of Positive Behavior Interventions, 3*, 237–250. doi: 10.1177/109830070100300405

Morse, T. E., & Schuster, J. W. (2000). Teaching elementary students with moderate intellectual disabilities how to shop for groceries. *Exceptional Children, 66*, 273–288.

Morse, T. E., & Schuster, J. W. (2004). Simultaneous prompting: A review of the literature. *Education and Training in Developmental Disabilities, 39*, 153–168.

Mosk, M. D., & Bucher, B. (1984). Prompting and stimulus shaping procedures for teaching visual-motor skills to retarded children. *Journal of Applied Behavior Analysis, 17*, 23–34.

Mostert, M. P. (Ed.). (2010). Empirically unsupported interventions in special education [special issue]. *Exceptionality, 18*(1).

Mostert, M. P., & Crockett, J. B. (2000). Reclaiming the history of special education for more effective practice. *Exceptionality, 8*, 133–143.

Mudd, J. M., & Wolery, M. (1987). Training Head Start teachers to use incidental teaching. *Journal of the Division for Early Childhood, 11*(2), 124–133.

Mueller, J. H. (1979). Anxiety and encoding processes in memory. *Personality and Social Psychology Bulletin, 5*, 288–294.

Murphy, J. L., Hatton, D., & Erickson, K. (2008). Exploring the early literacy practices of teachers of infants, toddlers, and preschoolers with visual impairments. *Journal of Visual Impairment and Blindness, 102*, 133–146.

Murray-Branch, J., Udvari-Solner, A., & Bailey, B. (1991). Textured communication systems for individuals with severe intellectual and dual sensory impairments. *Language, Speech, and Hearing Services in Schools, 22*, 260–268.

Najdowski, A. C., Wallace, M. D., Penrod, B., Tarbox, J., Reagon, K., & Higbee, T. S. (2008). Caregiver-conducted experimental functional analyses of inappropriate mealtime behavior. *Journal of Applied Behavior Analysis, 41*, 459–465.

Narr, R. F. (2008). Phonological awareness and decoding in deaf/hard of hearing students who use Visual Phonics. *Journal of Deaf Studies and Deaf Education, 13*, 405–416.

Narr, R. F., & Cawthon, S. (2010). The "Wh" questions of visual phonics: What, who, where, when, and why. *Journal of Deaf Studies and Deaf Education,* Advance online publication. doi:10.1093/deafed/enq038

Nathanson, R., Crank, J., Saywitz, K., & Ruegg, E. (2007). Enhancing the oral narratives of children with learning disabilities. *Reading & Writing Quarterly, 23*, 315–331.

National Autism Center. (2009). *National standards report: National standards* project—Addressing the need for evidence-based practice guidelines for autism spectrum disorders. Randolph, MA: National Autism Center.

National Center for Culturally Responsive Educational Systems. (2008). *Culturally responsive literacy.* Professional Learning Series. Tempe, AZ: Author.

National Consortium on Deaf-Blindness (NCDB). (2009). *2009 National deaf-blind child count maps.* Retrieved from http://www.nationaldb.org/censusMaps.php

National Early Literacy Panel. (2009). *Executive summary. Developing early literacy: Report of the National Early Literacy Panel (NELP).* Louisville, KY: National Institute for Literacy.

National Research Council. (2001). *Educating children with autism.* Committee on Educational Interventions for Children with Autism, Division of Behavioral and Social Sciences and Autism, Washington, D.C.: National Academy Press.

National Secondary Transition Technical Assistance Center Research to Practice Lesson Plan Starter Library. Retrieved from http://www.nsttac.org/LessonPlanLibrary/Main.aspx

Neef, N. A., Walters, J., & Egel, A. L. (1984). Establishing generative yes/no responses in developmentally disabled children. *Journal of Applied Behavior Analysis, 17,* 453–460.

Nehring, A. D., Nehring, E. E., Bruni, J. R., & Randolph, P. L. (1992). *Learning Accomplishment Profile-Diagnostic Standardized Assessment.* Lewisville, NC: Kaplan Press.

Neitzel, J., Boyd, B., Odom, S. L., & Edmondson-Pretzel, R. (2008). *Peer-mediated instruction and intervention for children and youth with autism spectrum disorders: Online training module.* Chapel Hill, NC: National Professional Development Center on Autism Spectrum Disorders, FPG Child Development Institute, UNC-Chapel Hill.

Nelson, C., McDonnell, A. P., Hohnston, S. S., Crompton, A., & Nelson, A. R. (2007). Keys to Play: A strategy to increase the social interactions of young children with autism and their typically developing peers.

Education and Training in Developmental Disabilities, 42,* 165–181.

New York Department of Health. (1999). *Clinical practice guideline: Report of the recommendations. Autism/pervasive developmental disorders: Assessment and intervention for young children (age 0–3 years).* Albany, NY: New York Department of Health.

Newman, L., Wagner, M., Cameto, R., & Knokey, A. M. (2009). *The post-high school outcomes of youth with disabilities up to 4 years after high school. A report from the National Longitudinal Transition Study-2 (NLTS2)* (NCSER 2009-3017). Menlo Park, CA: SRI International.

Nietupski, J., Hamre-Nietupski, S., Clancy, P., & Veerhusen, K. (1986). Guidelines for making simulation an effective adjunct to in vivo community instruction. *Journal of the Association for Persons with Severe Handicaps, 11,* 12–18.

Nietupski, J., Welch, J., & Wacker, D. (1983). Acquisition, maintenance, and transfer of grocery item purchasing skills by moderately and severely handicapped students. *Education and Training in Mental Retardation, 18,* 279–286.

No Child Left Behind Act of 2001, Pub. L. No. 107-110, 115 Stat. 1425 (2002).

Nolte, R., & Singer, H. (1985). Active comprehension: Teaching a process of reading comprehension and its effects on achievement. *The Reading Teacher,* 39, 24–31.

Noonan, M. J., & McCormick, L. (2006). *Young children with disabilities in natural environments: Methods and procedures.* Baltimore: Brookes.

Norland, J. J. (2005). *English language learners interactions with various science curriculum features.* (Doctoral dissertation). Available from Proquest Dissertation and Theses database. (UMI No. 885692991)

Notari-Syverson, A., O'Conner, R. E., & Vadasy, P. F. (1998). *Ladders to literacy.* Baltimore: Brookes.

O'Neill, R., Horner, R., Albin, R., Sprague, J., Storey, K. & Newton, S. (1997). *Functional assessment and program development for problem behavior.* Pacific Grove, CA: Brookes-Cole.

O'Reilly, M., Sigafoos, J., Lancioni, G., Edrisinha, C., & Andrews, A. (2005).

An examination of the effects of a classroom activity schedule on levels of self-injury and engagement for a child with severe autism. *Journal of Autism and Developmental Disorders, 35,* 305–311.

Obiakor, F. E. (1999). Teacher expectations of minority exceptional learners: Impact on accuracy of self-concepts. *Exceptional Children, 65,* 39–53.

Ochoa, S. H., Robles-Piña, E., Garcia, S. B., & Breunig, N. (1999). School psychologists' perspectives on referrals of language minority students. *Multiple Voices for Exceptional Learners, 3,* 1–14.

Odom, S. L., Chandler, L. K., Ostrosky, M., McConnell, S. R., & Reaney, S. (1992). Fading teacher prompts from peer-initiation interventions for young children with disabilities. *Journal of Applied Behavior Analysis, 25,* 307–317.

Odom, S. L., McConnell, S. R., Ostrosky, M., Peterson, C., Skellenger, A., Spicuzza, R., . . . Favazza, P. C. (1993). *Play time/social time: Organizing your classroom to build interaction skills.* Tucson, AZ: Communication Skill Builders.

Ogle, D. M. (1986). K-W-L: A teaching model that develops active reading of expository text. *The Reading Teacher, 39,* 564–570.

Oliver, C. B., & Halle, J. W. (1982). Language training in the everyday environment: Teaching functional sign use to a retarded child. *Journal of the Association for the Severely Handicapped, 8,* 50–62.

Omanson, R. (1982). An analysis of narratives: Identifying central, supportive, and distracting content. *Discourse Processes, 5,* 195–224.

Osguthorpe, R. T., & Scruggs, T. E. (1986). Special education students as tutors: A review and analysis. *Remedial and Special Education, 7*(4), 15–26.

Owen-DeSchryver, J. S., Carr, E. G., Cale, S. I., & Blakely-Smith, A. (2008). Prompting social interactions between students with autism spectrum disorders and their peers in inclusive school settings. *Focus on Autism and Other Developmental Disabilities, 23,* 15–28.

Padden, C., & Ramsey, C. (2000). American Sign Language and reading ability in deaf children. In C. Chamberlain, J. P. Morford, & R. I. Mayberry (Eds.), *Language acquisition by eye* (pp. 165–189). Mahwah, NJ: Erlbaum.

Parent, W., & Wehman, P. (2011). Writing the transition individualized education program. In P. Wehman (Ed.). *Essentials of transition planning* (pp. 95–109). Baltimore: Brookes.

Parette, H. P., & Peterson-Karlan, G. R. (2007). Facilitating student achievement with assistive technology. *Education and Training in Developmental Disabilities, 42,* 387–397.

Parker, M., Cunningham, S., Enderby, P., Hawley, M., & Green, P. (2006). Automatic speech recognition and training for severely dysarthric users of assistive technology: The STARDUST project. *Clinical Linguistics and Phonetics, 20*(2/3), 149–156.

Paul, P. V. (2009). *Language and deafness* (4th ed.). Sudbury, MA: Jones and Bartlett.

Pearson, P. D., & Duke, N. K. (2002). Comprehension instruction in the primary grades. In C. Collins-Block & M. Pressley (Eds.), *Comprehension instruction: Research based best practices* (pp. 247–258). New York: Guilford Press.

Peck, C. A., Killen, C. C., & Baumgart, D. (1989). Increasing implementation of special education instruction in mainstream preschools: Direct and generalized effects of nondirective consultation. *Journal of Applied Behavior Analysis, 22,* 197–210.

Peeters, M., Verhoeven, L., & de Moor, J. (2009). Predictors of verbal working memory in children with cerebral palsy. *Research in Developmental Disabilities, 30,* 1502–1511.

Peeters, M., Verhoeven, L., de Moor, J., & van Balkom, H. (2009). Importance of speech production for phonological awareness and word decoding: The case of children with cerebral palsy. *Research in Developmental Disabilities, 30,* 712–726.

Pelham, W. F., Fabiano, G. A., & Massetti, G. M. (2005). Evidence-based assessment of attention deficit hyperactivity disorder in children and adolescents. *Journal of Clinical Child and Adolescent Psychology, 34,* 449–476.

Pellegrini, A. D., Galda, L., Jones, I., & Perlmutter, J. (1995). Joint reading between mothers and their Head Start children: Vocabulary development in two text formats. *Discourse Processes, 19,* 441–463.

Pepper, J., & Weitzman, E. (2004). *It takes two to talk: A practical guide for parents of children with language delays* (2nd ed.). Toronto: The Hanen Centre.

Perrin, C. J., Perrin, S. H., Hill, E. A., & DiNovi, K. (2008). Brief functional analysis and treatment of elopement in preschoolers with autism. *Behavioral Interventions, 23,* 87–95.

Perry, A., & Condillac, R. A. (2003). *Evidence-based practices for children and adolescents with autism spectrum disorder: Review of the literature and practice guide.* Toronto: Children's Mental Health, Ontario.

Peterson-Karlan, G., Hourcade, J. J., & Parette, P. (2008). A review of assistive technology and writing skills for students with physical and educational disabilities. *Physical Disabilities: Education and Related Services, 26*(2), 13–32.

Piaget, J. (1954). *The construction of reality in the child.* New York: Basic Books.

Pierce, K., & Schreibman, L. (1997). Multiple peer use of pivotal response training to increase social behaviors of classmates with autism: Results from trained and untrained peers. *Journal of Applied Behavior Analysis, 30,* 156–160.

Pikulski, J. J. (2006). Fluency: A developmental and language perspective. In S. J. Samuels & A. E. Farstrup (Eds.), *What research has to say about fluency instruction.* Newark, DE: International Reading Association.

Planty, M., Hussar, W., Snyder, T., Provasnik, S., Kena, G., Dinkes, R., . . . Kemp, J. (2008). *The condition of education 2008* (NCES 2008-031). Washington, DC: National Center for Education Statistics, Institute of Education Sciences, U.S. Department of Education.

Post, M., & Storey, K. (2002). A review of using auditory prompting systems with persons who have moderate to severe disabilities. *Education and Training in Mental Retardation and Developmental Disabilities, 37,* 317–327.

Powers, M. D. (1992). Early intervention for children with autism. In D. E. Berkell (Ed.), *Autism: Identification, education, and treatment* (pp. 225–252). Hillsdale, NJ: Erlbaum.

Pretti-Frontczak, K. L., Barr, D. M., Macy, M., & Carter, A. (2003). Research and resources related to activity-based intervention, embedded learning opportunities, and routines-based instruction. *Topics in Early Childhood Special Education, 23,* 29–39.

Pretti-Frontczak, K. L., & Bricker, D. D. (2001). Use of the embedding strategy by early childhood education and early childhood special education teachers. *Infant and Toddler Intervention: The Transdisciplinary Journal, 11,* 111–128.

Psychological Corporation. (2002). *Wechsler individual achievement test* (2nd ed.). San Antonio, TX: Harcourt Assessment.

Rao, S., & Kane, M. T. (2009). Teaching students with cognitive impairment chained mathematical task of decimal subtraction using simultaneous prompting. *Education and Training in Developmental Disabilities, 44,* 244–256.

Ratner, V. L., & Harris, L. R. (1994). *Understanding language disorders: The impact on learning.* Eau Claire, WI: Thinking Publications.

Reese, G. M., & Snell, M. E. (1991). Putting on and removing coats and jackets: The acquisition and maintenance of skills by children with severe multiple disabilities. *Education and Training in Mental Retardation, 26,* 398–410.

Reichle, J. (1990). *National Working Conference on Positive Approaches to the Management of Excess Behavior: Final report and recommendations.* Minneapolis, MN: Institute on Community Integration, University of Minnesota.

Reichle, J. (1997). Communication intervention with persons who have severe disabilities. *Journal of Special Education, 31,* 110–134.

Reid, R., Gonzalez, J. E., Nordness, P. D., Trout, A., & Epstein, M. H. (2004). A meta-analysis of the academic status of students with emotional/behavioral disturbance. *The Journal of Special Education, 38,* 130–143.

Repp, A. C., Karsh, K. G., & Lenz, M. W. (1990). Discrimination training for persons with developmental disabilities: A comparison of the task demonstration model and the standard prompting hierarchy. *Journal of Applied Behavior Analysis, 23*, 43–52.

Rescorla, L., Roberts, J., & Dahlsgaard, K. (1997). Late talkers at 2: Outcome at age 3. *Journal of Speech, Language, and Hearing Research, 40*, 556–566.

Reutzel, R. (1985a). Reconciling schema theory with the basal reading lesson. *The Reading Teacher, 39*, 194–197.

Reutzel, R. (1985b). Story maps improve comprehension. *Reading Teacher, 38*, 400–404.

Rex, E. J., Koenig, A. J., Wormsley, D. P., & Baker, R. L. (1994). *Foundations of braille literacy.* New York: AFB Press.

Reyna, V. (2004). Why scientific research: The importance of evidence in changing educational practice. In P. McCardle & V. Chhabra (Eds.), *The voice of evidence in reading research.* Baltimore: Brookes.

Rice, M. L., & Wexler, K. (1996). Toward tense as a clinical marker of specific language impairment in English-speaking children. *Journal of Speech and Hearing Research, 39*, 1239–1257.

Rice, M. L., Wexler, K., & Hershberger, S. (1998). The longitudinal course of tense acquisition in children with specific language impairment. *Journal of Speech, Language, and Hearing Research, 41*, 1412–1431.

Riley-Tillman, T. C., Chafouleas, S. M., Sassu, K. A., Chanese, J. A. M., & Glazer, A. D. (2008). Examining the agreement of direct behavior ratings and systematic direct observation data for on-task and disruptive behavior. *Journal of Positive Behavior Intervention, 10*, 136–143.

Rogers-Warren, A., & Warren, S. F. (1980). Mands for verbalization: Facilitating the display of newly-taught language. *Behavior Modification, 4*, 361–382.

Rohwer, W. D., Jr., Raines, J. M., Eoff, J., & Wagner, M. (1966). The development of elaborative propensity in adolescence. *Journal of Experimental Child Psychology, 23*, 472–492.

Rosen, K., & Yampolsky, S. (2000). Automatic speech recognition and a review of its functioning with dysarthric speech. *Augmentative and Alternative Communication, 16*, 48–60.

Rowland, C. (1996). *Communication matrix.* Portland, OR: Oregon Health Sciences University.

Rowland, C., & Schweigert, P. (1989). Tangible symbols: Symbolic communication for individuals with sensory impairments. *Augmentative and Alternative Communication, 5*, 226–234.

Rowland, C., & Schweigert, P. (1990). *Tangible symbol systems.* Tucson, AZ: Communication Skill Builders.

Rowland, C., & Schweigert, P. (2000). Tangible symbols, tangible outcomes. *Augmentative and Alternative Communication, 16*, 61–78.

Rowley-Kelly, F. L., & Reigel, D. H. (1993). *Teaching the student with spina bifida.* Baltimore: Brookes.

Rumelhart, D. E. (1975). Notes on a schema for stories. In D. G. Brown & A. Collins (Eds.), *Representation and understanding: Studies in cognitive science* (pp. 211–236). New York: Academic Press.

Ryndak, D. L., Moore, M. A., Orlando, A. M., & Delano, M. (2008/2009). Access to the general curriculum: The mandate and the role of context in research-based practice for students with extensive support needs. *Research and Practice for Persons with Severe Disabilities, 33/34*, 199–213.

Sáenz, L. M., Fuchs, L. S., & Fuchs, D. (2005). Peer-assisted learning strategies for English language learners with learning disabilities. *Exceptional Children, 71*, 231–247.

Sáenz, L. M., McMaster, K. L., Fuchs, D., & Fuchs, L. S. (2007). Peer-assisted learning strategies in reading for students with different learning needs. *Cognitive Education and Psychology, 6*, 395–410.

Sagan, C. (1996). *The demon-haunted world: Science as a candle in the dark.* New York: Ballantine Books.

Samson, J. F., & Lesaux, N. K. (2009). Language-minority learners in special education: Rates and predictors of identification for services. *Journal of Learning Disabilities, 42*, 148–162.

Sandall, S., Hemmeter, M. L., Smith, B. J., & McLean, M. E. (Eds.). (2005). *DEC recommended practices: A comprehensive guide for practical application in early intervention/early childhood special education.* Longmont, CO: Sopris West.

Sandknop, P. A., Schuster, J. W., Wolery, M., & Cross, D. P. (1992). The use of an adaptive device to teach students with moderate mental retardation to select lower priced grocery items. *Education and Training in Mental Retardation, 27*, 219–229.

Sanford, L., & Burnett, R. (2008). *Functional vision and learning media assessment. A practitioner's guide.* Louisville, KY: American Printing House for the Blind.

Sasso, G. M., Mundschenk, N. A., Melloy, K. J., & Casey, S. D. (1998). A comparison of the effects of organismic and setting variables on the social interaction behavior of children with developmental disabilities and autism. *Focus on Autism and Other Developmental Disabilities, 13*, 2–16.

Scarborough, H. (1990). Very early language deficits in dyslexic children. *Child Development, 61*, 1728–1743.

Schalock, R. L., Borthwick-Duffy, S. A., Bradley, V. J., Buntinx, W. H. E., Coulter, D. L., Craig, E. M., . . . Yeager, M. H. (2010). *Intellectual disability: Definition, classification, and systems of supports* (11th ed.). Washington, DC: American Association on Intellectual and Developmental Disabilities.

Schalock, R. L., Harber, R. S., & Genung, T. (1981). Community integration of mentally retarded adults: Community placement and program success. *American Journal of Mental Deficiency, 85*, 478–488.

Scheerenberger, R. C. (1977). Deinstitutionalization in perspective. In J. Paul, D. Stedman, & G. Neufeld (Eds.), *Deinstitutionalization program and policy development* (pp. 3–14). Syracuse: Syracuse University Press.

Schepis, M. M., Reid, D. H., Behrmann, M. M., & Sutton, K. A. (1998). Increasing communicative interactions of young children with autism using a voice output communication aid and naturalistic teaching. *Journal of Applied Behavior Analysis, 31*, 561–578.

Schepis, M. M., Reid, D. H., Ownbey, J., & Parsons, M. B. (2001). Training support staff to embed teaching within natural routines of young children with disabilities in an inclusive preschool. *Journal of Applied Behavior Analysis, 34,* 313–327.

Schirmer, B. R., & McGough, S. M. (2005). Teaching reading to children who are deaf: Do the conclusions of the National Reading Panel apply? *Review of Educational Research, 75,* 83–117.

Schloss, P. J., Alper, S., Young, H., Arnold-Reid, G., Aylward, M., & Dudenhoeffer, S. (1995). Acquisition of functional sight words in community-based recreation settings. *The Journal of Special Education, 29,* 84–96.

Schoen, S. F., & Ogden, S. (1995). Impact of time delay, observational learning, and attentional cuing upon word recognition during integrated small-group instruction. *Journal of Autism & Developmental Disorders, 25,* 503–519.

Schreibman, L. (1975). Effects of within-stimulus and extra-stimulus prompting on discrimination learning in autistic children. *Journal of Applied Behavior Analysis, 8,* 91–112.

Schwartz, I. S., Staub, D., Peck, C. A., & Gallucci, C. (2006). Peer relationships. In M. E. Snell & F. Brown (Eds.) *Instruction of students with severe disabilities* (6th ed.). Upper Saddle River, NJ: Pearson.

Scott, M. S., Perou, R., Greenfield, D. B., & Swanson, L. (1993). Rhyming skills: Differentiating among mildly mentally retarded, learning disabled, and normally achieving students. *Learning Disabilities Research & Practice, 8,* 215–222.

Scott, T. M., & Nelson, C. M. (1999). Using functional assessment to develop effective intervention plans: A practical classroom application. *Journal of Positive Behavioral Support, 1,* 242–251.

Scruggs, T. E., & Cohn, S. J. (1983). Learning characteristics of verbally gifted students. *Gifted Child Quarterly, 27,* 169–172.

Scruggs, T. E., & Mastropieri, M. A. (1986). Academic characteristics of behaviorally disordered and learning disabled children. *Behavioral Disorders, 11,* 184–190.

Scruggs, T. E., & Mastropieri, M. A. (1988). Acquisition and transfer of learning strategies by gifted and nongifted students. *Journal of Special Education, 22,* 153–166.

Scruggs, T. E., & Mastropieri, M. A. (1989a). Mnemonic instruction of learning disabled students: A field-based evaluation. *Learning Disability Quarterly, 12,* 119–125.

Scruggs, T. E., & Mastropieri, M. A. (1989b). Reconstructive elaborations: A model for content area learning. *American Educational Research Journal, 26,* 311–327.

Scruggs, T. E., & Mastropieri, M. A. (1990). Mnemonic instruction for learning disabled students: What it is and what it does. *Learning Disability Quarterly, 13,* 271–281.

Scruggs, T. E., & Mastropieri, M. A. (1992). Classroom applications of mnemonic instruction: Acquisition, maintenance, and generalization. *Exceptional Children, 58,* 219–229.

Scruggs, T. E., & Mastropieri, M. A. (2000). The effectiveness of mnemonic instruction for students with learning and behavior problems: An update and research synthesis. *Journal of Behavioral Education, 10,* 163–173.

Scruggs, T. E., Mastropieri, M. A., & Berkeley, S., & Graetz, J. (2010). Do special education interventions improve learning of secondary content? A meta-analysis. *Remedial and Special Education, 31,* 437–449.

Scruggs, T. E., Mastropieri, M. A., Brigham, F. J., & Sullivan, G. S. (1992). Effects of mnemonic reconstructions on the spatial learning of adolescents with learning disabilities. *Learning Disability Quarterly, 15,* 154–162.

Scruggs, T. E., Mastropieri, M. A., & Levin, J. R. (1986). Can children effectively re-use the same mnemonic pegwords? *Educational Communication and Technology Journal, 34,* 83–88.

Scruggs, T. E., Mastropieri, M. A., & Levin, J. R. (1987). Implications of mnemonic strategy research for theories of learning disabilities. In H. L. Swanson (Ed.), *Memory and learning disabilities: Advances in learning and behavior disabilities* (pp. 225–244). Greenwich, CT: JAI Press.

Scruggs, T. E., Mastropieri, M. A., Levin, J. R., & Gaffney, J. S. (1985). Facilitating the acquisition of science facts in learning disabled students. *American Educational Research Journal, 22,* 575–586.

Scruggs, T. E., Mastropieri, M. A., & Marshak, L. (2009). *Peer-mediated instruction in inclusive secondary social studies classrooms: A randomized field trial.* Fairfax, VA: George Mason University, College of Education and Human Development.

Scruggs, T. E., Mastropieri, M. A., Marshak, L., & Mills, S. (2009, April). *How to differentiate instruction without differentiating it: Results of recent research.* Paper presented at the annual meeting of the Council for Exceptional Children, San Diego.

Scruggs, T. E., Mastropieri, M. A., & McDuffie, K. A. (2007). Co-teaching in inclusive classrooms: A meta-synthesis of qualitative research. *Exceptional Children, 73,* 392–416.

Scruggs, T. E., Mastropieri, M. A., McLoone, B. B., Levin, J.R., & Morrison, C. (1987). Mnemonic facilitation of learning disabled students' memory for expository prose. *Journal of Educational Psychology, 79,* 27–34.

Scull, J. A., & Bianco, J. L. (2008). Successful engagement in early literacy intervention. *Journal of Early Childhood Literacy, 8,* 123–150.

Seguin, J. R., Pihl, R. O., Harden, P. W., Tremblay, R. E., & Boulerice, B. (1995). Cognitive and neuropsychological characteristics of physically aggressive boys. *Journal of Abnormal Psychology, 104,* 614–624

Semel, E., Wiig, E. H., & Secord, W. A. (2003). *Clinical Evaluation of Language Fundamentals, Fourth Edition (CELF-4).* Toronto, Canada: Psychological Corporation/ Harcourt Assessment.

Sewell, T. J., Collins, B. C., Hemmeter, M. L., & Schuster, J. W. (1998). Using simultaneous prompting within an activity-based format to teach dressing skills to preschoolers with developmental delays. *Journal of Early Intervention, 21,* 132–145.

Shanahan, T., & Beck, I. L. (2006). Effective literacy teaching for English-language learners. In D. L. August & T. Shanahan (Eds.), *Developing literacy in a second language: Report of the National Literacy Panel.* Mahwah, NJ: Erlbaum.

Sharpe, M., McNear, D., & Bosma, J. (1995). The development of a scale to facilitate reading mode decisions. *Journal of Visual Impairment & Blindness, 89,* 83–89.

Sheehy, K. (2002). The effective use of symbols in teaching word recognition to children with severe learning difficulties: A comparison of word alone, integrated picture cueing and the handle technique. *International Journal of Disability, Development, and Education, 49,* 47–59.

Shermer, M. (2002). *Why people believe weird things.* New York: Henry Holt.

Short, E. J., & Ryan, E. B. (1984). Metacognitive differences between skilled and less skilled readers: Remediating deficits through story grammar and attribution training. *Journal of Educational Psychology, 76,* 225–235.

Sigafoos, J., Didden, R., Schlosser, R., Green, V. A., O'Reilly, M. F., & Lancioni, G. E. (2008). A review of intervention studies on teaching AAC to individuals who are deaf and blind. *Journal of Developmental and Physical Disabilities, 20,* 71–99.

Silliman, E., Diehl, S., Huntley-Bahr, R., Hnath-Chisolm, T., Zenko, C., & Friedman, S. (2003). A new look at theory of mind tasks by adolescents with ASD. *Language Speech and Hearing Services in Schools, 34,* 236–252

Simpkins, P. M., Mastropieri, M. A., & Scruggs, T. E. (2009). Differentiated curriculum enhancements in inclusive 5th grade science classes. *Remedial and Special Education, 30,* 300–308.

Simpson, R. (2005). Evidence-based practices and students with autism spectrum disorder. *Focus on Autism and Other Developmental Disabilities, 20,* 140–149.

Simpson, R., Koester, H., & LoPresti, E. (2006). Evaluation of an adaptive row/column scanning system. *Technology and Disability, 18,* 127–138.

Simpson, R., & Myles, B. (1998). Understanding and responding to the needs of students with autism. In R. Simpson & B. Myles (Eds.). *Educating children and youth with autism: Strategies for effective practice* (pp. 1–24). Austin, TX: Pro-Ed.

Singer, H., & Donlan, D. (1982). Active comprehension: Problem-solving schema with question generation for comprehension of complex short stories. *Reading Research Quarterly, 17,* 166–186.

Sitko, M. C., Laine, C. J., & Sitko, C. J. (2005). Writing tools: Technology and strategies for struggling writers. In D. L. Edyburn, K. Higgins, & R. Boone (Eds.), *Handbook of special education technology research and practice* (pp. 571–598). Whitefish Bay, WI: Knowledge by Design.

Skinner, B. F. (1953). *Science and human behavior.* New York: Macmillan.

Smith, A. (2003). Scientifically based research and evidence-based education: A federal policy context. *Research and Practice for Persons with Severe Disabilities, 28,* 126–132.

Smith, D. J., & Nelson, R. (1997). Goal setting, self-monitoring, and self-evaluation for students with disabilities. In M. Agran (Ed.), *Student-directed learning: Teaching self-determination skills* (pp. 80–110). Pacific Grove, CA: Brookes/Cole.

Smith, M. L. (2004). *Political spectacle and the fate of American schools.* New York: Routledge-Falmer.

Smith, M. W., & Dickinson, D. K. (1994). Describing oral language opportunities and environments in head start and other preschool classrooms. *Early Childhood Research Quarterly, 9,* 345–366.

Smith-Bird, E., & Turnbull, A. P. (2005). Linking positive behavior support to family quality-of-life outcomes. *Journal of Positive Behavior Interventions, 7,* 174–180.

Smith-Bird, E., Turnbull, A. P., & Koegel, R. L. (2005). Linking positive behavior support to family quality-of-life outcomes. *Journal of Positive Behavior Interventions, 7,* 174–180.

Snell, M. E., & Brown, F. (2011). Selecting teaching strategies and arranging educational environments.

In M. E. Snell & F. Brown (Eds.), *Instruction of students with severe disabilities* (7th ed.). Upper Saddle River, NJ: Pearson.

Snell, M. E., & Janney, R. (2000). *Social relationships and peer support.* Baltimore: Brookes.

Snow, C. (2006). What counts as literacy in early childhood? In K. McCartney & D. Phillips (Eds.), *Handbook of early child development* (pp. 274–294). Oxford: Blackwell.

Snow, C., Burns, M. S., & Griffin, P. (Eds.). (1998). *Preventing reading difficulties in young children.* Washington, DC: National Academy Press.

Song, A., Jones, S., Lippert, J., Metzger, K., Miller, J., & Borreca, C. (1980). *Wisconsin behavior rating scale.* Madison, WI: Wisconsin Central Center for the Developmentally Disabled.

Spackman, M. P., Fujiki, M., & Brinton, B. (2006). Understanding emotions in context: The effects of language impairment on children's ability to infer emotional reactions. *International Journal of Language & Communication Disorders, 41,* 173–188.

Sprague, J. R., & Rian, V. (1993). *Support systems for students with severe problems in Indiana: A descriptive analysis of school structure and student demographics.* Unpublished manuscript. Bloomington, IN: Indiana University Institute for the Study of Developmental Disabilities.

Sprick, M., Howard, L., & Fidanque, A. (1998). *Read well.* Longmont, CO: Sopris West.

Spungin, S. (1990). *Braille literacy: Issues for blind persons, families, professionals and producers of braille.* New York: AFB Press.

Stager, G. H., Singer, J., & Horner, R. H. (1987). Using pretask requests to increase the probability of compliance for students with severe disabilities. *Journal of the Association for Persons with Severe Handicaps, 12,* 287–291.

Stein, N. L., & Glenn, C. (1979). An analysis of story comprehension in elementary school children. In R. O. Freedle (Ed.), *New directions in discourse processing* (Vol. 2, pp. 53–120). Norwood, NJ: Ablex.

Steinberg, S., & Kincheloe, J. (2004). *19 urban questions: Teaching in the city.* New York: Peter Lang.

Steinman, B. A., LeJeune, B. J., & Kimbrough, B. T. (2006). Developmental stages of reading processes in children who are blind and sighted. *Journal of Visual Impairment & Blindness, 100,* 36–46.

Stillman, R., & Battle, C. W. (1986). *Callier-Azusa Scale H: Cognition and communication.* Dallas, TX: University of Texas at Dallas.

Stokes, T. F., & Baer, D. M. (1977). An implicit technology of generalization. *Journal of Applied Behavior Analysis, 10,* 349–367.

Storey, K., Smith, D., & Strain, P. (1993). Use of classroom assistants and peer-mediated intervention to increase integration in preschool settings. *Exceptionality, 4*(1), 1–16.

Strain, P. S., & Hoyson, M. (2000). The need for longitudinal, intensive social skill intervention: LEAP follow-up outcomes for children with autism. *Topics in Early Childhood Special Education, 20,* 116–122. doi: 10.1177/027112140002000207

Strain, P. S., Kerr, M. M., & Ragland, E. U. (1979). Effects of peer-mediated social initiations and prompting/reinforcement procedures on the social behavior of autistic children. *Journal of Autism and Developmental Disorders, 9,* 41–54.

Strain, P. S., & Odom, S. L. (1986). Effective intervention for social skill development of exceptional children. *Exceptional Children, 52,* 543–551.

Strand, S. C., & Morris, R. C. (1986). Programmed training of visual discriminations: A comparison of techniques. *Applied Research in Mental Retardation, 7,* 165–181.

Street, B. V. (1984). *Literacy in theory and practice.* Cambridge: Cambridge University Press.

Street, B. V. (1995). *Social literacies: Critical approaches to literacy in development, ethnography, and education.* London/New York: Longman.

Stumbo, N. J., Martin, J. K., & Hedrick, B. N. (2009). Assistive technology: Impact on education, employment, and independence of individuals with physical disabilities. *Journal of Vocational Rehabilitation, 30,* 99–110.

Suárez-Orozco, M., Roos, P. M., & Suárez-Orozco, C. (2000). Culture, education, and legal perspective on immigration: Implications for school reform. In J. P. Heubert (Ed.), *Law and school reform: Six strategies for promoting educational equity* (pp. 160–204). New Haven, CT: Yale University Press.

Swanson, L. (2000). What instruction works for students with learning disabilities: Summarizing the results from a meta-analysis of intervention studies. In R. M. Gersten, E. P. Schiller, & S. Vaughn (Eds.), *Contemporary special education research* (pp. 1–30). Mahwah, NJ: Erlbaum.

Swanson, L. A., Fey, M. E., Mills, C. E., & Hood, L. S. (2005). Use of narrative-based language intervention with children who have specific language impairment. *American Journal of Speech-Language Pathology, 14,* 131–143.

Swanson, L., Trainin, G., Necoechea, D. M., & Hammill, D. (2003). Rapid naming, phonological awareness, and reading: A meta-analysis of the correlation evidence. *Review of Educational Research, 73,* 407–440.

Swinehart-Jones, D., & Heller, K. W. (2009). Teaching students with severe speech and physical impairments strategy using internal speech and motoric indicators. *The Journal of Special Education, 43,* 131–144.

Taber, T. A., Alberto, P. A., Hughes, M., & Seltzer, A. (2002). A strategy for students with moderate disabilities when lost in the community. *Research and Practice for Persons with Severe Disabilities, 27,* 141–152.

Tam, K. Y., Heward, W. L., & Heng, M. A. (2006). A reading instruction intervention program for English-language learners who are struggling readers. *Journal of Special Education, 40,* 79–93.

Tam, S. F. (2000). The effects of a computer skill training programme adopting social comparison and self-efficacy enhancement strategies on self-concept and skill outcome in trainees with physical disabilities. *Disability and Rehabilitation, 22,* 655–664.

Tamis-LeMonda, C. S., Bornstein, M. H., & Baumwell, L. (2001). Maternal responsiveness and children's achievement of language milestones. *Child Development, 72,* 748–767.

Tankersley, M., Harjusola-Webb, S., & Landrum, T. J. (2008). Using single-subject research to establish the evidence base of special education. *Intervention in School and Clinic, 44,* 83–90.

Taylor, P., Collins, B. C., Schuster, J. W., & Kleinert, H. (2002). Teaching laundry skills to high school students with disabilities: Generalization of targeted skills and nontargeted information. *Education and Training in mental Retardation and Developmental Disabilities, 37,* 172–183.

Téllez, K. & Waxman, H. (2006). *Preparing quality educators for English language learners: Research, policies, and practices.* Mahwah, NJ: Erlbaum.

Test, D. W., Fowler, C. H., Richter, S. M., Mazzotti, V., White, J., Walker, A. R., … Kortering, L. (2009). Evidence-based practices in secondary transition. *Career Development for Exceptional Individuals, 32,* 115–128.

Test, D. W., Mason, C., Hughes, C., Konrad, M., Neale, M., & Wood, W. M. (2004). Student involvement in individualized education program meetings: A review of the literature. *Exceptional Children, 70,* 391–412.

Test, D. W., Mazzotti, V. L., Mustian, A. L., Fowler, C. H., Kortering, L., & Kohler, P. (2009). Evidence-based secondary transition predictors for improving post-school outcomes for students with disabilities. *Career Development for Exceptional Individuals, 32,* 160–181.

Test, D. W., & Neale, M. (2004). Using the *Self-Advocacy Strategy* to increase middle graders' IEP participation. *Journal of Behavioral Education, 13,* 135–145.

Thiemann, K. S., & Goldstein, H. (2004). Effects of peer training and written text cueing on social communication of school-age children with pervasive developmental disorder. *Journal of Speech, Language, and Hearing Research, 47,* 126–144. doi: 1092-4388/04/4701-0126

Tomblin, J. B., Records, N., Buckwalter, P., Zhang, X., Smith, E., & O'Brien, M. (1997). Prevalence of specific language impairment in kindergarten children. *Journal of Speech,*

Language, and Hearing Research, 40, 1245–1260.

Tomlinson, C. A. (2001). *How to differentiate instruction in mixed-ability classrooms* (2nd ed.). Alexandria, VA: Association for Supervision and Curriculum Development.

Torgesen, J. K. (1977). Memorization process in reading-disabled children. *Journal of Educational Psychology, 69*, 571–578.

Torgesen, J. K., & Goldman, T. (1977). Verbal rehearsal and short-term memory in reading disabled children. *Child Development, 48*, 56–60.

Trabasso, T. (2005). The role of causal reasoning in understanding narratives. In T. Trabasso, J. Sabatini, D. Massaro, & R. Calfee (Eds.), *From orthography to pedagogy: Essays in honor of Richard L. Venezky* (pp. 81–106). Mahwah, NJ: Erlbaum.

Trabasso, T., & Magliano, J. P. (1996). How do children understand what they read and what can we do to help them? In M. F. Graves, P. van den Broek, & B. M. Taylor (Eds.), *The first R: Every child's right to read* (pp. 160–187). New York: Teachers College Press.

Trabasso, T., Secco, T., & van den Broek, P. W. (1984). Casual cohesion and story coherence. In H. Mandl, N. L. Stein, & T. Trabasso (Eds.), *Learning and comprehension of text* (pp. 83–111). Hillsdale, NJ: Erlbaum.

Trabasso, T., Suh, S., Payton, P., & Jain, R. (1995). Explanatory inferences and other strategies during comprehension and their effect on recall. In R. F. Lorch & E. J. O'Brien (Eds.), *Sources of coherence in reading* (pp. 219–239). Hillsdale, NJ: Erlbaum.

Trabasso, T., & van den Broek, P. (1985). Casual thinking and the representation of narrative events. *Journal of Memory and Language, 24*, 612–630.

Trabasso, T., van den Broek, P., & Suh, S. (1989). Logical necessity and transitivity of causal relations in stories. *Discourse Processes, 12*, 1–25.

Trent, S. D., & Truan, M. B. (1997). Speed, accuracy, and comprehension of adolescent braille readers in a specialized school. *Journal of Visual Impairment & Blindness, 91*, 494–500.

Trezek, B. J., & Malmgren, K. W. (2005). The efficacy of utilizing a phonics

treatment package with middle school deaf and hard of hearing students. *Journal of Deaf Studies and Deaf Education, 10*, 256–271.

Trezek, B. J., & Wang, Y. (2006). Implications of utilizing a phonics-based reading curriculum with children who are deaf or hard of hearing. *Journal of Deaf Studies and Deaf Education, 11*, 202–213.

Trezek, B.J., Wang, Y., & Paul, P.V. (2010). *Reading and deafness: Theory, research, and practice.* Clifton Park, NY: Delmar, Cengage Learning.

Trezek, B. J., Wang, Y., Woods, D. G., Gampp, T. L., & Paul, P. V. (2007). Using Visual Phonics to supplement beginning reading instruction for students who are deaf/hard of hearing. *Journal of Deaf Studies and Deaf Education, 12*, 373–384.

Trief, E. (2007). The use of tangible cues for children with multiple disabilities and visual impairment. *Journal of Visual Impairment & Blindness, 101*, 613–619.

Troia, G. A. (2004). Migrant students with limited English proficiency: Can Fast ForWord Language make a difference in their language skills and academic achievement? *Remedial and Special Education, 25*, 353–366.

Truan, M. B., & Trent, S. D. (1997). Impact of adolescents' adjustment to progressive vision loss on braille reading skills: Case studies. *Journal of Visual Impairment and Blindness, 91*, 301–308.

Tumlin, J., & Heller, K. W. (2004). Using word prediction software to increase typing fluency with students with physical disabilities. *Journal of Special Education Technology, 19*, 5–14.

Turnbull, H. R., III. (2005). Individuals with Disabilities Education Act Reauthorization: Accountability and personal responsibility. *Remedial and Special Education, 26*, 320–326.

Turnell, R., & Carter, M. (1994). Establishing a repertoire of requesting for a student with severe and multiple disabilities using tangible symbols and naturalistic time delay. *Australia and New Zealand Journal of Developmental Disabilities, 19*, 193–207.

Tyler, A. A., & Sandoval, K. T. (1994). Preschoolers with phonological and language disorders: Treating different linguistic domains. *Language, speech, and hearing services in schools, 25*, 215–234.

Uberti, H. Z., Scruggs, T. E., & Mastropieri, M. A. (2003). Keywords make the difference! Mnemonic instruction in inclusive classrooms. *Teaching Exceptional Children, 35*(3), 56–61.

Ukrainetz, T. A. (1998a). Stickwriting stories: A quick and easy narrative representation strategy. *Language, Speech, and Hearing Services in Schools, 29*, 197–206

Ukrainetz-McFadden, T. (1998b). The immediate effects of pictographic representation on children's narratives. *Child Language Teaching and Therapy, 14*, 51–67.

Underwood, B. J., & Shultz, R. W. (1960). *Meaningfulness and verbal learning.* Chicago: Lippincott.

United Nations Educational, Scientific and Cultural Organization (n.d.) *Best practices.* Retrieved from http://www.unesco.org/new/en/social-and-human-sciences/themes/social-transformations/international-migration/best-practices/

U.S. Department of Education. (2006). *Twenty-eighth annual report to congress on the implementation of the Individuals with Disabilities Education Act, Parts B and C.* Retrieved from http://www2.ed.gov/about/reports/annual/osep/2006/parts-b-c/index.html

U.S. Department of Education. (2007). *The 29th annual report to Congress on the implementation of the Individuals with Disabilities Education Act.* Washington, DC: Author.

U.S. Department of Education, National Center for Education Statistics. (2010). *The condition of education 2010.* Washington, DC: Author.

Utley, C. A., Mortweet, S. L., & Greenwood, C. R. (1997). Peer-mediated instruction and interventions. *Focus on Exceptional Children, 27*, 167–181.

Vakil, E., Shelef-Reshef, E., & Levy-Shiff, R. (1997). Procedural and declarative memory processes: Individuals with and without mental retardation. *American Journal on Mental Retardation, 102,* 147–160.

Valdés, G. (2001). *Learning and not learning English.* New York: Teachers College Press.

Vallar, G., & Cappa, S. F. (1987). Articulation and verbal short-term memory. Evidence from anarthria. *Cognitive Neuropsychology, 4,* 55–78.

van Dijk, J. (1967). The first steps of deaf-blind children towards language. *The International Journal for the Education of the Blind, 15*(4), 112–114.

Van Reusen, A. K., & Bos, C. S. (1994). Facilitating student participation in the individualized education programs through motivation strategy instruction. *Exceptional Children, 60,* 466–475.

Van Reusen, A. K., Deshler, D. D., & Schumaker, J. B. (1989). Effects of a student participation strategy in facilitating the involvement of adolescents with learning disabilities in the individualized educational program planning process. *Learning Disabilities, 1,* 23–34.

Vaughn, S., Linan-Thompson, S., Mathes, P. G., Cirino, P. T., Carlson, C. D., Hagan, E.C., . . . Francis, D. J. (2006). Effectiveness of Spanish intervention and an English intervention for first-grade English language learners at risk for reading difficulties. *Journal of Learning Disabilities, 39,* 56–73.

Vaughn, S., Mathes, P., Linan-Thompson, S., Cirino, P., Carlson, C., Pollard-Durodola, S. . . . Francis, D. J. (2006). Effectiveness of an English intervention for first-grade English language learners at risk for reading problems. *The Elementary School Journal, 107,* 154–180.

Venn, M. L., & Wolery, M. (1992). Increasing daycare staff members' interactions during caregiving routines. *Journal of Early Intervention, 16,* 304–319.

Venn, M. L., Wolery, M., Wertz, M. G., Morris, A., DeCesare, L. D., & Cuffs, M. S. (1993). Embedding instruction in art activities to teach preschoolers with disabilities to imitate their peers. *Early Childhood Research Quarterly, 8,* 277–294.

Vermeer, A., & Dekker, L. F. D. (1993). Assessment of learning potential in children with cerebral palsy. *Issues in Special Education & Rehabilitation, 8,* 83–90.

Vygotsky, L. S. (1978). *Mind in society: The development of higher psychological processes.* (M. Cole, V. John-Steiner, S. Scribner, & E. Souberman, Eds.). Cambridge, MA: Harvard University Press.

Vygotsky, L. (1934/1986). *Thought and language.* Cambridge, MA: MIT Press.

Wagner, M., Newman, L., Cameto, R., Garza, N., & Levine, P. (2005). *After high school: A first look at the postschool experiences of youth with disabilities. A report from the National Longitudinal Transition Study-2 (NLTS2).* Menlo Park, CA: SRI International.

Wagner, M., Newman, L., Cameto, R., Levine, P., & Garza, N. (2006). An overview of findings from Wave 2 of the National Longitudinal Transition Study-2 (NLTS2). *National Center for Special Education Research.* (ERIC Document Reproduction Service No. ED495660). Menlo Park, CA: SRI International. Available at www.nlts2.org/reports/2006_08/nlts2_report_2006_08_complete.pdf

Walker, A. R., Uphold, N. M., Richter, S., & Test, D. W. (2010). A review of literature on community based instruction across grade levels. *Education and Training in Developmental Disabilities, 45,* 242–267.

Wall, M. E., & Gast, D. L. (1999). Acquisition of incidental information during instruction for a response-chain skill. *Research in Developmental Disabilities, 20,* 31–50.

Wall Emerson, R., Holbrook, C., & D'Andrea, F. M. (2009). Acquisition of literacy skills in young blind children: Results from the ABC Braille Study. *Journal of Visual Impairment and Blindness, 103,* 610–624.

Wall Emerson, R., Sitar, D., Erin, J. N., Wormsley, D. P. & Herlich, S. L (2009). The effect of consistent structured reading instruction on high and low literacy achievement in young children who are blind. *Journal of Visual Impairment and Blindness, 103,* 595–609.

Walls, R. T., Dowler, D. L., Haught, P. A., & Zawlocki, R. J. (1984). Progressive delay and unlimited delay of prompt in forward chaining and whole task training strategies. *Education and Training of the Mentally Retarded, 19,* 276–284.

Walls, R. T., Zane, T., & Ellis, W. B. (1981). Forward and backward chaining, and whole task methods. *Behavior Modification, 5,* 61–74.

Walsh, B. F., & Lamberts, F. (1979). Errorless discrimination and picture fading as techniques for teaching sight words to TMR students. *American Journal of Mental Deficiency, 84,* 473–479.

Ward, M. J. (1988). The many facets of self-determination. *NICHCY transition summary: National Information Center for Children and Youth with Disabilities, 5,* 2–3.

Warren, S. F., & Gazdag, G. (1990). Facilitating early language development with milieu teaching procedures. *Journal of Early Intervention, 14,* 62–86.

Warren, S. F., & Kaiser, A. P. (1986). Incidental language teaching: A critical review. *Journal of Speech and Hearing Disorders, 51,* 291–299.

Warren, S. F., & Kaiser, A. P. (1988). Research in early language intervention. In S. L. Odom & M. B. Karnes (Eds.), *Early intervention for infants and children with handicaps: An empirical base* (pp. 89–108). Baltimore: Brookes.

Warren, S. F., McQuarter, R. J., & Rogers-Warren, A. K. (1984). The effects of mands and models on the speech of unresponsive socially isolate children. *Journal of Speech and Hearing Disorders, 47,* 42–52.

Warren, S. F., & Yoder, P. J. (1997). Emerging model of communication and language intervention. *Mental Retardation and Developmental Disabilities, 3,* 358–362.

Warren, S. F., Yoder, P. J., Gazdag, G. E., Kim, K., & Jones, H. A. (1993). Facilitating prelinguistic communication skills in young children with developmental delay. *Journal of Speech and Hearing Research, 36,* 83–97.

Watkins, R., Rice, M., & Molz, C. (1993). Verb use by language-impaired and normally developing children. *First Language, 37,* 133–143.

Watts, F. N. (1995). Depression and anxiety. In A. D. Baddeley, B. A. Wilson, & F. N. Watts (Eds.), *Handbook of memory disorders* (pp. 293–317). Oxford, UK: John Wiley & Sons.

Webster-Stratton, C. (1992). *The incredible years: A trouble-shooting guide for parents of children ages 3–8 years.* Toronto: Umbrella Press.

Wehman, P., & Kregel, J. (2003). *Functional curriculum for elementary, middle, and secondary age students with special needs.* Austin, TX: Pro-Ed.

Wehmeyer, M. L. (1992). Self-determination and the education of students with mental retardation. *Education and Training in Mental Retardation, 27,* 302–314.

Wehmeyer, M. L. (1996). Self-determination in youth with severe cognitive disabilities: From theory to practice. In L. E. Powers, G. H. S. Singer, & J. Sowers (Eds.), *On the road to autonomy: Promoting self-competence for children and youth with disabilities* (pp. 17–36). Baltimore: Brookes.

Wehmeyer, M. L., Agran, M., & Hughes, C. (2000). A national survey of teachers' promotion of self-determination and student-directed learning. *Journal of Special Education, 34,* 58–68.

Wehmeyer, M. L., & Palmer, S. B. (2003). Adult outcomes for students with cognitive disabilities three-years after high school: The impact of self-determination. *Education and Training in Developmental Disabilities, 38,* 131–144.

Weitzman, E., & Greenberg, J. (2002). *Learning language and loving it: A guide to promoting children's social, language, and literacy development in early childhood settings* (2nd ed.). Toronto, Canada: The Hanen Centre.

Wellman, H. M. (1990). *The child's theory of mind.* Cambridge, MA: MIT Press.

Werner, H., & Kaplan, B. (1963). *Symbol formation: An organismic-developmental approach to language and expression of thought.* New York: John Wiley.

Wertlieb, E. C. (1992). Automatic and purposive semantic processing in learning disabled individuals. *Journal of Special Education, 23,* 450–462.

Werts, M. G., Caldwell, N. K., & Wolery, M. (1996). Peer modeling of response chains: Observational learning by students with disabilities. *Journal of Applied Behavior Analysis, 29,* 53–66.

Westby, C. E. (1984). Development of narrative language abilities. In G. P. Wallach & K. G. Butler (Eds.), *Language learning disabilities in school-age children* (pp. 103–127). Baltimore: Williams & Wilkins.

Westerveld, M. F., & Gillon, G. T. (2008). Oral narrative intervention for children with mixed reading disability. *Child Language Teaching and Therapy, 24,* 31–54.

Westling, D. L., & Fox, L. (2009). *Teaching students with severe disabilities* (4th ed.). Upper Saddle River, NJ: Merrill/Pearson.

Whitehurst, G. J., Falco, F., Lonigan, C. J., Fischal, J. E., DeBaryshe, B. D., Valdez-Manchaca, M. C., & Caulfield, M. (1988) Accelerating language development through picturebook reading. *Development Psychology, 24,* 552–559.

Willis, A., & Harris, V. (2000). Political acts: Literacy learning and teaching. *Reading Research Quarterly, 35,* 72–88.

Wilson, B. (1996). *Wilson reading system.* Millbury, MA: Wilson Language Training.

Wolery, M., Ault, M. J., Gast, D. L., Doyle, P. M., & Griffen, A. K. (1990). Comparison of constant time delay and the system of least prompts in teaching chained tasks. *Education and Training in Mental Retardation, 25,* 243–257.

Wolery, M., Holombe, A., Cybriwsky, C., Doyle, P. M., Schuster, J. W., Ault, M. J., & Gast, D. L. (1992). Constant time delay with discrete responses. A review of effectiveness and demographic, procedural, and methodological parameters. *Research in Developmental Disabilities, 13,* 239–266.

Wolery, M., & Schuster, J. W. (1997). Instructional methods with students who have significant disabilities. *Journal of Special Education, 31,* 61–79.

Wolfe, P. S. (1994). Judgment of the social validity of instructional strategies used in community-based instructional sites. *Journal of the Association of Persons with Severe Handicaps, 19,* 43–51.

Wolfensberger, W. (1972). *The principle of normalization in human services.* Toronto: National Institute on Mental Retardation.

Wolgemuth, J. R., Cobb, B. R., & Alwell, M. (2008). The effects of mnemonic interventions on academic outcomes for youth with disabilities: A systematic review. *Learning Disabilities Research & Practice, 23,* 1–10.

Wormsley, D. P. (1996). Reading rates of young braille-reading children. *Journal of Visual Impairment and Blindness, 90,* 278–282.

Wright, C. W., & Schuster, J. W. (1994). Accepting specific versus functional student responses within training chained tasks. *Education and Training in Mental Retardation and Developmental Disabilities, 29,* 43–56.

Yang, C. H., Chuang, L. Y., Yang, C. H., & Luo, C. H. (2003). Morse code application for wireless environmental control systems for severely disabled individuals. *IEEE Transactions on Neural Systems and Rehabilitation Engineering, 2*(4), 463–469.

Yates, R. A. (1966). *The art of memory.* Chicago: University of Chicago Press.

Yell, M. L., & Drasgow, E. (2000). Litigating a free appropriate public education: The Lovaas hearings and cases. *The Journal of Special Education, 53,* 205–214.

Yoder, P. J., Kaiser, A. P., Goldstein, H., Alpert, C., Mousetis, L. Kaczmarek, L., & Fischer, R. (1995). An exploratory comparison of milieu teaching and responsive interaction in classroom applications. *Journal of Early Intervention, 19,* 218–242.

Yoder, P., Warren, S., Kim, K., & Gazdag, G. (1994). Facilitating prelinguistic communication skills in young children with developmental delay II: Systematic replication and extension. *Journal of Speech and Hearing Research, 37,* 841–851.

Yopp, H. K. (1988). The validity and reliability of phonemic awareness tests. *Reading Research Quarterly, 23,* 159–177.

Zehler, A. M., Fleischman, H. L., Hopstock, P. J., Stephenson, T. G., Pendzick, M. L., & Sapru, S. (2003). *Descriptive study of services to LEP students and LEP students with disabilities: Policy report—Summary of findings related to LEP and SPED-LEP student.* Washington, DC: Development Associates.

Zimmerman, I. L., Steiner, V. G., & Evatt Pond, R. (2002). *Preschool Language Scale-Revised* (PLS-R) (4th ed.). San Antonio, TX: Psychological Corporation.

Name Index

Abbott, M., 6
Abedi, J., 45
Ada, A. F., 53, 54
Adams, M. J., 49, 52
Adlington, R., 86
Ager, C., 41
Agran, M., 39, 40, 42
Ahlgrim-Delzell, L., 32
Aiken, S., 108, 110
Akamatsu, C., 101
Alberto, P. A., 31, 37, 39, 41, 88, 89, 92, 119, 125
Alcantra, P. R., 119, 123
Alexander, R., 51
Algeria, J., 101
Allen, S., 121
Allen, S. K., 117
Alpert, C. L., 16
Alwell, M., 25, 117
Amari, A., 37
Amaya-Williams, M., 89
American Printing House (APH), 105
American Psychiatric Association, 73
Americans with Disabilities Act, 9
Andrews, A., 84
Angelo, J., 95
Anglin, G., 25
Anthony, T. L., 106
Arguelles, M. E., 6
Arndt, S. A., 117
Arntzen, E., 39
Artiles, A. J., 45
Arunachalam, V., 2
Ary, D., 48
Atkinson, R., 20
Atwater, J. B., 9
Au, K. H., 50, 55
August, D. L., 45, 46, 48
Ault, M. J., 32, 33, 34

Baddeley, A., 89
Baer, D. M., 12, 15, 16
Bailey, B., 109
Bailey, E., 11
Baker, J. N., 31, 32
Baker, R. L., 106
Bakkaloglu, H., 11
Bakken, J. P., 21, 24
Bambara, L. M., 16, 41
Banda, D. R., 34, 35, 36
Barone, D., 86
Barr, D. M., 11
Bartsch, K., 68
Bates, E., 110

Bates, P. E., 119, 122, 123, 124, 125, 127
Battle, C. W., 110
Bauer, R., 19
Baumgart, D., 11
Baumwell, L., 65
Beck, I. L., 46
Beeler, T., 52
Behrmann, M. M., 16
Beirne-Smith, M., 30, 31
Benigni, L., 110
Benitez, D. T., 117
Bereiter, C., 49
Berkeley, S., 29
Berkeley, T. R., 9
Bernhard, J. K., 45, 50, 51, 53, 54, 56
Best, S. J., 31, 87
Bianco, J. L., 47, 48, 50, 59
Biglan, A., 48
Bingham, C., 63, 69, 70
Bishop, D., 89
Blackorby, J., 115
Blakeley-Smith, A., 75
Blauvelt-Harper, C., 78
Bleiker, C., 54
Bloom, Y., 110
Boardman, A. G., 6
Bopp, K. D., 84
Borell, L., 88
Bornstein, M. H., 65
Borthwick-Duffy, S. A., 79
Bos, C. S., 117
Bosma, J., 106
Boulerice, B., 19
Boulinea, T., 70
Boyd, B., 75
Brady, M. P., 41
Brainerd, C., 19
Branham, R. S., 119
Bransford, J., 50
Branson, T. A., 33
Brazeau, K. C., 79
Bredekamp, S., 9
Brent, M. R., 62
Bretherton, I., 110
Breunig, N., 45
Bricker, D., 9, 10, 11, 12, 13, 14, 18
Bricker, D. D., 11
Bricker, W., 9
Brienza, D. M., 95
Brigham, F. J., 25
Brineman, D. G., 88, 92
Brinton, B., 67
Brophy, J., 5
Browder, D., 32, 38, 39

Browder, D. M., 31, 32, 33, 38
Brown, A., 50
Brown, F., 33, 34, 35, 38
Brown, K. E., 84
Brown, L., 31, 119
Browning, N., 86, 88
Bruce, S. M., 110
Bruder, M. B., 9, 11
Bruner, E. C., 49, 103
Bruner, J., 65
Bruner, J. S., 15
Bruni, J. R., 53
Bruteig, J. M., 107, 113
Bryan, D., 49, 56
Bucher, B., 34
Buendía, E., 46
Bulgren, J. A., 24
Burke, M., 70
Burnett, R., 106
Burns, M. K., 6
Burns, M. S., 45
Burta, M., 41
Butler, L. R., 85
Buultjens, M., 108

Cabello, B., 9
Caldwell, J., 50
Cale, S. I., 75
Camaioni, L., 110
Cameto, R., 115, 116
Campbell, P. H., 11
Campoy, F. I., 54
Campoy, I., 53
Carney, R., 25
Carnine, D., 6
Carpenter, M. H., 16
Carr, E. G., 10, 75, 79
Carta, J. J., 9
Carter, A., 11
Carter, E. W., 75
Carter, M., 38, 109, 111, 114
Case, R., 49
Case, R. E., 45
Casey, A. M., 9, 16
Casey, S. D., 76
Casto, G. C., 29
Cathers, T., 88
Cavalier, A. R., 42, 97
Cavallaro, C. C., 9, 16
Cawthon, S., 101, 103, 105
Ceci, S., 19
Center for Applied Special Technology (CAST), 105
Certo, N., 122, 123

Cestone, C. M., 7
Chabris, C., 2
Chafouleas, S. M., 80, 81
Chall, J., 106
Chamberlain, C., 101
Chambers, J., 62
Chandler, L. K., 77
Chandler, W., 37
Chanese, J. A. M., 81
Chapman, R., 65
Charlop-Christy, M. H., 16
Chávez, L., 44
Chen, D., 108, 109
Chen, J., 48
Chen, S., 33
Christ, T. J., 80
Christensen, L. L., 84
Christensen, W. R., 117, 119
Christian, D., 45
Chuang, L. Y., 95
Chung, K. M., 77
Cihak, D. F., 41, 88, 119, 124, 125
Clancy, P., 127
Clark, C., 108
Clarke, S., 84
Cleave, P. L., 63, 64, 65, 66, 67
Clifford, S. M., 74
Cobb, B. R., 25, 117
Cocking, R., 50
Cohen, E. T., 87
Cohen, J., 50, 56
Cohn, S. J., 20
Cole, K., 66
Coleman, M. B., 94, 95, 96
Coleman-Martin, M. B., 86, 87, 88, 92, 93, 95
Collins, B. C., 11, 32, 33, 36, 37, 119
Condillac, R. A., 74
Conti-Ramsden, G., 63
Cook, B. G., 1, 4, 5, 6, 7
Cook, D. M., 40
Cook, L., 4
Cook, S., 29
Cooney, J., 19, 101
Cooper, J. O., 31, 32, 33, 34, 37, 39, 42, 79, 125
Cooper, K. J., 38
Copeland, S., 45
Copeland, S. R., 39, 40, 41
Copple, C., 9
Cornwall, A., 19
Council for Exceptional Children (CEC), 3, 105
Crank, J., 70
Cress, P. J., 42
Cripe, J., 10, 11, 12, 13, 14, 18
Crockett, J. B., 2
Crompton, A., 77
Crosland, K., 46
Cross, C. T., 45
Cross, D. P., 123
Cummins, J., 50, 53, 54
Cunningham, S., 98
Cuvo, T., 119

Dacy, B. J. S., 7
Dahlsgaard, K., 62
Dale, P., 66
Dammann, J. E., 2, 6
D'Andrea, F. M., 106
Daugherty, S., 11
Davies, D. K., 41
Davis, C. A., 41
Davis, Z. T., 67
Dawson, G., 74
Deci, E. L., 116
DeFord, D., 104
Deitz, S. J., 105

Dekker, L. F. D., 87
Delano, M., 39
De La Paz, S., 96, 97
Delpit, L., 50, 54
Demchak, M., 33, 34
de Moor, J., 89
Dennison, L., 9
Denny, M., 32, 33, 36
Deno, S. L., 5
Denton, C. A., 49, 56
Deshler, D. D., 24, 117
Detrich, R., 73, 74
De Valenzuela, J., 45
Dewey, J., 10
Diaz, R. M., 89
Dickinson, D. K., 66
Dickson, D., 2
Didden, R., 109
Diemer, S. M., 79
Diggs, C. A., 88, 92
DiNovi, K., 84
DiPipi-Hoy, C., 124, 125
Dissanayake, C., 74
Division for Early Childhood (DEC), 9
Dogoe, M., 34, 35, 36
Donlan, D., 70
Donovan, M. S., 45
Doumbia, F., 46
Dowler, D. L., 33
Downing, J. E., 108, 109
Doyle, P. M., 32, 33, 34, 35, 38
Doyle, W., 5
Driscoll, A., 44
Duda, M. A., 84
Duke, N. K., 69
Dunlap, G., 74, 79, 80, 81, 84, 85
Dunst, C. J., 9, 11
Durán, R. P., 44, 45
Dykes, M. K., 87

Edmonds, C. J., 107
Edmondson-Pretzel, R., 75
Edrisinha, C., 84
Education Trust, 45
Edyburn, D. L., 94
Egel, A. L., 16
Ellis, D. N., 42
Emerick, K., 24
Enderby, P., 98
Engelmann, S., 49, 103
Eoff, J., 20
Epstein, M. H., 19
Erickson, A. M., 41
Erickson, K., 106, 108
Erickson, K. A., 108
Erin, J. N., 106
Evatt Pond, R., 53
Eyre, J. T., 108
Ezell, H. K., 65

Fabiano, G. A., 80
Fantuzzo, J. W., 40
Farlow, L. J., 37
Farrell, D. A., 37
Felton, E. A., 95, 96
Feng, J., 96
Ferguson, B., 38, 122, 123
Ferreira, J., 88
Ferrell, K. A., 105
Ferretti, R. P., 42
Fey, M. E., 63, 64, 65, 66, 67, 70
Fickel, K. M., 32, 35
Fidanque, A., 49
Field, S., 40, 116
Fierros, E., 45

Finestack, L. H., 65, 66
Fitzgerald, J., 70
Fitzgerald, S., 6
Fleming, J. L., 11
Flood, J., 54
Flowers, C., 117
Fodor-Davis, J., 40
Foley, B. E., 89
Fontana, J., 25, 28
Foorman, B. R., 52
Ford, J., 67
Fore, C., 70
Forness, S. R., 19, 20, 25
Forney, P. E., 31
Fowler, C. H., 40, 116, 117, 119, 121, 122, 124, 126, 127
Fowler, S. E., 40
Fox, D., 108
Fox, L., 11, 31, 79, 84, 85, 119
Francis, D., 45
Frea, W. D., 75, 78
Frederick-Dugan, A., 33
Fredrick, L. D., 87, 88, 92
Freedman, D. H., 2
Freire, P., 50
Fuchs, D., 26, 27, 49, 59
Fuchs, L. S., 26, 27, 49, 59
Fujiki, M., 67
Fulk, B. M., 23

Gaffney, J., 20
Gaffney, J. S., 21
Galda, L., 65
Gallucci, C., 31
Gambrell, L. B., 50
Gampp, T. L., 103
Gándara, P., 44
Ganger, J., 62
Ganz, J. B., 40, 42
Garcia, J., 79
Garcia, S. B., 45
Gardill, M. C., 67
Garrett, J., 98
Garrett, Z., 63
Garza, N., 115, 116
Gast, D. L., 32, 33, 38, 41
Gaule, K., 122, 123
Gay, G., 54
Gazdag, G., 11, 16, 18
Gazdag, G. E., 16, 62
Gee, J. P., 46, 50
Genesee, F., 45
Genung, T., 8
Gerber, M. M., 47, 57, 58
Gersten, R., 52, 126
Geva, E., 52
Gilberts, G. H., 42
Gilbertson, L., 95
Gillam, R., 63, 69, 70
Gillam, R. B., 71
Gillam, S., 63, 69, 70, 71, 72
Gillon, G. T., 70, 71
Gilpin, M., 88
Girolametta, L., 63, 64, 65, 66
Gitlin, A., 46
Glazer, A. D., 81
Glenn, C., 67, 68
Goldenberg, C., 45
Goldman, S., 68
Goldman, T., 19
Goldstein, H., 75, 78
Gomez-Bellenge, F. X., 48
Gonzalez, J. E., 19
Good, T. L., 5
Goossens, A., 41

Gordon, C. J., 70
Graesser, A. C., 68
Graetz, J., 29
Graetz, J. E., 28
Graff, R. B., 34
Graham, S., 96
Green, G., 34
Green, P., 98
Green, V. A., 109
Greenberg, J., 65
Greenfield, D. B., 26
Greenwood, C. R., 6, 26, 75
Greteman, C., 77
Griffen, A. K., 32, 37, 38
Griffin, P., 45
Grisham-Brown, J. L., 11
Grossi, T. A., 41
Gumerlock, S., 11
Gunn, B., 48, 52, 57
Günther, T., 19
Guralnick, M. J., 9
Gustafson, S., 88

Hagan-Burke, S., 70
Hagopian, L. P., 37
Hakuta, K., 48
Hall, M., 33
Halle, J. W., 16
Halpern, A. S., 115
Halstadtro, A., 39
Halstadtro, M., 39
Halverson, C. A., 97
Hamby, D., 11
Hammer, M. R., 117
Hammill, D., 54
Hamre-Nietupski, S., 127
Hancock, T. B., 11, 16
Haney, M., 9
Hanline, M. F., 11
Hannan, C. K., 107
Hansford, D., 86
Harber, R. S., 8
Harden, P. W., 19
Harjusola-Webb, S., 4, 5
Harper, C. B., 75
Harr, J., 62
Harris, L. R., 63
Harris, V., 46
Harrower, J. D., 79
Hart, B., 15, 16, 18, 65
Hatton, D., 108
Hatton, D. D., 106
Haught, P. A., 33
Hawley, M., 98
Hayward, D., 70
Heal, L. W., 79
Heath, S. B., 54
Hedrick, B. N., 93
Heller, K. W., 31, 86, 87, 88, 89, 92, 93, 94, 95, 96
Hemmeter, M. L., 9, 11, 12, 17
Hemmingston, H., 88
Hendrix, M. P., 88
Heng, M. A., 49, 59
Henry, L., 19
Herlich, S. L., 106
Heron, T. E., 31, 79, 125
Herpetz-Dahlmann, B., 19
Hershberger, S., 66
Hess, F., 3
Hester, P. P., 11, 16, 17, 18
Heward, W. L., 31, 49, 59, 79, 125
Hickman-Davis, P., 47
Highnam, C., 77

Hill, E. A., 84
Hirschberg, J., 49
Hoffman, A., 116
Hoggan, K., 68
Hogue, A., 6
Hohnston, S. S., 77
Holbrook, C., 106
Holbrook, M. C., 106, 107
Holtkamp, K., 19
Hood, L. S., 70
Horn, D. B., 97
Horn, E., 11
Horner, R. D., 37
Horner, R. H., 16, 79, 84, 123, 126
Hourcade, J. J., 86
Howard, L., 49
Howe, M., 19
Hoyson, M., 11, 75, 79
Huber, H., 74
Hughes, C., 40, 41, 42
Hughes, D., 67
Hughes, D. L., 67
Hughes, M., 119
Hughes, M. T., 6
Hurth, J., 74
Hux, K., 98

Iacino, R., 9
Iddon, J. L., 87
Idol, L., 70
Individuals with Disabilities Education Improvement Act (IDEA), 8, 9, 39, 100, 105
Iovannone, R., 74, 80, 81, 85
Irvine, A. B., 41
Irvine, K. L., 88
Izeman, S. G., 74

Jain, R., 68
Jameson, J. M., 36
Jamieson, B., 11, 79
Janney, R., 75
Jawitz, P. B., 50
Jenkins, V., 19
Jerman, R. L., 119
Jitendra, A. K., 67, 124
Johnson, J. E., 9
Johnson, J. W., 36
Johnson, K. M., 9
Jolles, J., 19
Jones, C. D., 75
Jones, H. A., 16, 62
Jones, I., 65
Jones, M., 63
Jones, M. L., 6
Joseph, D., 33
Junkala, J., 87
Justice, L. M., 61, 65

Kahn, N., 70
Kaiser, A., 15, 16, 17
Kaiser, A. P., 11, 15, 16, 17, 18
Kamps, D., 49, 57, 79
Kamps, D. M., 75
Kane, M. T., 32, 35, 37, 39
Kaplan, B., 109, 110
Karat, C. M., 96, 97
Karat, J., 97
Karsh, K. G., 34
Kauffman, J. M., 6
Kavale, K. A., 19, 20
Keetz, A., 15
Keilitz, I., 37
Keller-Allen, C., 45
Kelly, P. R., 48, 58

Kemp, C. R., 38
Kennedy, C. H., 75
Kern, L., 124
Kerr, M. M., 75
Kessler, K., 119, 125
Kessler, K. B., 41
Kieffer, M., 45
Killen, C. C., 11
Killoran, J., 108
Kim, K., 16, 62
Kim, S. H., 30
Kimbrough, B. T., 106
Kincaid, D., 74, 79, 80, 81
Kincheloe, J., 44
King, G. A., 88
King, T. W., 94
Kingma, J., 19
King-Sears, M. E., 24, 39
Kintsch, W., 68
Klaase, M., 41
Kleinert, H., 119
Klingner, J., 6, 45
Klingner, J. K., 45
Knokey, A. M., 115
Knowlton, M., 107, 113
Koegel, L. K., 40, 42, 75, 79
Koegel, R. L., 75, 79
Koenig, A. J., 106, 107
Koester, H., 95
Koester, H. H., 97, 98
Kohl, F. L., 38, 39
Kohler, F. W., 11, 74, 77
Konrad, K., 19
Konrad, M., 40, 117
Koppenhaver, D. A., 88
Korabek, C. A., 119
Kotler, A. L., 97, 98
Kouzekanani, K., 47
Krantz, P. J., 16
Kregel, J., 119
Krulik, T. E., 66

Labov, W., 67
Ladson-Billings, G., 46, 54
Laine, C. J., 96
Lamberts, F., 34
Lancaster, P. E., 117
Lancioni, G., 84
Lancioni, G. E., 41, 95, 109
Land, L., 37
Landrum, T. J., 2, 4, 6, 7
Lane, D. S., 44
Lang, R., 85
Lange, E., 33
Lapp, D., 54
Lattimore, J., 117
Laughlin, B., 37, 38
Lauritzen, E., 98
Law, J., 63
Law, S. G., 44
Leafstedt, J. M., 47, 52, 58
Lee, C., 54
Lee, S., 77
Lehmann, J., 117
LeJeune, B. J., 106
Lentini, R., 84
Lentz, M. W., 34
Leonard, L. B., 63
Lesaux, N., 45
Lesaux, N. K., 45
Leslie, L., 50
Levin, J., 25
Levin, J. R., 20, 21, 24, 25
Levine, P., 115, 116
Levy-Shiff, R., 19

Lewis, N. L., 95
Leybaert, J., 101
Li, S., 11
Lieber, J., 11
Light, J., 103
Light, J. C., 99
Limbos, M. M., 52
Linan-Thompson, S., 47, 49, 50, 52, 58, 60
Lindholm-Leary, K., 45
Lloyd, J. W., 3
Lloyd, P. A., 3
Loeb, D. F., 66
Loftin, R., 77
Long, S. H., 63, 65, 66, 67
LoPresti, E., 95
LoPresti, E. F., 95
Losardo, A., 11, 14
Losen, D. J., 45
Loveday, C., 87
Lovett, M. W., 49, 58
Luckner, J. L., 101, 104
Lucyshyn, J. M., 84
Ludlow, B. L., 9
Luiselli, J. K., 85
Lundberg, I., 52
Luo, C. H., 95
Lynch, J., 72
Lyon, G. R., 46, 51

MacArthur, C. A., 97
Macy, M., 11
Macy, M. G., 11
Madelaine, A., 4
Magill-Evans, J. E., 88
Magliano, J. P., 68
Malmgren, K. W., 103, 104
Malouf, D. B., 2
Manasse, N., 98
Marshak, L., 20, 25, 28, 29
Marshall, A. M., 16
Marshall, L. H., 119
Martin, J., 40
Martin, J. E., 117, 119
Martin, J. K., 93
Mason, D., 16
Massaro, D. W., 103
Massetti, G. M., 80
Mastropieri, M. A., 5, 19, 20, 21, 22, 23, 24, 25, 26, 28, 29
Mathes, P., 47, 49, 50, 52, 60
Maxson, L. M., 119
Maxwell-Jolly, J., 44
Mayberry, R., 100, 101
Mayer, C., 101
Mazzotti, V. L., 116, 117
McAvoy, C., 96
McBride, B. J., 11
McClannahan, L. E., 16
McConnell, S. R., 9, 77
McCormick, L., 12, 15
McCough, S. M., 104
McCoy, J. F., 34
McDonnell, A. P., 77
McDonnell, J., 36, 37, 38, 39, 122, 123
McDuffie, K. A., 2, 28, 29
McFarland, S., 37
McGee, G. G., 16, 34
McGillivray, L., 67
McGregor, K., 63
McKeough, A., 49
McLean, M. E., 12
McLoone, B., 20
McLoone, B. B., 20, 24, 25
McMaster, K. L., 6, 26, 27
McNaughton, D. B., 99

McNear, D., 106
McQuarter, R. J., 16
McWilliam, R. A., 9, 16
Mechling, L. C., 41, 123
Melloy, K. J., 76
Mercer, C. D., 24
Mezei, P., 87
Mike, D. G., 88
Miko, P., 33
Millar, D. C., 99
Millar, S., 107
Miller, R., 40
Miller, U. C., 33, 37, 38
Mills, C. E., 70
Mills, P., 66
Mills, S., 20, 28
Milosky, L., 67
Mims, P. J., 32
Miner, C. A., 119
Mirenda, P., 84, 96
Molz, C., 63
Montgomery, J., 70
Moore, M. A., 39
Moore, S. C., 40
Morgan, D. J. R., 87
Morris, R. C., 34
Morrison, C., 25
Morrison, L., 79
Morse, T. E., 32, 34, 37, 119, 123
Mortweet, S. L., 75
Mosk, M. D., 34
Mostert, M. P., 2
Mudd, J. M., 11
Mueller, J. H., 19, 20
Muir, S. G., 101
Mundschenk, N. A., 76
Murphy, J. L., 108
Murphy, M. J., 42
Murphy, R., 42
Murray-Branch, J., 109, 110, 114
Myles, B., 73

Najdowski, A. C., 84
Narr, R. F., 101, 103, 104, 105
Nathanson, R., 70
National Association for the Education of
    Young Children (NAEYC), 9
National Autism Center, 74
National Center for Culturally Responsive
    Educational Systems, 55
National Consortium on Deaf-Blindness
    (NCDB), 108
National Research Council (NRC), 73, 74, 79, 85
National Secondary Transition Technical
    Assistance Center, 118, 121, 123,
    125, 126
Neal, C. J., 89
Neale, M., 118
Necoechea, D. M., 54
Neef, N. A., 16
Nehring, A. D., 53
Nehring, E. E., 53
Neitzel, J., 75
Nelson, A. R., 77
Nelson, C., 77
Nelson, C. M., 81
Nelson, R., 42
Newman, L., 115, 116
Newman-Gonchar, R., 117
New York Department of Health, 74
Nietupski, J., 122, 123, 127
Nihalani, P. K., 7
Nolte, R., 70
Noonan, M. J., 12
Nordness, P. D., 19

Norland, J. J., 28
Notari-Syverson, A., 52
Nye, C., 63

Obiakor, F. E., 44
Ochoa, S. H., 45
O'Conner, R. E., 52
Odom, S. I., 77
Odom, S. L., 75, 77
Ogden, S., 32, 33
Ogle, D. M., 50
Oliver, C. B., 16
O'Neil, R., 81
O'Reilly, M., 84
O'Reilly, M. F., 41, 109
Orfield, G., 45
Orlando, A. M., 39
Orlansky, M. D., 125
Osguthorpe, R. T., 26
Osterling, P., 74
Ostrosky, M., 77
Ostrosky, M. M., 16
Owen-DeSchryver, J. S., 75, 77
Ownbey, J., 11

Padden, C., 102
Palmer, J., 45
Palmer, S. B., 117
Parent, W., 127
Parette, H. P., 93
Parette, P., 86
Park, M., 45
Parker, D., 79
Parker, M., 98
Parrish, T., 62
Parsons, M. B., 11
Patton, J. R., 30
Paul, P. V., 101, 102, 103
Payton, P., 68
Pearce, P. S., 63
Pearson, N. A., 71
Pearson, P. D., 69, 70
Pease, L., 108
Peck, C. A., 11, 31
Peeters, M., 89
Pelham, W. F., 80
Pellegrini, A. D., 65
Pepper, J., 65
Perlmutter, J., 65
Perou, R., 26
Perrin, S. H., 84
Perry, A., 74
Petersen, D., 63, 69, 70
Peterson-Karlan, G., 86, 94
Peterson-Karlan, G. R., 93
Petrilli, M., 3
Piaget, J., 10
Pickard, J. D., 87
Pierce, K., 78
Pihl, R. O., 19
Pikulski, J. J., 105
Planty, M., 44
Polite, K., 40
Pollatsek, A., 89
Polychronis, S., 36
Post, M., 41
Powers, M. D., 74
Pretti-Frontczak, K., 11
Pring, L., 107
Proctor-Williams, K., 66
Psychological Corporation, 103
Pullen, P. C., 3

Qi, C., 45
Quinn, G., 40

Raab, M., 11
Radwin, R. G., 95
Ragland, E. U., 75
Raines, J. M., 20
Ramsey, C., 102
Randolph, P. L., 53
Rankin-Erickson, J., 98
Rao, S., 32, 35, 37, 39
Raphael, T., 50
Raschke, D., 77
Ratner, V. L., 63
Reaney, S., 77
Reese, G. M., 33, 37, 38
Reichle, J., 31, 79
Reid, D. H., 11, 16
Reid, R., 19
Reigel, D. H., 87
Renne, D., 108
Repp, A. C., 34
Rescorla, L., 62
Restall, G., 88
Reutzel, R., 67
Rex, E. J., 106, 107
Reyna, V., 46
Rian, V., 79
Rice, M., 63
Rice, M. L., 66
Richards, C., 47, 58
Richter, S., 121
Riesen, T., 36
Riley-Tillman, T. C., 80, 81
Risley, T. R., 15, 16, 18, 65
Rivera, H., 45
Rivera, M., 45
Robbins, F. R., 74
Roberts, J., 62
Robinson, D. H., 7
Robles-Piña, E., 45
Robson, J., 89
Rogers, S. J., 74
Rogers-Warren, A., 16
Rogers-Warren, A. K., 15, 16
Rohwer, W. D., Jr., 20
Roit, M., 49
Rönnberg, J., 88
Roos, P. M., 45
Rosen, K., 97
Rowland, C., 108, 109, 110, 111, 114
Rowley-Kelly, F. L., 87
Roy, V., 108
Rueda, R., 45
Ruegg, E., 70
Rumelhart, D. E., 68
Ryan, E. B., 67
Ryan, R. H., 116
Ryndak, D. L., 39

Sáenz, L. M., 26, 49, 59
Sagan, C., 5
Sahakian, B. J., 87
Salazar, J. J., 45
Samson, J. F., 45
Sandall, S., 11, 12, 18
Sandknop, P. A., 123
Sandoval, K. T., 64
Sanford, L., 106
Sasso, G. M., 76
Sassu, K. A., 81
Saunders, R. R., 79
Saunders, W., 45
Sawyer, L. B., 11
Saywitz, K., 70
Scarborough, H., 62
Schalock, R. L., 8, 30
Scheerenberger, R. C., 8

Schepis, M. M., 11, 16
Schiller, E. P., 2
Schirmer, B. R., 6, 104
Schloss, P. J., 119
Schlosser, R., 109
Schmidek, M., 67
Schneider, P., 70
Schoen, S. F., 32, 33
Schreibman, L., 34, 78
Schultz, I. Z., 88
Schulz, M. M., 48
Schumaker, J. B., 117
Schuster, J., 32
Schuster, J. W., 11, 32, 34, 37, 39, 119, 123
Schwartz, I., 11
Schwartz, I. S., 9, 11, 31, 75
Schwartzman, M. N., 31, 87
Schweigert, P., 108, 109, 110, 111, 114
Scott, M. S., 26
Scott, T. M., 81
Scruggs, T. E., 5, 19, 20, 21, 22, 23, 24, 25, 26, 28, 29
Scull, J. A., 47, 48, 50, 59
Sears, A., 96
Sebald, A. M., 101
Secco, T., 68
Secord, W. A., 71
Seguin, J. R., 19
Seltzer, A., 119
Semel, E., 71
Sewell, T. J., 11
Shanahan, T., 46
Sharpe, M., 106
Shaw, A. R., 105
Shaw, E., 74
Sheehan, R., 11
Sheehy, K., 34
Shelef-Reshef, E., 19
Shermer, M., 5
Short, E. J., 67
Shultz, R. W., 20
Shumaker, J. B., 24
Sigafoos, J., 42, 84, 109
Silliman, E., 68
Simons, D., 2
Simpkins, P. M., 28, 29
Simpson, R., 73, 74, 95
Sindelar, P., 24
Singer, G. H. S., 41
Singer, H., 70
Singer, J., 84
Singer, M., 68
Sitar, D., 106
Sitko, C. J., 96
Sitko, M. C., 96
Skinner, B. F., 79
Smagorinsky, P., 54
Smith, A., 3, 121
Smith, A. C., 117
Smith, B. J., 12
Smith, D. J., 42
Smith, G. J., 1
Smith, M. L., 54
Smith, M. W., 66
Smith, S. C., 76
Smith-Bird, E., 84
Smolkowski, K., 48
Snell, M. E., 33, 34, 35, 37, 38, 75
Snow, C., 46
Snow, C. E., 45
Song, A., 110
Spackman, M. P., 67
Spellman, C. R., 42
Spiegel, D. L., 70

Spooner, F., 31, 32
Spradlin, J. E., 16
Sprague, J., 16
Sprague, J. R., 79
Sprick, M., 49
Spungin, S., 106
Stager, G. H., 84
Stahlberg, D., 41
Staub, D., 31
Steel, K., 88
Stein, N. L., 67, 68
Steinberg, S., 44
Steiner, V. G., 53
Steinman, B. A., 106
Stettner-Eaton, B. A., 38, 39
Stevens, K. B., 37
Stillman, R., 110
Stinson, D. M., 37
Stock, S. E., 41
Stokes, T. F., 12, 15, 16
Storey, K., 41, 76
Strain, P., 76
Strain, P. S., 11, 74, 75, 79
Street, B. V., 46, 50, 51
Strong, C., 68
Stumbo, N. J., 93
Suárez-Orozco, C., 45
Suárez-Orozco, M., 45
Suh, S., 68
Sullivan, A., 45
Sullivan, G. S., 25
Surratt, A., 79
Sutton, K. A., 16
Swanson, H., 19
Swanson, L., 26, 46, 54
Swanson, L. A., 70, 71
Sweda, J., 25
Swinehart-Jones, D., 86, 87, 88, 92, 93
Symon, J. B. G., 75, 78

Taber, T. A., 119, 125
Talbot, M. L., 87
Tam, C., 97, 98
Tam, K. Y., 49, 59
Tam, S. F., 88
Tamis-LeMonda, C. S., 65
Tankersley, M., 3, 4, 5, 6, 7
Tankersley, M. T., 6
Taylor, P., 119
Taylor, S. S., 45
Téllez, K., 45
Test, D., 121
Test, D. W., 33, 37, 38, 40, 116, 117, 118, 119, 121, 122, 124, 126, 127
Thiemann, K. S., 75, 78
Thomas-Stonell, N., 98
Tomblin, J. B., 62
Tomlinson, C. A., 26
Torgesen, J. K., 19, 49
Trabasso, T., 68
Trainin, G., 54
Trela, K., 31
Tremblay, R. E., 19
Trent, S. C., 45
Trent, S. D., 107, 113
Trezek, B. J., 101, 102, 103, 104, 105
Trief, E., 108, 111, 114
Trivette, C. M., 11
Troia, G. A., 48, 59
Trout, A., 19
Troutman, A. C., 37, 39
Truan, M. B., 107, 113
Tumlin, J., 88, 92, 96
Turnbull, A. P., 84
Turnbull, H. R., 3

Turnell, R., 109, 111, 114
Turoldo, K., 96
Tyler, A. A., 64

Uberti, H. Z., 24, 25
Udvari-Solner, A., 109
Underwood, B. J., 20
Uphold, N. M., 121
U.S. Department of Education, 8, 19, 45
Utley, C. A., 75

Vadasy, P. F., 52
Valdés, G., 46
Vallar, G., 89
van Balkom, H., 89
van den Broek, P., 68
van den Broek, P. W., 68
van Dijk, J., 110
van Dijk, T. A., 68
Van Dycke, J. L., 117, 119
Van Reusen, A. K., 117
Varn, L., 33
Varnhagen, C. K., 68
Vaughn, S., 2, 6, 47, 49, 50, 52, 56, 60
Veerhusen, K., 127
Venn, M. L., 11
Verhoeven, L., 89
Vermeer, A., 87
Volterra, V., 110
Vygotsky, L., 10, 88

Wacker, D., 123
Wagner, M., 20, 115, 116
Wakeman, S., 31
Walker, A. R., 40, 117, 121

Wall, M. E., 38
Wall Emerson, R., 106, 107
Walls, R. T., 33, 37
Walsh, B. F., 34
Walters, J., 16
Wang, Y., 101, 102, 103, 105
Ward, M., 40
Ward, M. J., 116
Warren, S., 16
Warren, S. F., 11, 15, 16, 18, 62
Watkins, R., 63
Watts, F. N., 19
Waxman, H., 45
Webster-Stratton, C., 48
Wehman, P., 119, 127
Wehmeyer, M., 40, 42
Wehmeyer, M. L., 39, 41, 116, 117
Weitzman, E., 63, 65, 66
Welch, J., 123
Wellman, H. M., 68
Wengelin, Å., 88
Werner, H., 109, 110
Wertlieb, E. C., 19
Werts, M. G., 38, 39
Westerveld, M. F., 70, 71
Westling, D. L., 119
Wetzel, R., 107, 113
Wexler, J., 49, 56
Wexler, K., 66
Whaley, K., 74
Whedon, C., 21
Wheldall, K., 4
Whittaker, M. E. S., 24
Wiig, E. H., 71
Wilcox, B., 16

Williams, A. R., 88
Williams, J. A., 123
Williams, J. C., 95
Williams, R. E., 41
Willis, A., 46
Wills, S. A., 95
Wilson, B., 49, 89
Wilson, K., 85
Winsler, A., 54
Wolery, M., 11, 32, 33, 34, 37, 39, 123
Wolfe, P. S., 119, 121
Wolfensberger, W., 8
Wolgemuth, J. R., 25
Wood, W., 121
Wood, W. M., 40, 117
Woods, D. G., 103
Wormsley, D. P., 106, 107, 113
Wright, C. W., 37, 39
Wright, T. E., 86

Yampolsky, S., 97
Yang, C. H., 95
Yang, C. H., 95
Yates, R. A., 20
Yoder, P., 15, 16
Yoder, P. J., 16, 62
Yopp, H. K., 52
Young, J., 101
Ysseldyke, J. E., 6

Zawlocki, R. J., 33
Zehler, A. M., 45
Zhang, J., 33
Zimmerman, I. L., 53
Zucker, S. F., 20

Subject Index

AAC (augmentative and alternative communication) devices, 16, 90, 92, 99
ABI. *See* Activity-based intervention (ABI)
Academic achievement, high-incidence
disabilities, 20, 26, 29
Academic skills outcomes
prompts and, 32, 36
research-based practices in, 7
research-to-practice gap and, 6
Access to writing. *See also* Written expression
physical disabilities, 95–96, 99
Accuracy, speech recognition, 98
Achievement tests. *See specific tests*
Activity-based intervention (ABI)
developmentally appropriate practices
and, 9–10
group activity matrix, 13
implementation, 10, 12–14, 18
research on, 11–12
theoretical underpinnings, 10–11
ADA (Americans with Disabilities Act), 9
Adaptations
mnemonic strategies and, 25–26
physical disabilities and, 92
Adaptive skills, 10
Aggressive, coercive behavior
autism spectrum disorders and, 84
function-based approach to problem
behaviors, 84
verbal learning deficits and, 19
Alternative assessments. *See* Modifications
American Association on Intellectual
and Developmental Disability
(AAIDD), 30
American Association on Mental
Retardation, 30
American Sign Language (ASL), 101, 104
Americans with Disabilities Act (ADA), 9
Amyotropic lateral sclerosis, 96
Anarthric speech, 88, 92
Antecedent prompts
description of, 31–36, 40–42
implementation of, 41–42
types of, 41
Antisocial behavior. *See* Aggressive, coercive
behavior
Anxiety, verbal learning deficits, 19
Arthritis, 87
ASL (American Sign Language), 101, 104
Asperger's syndrome, 98
Assessment. *See also* Response to
Intervention (RtI)
learning media assessments, 105, 106, 108
limited English proficiency and, 45

research-based practices in, 7
task analysis and, 37
Assistive technology (AT) for writing
access to writing and, 95–96, 99
definition and theoretical underpinnings
of, 93–94
physical disabilities and, 86, 93–99
research on, 94–99
Attention, illusions of, 2
Augmentative and alternative communication
(AAC) devices, 16, 90, 92, 99
Autism
language disorders and, 62, 73
milieu teaching and, 16, 17
Autism spectrum disorders (ASD)
characteristics of, 73–74
functional approach to problem behaviors,
74, 79–85
Nonverbal Reading Approach and, 93
peer-mediated interventions, 74–79
physical disabilities and, 88
story structure intervention and, 67–68

Background noise, speech recognition
software, 97
Backward chaining, 37–38
Baker's Basic Ergonomic Equation, 94
Baldi computer program, 103
Behavioral chains, 36–37
Behavioral outcomes, research-based
practices in, 7
Behavioral supports. *See* Positive behavior
support (PBS)
Behavioral theory, 15, 125–126
Behavior challenges, deaf-blindness, 108
Behavior rating scales, 80–81
Behavior support plans, 82–84
Blindness. *See also* Deaf-blindness (DB);
Visual impairments (VI)
early identification of potential braille
readers and, 105–108
as sensory disabilities, 100
tangible symbols and, 108–112
Boardmaker Plus, 96
Braille, early identification of potential readers,
105–108, 113

CAI (computer-assisted instruction), 88, 93
Callier Azusa Scale-H, 110
Capitalization, speech recognition
software, 97
Causality, 2, 4
CBI. *See* Community-based instruction (CBI)
CEC (Council for Exceptional Children), 3

CELF-4 (Clinical Evaluation of Language
Fundamentals, Fourth Edition), 71
Cerebral palsy, 87, 93, 98
Checklists. *See also* Fidelity checklists
for response prompts, 35–36
Child-selected situations, 15
Clausal complements, 67
Clinical Evaluation of Language Fundamentals,
Fourth Edition (CELF-4), 71
Cochlear implants, 101, 103
Cognitive abilities, physical disabilities, 86–87
Cognitive disabilities. *See also* Intellectual
disabilities
language disorders, 62
Cognitive effort, assistive technology for
writing, 93–94
Cognitive impairments
deaf-blindness and, 108
milieu teaching and, 17
physical disabilities and, 94
Colleagues, personal experiences of, 1, 3
Communication, definition of, 61
Communication impairments, autism spectrum
disorders, 73
Communication skills
milieu teaching and, 15–18
tangible symbols and, 108–110
Community-based instruction (CBI)
description of, 119
employment skills using, 123–127
grocery shopping using, 122–123, 126–127
research on, 119, 121–122, 124–125
Community living, transition to
adulthood, 115
Compensatory education, 8
Comprehension. *See also* Reading
comprehension
language and, 61
literacy interventions for English Language
Learners, 47, 49
Computer-assisted instruction (CAI), 88, 93
Confidence, illusions of, 2
Constant Time Delay, 33–34, 35–36, 38,
95, 124
Continuous speech recognition, 97
Contrasts, focused stimulation, 63–64
Control groups, 4
Council for Exceptional Children (CEC), 3
Credible measures, 4
Cultural diversity, literacy outcomes, 45
Culturally responsive literacy interventions,
53–55
Culturally Responsive Literacy learning
module, 55

Deaf-blindness (DB)
  as sensory disabilities, 100
  tangible symbols and, 108–112, 114
Deafness. *See* Deaf-blindness (DB); Deaf or
      hard of hearing (DHH); Hearing
      impairment; Hearing loss
Deaf or hard of hearing (DHH)
  description of students, 100–101
  visual phonics and, 100–105
Decoding
  guided practice and, 89–91
  literacy interventions for English Language
      Learners, 47
  Nonverbal Reading Approach and, 92–93, 99
  phonological awareness and, 52
  Reading Mastery and, 48
  Visual Phonics and, 101, 104
Decontextualization, 109–110
Degenerative conditions, 87
Delay procedure, 17, 33–34
Denaturalization, 109–110
Depression, verbal learning deficits, 19
Developmental disabilities, early childhood
      special education, 8, 16
Developmental language disorders, 62
Developmentally appropriate practice (DAP),
      early childhood special education,
      8, 9–10, 18
Dewey, J., 10–11
DHH. *See* Deaf or hard of hearing (DHH)
*Diagnostic and Statistical Manual of Mental
      Disorders IV,* autism spectrum
      disorders, 73
Diagnostic distractor arrays, 91, 92
Dictation, speech recognition software, 96–99
Differentiated activities, 27, 28
Differentiated curriculum enhancements
  description and implementation of, 26–28
  rationale for, 26
  research on, 28–29
  as strategy, 20
Differentiated instruction, 26
Direct instruction model, 46–47, 52–53, 103
Direct Instruction reading programs, 92–93
Discrete-utterance speech recognition, 97–98
Discriminative stimulus, 31
Diversity
  disproportionate representation and, 45–46
  linguistic diversity, 44–45, 47–48, 49, 50–53
  research on differentiated curriculum
      enhancements and, 28
  research on mnemonic strategies and, 25
Dominie Reading and Writing Assessment
      Portfolio, 104
Down Syndrome, language disorders, 62
Drop-out rates, 44–45
Dysarthric speech, 88, 92, 98

Early Authors Program (EAP), 50, 53
Early childhood special education (ECSE)
  activity-based intervention, 9–14
  milieu teaching, 15–18
  perspectives on, 8–9
  research on, 10–12, 15–17
Early identification of potential braille readers
  description and implementation of practice,
      105–106
  description of students, 105
  recommendations for practice, 108
  research on, 106–108
  strengths and limitations of research base,
      107–108
  summary of studies, 113
  theoretical underpinnings, 106
  visual impairments and, 105–108

Early intervention, autism spectrum disorders, 74
Early Interventions in Reading (EIR),
      research on, 49
EBDs. *See* Emotional and behavioral disorders
      (EBDs)
EBSCO database, 46
Economic disadvantages, milieu teaching, 16
Economic Opportunity Act Amendments, 8
ECSE. *See* Early childhood special
      education (ECSE)
Education for All Handicapped Children Act
      (EHA), early childhood special
      education, 8
Effective practices
  caveats regarding, 5
  limitations of traditional determining
      factors, 2
  need for in-depth information on, 1
  relation between reality and educator's
      judgments, 3
  research as basis for, 3–6
  research-to-practice gap, 6–7
Effective teaching, research-based practices, 5
EHA. *See* Education for All Handicapped
      Children Act (EHA)
EIR. *See* Early Interventions in Reading (EIR)
Elaboration, requests for, 64
ELLs. *See* English Language Learners (ELLs)
Embedded mnemonic elaborations, 28
Emotional and behavioral disorders (EBDs),
      mnemonic strategies, 24
Employment, transition to adulthood, 115–116,
      119, 123–125
Employment skills, teaching using community-
      based instruction, 123–127
EMT (enhanced milieu teaching), 15, 17–18
English Language Acquisition, Language
      Enhancement, and Academic
      Achievement Act, 47
English Language Learners (ELLs)
  culturally responsive interventions, 53–55
  deaf or hard of hearing students as, 101
  differentiated curriculum enhancements
      and, 29
  linguistic diversity and, 44–45, 47–48, 49,
      50–53
  literacy interventions for, 44–60
  literacy needs of, 45–46
  mnemonic strategies and, 25
  Peer-Assisted Learning Strategies, 49
  research on literacy interventions, 46–54
  special education placement and, 45
  summary of interventions for, 56–60
  supporting practices for literacy
      development, 51–53
Enhanced milieu teaching (EMT), 15, 17–18
Environmental arrangements
  for early childhood special education, 8, 9,
      15–16
  milieu teaching, 18
Environmental barriers, literacy instruction for
      individuals with physical disabilities,
      87–88, 93, 99
ERIC online catalog, 46
Error analysis, 91–92
Error correction, speech recognition software, 97
Errors, severe intellectual disabilities, 32, 39
Evaluation component, Nonverbal Reading
      Approach, 90, 91–92
Expectations, 2, 31, 42, 44, 88
Experimental groups, 4
Expert opinion, 1–2, 3, 4, 5, 7
Explicit instruction, 46
Expression, and language, 61
Eye blinks, assistive technology for writing, 96

Fact sheets, differentiated curriculum
      enhancements, 26–27, 28, 29
Fading response prompts, 32–33
False assertions, 64
False positives and negatives, safeguards
      against, 3–6
Fast ForWord Language, 48
Federal Quota Census, 105
Feigned misunderstanding, 64
Fetal alcohol syndrome, 62
Fidelity checklists
  differentiated curriculum enhancements
      and, 28
  function-based support plans and, 83–84
  mnemonic strategies and, 22–24, 25
Fixated interests, autism spectrum
      disorders, 73
Fluency
  braille reading and, 107
  literacy interventions for English Language
      Learners, 47, 49
  physical disabilities and, 99
  Reading Mastery and, 48
Focused stimulation
  definition and overview of, 63–65
  implementation guide, 65, 66
  specific language impairments and, 66–67
  theoretical underpinnings, 65
  vocabulary delays and, 66
Forced-choice questions, 64
Forward chaining, 37–38
Functional behavioral assessment, autism
      spectrum disorders, 79–84
Functional impacts of physical disabilities, 87
Functional order, 38–39
Functional skills, 10
Functional visual assessment, 106
Function-based approach to problem behaviors
  autism spectrum disorders, 74, 79–85
  description of, 79–80
  as research-based strategy, 85
  research on, 84–85
  steps of, 80–84
Function-based supports, 79, 83–85

General education classrooms
  physical disabilities and, 88
  prompting and, 36
  severe intellectual disabilities and, 31, 39
  students with high-incidence disabilities,
      19–20
Generalization, 31
Generative skills, 10
Gifted students, mnemonic strategies, 24
Goals
  focused stimulation and, 64–65
  function-based approach to problem
      behaviors, 80–81
Good practices, literacy interventions for
      English Language Learners, 51–52
Graduated guidance, 33, 36
Grammar, language disorders, 61, 64–65,
      66–67, 72
Graphic cues, prompts, 41–42
Graphic organizers, 68, 71
Grocery shopping, teaching using
      community-based instruction,
      122–123, 126–127
Group activity matrices, 12–13
Group experimental research, 4
Guided practice
  computer-assisted instruction and, 93
  decoding and, 89–91
  optional components, 91
  self-instruction and, 90–91

Hand cues, 101
Handwriting, 94
Head-controlled devices, 95
Head Start, 8, 9
Hearing impairment. *See also* Deaf or hard of hearing (DHH)
 as disability category, 100
 visual phonics and, 100–105
Hearing loss
 deaf-blindness and, 108, 110
 language disorders and, 62
 research on tangible symbols and, 110
High-incidence disabilities. *See also specific disabilities*
 differentiated curriculum enhancements and, 26–29
 introduction, 19–20
 mnemonic strategies and, 20–26
Highly concentrated presentations, 63
How People Learn model, 50
Hydrocephalus, 87

ICLI (International Communication Learning Institute), 102
IDEA. *See* Individuals with Disabilities Education Improvement Act (IDEA)
IEPs. *See* Individualized education programs (IEPs)
Illustrations
 mnemonics and, 22–24
 tangible symbols, 108–111
Imbedded instruction, 10–14, 15–18, 36
Implementation
 activity-based intervention, 10, 12–14, 18
 differentiated curriculum enhancements, 28–29
 focused stimulation, 65
 milieu teaching, 17–18
 mnemonic strategies, 25
 peer-mediated interventions, 75–77
 prompting, 32, 34
 self-monitoring systems, 42
 story structure interventions, 69–70
 tangible symbols, 108–109
 task analysis, 39
Incidental teaching, 15–18
Inclusion
 early childhood special education and, 8
 high-incidence disabilities and, 20, 24–26, 28, 29
 severe intellectual disabilities and, 39
Incredible Years Training for Children, 48
Independent living, transition to adulthood, 115–116
Individualized education programs (IEPs)
 early childhood special education and, 10
 early identification of potential braille readers and, 105, 106
 self-determination and, 116–119, 127
Individualized instruction
 autism spectrum disorders and, 74
 high-incidence disabilities and, 20
Individuals with Disabilities Education Improvement Act (IDEA)
 assistive technology and, 93
 deafness and hearing impairments and, 100
 early childhood special education and, 8, 9
 early identification of potential braille readers and, 105
 English Language Learners and, 55
 orthopedic impairment and, 86–87
 research-based practices and, 3
Inner speech, 89–92
Instructional practices. *See also* Effective practices
 research-to-practice gap and, 6–7

Intellectual disabilities. *See also* Severe intellectual disabilities
 community-based instruction and, 122
 memory deficits and, 19
 milieu teaching and, 16
 mnemonic strategies and, 24
 physical disabilities and, 88, 94
 sensory disabilities and, 100
Intelligence quotient (IQ), severe intellectual disabilities, 30
Internal responses, 67
International Communication Learning Institute (ICLI), 102
Internet, unproven treatments on, 73–74
Interventions. *See also* Activity-based intervention (ABI); Early Interventions in Reading (EIR); Peer-mediated interventions; Response to Intervention (RtI); Story structure interventions
 activity-based interventions, 9–14
 augmentative and alternative communication devices and, 99
 autism spectrum disorders, 73–74, 74–79, 79–85
 community-based instruction, 119–125
 definition of, 46
 delay and, 33–34
 focused stimulation, 63–67
 language disorders and, 62–63
 literacy interventions for English Language Learners, 44–60
 milieu teaching, 9, 15–18
 physical disabilities and, 87
 reading interventions, 49, 52–53
 Self-Advocacy Strategy, 117–118, 126–127
 single-subject research and, 4
 story structure intervention, 67–72
 tangible symbols, 108–112
 Visual Phonics, 100–105
Intracranial medical intervention, 87
IPLAN strategy, 117
IQ. *See* Intelligence quotient (IQ)
It Takes Two to Talk, 65

Keyboarding, assistive technology for, 94
Keyword mnemonic method, 20–21
Key-word strategies, 20–21
Knowledge, illusions of, 2
K-W-L charts, 50

Ladders to Literacy, 52
Language, definition of, 61
Language acquisition. *See also* Literacy acquisition
 social-interactionist theories of, 65
Language delays, deaf or hard of hearing, 100–101
Language disorders
 autism spectrum disorders and, 62, 73
 common indicators of, 63
 description of, 61–62, 63
 focused stimulation and, 63–67
 interventions and, 62–63
 research on, 65–67
 story structure intervention and, 67–72
Language interventions, incidental and milieu teaching, 16–17
LAP-D (Learning Accomplishment Profile-Diagnostic Edition), 53
LD. *See* Learning disabilities (LD)
LEAP (Learning Experiences: An Alternative Program for Preschoolers and Parents), 79
Learning Accomplishment Profile-Diagnostic Edition (LAP-D), 53

Learning disabilities (LD)
 English Language Learners and, 45, 46–53
 mnemonic strategies and, 24
 physical disabilities and, 94, 99
 self-determination and, 117
 story structure intervention and, 70
Learning Experiences: An Alternative Program for Preschoolers and Parents (LEAP), 79
Learning Language and Loving It, 65
Learning media assessments (LMA), 105, 106, 108
Least restrictive environment (LRE), early childhood special education, 9
Least-to-most prompting hierarchy, 33–34, 35
LEP. *See* Limited English Proficiency (LEP)
Letter mnemonic strategies, 21–22
Letter recognition, stimulus prompts, 34
Limited English Proficiency (LEP)
 deaf or hard of hearing students and, 101
 English Language Learners and, 44, 45, 46–47
Linguistic diversity, English Language Learners, 44–45, 47–48, 49, 50–53
Literacy
 conceptualizations of, 46
 ideological model of, 51
Literacy acquisition
 barriers for individuals with physical disabilities, 86–88, 93, 99
 motor disabilities and, 86, 87, 94
 Nonverbal Reading Approach and, 88–93
Literacy interventions
 culturally responsive literacy interventions, 53–55
 for English Language Learners, 44–60
 phonological awareness and, 47–48, 49, 52–53
 process-oriented literacy interventions, 46, 54
 for reading as reciprocal, interaction-oriented process, 50–51
 for specific reading subskills, 47–50
 summary information on, 56–60
Literacy outcomes, English Language Learners, 45–47
LMA (learning media assessments), 105, 106, 108
Low expectations
 English Language Learners and, 44
 physical disabilities and, 88
 severe intellectual disabilities and, 31, 42
LRE. *See* Least restrictive environment (LRE)

Mand-model procedure, 17
Measures
 baseline measures, 4
 credibility of, 3–4
Memory
 blindness and, 107
 illusions of, 2
 mnemonic strategies and, 20–26
 physical disabilities and, 87
 severe intellectual disabilities and, 31
Memory deficits, intellectual disabilities, 19
Microphone controls, speech recognition software, 97
Milieu teaching
 as early childhood special education practice, 9
 implementation, 17–18
 research on, 16–17
 theoretical underpinnings, 15–16
Miscue and error analysis, 91–92

Mnemonic strategies
description of, 22–24
effectiveness of, 29
embedded mnemonic elaborations, 28
fidelity checklist, 22–24, 25
Nonverbal Reading Approach and, 90–91
rationale for, 20
research on, 24–26
types of, 20–22
Model procedure, 17
Models, focused stimulation, 63–64
Modifications, mnemonic strategies, 25–26
Morphology, story structure intervention, 71, 72
Most-to-least prompting hierarchy, 33–34, 35
Motivation, assistive technology for writing, 94
Motor abilities, speech recognition software, 97
Motor disabilities
literacy acquisition and, 86, 87, 94
sensory disabilities and, 100
task analysis and, 37
Motoric indicators, decoding, 89–90
Multiple disabilities, visual impairments, 105
Muscular dystrophy, 87, 98
Musculoskeletal disabilities, 87

NAEYC (National Association for the Education
of Young Children), 9
Narrative elaboration treatment (NET), 70–71
Narratives, 67, 68. *See also* Story structure
interventions
National Association for the Education of
Young Children (NAEYC), 9
National Center for Culturally Responsive
Educational Systems, 55
National Center for Education Evaluation and
Regional Assistance, 52
National Deaf-Blind Child Count, 108
National Longitudinal Transition Study
(NLTS), 115
National Standards Project, 74
Native English Speaking (NES), 48
Natural environments, for early childhood
special education, 8, 9, 15–16
Naturalistic settings, peer-mediated
interventions, 76–77
Natural learning opportunities, 9
NCLB. *See* No Child Left Behind Act (NCLB)
NES (Native English Speaking), 48
NET (narrative elaboration treatment), 70–71
Neuromotor impairments, 87
NLTS (National Longitudinal Transition
Study), 115
No Child Left Behind Act (NCLB)
interventions and, 46
research-supported effective practices and, 3
Nonresponders, 5
Nonverbal Reading Approach (NRA)
definition and theoretical underpinnings of,
88–89
evaluation component, 90, 91–92
expansion strategies, 92
guided practice, 89–91
physical disabilities and, 86, 88–93
research on, 92–93
speech and, 99
NRA. *See* Nonverbal Reading Approach (NRA)
Number recognition, stimulus prompts, 34

Occasion for instruction, 15
Open Court, 49
Oral language, severe intellectual disabilities, 31
Orthopedic impairment
deaf-blindness and, 108
as disability category, 86–87
state certifications in, 88

PALS. *See* Peer-Assisted Learning Strategies
(PALS)
Parental involvement
autism spectrum disorders and, 74
focused stimulation and, 67
Parental permission, for peer-mediated
interventions, 75
PBS. *See* Positive behavior support (PBS)
PCP. *See* Person-centered planning (PCP)
Peer-Assisted Learning Strategies (PALS),
English Language Learners, 49
Peer-Mediated Instruction and Intervention
(PMI), 75
Peer-mediated interventions
description of, 74–75
fidelity measure for, 77, 78
peer-planning form schedule, 77
as research-based strategies, 85
research on, 77–79
scripts for, 75–76
steps of, 75–77
Peer selection and training, 75–76
Peer tutoring, high-incidence disabilities,
26–28
Pegword mnemonic method, 21
Pencil grips, 94
Personal experiences, 1–5, 7
Person-centered planning (PCP),
self-determination, 117
PHAST (Phonological and Strategy Training)
Decoding Program, 49
Phonemic awareness
deaf or hard of hearing students and, 101,
103–105
English Language Learners and, 52
Phonemic Awareness in Young Children, 52
Phonics. *See also* Visual Phonics
literacy skills acquisition and, 88
Phonological Analysis and Blending/Direct
Instruction Decoding Program, 49
Phonological and Strategy Training (PHAST)
Decoding Program, 49
Phonological awareness
literacy interventions for English Language
Learners, 47–48, 49, 52–53
subskills of, 53
Visual Phonics and, 104
Phonologic-based reading interventions, 49,
52–53
Phonology, and language disorders, 61, 64–65
Physical disabilities
assistive technology for writing and, 86,
93–99
characteristics that impede literacy
acquisition, 86–88, 93, 99
early childhood special education and, 12
Nonverbal Reading Approach, 86, 88–93
Physical effort, assistive technology for writing,
94, 98
Piaget, J., 10–11
Pictures. *See* Illustrations
Placement decisions, English Language
Learners, 45
PLS-R (Preschool Language Scale-Revised
Fourth Edition), 53
PMI (Peer-Mediated Instruction and
Intervention), 75
Positive behavior support (PBS), autism
spectrum disorders, 79
Postschool outcomes
self-determination and, 117
transition to adulthood, 115–116
Postsecondary education, transition to
adulthood, 115
Pragmatics, and language disorders, 61, 65

Prelinguistic skills, 62
Prematurity/low birth weight, 62
Prepackaged literacy interventions, English
Language Learners, 48
Preschool Language Scale-Revised Fourth
Edition (PLS-R), 53
Prevent-Teach-Reinforce (PTR), 80, 85
Primary language disorder, 62
Problem behavior interventions, autism
spectrum disorders, 79–85
Problem behavior prevention strategies,
functional approach, 74, 79–85
Problem solving, self-management, 40
Process-oriented literacy interventions, 46, 54
Progressive time delay, 33–34, 35
Progress monitoring
function-based support plans and, 83–84
peer-mediated interventions and, 77
research-based practices and, 5
task analysis and, 37
Prompts
antecedent prompts, 31–36, 40–42
definition of, 31
graphic cues and, 41–42
research on, 33–34, 36
response prompts, 32–34, 35–36
stimulus prompts, 34
teaching employment skills and, 124
Pseudoword decoding, 103
Psychosocial impacts of physical disabilities,
87–88
PTR (Prevent-Teach-Reinforce), 80, 85
Public examination, scientific research, 4
Punctuation, speech recognition software, 97

Qualitative Reading Inventory-3, 50

Race/ethnicity
differentiated curriculum enhancements
and, 28
disproportionate representation and, 45–46
English Language Learners and, 44–45, 48
mnemonic strategies and, 25
Self-Advocacy Strategy and, 117
Self-Directed IEP and, 119
RBT. *See* Replacement behavior training (RBT)
Reading. *See also* Literacy interventions;
Reading comprehension;
Technological aids; Vocabulary
interventions, 49, 52–53
Reading comprehension
mnemonic strategies and, 23
physical disabilities and, 99
story structure intervention and, 67, 68–69,
70, 72
Visual Phonics and, 105
Reading disabilities
limited English proficiency and, 45
story structure intervention and, 70
Reading Mastery, 48, 49
Reading rates, for braille, 107
Reading Recovery, 48
Reading skills
braille and, 106
speech recognition software and, 97
Reading subskills, in literacy interventions for
English Language Learners, 46–47,
49, 51–55
Read Naturally, 49
Read Well, 48, 49
Recasts, focused stimulation, 63–64
Reciprocal, interaction-oriented literacy
instruction, 46–47, 50–51
Reconstructive elaboration mnemonic
strategies, 22

Reinforcement
    behavior support plans and, 82, 83
    Nonverbal Reading Approach and, 91
    task analysis and, 37
Reliability, of measures, 3
Repetitive behaviors, autism spectrum
    disorders, 73
Replacement behavior training (RBT), autism
    spectrum disorders, 82, 83–84
Research
    on activity-based intervention, 11–12
    on assistive technology for writing, 94–99
    on community-based instruction, 119,
        121–122, 124–125
    on differentiated curriculum enhancements,
        28–29
    directions for future research, 29, 99, 105,
        108, 112, 127
    on early childhood special education, 10–12,
        15–17
    on early identification of potential braille
        readers, 106–108
    on Early Interventions in Reading, 49
    effective practices based on, 3–6
    on function-based approach to problem
        behaviors, 84–85
    on language disorders, 65–67
    on literacy interventions, 46–54
    on milieu teaching, 16–17
    on mnemonic strategies, 24–26
    on Nonverbal Reading Approach, 92–93
    open and iterative nature of science and, 4–5
    on peer-mediated interventions, 77–79
    research-to-practice gap, 6–7
    safeguards in, 4–6
    on specific language impairments, 66–67
    on story structure interventions, 70–72
    on tangible symbols communication,
        110–112
    on task analysis, 39
    on transition to adulthood, 116, 126–127
    on visual phonics, 103–105, 112
Research-based practices, as basis for effective
    practices, 3–6
Research-to-practice gap, 6–7
Research-to-practice lessons
    employment skills, 124–125
    grocery shopping, 122–123
    lesson-plan development, 117
    Self-Advocacy Strategy, 118
    Self-Directed IEP, 120–121
Response prompts, 32–36
Response to Intervention (RtI), English
    Language Learners literacy
    interventions, 49
Responsive interaction, milieu teaching, 18
RtI. *See* Response to Intervention (RtI)

Samples, size and composition of, 4
Scanning, assistive technology for writing, 94
Schema theory, 68–69
Scoliosis, 87
See the Sound/Visual Phonics. See Visual
    Phonics
Self-Advocacy Strategy, 116, 117–118,
    126–127
Self-analysis, as practice for students with
    severe intellectual disabilities, 31
Self-care, stimulus prompts, 34
Self-determination
    individualized education programs and,
        116–119, 127
    research on, 117–119
    Self-Advocacy Strategy, 117–118
    self-management strategies and, 40

Self-Directed IEP, 60, 116, 119, 120–121,
    126–127
Self-esteem, physical disabilities, 87–88
Self-injurious behaviors, 84
Self-instruction, 88–89, 90–93
Self-management
    self-monitoring and, 42
    severe intellectual disabilities and, 39–43
Self-monitoring, 42
Semantics
    language disorders and, 61, 64–65
    Visual Phonics and, 101
Sensory disabilities
    braille and, 105–108
    tangible symbols and, 108–112, 114
    task analysis and, 37
    visual phonics and, 100–105
Sensory impairments, research on tangible
    symbols, 110
SES. *See* Socioeconomic status (SES)
Settings, naturalistic settings, 76–77
Severe intellectual disabilities
    description of, 30
    learning characteristics of, 31
    prompting and, 31–36
    research on tangible symbols and, 110
    self-management and, 39–43
    task analysis and, 31, 36–39
Sign language, 100–101
Simultaneous prompting, 32, 35
Single-subject research, 4
Skill-based literacy interventions, 46, 49, 52,
    53–54
SLDs. *See* Speech and language disorders
    (SLDs)
SLI (specific language impairments),
    62, 66–67
SLPs (speech-language pathologists), 62, 66
Social behavior improvement
    autism spectrum disorders and, 74–79
    transition to adulthood and, 127
Social interaction impairments, autism spectrum
    disorders, 73
Social-interactionist theories of language
    acquisition, 65
Social networks, early childhood special
    education, 9
Social skills
    autism spectrum disorders and, 74–79
    placement decisions and, 88
    severe intellectual disabilities and, 31
Social validity. *See also* Validity
    Visual Phonics and, 104
Sociocultural process of literacy, 53
Socioeconomic status (SES)
    early childhood special education and, 17
    English Language Learners and, 45
Spastic quadriplegic cerebral palsy, 86, 88
Special education. *See also* Early childhood
    special education (ECSE)
    English Language Learners and, 45
    severe intellectual disabilities and, 30–43
Special education practices. *See* Effective
    practices
Special education teachers
    personal experiences of, 1–5
    research-based practices and, 2–3
    research-to-practice gap and, 6–7
Specialized curriculum
    autism spectrum disorders, 74
    visual impairment and, 106
Specific language impairments (SLI), 62, 66–67
Speech, definition of, 61
Speech and language disorders (SLDs), early
    childhood special education, 8, 16, 17

Speech impairments
    literacy skills acquisition and, 86, 87, 88, 89
    speech recognition and, 98
Speech-language pathologists (SLPs), 62, 66
Speech reading, 101
Speech recognition software, 94, 96–99
Spelling checkers, 94
Spina bifida
    assistive technology for writing, 98
    literacy skills acquisition and, 87
Spinal muscular atrophy, 87, 98
Stimulus modification, 34
Stimulus prompts, 34
Story maps, 68, 69, 70, 71
Story structure interventions
    definition and overview of, 67–68
    implementation, 69–70
    research on, 70–72
    theoretical underpinnings, 68–69
Story-telling skills, 67, 72
Strokes, Nonverbal Reading Approach, 93
Structured learning environments, autism
    spectrum disorders, 74
Struggling readers, English Language Learners
    as, 45–53
Student-directed learning strategies, 39–43. *See*
    also Self-management
Student outcome. *See* Academic skills
    outcomes
Student performance, credible measures of, 4
Students with disabilities
    early childhood special education and, 8–18
    language disorders and, 61–72
    mnemonic strategies and, 20–26
    modifications and, 25–26
    need for effective practices, 1–2, 3
    transition to adulthood, 115–127
Study descriptions, literacy interventions for
    English Language Learners, 56–60
Study design
    community-based instruction, 124–125
    early childhood special education and, 16
    English Language Learners, 46–47
    focused stimulation and, 67
    Nonverbal Reading Approach and, 92–93
    Self-Advocacy Strategy, 117, 126
    story structure intervention, 70–72
    tangible symbols and, 110–112
    transition to adulthood and, 116
    Visual Phonics, 104–105
Supplemental direct instruction, phonological
    awareness, 52–53
Support levels
    focused stimulation and, 65–66
    research on differentiated curriculum
        enhancements and, 28–29
    research on mnemonic strategies and, 25
Supports-based classification, 30
Symbols
    braille and, 106
    tangible symbols, 108–112, 114
Syntax, story structure intervention, 71, 72
Systematic instruction, autism spectrum
    disorders, 74
System of most/least prompts, 32–34, 38

Tangible symbols
    definition and implementation, 108–109
    directions for future research, 112
    recommendations for practice, 112
    research on, 110–112
    strengths and limitations of research base,
        111–112
    summary of studies on, 114
    theoretical underpinnings, 109–110

Target groups. *See also specific types of disabilities*
  research-based practices and, 5, 7
Task analysis
  description of, 36–37
  implementation, 39
  instructing students in, 38–39
  as practice for students with severe intellectual disabilities, 31, 36–39
  research on, 39
  teaching employment skills and, 124
  types of, 37–38
Teacher behaviors, 5
Teacher certified in visual impairments (TVI), 105–106
Teaching practices. *See* Effective practices; Instructional practices
Technological aids
  assistive technology for writing and, 93–99
  severe intellectual disabilities and, 41
Test of Narrative Language (TNL), 71
Text structure theory, 68
Three step decoding, 89–91, 93
Time delays
  Constant Time Delay, 33–34, 35–36, 38, 95, 124
  delay procedure, 17, 33–34
Total Communication, 103–104
Total task presentation, 37–38
Traditions, 1–2, 3
Training time, speech recognition software, 96

Transition to adulthood
  community-based instruction, 119–125
  instructional approaches, 125–126
  postschool outcomes, 115–116
  research on, 116, 126–127
  Self-Advocacy Strategy, 116, 117–118
  self-determination and, 116–119
  suggestions for future research, 127
Traumatic brain injury, literary skills acquisition, 87
Treatment delays, 33–34
Treatment fidelity, focused stimulation, 66
Treatment resistors, 5
Tutoring, high-incidence disabilities, 26–28
TVI (teacher certified in visual impairments), 105–106

United Nations Educational, Scientific, and Cultural Organization (UNESCO), 51
Universal Design for Learning (UDL), Visual Phonics, 105

Validity. *See also* Social validity
  of functional behavior assessment, 79
  of learning media assessment, 106
  of measures, 3
  of transition to adulthood, 126
Verbal learning and memory, high-incidence disabilities, 19–20
Verbal learning deficits, 19
VI. *See* Visual impairments (VI)
Violence. *See* Aggressive, coercive behavior

Visual impairments (VI). *See also* Blindness; Deaf-blindness (DB)
  early identification of potential braille readers and, 105–108, 113
  physical disabilities and, 87
  as sensory disability, 100
Visual phonics
  description and implementation of, 101–102
  description of students, 100–101
  recommendations for practice, 105
  research on, 103–105, 112
  strengths and limitations of research base, 104–105
  as supplement to phonics reading lesson, 102
  theoretical underpinnings of, 101
Vocabulary
  mnemonic strategies and, 22–24
  Visual Phonics and, 101–103
Vocabulary delays, focused stimulation, 66
Voice-detecting sensors, 95
Vygotksy, Lev, 10–11, 88–89

Weschler Individual Achievement Test-II (WIAT-II), 103
Wilson Reading System, 49
Wisconsin Behavior Rating Scale, 110
Word-prediction software, 94, 96
Word processors, 94–96
Writing instruction, speech recognition software, 97
Writing With Symbols, 96
Written expression, physical disabilities, 94–95
Written productivity, 94, 95, 96–99